VERGIL'S *AENEID*:
AUGUSTAN EPIC AND POLITICAL CONTEXT

VERGIL'S *AENEID*
Augustan Epic and Political Context

Editor
Hans-Peter Stahl

Contributors
Elaine Fantham, Don Fowler, Reinhold F. Glei,
Gunther Gottlieb, Philip Hardie, Stephen Harrison,
Egil Kraggerud, Eckard Lefèvre,
Alexander G. McKay, Llewelyn Morgan,
Anton Powell, Hans-Peter Stahl,
Richard F. Thomas, David West

The Classical Press of Wales

First published in hardback in 1998
This paperback edition 2009

The Classical Press of Wales
15 Rosehill Terrace, Swansea SA1 6JN
Tel: +44 (0)1792 458397
Fax: +44 (0)1792 464067
www.classicalpressofwales.co.uk

Distributor
Oxbow Books,
10 Hythe Bridge Street,
Oxford OX1 2EW
Tel: +44 (0)1865 241249
Fax: +44 (0)1865 794449

Distributor in the United States of America
The David Brown Book Co.
PO Box 511, Oakville, CT 06779
Tel: +1 (860) 945–9329
Fax: +1 (860) 945–9468

© 2009 The contributors

All rights reserved. No part of this publication may be reproduced, stored in a retrieval system, or transmitted, in any form or by any means, electronic, mechanical, photocopying, recording or otherwise, without the prior permission of the publisher.

ISBN 978–1–905125–33–3

A catalogue record for this book is available from the British Library
Printed and bound in Great Britain by
CPI Antony Rowe, Chippenham and Eastbourne

CONTENTS

List of Contributors and Chapter Summaries	vii
Preface	xiii
Editor's Introduction	xv
1. Vergil Announcing the *Aeneid*. On *Georg.* 3.1–48 *Egil Kraggerud* (Oslo, Norway)	1
2. Religion in the Politics of Augustus (*Aen.* 1.278–91; 8.714–23; 12.791–842) *Gunther Gottlieb* (Augsburg, Germany)	21
3. Political Stop-overs on a Mythological Travel Route: from Battling Harpies to the Battle of Actium (*Aen.* 3.268–93) *Hans-Peter Stahl* (Pittsburgh, Pa., U.S.A.)	37
4. The Peopling of the Underworld (*Aen.* 6.608–27) *Anton Powell* (Swansea, U.K.)	85
5. Vergil as a Republican (*Aen.* 6. 815–35) *Eckard Lefèvre* (Freiburg, Germany)	101
6. The Show Must Go on: the Death of Marcellus and the Future of the Augustan Principate (*Aen.* 6.860–86) *Reinhold F. Glei* (Bochum, Germany)	119
7. Allecto's First Victim: a Study of Vergil's Amata (*Aen.* 7.341–405 and 12.1–80) *Elaine Fantham* (Princeton, N.J., U.S.A.)	135
8. Opening the Gates of War (*Aen.* 7.601–40) *Don Fowler* (Oxford, U.K.)	155
9. Assimilation and Civil War: Hercules and Cacus (*Aen.* 8.185–267) *Llewelyn Morgan* (Dublin, Republic of Ireland)	175

Contents

10. *Non enarrabile textum?* The Shield of Aeneas and
    the Triple Triumph in 29 BC   (*Aen.* 8.630–728)   199
    Alexander G. McKay (Hamilton, Ontario, Canada)

11. The Sword-Belt of Pallas: Moral Symbolism and
    Political Ideology   (*Aen.* 10.495–505)   223
    Stephen Harrison (Oxford, U.K.)

12. Fame and Defamation in the *Aeneid*: the Council of Latins 243
    (*Aen.* 11.225–467)
    Philip Hardie (Cambridge, U.K.)

13. The Isolation of Turnus   (*Aeneid*, Book 12)   271
    Richard F. Thomas (Cambridge, Mass., U.S.A.)

14. The End and the Meaning   (*Aen.* 12.791–842)   303
    David West (Newcastle-upon-Tyne, U.K.)

Index   319

LIST OF CONTRIBUTORS AND CHAPTER SUMMARIES

ELAINE FANTHAM, Giger Professor of Latin at Princeton since 1986, was educated at Oxford, and taught for many years at the University of Toronto. Besides a number of articles on Roman epic from Vergil to Statius she has published commentaries on Seneca's *Trojan Women*, on Lucan's *Civil War* Book 2, on Book 4 of Ovid's *Fasti* (forthcoming), and most recently *Roman Literary Culture* (Johns Hopkins UP 1996).

This re-examination of Amata takes its starting point from one pre-Vergilian tradition which presented the queen as murderer of Latinus' sons. Vergil suppressed this legend to make Amata a matriarch misguided by a conception of family that refused to accept Latinus' divine imperative: as with Turnus, her resistance seems reasonable if one does not accept Aeneas as the hero whose success is fated. It is argued that Vergil has shaped Amata's role to echo the passion and self-destruction of Dido, but has also, as the poem approaches the tragedy of Turnus in Book 12, colored her behavior with elements of both Hecuba in *Iliad* 22, and Vergil's own Juno in her insubordination to Jupiter's divine purpose.

DON FOWLER is Fellow and Tutor in Classics at Jesus College, Oxford, and University Lecturer in Greek and Latin Literature. He has a particular interest in critical theory, and is currently writing a book on the book in Roman poetry.

In this paper, Don Fowler examines the passage in Book Seven of the *Aeneid* where Juno opens the 'Gates of War' in the light of the imagery of opening and closing in the rest of the *Aeneid* and more generally in Roman culture. In particular, the paper suggests that her action encodes an energy which is essential to the very idea of being Roman and highlights the complexity and ambiguity at the heart of Roman cultural self-definition.

REINHOLD F. GLEI is Professor of Latin at the Ruhr-Universität Bochum, Germany. His scholarship interests focus on Vergil and his later reception; on ancient and medieval philosophy; the Argonaut myth; and the dialogue between Christianity and Islam in the Middle Ages and in the Renaissance.

List of Contributors

In the *Aeneid*, the future of the Augustan principate appears to be overshadowed by the death of Marcellus (23 BC). There are however indications that Vergil viewed this event not as endangering the principate but took it as a 'warning' by the gods, to which Augustus reacted in an appropriate fashion both politically and personally. Beyond this aspect, the role of the *nepotes*, repeatedly emphasized in the *Aeneid*, possibly points to a concrete dynastic background (the birth of C. Caesar in 20 BC).

GUNTHER GOTTLIEB has been since 1975 Professor (Chair) for Ancient History at the University of Augsburg (Germany); 1993–5 vice rector; Dr. h.c. (University of Osijek, Croatia); representative for the partnership between the Universities of Augsburg and Osijek. Main fields of research: Herodotus, Roman Empire and Christian Church, religious politics in general, southern Germany in Roman times, reception of Greek and Roman historiography in early modern times.

Based on three passages from Vergil's *Aeneid* the author analyzes the fundamental positions of Augustus' religious politics in the following aspects: the use of symbols in politics, political propaganda and its function, political community and cult community.

PHILIP HARDIE is a University Lecturer in Classics in the University of Cambridge, and a Fellow of New Hall. He is the author of *Virgil's Aeneid: Cosmos and Imperium* (Oxford, 1986), *The Epic Successors of Virgil* (Cambridge, 1993), and a commentary on *Aeneid* 9 (Cambridge Greek and Latin Classics, 1994). He is currently working on Ovid and a book on *Fama*.

In the debate between Drances and Turnus in the Council of Latins may be heard echoes of the heated political debate of the late Republic. This paper examines the relationship between the persuasive goals of the rhetoric of deliberation and invective in this episode and the authority of the epic narrator's voice, in order to raise wider questions about the place of rhetoric within the *Aeneid*.

S.J. HARRISON is Fellow and Tutor in Classics at Corpus Christi College, Oxford, and University Lecturer in Classical Languages and Literature. He is author of a commentary on Vergil, *Aeneid* 10 (1991), and editor of *Oxford Readings in Virgil's* Aeneid (1990) and *Homage to Horace* (1995).

The Danaid iconography of Pallas' sword-belt at *Aeneid* 10.497–9 has a significant moral and narrative function in the poem; it looks back to the death of Pallas as well as forward to the death of Turnus, and stresses the tragedy of their early deaths rather than the criminality of their killings. It is related to the Danaid iconography of the sculptural decorations of Augustus' contemporary Palatine temple, which expresses triumph over Egypt and Cleopatra, a propaganda statement very different from the Vergilian meditation on the tragedy of war.

EGIL KRAGGERUD has been Professor of Classical Philology since 1969 at Oslo University. Areas of particular interest: Augustan literature (Vergil and Horace), medieval Latin and Neolatin from Norway – translations of classical literature: Greek tragedy, Vergil, Boethius.

In his line-by-line comment on the proem to *Georgics* 3.1–48 Kraggerud holds that the poem honouring Caesar (Octavian) alluded to was an *Aeneid* in largely the same form as we have it. The idea that Vergil changed his plans from a contemporary epic on Caesar to a mytho-historical epic on Aeneas cannot be built safely on an analysis of the proem. In the author's view the presence of Aeneas is tangibly close.

ECKARD LEFÈVRE has been a Professor of Classics and Head of the Classics Department of Freiburg University since 1977. In his research he mainly deals with Greek and Roman drama (tragedy and comedy) and with Augustan literature.

In Professor Lefèvre's paper *Aeneid* 6.815–35 are thoroughly analysed. Thereby Vergil is shown to be a 'Republican' to some extent, since he presents the heroes of the old Republic remarkably favourably, but displays a critical attitude to Caesar, the 'forerunner' of the Principate.

ALEXANDER G. MCKAY, Professor Emeritus of Classics at McMaster University, Hamilton, Ontario, Honorary President for Life of The Vergilian Society, has written extensively on Vergil, on Roman Lyric and Satiric Poetry, and on the topography and monuments of Cumae and The Phlegraean Fields.

Professor McKay's paper sets the scenes of Vulcan's shield into the perspective of the *pompa triumphalis* and of monuments and landmarks along its route, thereby anchoring the shield's panegyric message in Rome's present-day environment and in the context of the *pax Augusta*.

LLEWELYN MORGAN is Assistant Lecturer in the Department of Classics, University College Dublin. He has published on Vergil, Gallus, Caesar and Domitian, and his particular interest is in civil conflict as the

List of Contributors

context, theme or determinant of literary production. He is currently completing a monograph on the politics of Vergil's *Georgics*.

Morgan analyses certain recent political interpretations of the *Hercules and Cacus* episode in *Aeneid* 8, and in particular that of Lyne, who argues that the propaganda superficially presented in *Hercules and Cacus* is undercut by disquieting 'further voices': Vergil is thus politically ambivalent. Morgan suggests, however, that in the light of a more sophisticated notion of propaganda the disquieting elements identified by Lyne can after all be shown to serve the requirements of the Augustan regime.

ANTON POWELL was the founder and is now the Director of the University of Wales Institute of Classics; author of *Athens and Sparta* (1988); editor of *Roman Poetry and Propaganda in the Age of Augustus* (1992) and *The Greek World* (1995).

Powell examines Vergil's choice of offenders to portray in Tartarus. He argues that Vergil uses his mythic underworld to point implicitly at historical enemies, opponents of Octavian's faction and of Augustan values. Powell traces, amid the sins to which Vergil refers, a pattern of significant omissions which served Augustus' personal interest.

HANS-PETER STAHL is Andrew W. Mellon Professor of Classics at the University of Pittsburgh. Emphasizing close structural analysis, he has published on planning and outcome in Herodotus and Thucydides; Euripidean dramaturgy; Plato's propositional logic; Horace's *Satires*; Propertius ("Individual and State under Augustus"); political aspects of Vergil's *Aeneid*.

Aeneas' stop-overs around Greece legitimize his descendant Augustus as the heir to the kings of Troy. Potential rivals are eliminated (King Priam's sons Polydorus and Helenus). Any Cretan priority claims on Pergamon are obviated (Aeneas the founder of Pergam[e]a on Crete). Augustus' Actian propaganda is fatefully prefigured in his ancestor's victory memorial. Physical remains help to verify the politically motivated action line of *Aeneid* 3.

RICHARD F. THOMAS is Professor of Greek and Latin at Harvard University, where he writes and teaches on Hellenistic Greek poetry and Latin literature, chiefly of the late Republican and Augustan periods. He is interested in a variety of critical approaches (chiefly philological, intertextual, narratological), and in literary history, metrics and prose stylistics, genre studies, and the reception of Classical literature and culture, particularly as relates to Vergil.

Richard Thomas's article, 'The Isolation of Turnus', begins by taking issue with certain strongly Augustan readings of Turnus, which inevitably see him from the perspective of Aeneas, and judge him in terms of the impediments he raises to the mission of Aeneas; Thomas proposes instead to explore, with equal emphasis, the way the world looks through the lens of Turnus.

DAVID WEST is Emeritus Professor of Latin in the University of Newcastle-upon-Tyne and author of *Reading Horace* (1967), *The Imagery and Poetry of Lucretius* (1969 and, with additional chapter, 1994), *Vergil's* Aeneid: *a New Prose Translation* (1990) and Carpe Diem: *Horace Odes I* (1996).

Recent work on the gods in the *Aeneid* has concentrated on theological questions. This study draws attention to the humour in the final conversation between Jupiter and Juno and sees the episode as Vergil's means of shaping the end of the plot in order to support the Augustan message of the poem.

PREFACE

The volume presented here to the public was made possible only through help from various sides.

First, I gratefully acknowledge institutional assistance. The Faculty of Arts and Sciences of the University of Pittsburgh, the University Honors College, the University Center for International Studies, and the Department of Classics provided financial support for the first conference, which took place in Pittsburgh, Pa./USA, in September 1995. Next, heart-felt thanks are due to individual helpers. As discussion coordinators, Professors John F. Miller of the University of Virginia and Mark Possanza of the University of Pittsburgh did their part to keep the discussions on a smooth course. The dedication to organizational details shown by the Department's Managerial Assistant, Mrs Arlene Woodward, is unrivalled. Last, but not least, the Department's graduate students spent much time and energy to make the conference a success and an enjoyable experience for all present.

The second conference, held in July of 1996 in Oxford/England, not only benefited from the hospitality of Oxford University which provided an ideal location at the *Institutio Tayloriana* of the Ashmolean Museum. It also was able to draw on support granted by the University of Wales and the University of Pittsburgh as well as by the speakers' home universities and private expenses. As discussion coordinators there are gratefully acknowledged Dr Joan Booth and Professor Rosemary Wright of the University of Wales. Special thanks go to Dr Stephen J. Harrison of Corpus Christi College, Oxford, and Dr Anton Powell of the University of Wales Institute of Classics: without their unselfish devotion and unstinting commitment to organizational details the second conference would not have taken place.

Further thanks are owed to the publisher, Dr Anton Powell, whose Classical Press of Wales, in cooperation with Duckworth Ltd., brought out the volume with great speed and efficiency. Dr Powell deserves special acknowledgement for his indulgence shown toward those exceeding the originally planned size for individual contributions. Here, quite a number of us have experienced unexpected leniency, and I myself wish to express my gratitude for having even been encouraged

Preface

to provide a fuller account of my own topic. Dr Powell also helped by arranging the bibliographies and by going over the chapters of contributors whose native language is not English. Last but not least, the volume is indebted to him for preparing the index.

Ultimately, the success of a conference depends on those who participate in it, speakers as well as audience. If the organizer is not mistaken, mutual contacts and interactions among those attending (they came from more than a dozen countries on three continents) were extraordinarily active and harmonious (as well as spirited), both inside and outside the lecture halls. May the collection of contributions united in this volume be granted the same kind of stimulating reaction from its readers.

Pittsburgh, Pa., U.S.A., August 1997   Hans-Peter Stahl

EDITOR'S INTRODUCTION
Changing Views of the Political *Aeneid**

The collection of interpretations submitted to a broader public in this volume is not designed to promote any orthodoxy or to favor a certain methodology over others. On the contrary, the editor has aimed at bringing together a wide variety of approaches (including mutually contradictory ones), to be presented in concise contributions that might be easily surveyed, examined and compared. The result is that a wide-ranging international blend of "schools" is represented here; ranging from Vergil viewed as endorsing Rome's imperial warfare, to Vergil lending his voice to the victims of Roman imperialism; from the present-day literary critic's denial that any application of political context is feasible, to Vergil seen as holding up the ideal of the old republic to Rome's new master, the Emperor Augustus; from bringing out the political implications embedded in the dramatic perspectives of the *Aeneid*'s characters, to showing how the events and locales of the epic's mythical narrative can draw their *raison d' être* from the poet's contemporary political environment; etc. A complete list of the contributors, together with their research profiles and summaries of their contributions, is provided on page vii.

The *Aeneid* may be considered a test case for influential strands in the Western tradition. Does the epic stand for the subordination of the individual to the interests of the leadership in a hierarchically structured state, or does there run below the imperial surface a cross-current of wide human appeal? If the latter is the case, is the poem's human message non-partisan and all-embracing, or does the poet perhaps skillfully channel his reader's human capacity for compassion in a direction which would serve the power center of his time?

How is one to decide which of competing interpretations (or which combination of interpretative methodologies) is best qualified to secure the author's intention? Or is the "intentionalist" poet (as well as the "intentionalist" interpreter) perhaps an aberrant fiction of the naive classicist, rightly frowned upon by "unintentionalists" who would advise *a priori* to discard, in favor of *polysemy* or even *multifocality*,

Editor's Introduction

the (in their eyes) utopian idea of an author's identifiable intention? Does perhaps (as some would argue) the *Aeneid* itself support a variety of readings by offering different, even contradictory, focalizations?

Assuming, for the sake of argument, that the work does contain an identifiable intention (but how few are there who would in seriousness deny the poet a specific motive and message?), there arises the problem of tracking it down. How do we verify that, when assigning priority to the perspective of one character in the work over another – e.g., to Italian King Turnus over King Aeneas (his Trojan[-Julian] counterpart), or *vice versa* – , we really are hearing the author's voice and are not making an arbitrary assignment? Unlike drama (where the author communicates with his audience over the heads of his characters), our epic's narrative manifestly offers the author's voice many times, often enhanced by the poet's seemingly personal interventions, narrative endorsements or vituperations. But can even the narrator's interventions legitimately be taken to be the poet's personal voice? If not, is there a "private voice" behind the published stance? If so, what reliable indicator does one have that would demonstrably validate the "private voice" one believes to hear in a given passage as being truly the genuine voice of the poet?

And what about the author's honesty and sincerity if his true feelings must be assumed to be hidden under his work's encomiastic surface? Would we not risk making him a lackey of the regime (perhaps even a paid lackey – after all, he died disproportionately rich)?

Or should one rather dispense with all search for the author's opinions because they are not important for us since every generation reads "its own Vergil" anyway? Should the scholarly interpreter (like a creative poet who, while reworking a work handed down by tradition, imbues the subject matter with new meaning and spirit) feel free to disregard the historical conditions of the work's original setting? Would that setting be recoverable anyway?

Theories abound. In evaluating them, one must not lose sight of the fact that, for all its endeavor to achieve objectivity, scholarship itself is known not to be immune to the tendencies of its time. This can be documented by sudden surges in the transplantation of methodologies from one discipline to another (and also from one continent to another). It is also seen in the results at which scholars arrive. Trendy methods tend to generate similar results in different areas of application. (And first-time applicators may win the title of "interdisciplinary" originality.) In other words, the meshes of the net which the scholar

Editor's Introduction

throws over the object in many a case determine the features his search comes up with.

One should add that, in the interpretative disciplines, methodologies sometimes appear entwined with certain attitudes or sub-surface convictions, which may eventually show up in the form in which the results are achieved and presented. Such underlying, occasionally unacknowledged or even unrecognized, attitudes and convictions can even influence the results in terms of content also.

Obviously, there is no agreement among different schools of interpretation on how appropriately to approach the epic's text. Opposing representatives of the scholarly spectrum often do not seem to know how to talk to each other any longer in terms that are understood by the other side (or by an uninitiated audience). How does one, in this situation, assist readers who are eager to encounter the *Aeneid* within as objective a framework as possible? One way would be to offer them a cross-section of current approaches, presented in a manner which would allow them to compare methodologies and form their own judgement.

The volume presented here combines contributions from two conferences on "Vergil's *Aeneid* : Augustan Epic and Political Context" convened by the editor. The first one was held in the United States at the University of Pittsburgh in September 1995, its follow-up in Britain in July 1996 at Oxford University.

The charge to the speakers was that everyone would deal with a passage of limited length (so it might be easily surveyable to the audience) which she or he considers important for understanding the epic, and then closely interpret the chosen passage in its context and (if applicable) in light of its references to political and historical facts or developments. The presentation should offer a practical demonstration of the individual interpreter's methodology and, ideally, the choice of passage should allow her/him to open a window on her/his understanding of the work as a whole and of its message. A translation of key lines was expressly welcomed.

There lie, it is hoped, several advantages for the reader in proceeding in this way. Above all, contributors do not set out to present an overarching theory of interpretation but tie themselves down to providing a close reading of a surveyable text section (and this includes attention paid to relevant historical facts); a welcome consequence is that readers can more easily follow the arguments offered (and verify the validity of the conclusions drawn) by individual contributors; and,

Editor's Introduction

by comparing positions and methodologies, they may find the volume useful beyond the information it supplies on current Vergilian scholarship: it may also help them in choosing and defining their own approach to the epic. To this extent, the conferences also were a testing ground: how do different methodologies prove themselves when dealing in detail with a limited passage, easily surveyable to the reader?

One distinguishing feature of the two conferences (its unifying effect is registered with deep appreciation by the convener) has been that so many scholars have willingly agreed to impose upon themselves such stringent requirements in presenting their findings. It is appropriate that I here once more express my sincere gratitude to all the speakers.

In a multi-authored volume, it is difficult for the editor to achieve homogeneity of presentation throughout, especially so where two kinds of English are involved as well as printing conventions originating from a number of different countries. It is conceivable that some contributors might not have felt at ease with a rigorously imposed common standard. The question even arises whether a volume which espouses respect for the diversity of current approaches should at all apply a strait-jacket of unified conventions. After all, individual contributors may rightly consider form an integral part of their presentation. This editor has, while mediating and equalizing in the interest of the common enterprise, tried to be mindful of his colleagues' rights on their own contribution and of their interest. His guiding principle has been to guarantee the reading public's expectation of and right to a clear, unified and accessible presentation.

The impulse and rationale for the undertaking sprang, in part, from precisely that Babylonian confusion in today's Vergilian studies I mentioned earlier (a confusion which they of course share with other areas of literature). This is not the place to give a comprehensive introduction to present-day scholarship on Vergil. There do exist several informative and easily accessible accounts. First to be mentioned are the annual bibliographies, often complemented by brief reviews, which A.G. McKay has provided for several decades in *Vergilius*, the periodical published by the *Vergilian Society of America*.[1] A pronounced, sometimes provocative, report on recent scholarship is offered in N. Horsfall's *Companion to Vergil*.[2] In the opening chapter of his collection entitled *Oxford Readings in Vergil's Aeneid*, S.J. Harrison presents a masterly survey, covering a wide spectrum of twentieth century interpretations.[3] Of special interest regarding questions of literary criticism are the introductory chapter on methodology of R.F. Glei's *Der Vater*

Editor's Introduction

der Dinge[4] and K. Galinsky's *Introduction* to his collection of papers on *The Interpretation of Roman Poetry: Empiricism or Hermeneutics?*[5]

Even though no large-scale historical survey can be given here (in itself, such an undertaking might require a book-length study), at least some of the methodological considerations which led to convening the two conferences and to formulating the charge for the speakers should be highlighted and expounded. For, even if the wide international participation seems to confirm a general scholarly interest in the topic of the *Aeneid*'s political dimension, the organizer should, especially in the light of some present-day trends in Vergilian scholarship, both be ready to account for and be willing to defend the choice of topic and the form of its presentation on his own grounds.

So the reader is invited here to participate in systematically exploring a few prominent strands in (past and) present-day interpretations of the *Aeneid* which deal with the question of Vergil's political stand. Some of them, if universally valid, might (even if the participants did not think so) seem to render the conferences idle. P. White, for instance, declares "the political interpretation of Augustan poetry" to be "a habit of thought" which "has to be combated head-on".[6] Together with a presentation of trends like this one, some alternative methodologies are mentioned. Along the way, attention is paid to recurrent political components in the work's interpretative history.

Overall interpretation of the *Aeneid* has almost always been entwined with reaction to the political conditions prevailing in the interpreter's own time. This is understandable if one considers the epic's own encomiastic emphasis on the political order created in the poet's time, i.e., the principate and empire of Augustus (31 BC–AD 14).

As is well known, there are three great prophecies offered by the work to its reader, and they all culminate in Julian Augustus. In Book 1, the reader hears the prediction of Jupiter, the highest Roman god, given to his daughter Venus, ancestral goddess of the Julian family. It ends with the guarantee of never-ending Roman rule and a pacified empire under Augustus, himself a candidate for deification (1.278–96). In Book 6, Aeneas visits his deceased father Anchises in the underworld and is comforted for his toils by a prospect which is crowned by Augustus' (i.e., his descendant's) re-establishment of a golden age and limitless extension of the empire's frontiers (6.791–807). In Book 8, the god Vulcan supplies the shield which will protect *pius Aeneas* in his final struggle against the impious Italian King Turnus. On the shield, Vulcan has depicted Augustus' (*sic*, 678) final victory over Queen Cleopatra of Egypt and Antony (i.e., the Battle of Actium, 31 BC), as well as the scene of the victor accepting the homage of nations (8.671–728).

It is, then, perhaps no wonder that the *Aeneid*'s strong political component, dressed in the garb of supernatural guidance, has easily engendered a strong reaction in many modern readers and interpreters, and that this reaction is often tinged by their own political convictions.

The interpreter's relationship to the *Aeneid* tends to be unproblematical as long as the interpreter himself lives in a hierarchically structured society whose tenets he shares. Formulating his *"Gesamturteil"* at the end of his compendious commentary on Book 6, E. Norden in 1916 finds the artifice *"worthy* of *the great time* (würdig der grossen Zeit) in which it came into being". Picturing Vergil reading the Book to Augustus, "we must then try to enter the soul of the *greatest son* of that *great time* (in die Seele des grössten Sohnes jener grossen Zeit müssen wir uns also zu versenken suchen)."[7] Obviously, Norden has no problem with the "moral, religious, and political ideals" of "imperial Rome" as he finds them depicted in "the Vergilian *Nekyia*".

Decades later (our systematic perspective allows us to jump ahead quickly), a critical historian's powerful account moves Augustus into the vicinity of the European tyrants of the 1930s. In Syme's *Roman Revolution*, Vergil is seen, along with Horace, as close to the usurper, helping to organize public opinion.[8] In the opposite European camp (where Augustus would be praised as a worthy forerunner of *Führer* or *Duce*) such closeness to the center of power is far from being considered a blemish on a writer's record.[9]

Over the next three decades, the picture of Vergilian criticism begins to take on new features. Whereas some continental European scholars see fit to compensate for the loss of empire by taking refuge in the idea of the Christian European empire (and this can on occasion be seen to begin already after World War I),[10] and others, less perturbed by the political upheaval associated with World War II, continue to endorse the *Aeneid*'s program of Roman world rule,[11] another branch of scholarship, centered in North America, avails itself of new methods in literary criticism, abandoning the perspective of rhetorical (logical) organization handed down from antiquity. These scholars draw a new and widely different picture of Vergil.

Symbolic imagery (made a key instrument of interpretation by Pöschl)[12] and verbal repetition (added as an analytical tool especially by Putnam),[13] when interpreted independently from plotline, i.e.,

Editor's Introduction

from the work's overall train of thought, can suggest new perspectives which allow the interpreter to view Vergil as separate from – or even see him display a critical attitude toward – his Aeneas as well as toward Augustus. This has been the tendency of the so-called Harvard school.[14] In its more developed stage, the "school" has not been uninfluenced by a disinclination against what was seen as U.S. imperialism, and it has claimed Vergil for a more humane world view, in which the victims of Roman imperialism were granted at least as much consideration by the poet as victorious Rome. Once more, then, contemporary politics has played a part in Vergilian interpretation.

At the center of the debate has been the epic's final scene, in which Aeneas kills Turnus, who is both the Julian ancestor's political adversary on Italian soil and the brutal slayer of Aeneas' young ally, Pallas. Does (as interpreters close to the above-mentioned school would see it)[15] the poet himself criticize his *pius Aeneas* (and, implicitly, Augustus) for betraying the ideals of clemency and humanity, or does Augustan Vergil (as those would argue who view the poet's political commitment in accordance with his work's great prophecies) endorse the just punishment of both a malicious killer and an impious rebel against divine ordinances?[16] It seems that, by referring to the *Aeneid*'s text alone, scholars no longer find common ground. The two positions have been standing unreconciled up to this day.

Even a selective methodological survey like the present one can point out some significant developments in scholarship. Once separated from its (formerly appreciated) ties to Augustus, the *Aeneid* regains a literary status of innocence, and, exposed to further innovations in literary criticism, may even appear to confirm a focus (or foci) different from the Augustan perspective assigned to it by tradition.

More recently, an influential theoretical step was taken by Feeney, when he set out to dethrone Jupiter from his position as pronouncer of fate (fate being in this case identical with Jupiter's will). When, in Book 1, consoling his daughter Venus (who insists on a "promise" she allegedly received) about the present sufferings of her son Aeneas and his people, Jupiter's viewpoint (as seen by Feeney) "is not that of a detached author of events, for he speaks, first as a father, but more significantly, as the national god of the Roman state."[17] So Jupiter "does not here afford an impersonal vantage-point for the reader."[18] In this way, "the national force" of Jupiter restricts the god to the level and role of one character among others, offering "a mighty counterbalance to Juno's role as Carthage's chief deity".[19]

Editor's Introduction

   With the balancing of Jupiter by Juno the road has been opened to dual (or even multiple) focalization. The road is fortified further by the moral degradation of Jupiter, when Feeney characterizes the god's stern reaction to the liaison of Aeneas and Carthaginian Queen Dido with the term "inhuman".[20] Worse than Juno, who "can feel pity", Vergil's Jupiter (Feeney informs his reader) cannot feel pity (or anger), ever.[21] When Jupiter sends the *Dira* to make divine Juturna give up her support for her doomed mortal brother (i.e., for Turnus), he is, we hear, "a god paralysing his lover's brother, laying him open for the kill".[22] It appears only consistent that Feeney should arrive at the conclusion that "the narrator is ultimately unable to commit himself to Jupiter's perspective."[23]

   Scholarship has here arrived at a point where the poet's alienation is extended so as to reach beyond Aeneas and Augustus as far as the highest Roman god. To what extent this position, too, is historically conditioned (i.e., conditioned by a *Zeitgeist* that no longer values a central authority), readers may decide for themselves.

Whether or not one should specifically select Feeney's findings here is not the main question for our present discussion, which endeavors systematically to survey a variety of components with which Vergilian Interpretation has been operating, and among which political readings of the *Aeneid* have to locate themselves. One might as well, and with similar consequences, introduce B. Conte's distinction of epic code versus epic norm, and his assertion of (in the words of C. Segal) "a new 'polyphonic' epic that not only incorporates multiple viewpoints but even allows contradiction and incoherence as a fundamental part of its multilayered texture".[24]

   Conte likewise deals with Jupiter's *Dira*, in connection with Juturna's reaction to her brother's doom. Where traditional Augustan interpretation might argue that Juturna's innocent suffering is another consequence of her brother's theomachic[25] conduct and, thus, enhances Turnus' guilt, Conte ("this episode has no narrative justification") sees in her sorrowful and lamenting monologue "a lucid but isolated reflection, without any narrative sequel or dialectical contact with the 'positive' theodicy of the *Aeneid*".[26]

   For what he calls Vergil's "polyphonic way of writing", Conte insists on "the coexistence of the worlds of Aeneas, Dido, Turnus, Mezentius, and Juturna", asserting that "they conflict with each other without the possibility that any one of them may overcome and annul that which stands in opposition to it."[27] An (almost 'democratic') multifocality like

Editor's Introduction

this one requires diminished emphasis on logical organization and plotline: "The dramatic component never goes deeper than the text's *surface structure*; it never affects the shaping of the deep content."[28]

The point of consequence for Vergilian studies today is the frequent assumption of multiple autonomous foci. Such an assumption is conducive to supporting the position that the interpreter is free to choose a perspective for interpreting the literary artifice (as it is also conducive to promoting the thesis of the poet's independence from the Augustanism professed in the work's three great prophecies and ascribed to him by earlier generations of scholars as well as by antiquity).

The difficulty of making legitimate choices of foci has led the organizer to invite the speakers to integrate wherever suitable the core passage of their lecture into what they consider the work's larger context; or, in other words, to provide an outlook on their overall perspective of the epic based on a close reading of the passage they chose for their lecture. After all, what is at stake in this volume is the larger picture of Vergil's political stance.

A specific problem was likewise constitutive for the framework given to the two conferences. It can be defined as the subsumption of linguistic details under the interpreter's overall thesis (a process moving in opposite direction to the inductive method stipulated for the two conferences). The problem is perhaps best illustrated where the translator is the interpreter.

The example is taken from Book 10. After Turnus has killed young Pallas, Aeneas takes four young enemy fighters prisoner to – in the acclaimed translation of Mandelbaum – "offer up" (as victims to Pallas' shade), *quos immolet* (10.519). In the epic's final scene, Aeneas, about to deliver the fatal blow, says to Turnus (in the words of the same translator): "It is Pallas…who sacrifices you"*Pallas te…immolat* (12.949 f.). No one will disagree that *immolare* here (as before at 10.519) is again translated appropriately, this time by "sacrifice".

But the same translator surprises his reader in a third passage where Aeneas, likewise in the aftermath of young Pallas' death, "sacrifices" (*immolat*, 10.541) Haemonides, a priest of Apollo and Diana, who, in shining accouterments, has been fighting against the Aeneadae. This time, Mandelbaum translates *immolat* by "slaughters", thus suggesting that Aeneas is a priest-butcher.

It is not my task here to make a case for translating the third passage consistently with the other two, as for instance again by "sacrifices".[29] My point has to be twofold. First, the example shows how the

xxiii

Editor's Introduction

translation of a single word in a key passage can have ramifications for our understanding of the whole epic. *Pius Aeneas* as a priest-butcher almost certainly would beg the reader to doubt that the poet stands behind his hero. *Pius Aeneas* "sacrificing" a belligerent priest of Apollo who has used his priestly attire when leading his flock to war in defiance of the oracle made public by the country's pious king and priest (cf. 7.81–105), – this Aeneas might appear to show how far the poet is willing to go along with his hero.

Second, our survey's findings suggest that one should check whether Mandelbaum's translation is somehow associated with a stanceconcerning contemporary politics. Perhaps he himself provides us with a clue in his introduction by making the claim about Vergil that "his humanity is constant", and "no man ever felt more deeply the part of the defeated and the lost". In addition, there is Mandelbaum's "personal discontent; this state (no longer, with the Vietnam war, that innocuous word 'society') has wrought the unthinkable, the abominable."[30]

Once more it appears possible that the interpreter's view of present-day politics may have influenced his understanding of the Latin text, this time to the degree that he does not see fit to grant the same translation to the same word in comparable contexts. Apparently, the translator does not see fit to picture the poet siding with (what moderns might call) Roman imperialism and (again, as moderns might call him) the proto-imperialist, Aeneas, against "the part of the defeated and the lost".

The example (which could easily be complemented by others) is apt to demonstrate how the understanding even of seemingly unambiguous linguistic details may be subject to the interpreter's or translator's overall view of the epic's general political line. This had, with an eye also on the audience, to be taken into account when formulating the framework for the conferences. The speakers were encouraged to prefix the key Latin passages they chose for their lectures with translations, preferably their own. This procedure, it was felt, would not only enhance our accountability, but also give the public easier access to the contributions.

Returning from the excursus on the role of linguistic detail to the selective survey of changing trends among *Aeneid* interpretations, one should add that the pendulum of scholarship may today be swinging still further away from the positions held around the middle of this century. Five decades after the end of World War II, the picture of the European tyrants of the thirties has begun to pale in the Western world; they have lost their burning immediacy. It appears that the picture and reputation of Augustus have profited from this development so that he is seen in a more benign (or, at least, in a less evil) light; and that the need to dissociate Vergil from his emperor is no longer felt with the same urgency. Consequently, the gap between power and poetry is nowadays beginning to lose its former appeal, since literary support for (or, at least, connectedness to) the regime need no longer automatically count as a stain on the writer's record.

In times past, the "Augustan" poets, especially Horace and Vergil, have often been viewed as propagating the ideas and tenets of the new regime (with Maecenas functioning as a sort of 'minister of propaganda'), along the lines discernible on the coinage of Augustus or in his building program, as, for instance, expressed in the increasing Julianization of the formerly republican *forum Romanum*.

Today there is also a tendency to discount the possibility of officious directives given to the poets. Some interpreters will argue in favor of mutual respect and of the Augustan poets' intellectual independence rather than resume the unpalatable line of court-inspired literary production, which prevailed largely unquestioned before World War II (and even World War I) when and wherever the first European emperor was held in high esteem. P. White, a pronounced representative of this tendency, being critical of what he calls "the political interpretation of Augustan poetry" (which "has to be combated head-on"),[31] asks the question: "If Augustus did not lay down the lines to be followed, how did these and other motifs related to him come to engross such an important place in contemporary poetry?" Apart from stating that our information "does not suggest that he intruded on their work more than other members of the elite" (a statement which, sixty years earlier, might have been sufficient to worry a historian like Syme), "the answer seems to be that the poets elaborated an Augustan thematic by themselves, independently both of Augustus and of one another."[32]

White's optimistic view of the Augustan poets' situation can easily be balanced by a less favorable scholarly evaluation.[33] For objectivity's sake, a case concerning Horace may serve as an illustration. Binder[34] draws an interesting parallel: as academic presentation of the past often is connected to the modern-day scholar's political convictions, so the *mores maiorum* could be manipulated according to the interests of the regime which invoked them. In this area (Binder maintains) contemporary writers could (and were supposed to) help form the ideology of the *Princeps*. Among examples of cooperation between power and poets Binder cites Horace's call for the restoration of dilapidated temples (*donec templa refeceris*, C. 3.6.2, etc.) and Augustus' claim to have done just that in 28 BC (*duo et octoginta templa...refeci*, R.G. 20). Of course, Horace does not raise a new demand but he reacts "to a programmatic promise of Augustus from the time before or right after Actium". "Augustus on his part could claim to have fulfilled the poet's 'demand'..."[35]

The literary critic may find problems in the approach pursued by White for adequately appreciating the art of the *Aeneid*; they would lie in the overall concept of literature: does a critical evaluation, building on "thematic", "motifs", and "theme",[36] do justice to the work's organization (which, according to ancient information, had been established before versification started)?[37]

But White's approach is not that of a literary critic (and, so, this aspect of his work may be dispensed with here). He first of all deals with the question of poetry which may have been written following a request (a condition he finds generally not applicable to poets working under Augustus, according to the quotation given earlier). He approaches the question from the angle of the social relationship that exists between poet and patron. Since this procedure involves "subordinating discussion of the poems to discussion of their social background throughout the book",[38] there seems to be sufficient room left for a text-oriented investigation into the *Aeneid*'s political context, especially under the variety of aspects which two multi-authored conferences can provide.

For our systematic survey, White's position supplies evidence on two fronts of an ongoing "liberalization" in a growing sector of Vergilian studies. Under this perspective, an Augustan poet needs neither be an executor of a political program set up by his ruler, nor any longer stand in (more or less disguised) subversive opposition to the regime.

It is not only the sociological perspective addressed by White which results in re-evaluating existing positions. Research on Augustan art has helped to suggest avenues which lead in the same direction. Referring to developments in literary criticism, one has maintained that works of Augustan art can display an intentional ambiguity or even multi-referentiality, and cited this feature in support of a literary critical position. In the words of one scholar, "we are dealing with an intentional and authorially defined polysemy", which is seen to be comparable to "a multi-referential, complex iconography".[39] So the aspect of "the complex, nuanced, and multi-referential nature of

Editor's Introduction

Augustan art" as developed by art historians contributes to a model which "can be fruitfully extended to other aspects of Augustan culture, too."[40]

Such an approach is fundamentally different from the interpretative analysis of an ambiguity which documents itself in and through the medium of logic employed by the poet.[41] What it is said to allow is extending the *Aeneid*'s meaning beyond the poem's historical roots that anchor it in its own time.

Under our perspective of a selective but systematic review the position taken by Galinsky is highly significant because it synthesizes in a fresh combination elements we have encountered in past and current readings of Vergil. What is especially interesting for rounding out our survey, is that this approach is utilized for shedding the old straitjacket of Vergilian interpretation, which our opening sections illustrated through the bipolarity of the imperialist and anti-imperialist approaches, each of them conditioned by its attitude toward Emperor Augustus. There we saw how a politically acceptable Augustus was provided with the company of a supportive and congenial Vergil; but a politically unacceptable Augustus may be denied the poet's sympathy (as his poetic ancestor Aeneas may be denied humanly attractive features). It was also indicated that, fifty years after the demise of the European tyrants, the picture of Augustus is more tempered and less condemning.

These ingredients come together in Galinsky's approach: the concepts and ideas of the Augustan age "are not explained by a mere preoccupation with power; genuine leadership goes beyond the accumulation of power."[42] And " 'ideology' and 'propaganda' are inadequate foundations for lasting political systems." "And we have also come to realize the need for true values, guiding ideas, and a sense of direction." These are some of the features to which Galinsky's book pays attention. In particular, the last-quoted sentence appears to revive the old desire ("*we* have...come to realize") to receive edifying moral guidance from the "classical" Roman poet. Whereas most scholars would unhesitatingly read Thucydides (or Tacitus, for that matter) for the insights he provides into the darker side of humanity, this is not generally the case with Vergil. Galinsky insists that Augustan culture "was inspired by ideas, ideals, and values".[43] This is assumed to be especially true of the *Aeneid*, and it is through the theoretical position addressed above that Vergil can be viewed as being both Augustan and perennial.

This is not the place to deal once more with "the intentional multiplicity of resonances" supposedly evoked in the reader by the literary ancestry of an epic character (Galinsky is extraordinarily detailed on

Editor's Introduction

Dido, as Feeney is on Juno). What is important for Galinsky's position (if I understand him correctly on a difficult point) is his acknowledgement that "an authorial center exists along with the intended polysemy".[44] On another occasion, he mentions "a strong authorial, and even moral, center".[45]

A serious problem of preceding scholarship was the question, 'how to deal with a Vergil who is tied to Augustus?' Viewing, on the one hand, the achievements of the first Roman emperor in a less negative light, Galinsky on the other hand suggests as part of his solution that "Vergil uses them [i.e., the Augustan ideas], however, not as 'propaganda' or 'ideology,' but as a springboard for meditations on humanity and heroism. The Augustan ideas are extended to the point where the scope of these meditations becomes universal."[46] In this way Galinsky sees "the *Aeneid's* permanence"[47] or "transcendence" established, which supposedly lifts the epic above and beyond its Augustan moorings.

The circle of our selective survey is closed. To a degree, the positions of White and Galinsky mean a qualified and cautious re-institution of elements found in the earliest example I cited of Vergilian interpretation, viz. in the stance of Norden (itself representative of its time). So the survey reveals at least as much about the historical conditioning of pendular swings in scholarship as it does about an appropriate approach to the Augustan poetry of Vergil. There can be no doubt that the *Aeneid* with its divine prophecies about the fated rule of Augustus and about the return of the golden age under his sway holds a key to the imperial ideology as well as to traditional western concepts about the relationship of individual and state. The epic's determining and lasting influence, exercised still on our own world and age, ought not to lie outside the scholar's view when investigating the *Aeneid*'s political context. With regard to the epic itself, it must be stated that the need to consider its political context and ramifications may have been blurred at times, but has never ceased to exist.

These considerations widen the volume's scope beyond the range of current approaches to Vergil. In taking stock, the collection implicitly also comments on integral aspects of western political thought as well as reflecting the changes in scholarship that inherently deal with those aspects. It is hoped that the volume's wide variety of methodological perspectives may entice the reader also to reflection on the tides of *Wissenschaftsgeschichte* (history of scholarship) and that the constant referencing to political history may also serve as a wholesome controlling device which may help to define apposite routes of interpretation.

Editor's Introduction

Notes

* My thanks go to Dr Anton Powell, Ms Jana Adamitis and Dr Gisela Stahl for helpful criticism of an earlier version.

1. For McKay's reports, see the attached bibliography.
2. For Horsfall, see the bibliography.
3. Harrison (1990) 1–20.
4. Glei (1991) 1–41.
5. Galinsky (1992) 1–40.
6. White (1993) 96.
7. Norden (1916) 362. Translation and italics mine.
8. Syme (1974) 461–5. First edition: 1939.
9. On the use of Augustan ideas in Nazi ideology see Binder (1987) 1–4, 44–58; on the ideological 'usurpation' of Livy (often viewed in close proximity to Vergil's *Aeneid*) and *Römertum* in Germany in the 1930s, see Thraede (1988) 394–9 (with notes 2–7); 404–23. Today's scholarship does not ask the question why the *Aeneid* could so easily be appropriated by the ideologies of the thirties.
10. This tendency is represented especially by Haecker (1931); it is felt also in Pöschl's book (first edition, 1950). In addition to Harrison (1990) and Glei (1991) as quoted above, see also Stahl (1981) 157; (1990) 178–82.
11. The leading major German works (following earlier articles) are Klingner (1967) and Büchner (1961, a separate edition of his article, "Publius Vergilius Maro. Der Dichter der Römer", in Pauly-Wissowa's *Realencyclopädie*). See also E. Burck (1979) 52.
12. See the subtitle of Pöschl's book: "*Bild und Symbol in der Aeneis*".
13. In a 1970 publication (reprinted in Putnam 1995; see there p. 107), Putnam refers to the tame stag of the Italian girl, Silvia; the animal was wounded by Aeneas' hunting son, Ascanius. "An obvious link between Turnus and the stag is only felt, not stated, in book 7 (the stag, for instance, is *forma praestanti*, 483, while Turnus, armed, is *praestanti corpore*, 783)."
14. On the history of this name (to a degree, a misnomer which has developed into common currency) and on the School, see Clausen in the *Appendix* to Horsfall (1995) pp. 313 f. Next to Clausen himself, A. Parry (1963) should be mentioned as another early representative, together with K. Quinn (1968). For the chronology, see also Glei (1991) 14 f. Connecting Vergilian interpretation to the American experience of the 1960s (and 1950s): Nethercut (1986) 325f. The term "Harvard school" seems to appear for the first time in Johnson (1976, 11; see also note 10 there), viewed in contrast to the "European school" (1976, 13).
15. See, for instance, the final chapter in Putnam (1965), and, especially, Putnam (1984).
16. See Stahl (1990); also, compare Galinsky (1988).
17. Feeney (1993) 140. (Commas are Feeney's.)
18. Feeney (1993) 141.
19. Feeney (1993) 141.
20. Feeney (1993) 144.
21. Feeney (1993) 144, with note 61.
22. Feeney (1993) 151.

Editor's Introduction

[23] Feeney (1993) 155.

[24] Conte (1986) 158.

[25] Augustan interpretation might have presented Turnus as knowing that Jupiter is his enemy (12.895) because Turnus started the war against Aeneas in defiance of the oracle obtained with due rites and made public by King Latinus (7.102–5a).

[26] Conte (1986) 158.

[27] Conte (1986) 157.

[28] Conte (1986) 162.

[29] It is, however, important for our discussion to see that the possibility of an alternative to Mandelbaum's translation (an alternative which would not change the lexicographical meaning of the verb *immolare*; cf. *OLD, s.v.*) cannot be categorically excluded. An interpreter seeing Vergil going along with Aeneas' act might wish to point to the fact that Serestus (one of Aeneas' honored chief officers, cf. 9.171–4, 778 f. His unexpected presence at the scene is perhaps due to an oversight) carries the arms of the killed priest away in order that they may – in due observance of the *Aeneid*'s code of military piety – be offered to the war god Mars (Gradivus) as a *tropaeum* (542). He might also wish to point to another priest of Apollo, Panthus, who in the night of Troy's fall carries the city's gods and holy objects to Aeneas in Anchises' house (2.318–21); so Aeneas can later ask his father to carry them when leaving the city on his son's shoulders (2.717).

There may also arise the question whether, under this alternative aspect, it would make sense (perhaps sarcastic sense, comparable to such comments by the narrator as at 8.643 or at 10.390–6) that Aeneas "sacrifices" Haemonides (dressed with the sacrificer's/victim's *infula*) because the priest-in-arms has betrayed the god whom he is supposed to serve. After all, Apollo is, in the *Aeneid*, the guiding divinity *par excellence* for Aeneas (to whom he even speaks directly, without a priestly mediator, 3.93, 99), and in a comparable function he is also claimed by Aeneas' greater descendant, Augustus, in his political life and career (Apollo and Diana reside in the temple adjacent to the Emperor's residence on the Palatine hill).

[30] Mandelbaum (1961) X f.

[31] White (1993) 96.

[32] White (1993) 206.

[33] "How strong the pressure was that was exerted 'from above', not in the last place by Augustus himself, will remain debated; just 'going along and pretending' ... would not correctly describe either the artistic climate in the environment of Augustus..." Binder (1987) 24 (my translation. "Wie stark der nicht zuletzt von Augustus selbst ausgeübte Druck 'von oben' war, wird strittig bleiben; blosses 'Mitmimen' ... dürfte das künstlerische Klima in der Umgebung des Augustus auch nicht richtig beschreiben...")

[34] Binder (1987) 2; cf. 32, 44 f.

[35] Binder (1987) 29, cf. 27–9. My translation.

[36] See also White (1993) 182–90 passim.

[37] See *vita Donati*, 23; Horsfall (1995) 16 f.

[38] White (1993) 19.

[39] Galinsky (1992) 12; cf. 1996, 231.
[40] Galinsky (1996) 5. On p. 229, he states that "as in the case of the Ara Pacis, the intentional multiplicity of resonances of the *Aeneid* and the *Metamorphoses*, for instance, can be experienced on several levels, depending on the intellectual and social horizon of the reader."
[41] For the type of logically verifiable ambiguity, see Stahl (1985), *Index* (p. 399), *s.v.* "Ambiguity"; and, for an example (1.18), pp. 75–8: "Using romantic scenery, Propertius plays a rococo game."
[42] These and the following quotations are from Galinsky (1996) 4–8.
[43] Galinsky (1996) 8.
[44] Galinsky (1996) 231.
[45] Galinsky (1992) 11.
[46] Galinsky (1996) 239.
[47] Galinsky (1996) 239. The section is entitled "Transcendence" (p. 237); it also refers to "the breadth of meanings inherent in a classic as it raises substantive questions about the human condition" (p. 237).

Select Bibliography

Binder, G.
    1987   "Einführung", in G. Binder (ed.) *Saeculum Augustum I. Herrschaft und Gesellschaft*, Wege der Forschung 266, 1–58, Darmstadt.

Büchner, K.
    1961   *P. Vergilius Maro: Der Dichter der Römer*, Stuttgart.

Burck, E.
    1979   "Vergils *Aeneis*", in id. (ed.) *Das römische Epos*, 51–119, Darmstadt.

Clausen, W.
    1964   "An Interpretation of the *Aeneid*", *HSCP* 68, 139–47.

Conte, G.B.
    1986   *The Rhetoric of Imitation: Genre and Poetic Memory in Virgil and Other Latin Poets*, tr. and ed. C. Segal. Cornell Studies in Classical Philology 44, Ithaca.

Feeney, D.
    1993   *The Gods in Epic. Poets and Critics of the Classical Tradition*, Oxford.

Galinsky, G.K.
    1988   "The Anger of Aeneas", *AJPh* 109, 321–48.
    1992   "The Interpretation of Roman Poetry and the Contemporary Critical Scene", in K. Galinsky (ed.) *The Interpretation of Roman Poetry: Empiricism or Hermeneutics?* Studien zur Klassischen Philologie (67), 1–40, Frankfurt am Main (etc.).
    1996   *Augustan Culture. An Interpretive Introduction*, Princeton, N.J.

Glei, R.F.
    1991   *Der Vater der Dinge: Interpretationen zur politischen, literarischen und kulturellen Dimension des Krieges bei Vergil*, Trier.

Haecker, Th.
    1958   *Vergil. Vater des Abendlandes*, Frankfurt am Main/Hamburg (first edition, 1931).

Editor's Introduction

Harrison, S. J. (ed.),
  1990 *Oxford Readings in Vergil's* Aeneid, Oxford.
  1991 *Vergil. Aeneid 10. With Introduction, Translation, and a Commentary*, Oxford.
Horsfall, N. (ed.),
  1995 *A Companion to the Study of Virgil*, Mnemosyne, suppl. vol. 151, Leiden.
Johnson, W.R.
  1976 *Darkness Visible. A Study of Vergil's* Aeneid, Berkeley.
Klingner, F.
  1967 *Virgil: Bucolica, Georgica, Aeneis*, Zürich.
Mandelbaum, A.
  1961 *The* Aeneid *of Vergil. A Verse Translation*, Toronto, etc.
McKay, A.G.
  1964– "Vergilian bibliography". Annual reports in *Vergilius*.
Nethercut, W.R.
  1986 "American Scholarship on Vergil in the Twentieth Century", in J.D. Bernhard (ed.) *Vergil at 2000. Commemorative Essays on the Poet and his Influence*, 303–30, New York.
Norden, E.
  1901 "Vergils *Aeneis* im Lichte ihrer Zeit", *NJA* 7, 249–82, 313–34.
  1957 *P. Vergilius Maro. Aeneis Buch VI.* Ed. with comm. 4th edn, Darmstadt (2nd edn, 1916).
Parry, A.
  1963 "The Two Voices of Virgil's *Aeneid*", *Arion* 2, 66–80.
Pöschl, V.
  1977 *Die Dichtkunst Virgils: Bild und Symbol in der* Aeneis, 3rd revised and enlarged edn, Berlin (first edition, 1950).
Putnam, M.C.J.
  1965 *The Poetry of the Aeneid: Four Studies in Imaginative Unity and Design*, Cambridge, Mass.
  1984 "The hesitation of Aeneas", in *Atti del Convegno mondiale scientifico di studi su Virgilio. Mantova, Roma, Napoli, 19-24 settembre 1981*, a cura dell' Accademia Nazionale Virgiliana, vol. 2, 233–52, Milan.
  1995 *Vergil's* Aeneid. *Interpretation and Influence*, Chapel Hill and London.
Quinn, K.
  1968 *Virgil's* Aeneid. *A Critical Description*, London.
Stahl, H.P.
  1981 "Aeneas – an 'Unheroic' Hero?", *Arethusa* 14, 157–77.
  1985 *Propertius: "Love" and "War". Individual and State Under Augustus*, Berkeley.
  1990 "The Death of Turnus: Augustan Vergil and the Political Rival", in K.A. Raaflaub and M. Toher (eds.) *Between Republic and Empire: Interpretations of Augustus and His Principate*, 174-211, Berkeley.
Syme, R.
  1974 *The Roman Revolution*, London (repr. of 1962 edn).

Thraede, K.
　1988　"Außerwissenschaftliche Faktoren im Liviusbild der neueren Forschung", in G. Binder (ed.) *Saeculum Augustum II. Religion und Literatur*, Wege der Forschung 512, 394–425, Darmstadt.

White, P.
　1993　*Promised Verse. Poets in the Society of Augustan Rome*, Cambridge.

1

VERGIL ANNOUNCING THE *AENEID*
On *Georgics* 3.1–48[1]

Egil Kraggerud

If we can trust the *Vita Donati* (§35), Vergil read his *Georgics* to Octavian at Atella in Campania in the summer of 29 BC.[2] I guess that the poet had sent him a copy before they met. Amidst the preparations for the triumphs and ensuing festivities in Rome[3] this recital was important enough to engage Octavian's attention for at least one hour and a half on four consecutive days. The reason why the poet was invited and shown so much attention was probably only partly due to his expert knowledge of agriculture. One can assume that Octavian had heard, via Maecenas, that Vergil planned to write an epic poem on Aeneas, his own ancestor and father of the nation. These plans were at any rate ripe enough at the time to be firmly embedded in the middle of the *Georgics*. That Octavian would care to listen to the poem there and then – attended of course by an audience of chosen *comites* – was no small token of confidence in Vergil. Octavian had probably never forgotten that Vergil paid him a handsome tribute in his First Eclogue (40–5). I am sure he had also invited the poet to take part in the celebrations to follow in Rome. We can easily see that there must have been much to interest Octavian in the *Georgics*, for instance with regard to old religion and to *mos maiorum* in general. He would have heard thoughts that were politically relevant and presented in a way he could sympathize with, perhaps be guided by. Used to flattery as he was, much of which must have been rather tasteless, he would have admired Vergil's dexterity in this respect and found him a useful mouthpiece for his own Western values. Vergil gave him something to ponder upon in the last part of Book I with his assessment of the difficult period from Caesar's death until it all was on the point of chaos (*Geo.* 1.463–514). Vergil had painted the situation before Actium as utterly gloomy and hopeless but for the prospect of Octavian's leadership (1.498–502),[4] and in all this Vergil had avoided making

Octavian party to the atrocities of the past. On all four days Octavian was honoured explicitly,[5] but on the third he would surely have been more attentive than ever when the poet commented on the most recent victories and promised to make them the subject of a future poem.

In the prologue to the whole poem (1.1–5a) the theme of Book 3 was announced as 'tending of cattle', *cura boum* (3), and 'the method for keeping a flock', *cultus habendo* | ...*pecori* (3–4), and Vergil had proceeded in the invocation part (5 ff.) to address the competent deities in that regard, the Fauni with the Dryades (10–12a), then Neptune who had created the horse (12b–14a); he had asked Pan to leave his pastures on the Lycaeus and the Maenalus (16–18a), and he had even appealed to a hero not mentioned by name (14–15),[6] but not too difficult to recognize, Aristaeus, the son of Apollo.[7]

Opening the Third Book, he mentions none of these, but invokes instead a couple of deities mentioned in the song of Mopsus in the Fifth Eclogue (35), the goddess Pales and Apollo Nomios:

I will sing of you too, mighty Pales, and of you, memorable shepherd of Amphrysus, and of you, Lycaean woods and rivers.

> Te quoque, magna Pales, et te memorande canemus
> pastor ab Amphryso, uos, siluae amnesque Lycaei.

These gods remind us of the pastoral world of the eclogues in a reassuring way. At the death of Daphnis they had left the countryside together,[8] now we are about to see them again exerting their beneficial influence on it. Only the place-name *Lycaeus* serves as a link to the presentation of Book 3 in the first prologue (1.16). Apollo is mentioned as *pastor ab Amphryso*. It would hardly have escaped Octavian that this was the first invocation of Apollo in the poem, indeed the first direct reference to his own guardian god. There had been no mention of him in the first prologue in the poet's kind of *dodekatheon* where four among that number had been invoked.[9] Instead the poet had concentrated on his son Aristaeus (1.14) as patron of cattle. And Apollo was almost conspicuously absent when the poet called on *Vesta mater* to extend her protection to *Romana Palatia* at the end of Book I (498b–499). When the god eventually appears in our proem it is in a rather unassuming way, it may seem. Apollo's pastoral career was usually presented as a punishment imposed on him by Zeus.[10] Vergil seems to have taken the sting out of such an interpretation by alluding to the famous second hymn of Callimachus[11] where Apollo was invoked as Nomios tending the horses of Admetos ἐπ' Ἀμφρυσσῷ (48); the menial task had been undertaken explicitly out of love for the young king (49).

Of course the reference to Callimachus' use of the name Amphrysus has long been recognized. Richard Thomas points to a number of other possible allusions to Callimachus in our prologue.[12] One should consider the total impact of these references. It emerges that Vergil, while in some respects a true Callimachean, is bent on going one better than Callimachus in others. Nobody could object to a presentation of Apollo Nomios in the introduction to a book dealing mainly with the tending of horses and cattle. But Vergil would have been both blind and deaf if he had not been aware of the god's true potential when addressing Caesar (Octavian) in 29.[13] And the Callimachean reference implies just such an awareness. The passage on Apollo Nomios in the Alexandrian poet functions as a modest rural prelude to a passage praising the god as a truly great Olympian. Callimachus proceeds to show that Apollo took a particular delight in founding cities (56-7a) and did so already as a boy on native Delos where he had founded his famous altar of goats' horns (57-64).[14] What was to crown the god's activities in this field was that he led Battus and his colonists from Thera to Libya by means of oracles and established Cyrene as a new home for them (65 ff.). Thereby the god had bestowed his blessings on the city, on Battus and his successors and on the poet as well since Callimachus was a relative of the royal family. As was only meet and proper, the city and its kings had gratefully honoured Apollo Karneios with a magnificent shrine, a festival and rich sacrifices (77 ff.). I believe that Callimachus' account of Apollo starting from Apollo Nomios and ending with a climactic tribute to Apollo Karneios of Cyrene has some bearing on our prologue.

> All else that might have held idle minds fast in song is now hackneyed
>
> > Cetera, quae vacuas tenuissent carmine[15] mentes,
> > omnia iam vulgata   (3-4a)

This seems at first glance, looking backwards, to serve as a defence for the poet's choice of theme for his *Georgics*, like the theme of cattle-tending just alluded to in the preceding invocation. As one continues, however, it becomes clear that the words form part of a syntagm together with *temptanda via est etc.* (8).[16]

The Callimachean reference in *omnia iam vulgata* is obvious enough, though Vergil softens the contempt in 'I loathe everything popular', σικχαίνω πάντα τὰ δημόσια *(Epigr.* 27.4) by leaving out the verb, 'loathe'. Moreover, *iam* grants that the trivial themes were at one time original and interesting. Illustrating examples follow, i.e., themes rejected by our poet:

Egil Kraggerud

Who is ignorant of cruel Eurystheus or the altar of the accursed Busiris? By whom has not (the story of) the boy Hylas been told, Latona's Delos, and Hippodame, and Pelops marked with an ivory shoulder, fierce with his horses?

>   quis aut Eurysthea durum
> 5 aut illaudati nescit Busiridis aras?
>   cui non dictus Hylas puer et Latonia Delos
>   Hippodameque umeroque Pelops insignis eburno,
>   acer equis?   (4b–8a)

The examples may seem somewhat baffling. We have learnt to see our poet as deeply familiar with Greek poetry, both modern and archaic. But his adherence to Greek models has obviously certain limits beyond which he cannot follow them. The Roman poet is now *de facto* rejecting the greatest themes of Greek epic and religious poetry, not only in the Callimachean way by declining 'cyclic poems',[17] but apparently wholesale. It cannot escape us that Vergil, having reminded us of Callimachus' Hymn to Apollo, is making a programmatic statement as important as those propounded in that same hymn (105–12) and elsewhere. Callimachus made it clear that it was impossible to attain to the level of the Homeric Oceanus, πόντος (106); if one tried, the result would be a muddy affair (108–9). Only the drops from a pure fountain were fit when honouring a god (110–12). The programme of Callimachus turned down one kind of poetic effort and extolled another. Vergil seems to refuse both these alternatives as viable roads to success, and so he makes us all the more curious to see the positive side of his programme.

In contrast to Callimachus, Vergil is specific about the subject matter to be avoided by an ambitious poet, first Hercules and his athla,[18] but evidently not only as a ποίημα κυκλικόν, but also in the episodic form favoured by Alexandrian poets and by Callimachus in particular. It strikes the reader that Vergil's remarks on the greatest of all Greek heroes imply certain reservations. Hercules was not a free hero. The magnificent deeds of civilization he performed were due to the orders of a cruel and unworthy master (4). He had joined the expedition of Jason, but his only claim to fame as an Argonaut was his amorous search for Hylas (6a).[19] Pelops, on the other hand, carries for ever a shoulder[20] reminding us of an inadvertent act of cannibalism of gods, and he won his Hippodame by cheating his father-in-law and killing his charioteer (7–8a).

Thus the themes of the great Alexandrian poets, and of Callimachus in particular, have become irrelevant not only because they had been treated already: their heroes are not always up to heroic standard either. This last-mentioned limitation, however, does not apply to *Latonia Delos* in l. 6, a reference as clear as one could wish to the Fourth Hymn of Callimachus. Callimachus had focused very much on the blessed island itself as a safe haven for the pregnant Leto. This one example at least indicates that Vergil's *recusatio* has nothing to do with the 'great book' (μέγα βιβλίον) issue, so often referred to with dubious justification. According to Vergil even a medium-sized hymn written in the most exquisite and learned style would have been dated. So the Callimachean programme has become inadequate, to say the least. Vergil is implicitly ironic: you may admire this poetry as much as you like; the fact that Callimachus (or others) treated a certain topic does not prevent it from being dated for me, a modern Roman poet.

But there is a more disturbing side to this example. In *Latonia Delos* Apollo again, albeit implicitly, comes into view only to be dismissed as a fit theme for a modern poem. Is not this a strange note to strike towards the native island of Apollo face to face with Octavian who favoured this god so much? That Hercules does not fare better than he does also calls for some qualification. Octavian was perhaps just then busy synchronizing his triumphant return to Rome with the calendar of the Hercules worship in the Forum Boarium, thus emphasizing his claim to be a new Hercules.[21]

The traditional Greek heroic and hymnic poetry, then, cannot claim either interest on the reader's part (*quis...nescit*) or originality on the poet's (*cui non dictus*) any longer. The poet is faced with two possibilities, either to go on writing poetry on themes like those belonging to the farmer's world – that would mean to sacrifice higher ambitions – or to find some virgin theme in epic or hymnic poetry. The Roman poet is already at the cross-roads where a decision is required. He is highlighting what is incongruous in his own situation. For the time being, that is within the poem itself, Vergil leaves his present enterprise and concentrates for a few moments on the future project, which the first reader knows is already under way.[22] Due to the fiction that his new plan is as it were still encapsulated in the *Georgics* as a poem still unfolding itself, we are all the more prepared to accept a certain eclecticism in what the poet is going to disclose about his 'future' plans.

The essential thing for the time being is that the poet has seen and seized on the true literary potential of Octavian's triumph. Due to the recent victories the poet has got an opportunity of becoming a *victor* himself. He could not possibly commit himself as a poet more totally to Octavian's cause than by making his own poetic success dependent on

Egil Kraggerud

Octavian's political one. There we have the positive side of Vergil's programme and one far beyond the horizon of the Callimachean one. In fact he is imparting to us a manifesto to counter Callimachus and open up for something like Homer's Ὠκεανός again. Considering that Caesar (Octavian) has won splendid victories (i.e. at least victories that can be made to look splendid), that the poet is facing the mightiest man on earth who is going to celebrate himself on a scale Rome had not seen since the days of Pompey, the general reader could not have been taken aback by the poet's choice of a great theme. The new hero differs from Hercules and Pelops in two respects: he is a living hero and he is a Roman. And compared with Hercules Caesar is subservient to the Roman people, and not to a despicable tyrant. Whereas Hercules had slain a barbaric Egyptian king, the new Roman hero had in fact conquered the whole Egyptian kingdom and become the successor of Alexander. Caesar was indeed a worthy substitute for Hercules and Pelops on the heroic side. An ambitious poet, then, could do nothing better than leave the traditional themes of distant mythology and turn to the most recent events on the world scene. This is the surface side of it, and on the basis of the obvious equation Hercules–Caesar the reader cannot be blamed for thinking in terms of a Caesar epic. This impression is well summed up by Mynors in his formula: 'We are, it seems, meant to think of an epic on Caesar with backward glances towards Troy, rather than the historical poem Vergil afterwards wrote, with its forward glances towards Caesar.'[23] All the same, it is difficult to believe that Vergil changed plans or found out at a later stage that a Caesar epic was not a good idea after all. Or that he had only vague ideas so far about the character of his new poem.

At this juncture in my reading I would like to anticipate my conclusion in a provisional way. I believe that the fairly recent additions to the Third Book of the *Aetia* have put our prologue in a new light.[24] Richard Thomas who so fruitfully has drawn our attention to the relevance of the new material for the interpretation of the proem has little if anything to say concerning the specific issue of an *Aeneid* versus a Caesar epic. The opening of the Third Book of the *Aetia* commemorated the win of Berenice's chariot at the Nemean games founded by Hercules. Vergil refers to these games in Callimachus with the expression 'the groves of Molorchus', *lucos Molorchi* (19). In tune with this topic of 'games arising from heroic actions' is Pelops, whose famous chariot race with Oinomaos was considered to be the inauguration of the Olympic games.[25] Pelops himself, however, was less deserving of epinician praise on account of his unfair means. The great panhellenic games, then, were established in the wake of great (or not so great) feats carried out by famous mythical heroes. And something similar could be seen in the case of the most recent Roman hero as well: his victories had led to Actian Games surpassing the old Greek games as they now point towards promised allegorical games from Vergil's side, that is a future poem.

But there is more to the Callimachean parallel than this. Just to recapitulate: Book 3 of the *Aetia* opened with the commemoration of Berenice's winning chariot at the Nemean Games (the *Victoria Berenices*) accompanied by the aetiological account of how the games were founded by Hercules; the hero was instructed to do so by Athena after he had slain the Nemean lion, a tale Callimachus had combined with the story of the peasant Molorchus with whom Hercules lodged immediately before he killed the destructive beast. Now, the concern of Callimachus is to link past and present by means of the αἴτιον. A great mythical hero, his achievement and the ensuing games are linked within the poem's framework with a chariot victory won by the poet's royal patroness, the Alexandrian queen. As for Vergil, he has a contemporary victor who far surpasses the royal person Callimachus had praised, to the extent that his Caesar had defeated Berenice's descendant, the last queen on the throne of the Ptolemies, Cleopatra. He is a hero who overshadows even the mythical Hercules. Only in one respect does Vergil seem deficient: the glorious past that provided Callimachus with his *aition* has apparently no counterpart in Vergil's version. The contemporary scene is dominant, his Caesar represents both Berenice and Hercules. But on further consideration this is not quite so. For those able to see a little bit below the surface there is a missing link to be found. Vergil has in mind something proportionate along the same lines, combining a living hero with a glorious past. He is in fact going to establish a much closer and richer link between the past and the present than Callimachus had ever been able to. Admittedly the required mythological figure is not there *in persona*. Vergil is playing hide and seek with us in a way Octavian would have relished. So far Vergil's point is this: my heroes, both the present and the past one, are no Greeks; instead of Hercules and Pelops on the mythical side you will find a Trojan, Aeneas, father of the nation, father of the *gens Iulia*, a true link between *illud tempus* and the contemporary scene. Important inferences will follow: Queen Berenice in Callimachus' poem was a *victrix* in the chariot race, Vergil's Pelops was also a *victor* in a chariot race, albeit a deceitful one, Callimachus' Hercules was a *victor* over the Nemean lion, Caesar is indeed a global *victor* surpassing even

Egil Kraggerud

Hercules.[26] Aeneas, however, though from the outset a loser, became in the end a new sort of *victor*. This is the heart of the matter. Just as Caesar is another sort of *victor* altogether – he has saved Rome and is its second founder – so Aeneas once saved the Trojans and founded a new nation. This theme of a new national heroism is already inherent in the gloomy end to the First Book of the *Georgics*. What was, compared to this, the *aition* of Hercules, the Greek hero whom Antony was so proud to reckon as his ancestor?[27] For now I leave the subtle suggestions provided by the Third Book of the *Aetia*.

Nothing in this proem deserves cursory treatment, but on the basis of the above interpretation I can proceed a little more rapidly returning to the Pelops example (7–8a). At this point the poet could have continued, 'Let me pursue the virgin woods and glades of the Dryads', *Dryadum silvas saltusque sequamur | intactos etc.*, i.e., l. 40 f., minus *interea*. But he refuses to resign himself to the situation, presenting instead a solution to the problem:

> a path must be ventured where I too may rise from earth and fly before the eyes of men.[28]
>
> ...temptanda via est, qua me quoque possim
> tollere humo victorque virum volitare per ora.

There is a lofty theme at hand, a great opportunity in fact, that can bring him laurels. By reminding the reader of Ennius' famous epitaph,[29] Virgil signals that his ambition will be to write a national epic, though he bypasses the *Annales* with his insistent *primus*.[30] His epic poem will be the result of a triumphant return to his country with the Muses. The poet will romanize heroic poetry, not by banishing the Greek impulse, but by making it subservient to his Roman subject-matter. This much I deduce metonymically from 'I will bring with me to my native land...the Muses from their Aonian peak', *in patriam mecum... | Aonio rediens deducam vertice Musas* (10–11).

The poet himself is a victor *expressis verbis* in ll. 9 and 17 whereas Caesar (Octavian) is so by patent implication (see especially 'the arms of victorious Quirinus',[31] *victoris...arma Quirini*, 27[32]). The parallelism between the poet and Caesar is sustained throughout the proem. As this aspect has been emphasized well enough by Buchheit, I will just make a couple of additional observations. Octavian was returning from the East, the Greek world, Egypt in particular; he was presenting himself as the conqueror of the East, of Alexandria in particular. The whole prestigious Ptolemaic kingdom had become his, and so all of a sudden the cultural pride of that city had become the conqueror's heritage and responsibility. In this proem Rome's leading poet shows himself aware of the implications. As Octavian was a successor to the Ptolemaic crown, so contemporary Roman poets were challenged to succeed the Alexandrian poets.

Vergil behaves like a victor and uses notions associated with Caesar as a triumphant general on his way to Rome; Vergil will bring *Idumaeas palmas* to his home Mantua (l. 12). Octavian must recently have passed through that region, and successfully so, as we know from his contact with Herod.[33] Arranging the festival, the poet will appear in Tyrian purple, *Tyrio...in ostro* (17). The city that had been conquered by Alexander after a long siege contributes its splendour to the great triumph. Vergil's temple and festival will supplant those of the Panhellenic world, the most important of which were the Olympic Games, taking place at the river Alpheus. As the Actian Games surpassed these in the real world, so the poet's allegorical ones serve to remind us that Roman poetry is from now on ambitious to take the lead.

Vergil gives his temple and its games a setting on the river Mincius, a bucolic landscape as the poet stresses by quoting himself.[34] Why does he not establish it all in Rome in order to underline the imperial aspect of his new poem? There are probably many factors at play, both positive and negative. The personal character of the cult is one thing; we have the piety of a Tityrus (*Ecl.* 1. 42–3) enlarged to a magnificent scale. And I for one guess that Vergil also would like to point out to Octavian something like this: not only my future poem will have your praise in its midst; it has been central in all my poetry from the *Bucolics* on. It is also much easier to accept the deification of the living Caesar in the heart of Vergil's own country than in the capital. Nor would the poet have liked to trespass on Octavian's own territory where he is about to celebrate his triumphs and dedicate new temples. And, not least, Mantua and the Mincius are Italian and Vergilian parallels to Olympia and the Alpheus of the Greeks.

There are few left today who will identify Vergil's allegorical project with the *Georgics* itself.[35] Nevertheless there is more than one grain of truth in this position. As a Roman poet could couch his *recusatio* in so much flattery that the person addressed was likely to feel compensated, so Vergil's promise of future praise is so detailed and exuberant that Octavian gets an encomiastic hors-d'oeuvre to dwell on. Vergil fulfills his immediate obligations as devoutly as had Callimachus in his *Aetia*. He kills two birds with one stone in that he combines immediate praise with his promise of still more to come.

Provided, then, that we are justified in believing that Vergil planned the *Aeneid* right from the beginning roughly as we have it, how could he best present his plans there and then in the *Georgics*? Not by focusing on Aeneas with something in the vein of *arma virumque can<u>am</u>, Troiae qui primus etc*. And who would have seen the relevance of, e.g., a cyclus of pictures from the *Aeneid* with the fall of Troy, the visit to the Underworld and so on? In the end Vergil needed nearly 9,000 lines to demonstrate the true potential of his new 'mythological' point of view. The obvious way was to turn the viewpoint upside down when he is announcing the *Aeneid* for the first time and to emphasize the present and panegyrical side (Caesar) at the expense of the past and epical one (Aeneas). The poem even insists on the present character of his praise, talking about a *pompa* with *immediate* sacrifices of bulls, a theme which otherwise fits very well into the context of the Third Book with its 'care of cattle', *cura boum* (1. 3):

> *already* it is a pleasure to lead the solemn procession to the shrine and watch the slaughter of bullocks...
>
> ...*iam nunc* sollemnis ducere pompas
> ad delubra iuvat caesosque videre iuvencos

The eulogy of Caesar's foreign policy starts already with the mention of *Britanni* on the scene curtains (25). The *Britanni* are shown in a subservient role: '[even now it is a pleasure...] to watch how the inwoven Britons raise the crimson curtains', *utque | purpurea intexti tollant aulaea Britanni* (25). They could hardly be part of the reliefs on the temple doors with their successful battles and victories as the expedition against them was still on the agenda.[36] The poet's reference to them as curtain raisers is compatible both with their present status and their future conquest.

Then Vergil becomes more specific about battles and war when he proceeds to describe the themes on the temple doors in 8 lines (26–33) giving a survey of Octavian's most recent achievements:

> On the doors I will fashion in solid gold and ivory the battle of the Ganges people and the arms of victorious Quirinus, and here (I will fashion) also the Nile surging with war and flooding mightily, and columns rising with the bronze of ships. I will add the vanquished cities of Asia, the routed Niphates, the Parthian relying on flight and arrows shot backward, the two trophies snatched in fight from enemies far separated from each other and the nations twice triumphed over on either shore.
>
> in foribus pugnam ex auro solidoque elephanto
> Gangaridum faciam victorisque arma Quirini,

>   atque hic undantem bello magnumque fluentem
>   Nilum ac navali surgentis aere columnas;
> 30   addam urbes Asiae domitas pulsumque Niphaten
>   fidentemque fuga Parthum versisque sagittis
>   et duo rapta manu diverso ex hoste tropaea
>   bisque triumphatas utroque ab litore gentes.

A good comment on this passage is to be found in the last part of Book 8 of the *Aeneid* where the poet so to speak fulfills his promise (675–728). There Vergil describes how Apollo Actius causes panic and flight not only among Egyptians but also among Indians (705). Vergil focuses audaciously on far-off nations in our proem. Caesar even surpasses Alexander as world conqueror. The Nile (28–9) needs no comment. The 'cities of Asia' (30) refer to events both before and after Alexandria, but above all to the time Octavian spent in Syria in late 30 BC.[37] The reference to two nations conquered on either coast in l. 33 had to be specified in the *Aeneid* as in the meantime the *Morini* (8.727) and the *Dahae* (8.728)[38] had faded out of people's memory. We have here to do with a chain of events following immediately upon the situation described at the end of the First Book. The prologue to the Third Book is almost the heaven-sent answer to the poet's ardent prayer when Rome was on the point of collapse, when Euphrates went to war on one side and Germany on the other (1.509).[39]

One important aspect of Vergil's encomium is connected with his use of the future tense. The trick of the future in such a context can be to create the impression that further, even greater, successes may follow before the poem has been finished; the phrasing is accordingly a bit vague.[40] Generally it would have been wise for Vergil everywhere to base his praise on victories already won. And so all the references in the passage 26–33 will function fully as panegyrics within the *Georgics* as suggested already. But at the same time Vergil does not exclude the possibility that he will have a stronger basis for praise by the time the new poem is finished. Should it happen, however, that Caesar would opt for a less aggressive foreign policy, the poet would have nothing to recant. The balance here is a subtle one. How clever Vergil is in phrasing Octavian's recent diplomacy can be seen from the use of participles in the accusative at 30 and 31: *addam urbes Asiae* domitas pulsum*que Niphaten* | fidentem*que fuga Parthum versisque sagittis*. Reading these lines you will almost unconsciously add *pulsum* to l. 31 as well, and find Vergil's words rather explicit about victory over the Parthians, but the line can also be read making *fidentem* parallel with *pulsum*. Then the line becomes more modest and is indeed more true to facts so far. In the end Vergil left the Parthians almost out in his *Aeneid*.[41]

The whole passage in question seems to speak eloquently in favour of a planned Caesar-epic. And if most of Vergil's contemporaries understood it that way, so much the better, Vergil must have thought. In the end he enlarged it something like ten times its length in the *Aeneid*. He surely never intended to do more. Even so he almost overstretched himself.

However, the next three lines (34–6) indicate as clearly as was expedient for the poet at the time the nature of his future epic:[42]

> There shall stand also Parian marbles, breathing statues, the progeny of Assaracus and the names of a race descended from Jove, father Tros and the Cynthian founder of Troy.

> stabunt et Parii lapides, spirantia signa,
> Assaraci proles demissaeque ab Iove gentis
> nomina, Trosque parens et Troiae Cynthius auctor.

What could Vergil have done with the Trojan past if a *Caesareis* had been his intention? It would probably have functioned as a sort of family background. It is my contention that the passage is fully relevant only with regard to the *Aeneid* kind of epic. *Assaraci proles* points to *Iliad* 20. The name Assaracus occurs only in the monologue where the Homeric Aeneas presents himself and his family (200–58): 'Assaracus begot Capys, and he again begot Anchises as his son, but Anchises (begot) me', Ἀσσάρακος δὲ Κάπυν, ὁ δ' ἄρ' Ἀγχίσην τέκε παῖδα | αὐτὰρ ἔμ' Ἀγχίσης (239 f.),[43] i.e. Assaracus first – Aeneas at the end of that particular Trojan line. Then follow 'sons after sons'[44] according to Poseidon a little later (308) – until the present Caesar, we would add. The *gens Iulia* had presented their Alban and Trojan ancestors more and more forcefully on Rome's political scene since the present Caesar's father had honored his deceased aunt Iulia in the Forum in the early 60s.[45] It is through these three lines that the idea of an *Aeneis* becomes quite tangible for the audience.

I for one think that Vergil's plans of an *Aeneid* would have been finalized at this stage, otherwise he would not have phrased his encomium in the form of a promised project at all. There had been ample time for the poet to contemplate what poetic enterprise he should launch after the *Georgics*. Caesar had won his decisive victory already in September 31. To write a contemporary epic would right from the beginning have been a breakneck project. The end of Book 1 of the *Georgics* tells us why. Almost the whole of Caesar's martial career was connected with civil war. It would indeed require extraordinary stamina and courage to depict this terrible saga on a broad canvas in the style of a contemporary epic. We can see how Vergil studiously avoids making Caesar party to civil war in the *Georgics*. Cleopatra was a god-sent gift for many reasons, not least because she almost freed him from the curse of civil war which was instead laid at the door of the Roman people, Laomedon or Romulus.[46]

Let us by no means forget the three words marking the climax of the passage on Troy, *Troiae Cynthius auctor* (36). There is hardly a phrase more fraught with meaning and implications in this proem or in the whole poem for that matter. To start with a simple question about the temple: where is Apollo to be found in terms of architectural decoration? The most natural place for Tros, Assaracus and the other Trojans would be in the Porticus. Then I would propose the pediment as the proper place for the god Apollo. One cannot help thinking of the west pediment of the Zeus temple at Olympia where the commanding figure of Apollo was in the middle.[47] Be that as it may. This is the third time Apollo is referred to in our prologue, and what an epiphany it turns out to be! The word *Cynthius* harks back to his birthplace and beloved abode. But now we are transcending the horizon of both hymns of Callimachus (2 and 4). The climax is no more the city-founding god of Callimachus, protector of Battus and his fellow colonists, establishing them in Cyrene. We have long since left the Greek world in favour of Troy. Commentaries refer to *Iliad* 7 where Poseidon tells that he and Apollo had built the city for Laomedon. But in Vergil the reference to the city-founding Apollo implies much more. As the family of Aeneas constitutes the nearest context, so Apollo's relation to that family in the *Iliad*, i.e., to Aeneas, is relevant in the first place. Had it not been for Apollo, Aeneas would have met his end in *Iliad* 5 (436 ff.). Albeit 'founder' of Troy, Apollo could not save the city – the perjury of Laomedon was one of the negative factors preventing this – but in saving and protecting Aeneas the god succeeded in saving the germ of Troy that was to lead to Rome and the distant descendant Caesar. Now one may argue that there is not a word here about Apollo Actius or Rome, not to mention the god's special relation to Caesar. But the common architectural setting is undeniable and speaks for itself: Apollo and Caesar are united in the same *templum*. This reminds one strongly of the Palatine arrangement with the quasi-cohabitation between Caesar and his god. And once again the Zeus temple at Olympia springs to mind; the presence of both Zeus and Apollo there contributed to the august character of that temple. The link, between the first reliefs on the temple doors about Actium on the one hand (26–9) and Apollo as the last item in the decoration programme on the other, strongly suggests that Apollo Actius is behind and above it all; Apollo's ever-present protection links the past with the present. Apollo and Caesar are as close to a *binitas* between man and god as ever there was in Roman religion. We can hardly find a better comment than Vergil's own description of the triumph in *Aeneid* 8, with Caesar sitting before the temple as the earthly representative of the god.[48]

The three concluding lines (37–9) have often baffled commentators.[49]

> Unlucky Envy[50] shall fear the Furies and the merciless river Cocytus, the twisted snakes of Ixion, the awful wheel and the stone not to be mastered.

> Invidia infelix Furias amnemque severum
> Cocyti metuet tortosque Ixionis anguis
> immanemque rotam et non exsuperabile saxum.

For one thing: is the temple allegory still valid? I think so. A painting is a possibility; my own idea is that the juxtaposition with Apollo points to a pediment group around Apollo as the central figure. As for the meaning, I will not reject the idea of Thomas that Vergil's *invidia* has some connection with the Phthonos theme at the end of Callimachus' *Hymn to Apollo*. *Phthonos*, i.e., envy against the poet, is banished there from Apollo's presence (107). Mynors among others denies that the *invidia* has anything to do with the poet. The idea should perhaps not be rejected altogether, as the interpretation of Thomas can be taken one step further (see my last remarks on this passage below). Thomas does not, however, succeed in explaining the Tartarus setting on the basis of Callimachus alone. Our passage is closer to a well-known passage in Lucretius, 5.1125–30, describing the negative effects of *invidia*:[51]

> Nevertheless ill-will[52] strikes them (rich and mighty men) from time to time like a lightning and hurls them scornfully down from the summit into horrible Tartarus; since the summits and everything that is elevated above other things are often ablaze with ill-will as with lightning, so that it is much better to obey in peace than to wish to govern by force and rule kingdoms.

> 1125   et tamen e summo, quasi fulmen, deicit ictos
>   invidia interdum contemptim in Tartara taetra;
>   invidia quoniam, ceu fulmine, summa vaporant
>   plerumque et quae sunt aliis magis edita cumque;
>   ut satius multo iam sit parere quietum
> 1130   quam regere imperio res velle et regna tenere.[53]

In Vergil orderly rule has been established so securely that the evil power of earlier times (cf. Lucretius) has no longer any power. Accordingly, envy cannot threaten the ruler and perhaps overturn him successfully, but will now have to face serious consequences if it lifts its head.

Vergil's Tartarus has an anti-lucretian, anti-epicurean ring not to be ignored. Many readers would have remembered Vergil's *makarismos* at *Geo.* 2.490–2: 'Blessed is he who has been able to understand the causes of things and has laid all kinds of fear and inexorable fate and the roar of the greedy Acheron under his feet', *Felix qui potuit rerum cognoscere causas | atque metus omnis et inexorabile fatum | subiecit pedibus strepitumque Acherontis avari*. What looked like a compliment to Lucretius/Epicurus[54] has to be modified somewhat in the light of the whole poem. In our passage on *Invidia* Vergil discards implicitly the claim of Epicurus to divine status and firmly marks his stance as akin to that of Plato (*Republic*). In a political context it is essential that ἀδικία will have to face punishments beyond death. This interpretation is especially significant if Buchheit is right in seeing our proem as a sort of antithesis to the eulogy of Epicurus in Lucretius' poem.[55] *Invidia* applies, of course, primarily to the enemies of Caesar. So far Vergil has said nothing about the painful civil side of Octavian's victories. In his account of Actium in *Aeneid* 8 he did not hide it altogether: *scissa gaudens vadit Discordia palla*; Antony was leader of the barbaric forces. Within such a frame the more euphemistic notion *invidia* suggests stronger terms as *impietas* and the like. This perspective plays an important role in the *Aeneid* in figures like Cacus, Mezentius, Turnus, Catilina,[56] Antony, who all have to answer for their ἀδικία. It is also relevant to point to the ambiguous use of the future tense again as there is also a prospective side to *metuet*: *invidiosi*, i.e. *impii, scelesti*, will have to face severe penalties in case they do not give heed in the future. The passage functions as a warning to the vanquished side. As for envy against the poet it remains to be said that Vergil and his hero are very much in the same boat all along. Vergil is keen to emphasize that they are both triumphant; the triumph of Vergil corresponds to and derives from that of Caesar. The poet is, or rather will be, responsible for this interpretation of it all. So envy is inseparable from the glory the poet will bestow on Caesar through his epic poem.

Some few words remain to be said about the possible inspiration from Roman monumental buildings on the proem as a whole. Some have thought that the temple of *Hercules Musarum* on the Campus Martius was Vergil's main inspiration.[57] This idea got some support from

Mynors.[58] It is mainly based on the prominent role Hercules plays in the prologue and on the fact that the poet brings the Muses home to Italy in a way corresponding to what Marcus Fulvius Nobilior did in the literal sense in the 180s BC when he built a temple for them and for Hercules as Mousagetes. I cannot here go into all the details. On the whole I find the theory less attractive. Vergil's allegory is no *templum Caesaris Musarum*. The Hercules figure of the prologue was never meant to loom large in our thoughts as the allegory unfolds. Other temples are more relevant. There were prestigious temples connected either with the divine descent of Caesar (the Temple of Venus Genetrix), with his murdered 'father' (the Temple of the Deified Julius Caesar) or with the living Caesar's patron god (the Temple of Apollo Palatinus). Though Vergil according to the *Vita Donati* (§11) seldom visited Rome, he must have been well informed about the ambitious building enterprises going on there, in particular about the *templum Divi Iulii* on the Forum which was to be dedicated and celebrated with sacrifices and games when Octavian returned to Rome.[59] Vergil's allegory is such that the readers would have been reminded of more than one temple. One and a half years before the assassination of Caesar the temple of Venus Genetrix had been dedicated (September 46). The festivities connected with it were celebrated on a regular basis by Octavian as *ludi Victoriae Caesaris*. Those in 44 BC, in late July, coincided with the comet that led to the apotheosis of Caesar and eventually to the temple of Divus Iulius in the Forum. The *Divi filius* had a certain part in it in so far as it was adorned with *rostra* from Actium. The reference to Apollo would have reminded the audience already in 29 that Apollo was going to be honoured with a splendid temple for the most important victories Octavian had won.

Notes

[1] The literature on the proem has grown considerably since Büchner's complaint in his *RE* article, 'Eine überzeugende Interpretation fehlt' (col. 269, 53 f.). Useful further references can be found in R.F. Glei 101, n. 29. Personally I am especially indebted to the studies of Buchheit and Thomas (1983 and 1988). For a recent succinct and competent account see N. Horsfall (1995) 96–8.

[2] *Georgica reverso post Actiacam victoriam Augusto atque Atellae reficiendarum faucium commoranti per continuum quadriduum legit, suscipiente Maecenate legendi vicem, quotiens interpellaretur ipse vocis offensione.*

[3] Conveniently presented with references in Binder 258 ff.

[4] Cf. Buchheit 42 f.

[5] The name *Caesar* (referring to Octavian) occurs more often in the *Georgics*

(7 times) than in the *Aeneid* (5 times): 1.25, 503; 2.170; 3.16, 47, 48; 4.560.

[6] *...et cultor nemorum, cui pinguia Ceae | ter centum nivei tondent dumeta iuvenci.*

[7] Lundström 164.

[8] *Ecl.* 5.34 f. 'since the fates snatched you (i.e., Daphnis), Pales and Apollo themselves have left the country' (*postquam te fata tulerunt, | ipsa Pales agros atque ipse reliquit Apollo*). Further comments in Buchheit 92 ff.

[9] Liber (7), Ceres (7), Neptune (14) and Minerva (18). Liber/Dionysus was not included among the Twelve Gods in the Forum (Livy 22.10.9; Ennius *Ann.* 240-1 Skutsch), but he was coupled with Ceres in Varro's introduction to his *Res rusticae* (1.1.4-6) and he was often included in the canon on Greek soil (Olympia, Parthenon). On this see Roscher s.v. 'Zwölfgötter' 776 and 782 (O. Weinreich = *idem, Ausgewählte Schriften* II, Amsterdam, 1973).

[10] The *locus classicus* is Euripides *Alc.* 6-7.

[11] Edited with commentary by Williams.

[12] Thomas (1988), p. 36 f. ad 3-8, 4, 7-8, 11, 13, 19-20, 28, 37-39.

[13] Gagé 479-522.

[14] For which see Williams ad loc.

[15] Nom. pl. *carmina* has strong manuscript support and should be seriously considered. It would have to mean 'subjects of song', 'poetical themes'; I can see no valid objection to this, see *OLD* s.v. *carmen* 2 c, citing, e.g., *Aetna* 4 (*Aetna mihi carmen erit*).

[16] The (asyndetic) parataxis, as often in poetry, corresponds to a causal hypotagm: '*Since* all other possible themes have now become hackneyed' (3-4a) – then follows a number of examples (4b-8a) – 'I have (accordingly) to try a path etc.' (8-9). Cf. Lundström 167.

[17] Cf. *Epigr.* 27.1 Ἐχθαίρω τὸ ποίημα τὸ κυκλικόν...

[18] His name is neither mentioned as Hercules (though the nominative *Hercules* is metrically impossible, both the abl. and the genitive and the adj. *Herculeus* would have been possible) nor by means of any substitute name (*Alcides* being the most common – 12 times in the *Aeneid*). To mention it along with that of Eurystheus, Busiris and Hylas would have been (1) otiose (and therefore un-Alexandrian), (2) almost tantamount to denying his fame and the trivial character of such poems and (3) variation is achieved with regard to the following hero who is mentioned by name (Pelops).

[19] Cf. Theocritus' poem 13 (Ὕλας) whose account stresses the hero's love for the young boy (ll. 6 and 65-6) while Hercules was reckoned by his comrades as a deserter (λιποναύτας, 73). Hylas was also treated by Apollonius (*Arg.* 1.1187-1357), Nicander, and many more, apparently also Callimachus (Thomas 1983, 94).

[20] On the possible connection with Pindar's *Olympian* 1 see Buchheit 148-50 (with n. 631); Lundström 169.

[21] Cf. also Binder 258 f. (with 141 ff.).

[22] That is according to the perspective of the first reader, the year of publication. For readers of later decades the prophecy would either have become true or at least testified to the poet's devout intentions.

[23] Mynors 181 (on 3.16).

[24] Parsons and *SH* no. 254-69.

[25] For Pelops and Olympia see *RE* 17, 2521 ff.

[26] Cf. *Aen.* 6.801–3.

[27] Plut., *Anton.* 4.3.

[28] On the double meaning of this line see the following note.

[29] *Varia* 17–18 (Vahlen) *Nemo me lacrimis decoret nec funera fletu | faxit. Cur? Volito vivus per ora virum* ('Let nobody honour me with tears or make my funeral crying. Why? I am flying alive from lips to lips of men'). It has been much debated whether Vergil's *virum...per ora* should be taken as 'before men's eyes' or 'on men's lips'. In view of Ennius the last alternative is favoured by many commentators (so Thomas, Mynors), but in view of the context (*Pelops...acer equis* 7–8 and 17–18, where also a victor is found) the first is no less valid (so Lundström 178 ff.). It goes without saying that *volitare* suits either meaning (*OLD s.v.* 2 and e.g. *Aen.* 12.328, whereas in Ennius both *OLD* 1 b and 2 b are applicable). It is a *tour de force*, typical of Vergil's imitation, to adapt a famous quotation to a new context, thereby modifying or changing its original meaning (see my paper '*Disiectorum voces poetarum*: On Imitation in Vergil's *Aeneid*', *SO* 72 (1997) forthcoming).

[30] Lucretius had hailed Ennius as the first who had brought down from beautiful Helicon a crown of evergreen leafage to win fame among the peoples of Italy (*Ennius...qui primus amoeno | detulit ex Helicone perenni fronde coronam | per gentis Italas hominum quae clara clueret* 1.117–19).

[31] Thomas (1988), Mynors and Buchheit 91 find an allusion here to Octavian.

[32] Octavian is a *victor* also in *Geo.* 2.171 and 4.561.

[33] For the whole subject see Smallwood 68–71.

[34] *tenera praetexit harundine ripas* corresponding to *hic viridis tenera praetexit harundine ripas* at *Ecl.* 7.12, leaving out what produced the golden line (*viridis*) in the *Eclogue*.

[35] But see Lundström 184.

[36] Meyer; Kienast 292f.

[37] Cass. Dio 51.18.

[38] This is my personal view on a difficult issue (see Mynors for other views). On the Morini and the Dahae see *EV* III 588 s.v. (R.F. Rossi) and I 973 s.v. Dai (M. Malavolta) respectively.

[39] The relation between the end of Book 2 and the proem to Book 3 has been dealt with in considerable detail by Buchheit 45–92.

[40] I have comments of a similar kind on *Aen.* 1.289 in *SO* 69 (1994), 92.

[41] *EV* III s.v. *Parti* 990–2 (M. Pani).

[42] Vergil's plans would most probably have been known already by those who had a certain claim to have his confidence or friendship (Maecenas, Octavian, and a few good colleagues).

[43] He was mentioned the first time as one of the three sons of Tros in l. 232.

[44] νῦν δὲ δὴ Αἰνείαο βίη Τρώεσσιν ἀνάξει | καὶ παίδων παῖδες, τοί κεν μετόπισθε γένωνται (*Il.* 20.307–8).

[45] *EV* II s.v. *Enea* 227–9 (N. Horsfall).

[46] Laomedon: particularly *Geo.* 1.502, Romulus: Horace *epod.* 7.19 f. (with D. Mankin's note).

[47] Ashmole and Yalouris 17 ff.

[48] On Apollo's role and importance in the *Aeneid* see Unte.

[49] A close examination (with many references) is provided by Romano.

[50] 'Envy' is hardly strong enough; 'ill-will' is probably better. Vergilian parallels of interest are *Aen.* 10.852 and 11.539, both cases referring to a struggle for political power.

[51] The parallel has been observed, but not the great difference between Lucretius and Vergil, by Sauron 505.

[52] I follow the recommended rendering by Bailey's commentary here.

[53] There is a reminiscence of this passage also in the famous command of Anchises at *Aen.* 6.851: *tu regere imperio populos, Romane, memento*, which is equally far from Epicurean quietism: Roman rule is a guarantee of peace and good life, not a constant threat to those values.

[54] But see Buchheit 74 (with n. 294).

[55] Buchheit 71 f., 99 ff.

[56] Cf. *Aen.* 8.666b–69 describing Catilina fearing the Furies' punishment in Tartarus: *hinc procul addit | Tartareas etiam sedes... et te, Catilina, minaci | pendentem scopulo Furiarumque ora trementem.*

[57] Lundström 175 ff. On the *Aedes Herculis Musarum* see now Sauron 84–98.

[58] Mynors 181 (on line 13).

[59] Cassius Dio 51.21.5–22.2.

Bibliography
Abbreviations

    EV: *Enciclopedia Virgiliana* I–V. Ed. F. Della Corte. Roma, 1984–91.
    RE: Pauly-Wissowa, *Realencyclopädie der classischen Altertumswissenschaft*
    Roscher: *Ausführliches Lexikon der griechischen und römischen Mythologie* I–VI, herausgeg. von W. Roscher. Leipzig, 1884–1937.
    SH: *Supplementum Hellenisticum*, ed. H. Lloyd-Jones and P.J. Parsons, 254–69. Berlin/New York, 1983.

Books and articles

Ashmole, B. and Yalouris, N.
    1967   *Olympia. The Sculptures of the Temple of Zeus*, London.
Binder, G.
    1971   *Aeneas und Augustus. Interpretationen zum 8. Buch der Aeneis.* Beiträge zur klassischen Philologie 38, Meisenheim.
Buchheit, V.
    1972   *Der Anspruch des Dichters in Vergils Georgika. Dichtertum und Heilsweg* (Impulse der Forschung, Bd. 8), Darmstadt.
Büchner, K.
    1959   *P. Vergilius Maro. Der Dichter der Römer* (off-print from *RE*), Stuttgart.
Gagé, J.
    1955   *Apollon romain*, Bibliothèque des écoles françaises d'Athènes et de Rome, Vol. 182, Paris.

Glei, R.F.
    1991   *Der Vater der Dinge. Interpretationen zur politischen, literarischen und kulturellen Dimension des Krieges bei Vergil*, Bochumer Altertumswissenschaftliches Colloquium, Bd. 7., Trier.

Grimal, P.
    1951   'Énée à Rome et le triomphe d'Octave', *REA* 53: 51–61.
            (German version in: G. Binder (ed.) *Saeculum Augustum* II (Wege der Forschung 512) 240–54, Darmstadt, 1988.)

Horsfall, N. (ed.)
    1995   *A Companion to the Study of Virgil*, Mnemosyne Suppl. 151, Leiden.

Kienast, D.
    1982   *Augustus. Prinzeps und Monarch*. Darmstadt.

Kraggerud, E.
    1994   'Caesar versus Caesar again: a reply.' *SO* 69, 83–93.

Lundström, S.
    1976   'Der Eingang des Proömiums zum dritten Buche der Georgica', *Hermes* 104, 163–91.

Meyer, H.D.
    1961   *Die Aussenpolitik des Augustus und die augusteische Dichtung*, Köln.

Mynors, R.A.B.
    1990   *Virgil: Georgics*, Oxford.

Parsons, P.J.
    1997   'Callimachus: Victoria Berenices', *ZPE* 25, 1–50.

Romano, D.
    1977   'Invidia infelix. Virgilio, *Georg*. III, 37–9', in *Atti del convegno virgiliano sul bimillenario delle Georgiche*, 505–13, Napoli.

Sauron, G.
    1994   *Quis deum? L'expression plastique des idéologies politiques et religieuses à Rome*, Bibliothèque des écoles françaises d'Athènes et de Rome, Vol. 285, Rome.

Smallwood, E.M.
    1976   *The Jews under Roman Rule*, Studies in Judaism in Late Antiquity, Vol. 20, Leiden.

Thomas, R.
    1983   Callimachus, the *Victoria Berenices* and Roman poetry', *CQ* 33, 92–113.
    1988   *Virgil: Georgics. Volume 2: Books III–IV*, Cambridge.

Unte, W.
    1994   'Die Gestalt Apollos im Handlungsablauf von Vergils Aeneis', *Gymnasium* 101, 204–57.

Williams, F.
    1978   *Callimachus: Hymn to Apollo*, Oxford.

To my friend Géza Alföldy

2

RELIGION IN THE POLITICS OF AUGUSTUS
Aeneid 1.278–91, 8.714–23, 12.791–842[1]

Gunther Gottlieb

Religion and politics

The Romans lived up to their conviction that they were a pious people. Roman piety and the experience of the gods' help, or their refusal of help, are very close together. Polybios was convinced that the Romans were the most pious amongst all people[2] and Vergil has Jupiter predict that one day the Romans will surpass men and gods in piety.[3] *Pietas* had a strong impact on the Romans' behaviour with respect to the gods, the fatherland, the family, and the ancestors. In relation to the gods, *pietas* was expressed by *religio*, which for the Romans was the *cultus deorum*. *Cultus deorum* means the performance of ritual acts, that is *sacra et ritus*. I quote G. Alföldy, who, in a famous article about the crisis of the Roman Empire and Rome's religion,[4] describes this as the essential characteristic of Roman religion. Both virtues, *pietas* and *religio*, belong together. We learn that the welfare of the Roman community or the Roman state (*res publica*) is inconceivable without compliance with the rules of *pietas* and *religio*. Cicero describes the high position of *religio* by emphasizing that other people may surpass the Romans in various qualities, but that the Romans themselves surpass all tribes and nations in *pietas* and *religio* as well as through the realization that the workings of the gods lead and guide all.[5] According to Livy, M. Furius Camillus, the so-called second founder of Rome, explained in a programmatic political speech, after the destruction of Rome through the Celts, what experience has taught: i.e., that the Romans are successful in everything whenever they follow the gods, but that, when neglecting the gods, they head for disaster.[6]

As old Babylonian chants proclaim, the supreme deity imposed religious service on men. Therefore to worship is man's destiny.[7] This is exactly what the Romans themselves felt. It was quite natural to combine in a second step the welfare of the state with worshipping the gods. This step had already been taken by the time the Romans emerged into the light of history. For the sake of survival, the political community has to be first and foremost a cult-community (I follow A. Dihle, who explains this anthropological key question in terms of a postulate[8]). This postulate is, I think, as old as political community itself. Accordingly, we get to know the Romans as a nation and political community which took this postulate extremely seriously. The increase and ideologization of *pietas* and *religio* apply to the continuous rise of the *res Romana*, based on ever new military and political successes. At each moment of success, whenever the help of the gods could be empirically recognized as a service in return for dutiful religious worship, the events underwent (in retrospect) an increase in value. Conversely, the Romans saw bad luck or mishaps as a punishment for the disregard of the cult rules.

Aristotle describes the cult of the gods as the most important thing among the basic needs which guarantee the existence of a political community.[9] Cicero reminds his readers of C. Flaminius, who had neglected the cult rules (*religione neglecta*) and who therefore lost the battle at Lake Trasimene, which seriously harmed the *res Romana*.[10] The Christian Emperor Constantius II imposed a law on his subjects to 'rejoice and glory in the faith', knowing that the Roman community – our state (*nostra res publica*) – is preserved more by religious service (*religiones*) than by physical and manual efforts.[11]

These general remarks and examples are meant to set the frame and clarify my starting position. We shall further discuss the question, in which way *religio* manifests itself, of what use it was to the Romans, and how the connection between the cult and *salus publica* was put into concrete form.

The Chair has generously allowed me to be free in organizing my subject. His intention was to give the historian the chance to address our symposium with positions and questions which are possibly not congruent with those of philologists. Thus my presentation is not the interpretation of a passage from Vergil's *Aeneid* in a strict sense, but is structured more generally. Of course I do not want to isolate myself, therefore I will take three passages from the *Aeneid* as my starting point about 'Religion in the Politics of Augustus'.

In the title I have used the term 'religion'. To prevent misunderstanding, I should use the terms *pietas*, *religio*, *ritus*, and *sacra* – in other words, everything that makes up *Roman* religion. It would be a mistake if we understood these elements of Roman religion as superficial. Roman religion, with its rituals, cults and festivals, represents, as

P. Barceló argues, the conviction that the gods are guarantors of victory and are jointly responsible for every public success.[12]

Consensus, *pax*, and *pietas*

I take *consensus*, *pax* and *pietas* to be the most important elements of Augustan politics, ideology and propaganda. Let us first look at three passages from Vergil's *Aeneid*.

1. *Jupiter's Promises (Aen. 1.278–91)*

Jupiter calms his daughter, Venus, who is concerned about the surviving Trojans and their Roman future. Jupiter emphasizes that he will never put limits to the Romans' rule and power, neither in time nor space. He has granted them never-ending rule and even Juno herself will change her mind and, together with him, will support the Romans, the 'lords of the world'. The Trojan Caesar, Julius, that is Augustus, will rule and be invoked by his subjects.[13] The times of torment will change into peaceful conditions of life when war ceases.

2. *Augustus' Pietas (Aen. 8.714–23)*

Caesar Augustus returns to Rome as triumphator. He dedicates three hundred magnificent temples to the Italian gods, as he had vowed. The streets resound with the jubilation, the games and the applause. In all the temples, groups of married women dance and priests sacrifice to the gods. Augustus himself sits clad in white on the steps of the temple of Apollo. He surveys the gifts made by the nations. The defeated tribes march past in a long parade.

3. *Reconciliation between Jupiter and Juno (Aen. 12.791–842)*

Jupiter and Juno are reconciled, as Jupiter had long promised. Let us remember Jupiter's promises in the first book of the *Aeneid* (1.278–91). Jupiter finally succeeds in calming down the angry and grumbling Juno. There are no more obstacles to prevent the happy rise of the *res Romana* in Italy. The new generation growing up will surpass men and gods in piety and will honour even Juno as nobody else does. Vergil refers to the Capitoline triad with Juno as one of the three supreme gods, who in the time of Vergil's readers are the guarantors of Roman welfare and prosperity.

Consensus was the imperative requirement for the reign of Augustus – *consensus omnium ordinum*, *consensus populi Romani*, *consensus* among all people under the Roman rule. This consensus was anticipated by the gods. In the same way *consensus* within a nation or a society and among the leading persons (cf. *concordia ordinum*) is a precondition for rise and success. The intensity with which Cicero during the civil war and Augustus after the civil war focus on this important subject may elucidate how the Romans were aware of the necessity of *consensus*.[14] The glory of Roman history is inconceivable without this *consensus* between the supreme gods. That is what Vergil will explain. *Consensus* and *pax* are donations from the gods – celestial gifts which can be promised to mankind. Under the care of the gods Augustus has realized peace. With their consent, the *consensus omnium* supports the reign of Augustus. As an example for all subjects, Augustus gives thanks to the gods with his unique *pietas*: he gives orders to build new temples, to restore and reconstruct ruined shrines, he watches over the priesthoods, the rituals, ceremonies and the solemn celebrations which include not only the members of the order, but also the whole population of the capital. This is the meaning of Vergil's text. It seems as if he were answering the question of what one can learn from history, of which even mythical times are a part (this is especially true for Vergil). It is the typical Roman way of thinking, when Vergil takes up the function of the historian as orator, who utilizes myth and history to pursue political aims. By combining past and present, his intention is to elucidate and to give pedagogical impulses.

I have opened my reflections about Vergil with the assessment that *consensus*, *pax* and *pietas* are among the most important elements of Augustan politics, ideology and propaganda. These concepts were in accordance with the divine and human order as the Romans imagined this order to be, and as it was described in the traditions. The correspondence between divine and human order is guaranteed by the cult, that is, by the ritualistic communication between men and gods. It is essential to the welfare of the state and the community. A. Dihle has analysed this relationship in the excellent article cited above.[15] According to him, the cult has a political function, which can be successfully realized only when the personal identity between cult community and political community is guaranteed. Dihle marks as the crucial point the preservation of the unity of cult community and political community within the framework of the existing state.[16] If we apply Dihle's concept to our case, then Augustus has renewed the unity of cult community and political community, or, we may say, he has re-established this unity. In any case, by his care for *cultus*, *religio* and *sacra*, he created the requirements which, in the Roman point of view, were the precondition for the prosperity of the *res publica Romana*.

Apart from the *res gestae Divi Augusti*, we find concrete contemporary evidence in Livy, for example Camillus' speech about Rome (5.51–4), and in Velleius Paterculus' *historia Romana*. Livy lets Camillus describe the unity of cult community and political community as an element of vital significance, including the place where the community so-defined has its domicile as willed by the gods. I am convinced that, when reading this passage, contemporaries already identified the place and time of Augustan Rome in the same way as they come to mind today.[17] Within the framework of another important event, Livy also illustrates the Augustan times in order to focus attention on the central points of the emperor's political order. I am referring to the introduction of the cult of Dionysos in 180 BC.[18]

On the basis of this analysis we may go one step further. The Roman imagination was strictly oriented towards tradition and continuity. On the other hand, the strong religious impulses which Augustus inaugurated presuppose a break – or, if we tone down our assumption, at least an interruption. Whether poetry, historiography or Augustus' self-portrayal, all the literary production focuses on a leading motif of Augustus' politics and ideology, that of emphasizing the continuity between the times before the civil war and its own present. I use this chronological frame to illustrate what I would like to explain: the Roman dominance over the world, which had long ago become a reality, has been empirically proved. This world dominance is connected with the will of the gods, who, in the imagination of the Augustan era, had promised Rome a continuous rise. But this favourable course of Roman history is based on the loyalty to the traditions of the fathers, which are distinguished mainly by *consensus*, *pietas*, and *religio*. The congruence between divine and human order had suffered lasting disturbance by the spread of internal *discordia*, by the loss of *consensus* and *pax*, by the neglect of *pietas* and *religio*, by the disregard of divine orders. All of these are evils, which began with the decline of the Roman virtues and which had reached their peak during the civil wars.

The use of symbols in politics

Within this context we come upon the insights of modern political science. Political science deals with the phenomenon of politics as ritual, and through that analyses the symbolic function of public institutions and political acting. Symbolic uses of politics refer to time or to places, to events, to myths, to history or values. These different kinds of symbolic uses and the political rituals which derive from them manifest themselves in the utilization of divine and human history, as well as in the construction of symbolic points of reference, local or temporal points of reference, ritualization of the year, the mental awareness of time in its social dimension, the creation of cognition through language and images, or the group- and class-oriented motivation of social formation. They serve such important aims as identity formation, legitimation, self-portrayal, crowd psychology or the satisfaction of needs. They are signs for charismatic leadership or military victories and even in defeat they offer useful help. From a structural point of view, we are dealing with facts of cultural anthropology and universal politics. In contrast to administrative, institutional or social concretions, which are typical for certain situations, these general phenomena can be taken out of their special context and can be treated in a general discourse. The universal uniformity or similarity of phenomena, independent of historical periods, is the methodological premise for utilizing insights coming from the field of social science. Contemporary political and social science has a supporting function by offering the theoretical qualifications which need only be put to use.[19]

Politics can be defined as the attempt to acquire power over subjects – no matter whether we look at Pericles, Augustus, Constantine, Charles de Gaulle or the American presidents. Political acts, speeches, and gestures involve either all subjects/citizens or only certain orders, strata and groups in politics. I think this has been the case ever since states existed, that is to say, since the formation of societies with a government, laws and subjects. Today, as it was a hundred, a thousand or two thousand years ago, under the reign of Augustus, the permanent legal and political institutions, symbols and rituals reassure people. They build identity, convey the feeling of security and form the people, as M. Edelman says, into a 'supporting bulwark, even while they respond to particular developments with fear and hope'. And again Edelman: 'The complement to this adaptive and acquiescent behavior on the part of spectators is cognitive and rational planning on the part of groups directly involved in maneuvering for tangible values...'[20] We could interpret: in maneuvering for rule and power. Within this framework, charismatic leadership (whether in a democracy or monarchy) has an important function. It satisfies the needs of the masses and, based on a common understanding, it serves their political and religious desires or dreams.

I return to Augustus, *consensus*, *pax*, and *pietas*. Using the interpretations of political scientists about symbols in politics, we may define *consensus*, *pax* and *pietas* as 'condensation symbols', especially in the shape which these phenomena took on under Augustus. M. Edelman has treated these questions and phenomena in his books *The Symbolic Uses of Politics* and *Politics as Symbolic Action*. I cite from *The Symbolic Uses of Politics*:

Condensation symbols evoke the emotions associated with the situation. They condense into one symbolic event, sign, or act patriotic pride, anxieties, remembrances of past glories or humiliations, promises of future greatness: some one of these or all of them. Where condensation symbols are involved, the constant check of the immediate environment is lacking.[21]

I emphasize the connection between single references and the condensation into an all-encompassing complex. This connection, realized by Augustus with *consensus* as well as with *pax* and *pietas*, shows how the politics of Augustus and his use of symbols are oriented towards utilization, empirical learning, and perception. The annual ceremonies at the *Ara Pacis* for example are one aspect which, within the context of all acts turned to *pax* and within the idealization of *pax* in Augustan poetry, makes *pax* itself into a condensation symbol. In the same way, we can demonstrate with regard to *consensus* or *pietas* the conglomeration of single aspects and the condensation into a key-symbol. It is not necessary to explain this in detail, the correlation is clear.

Political propaganda and its function

Political symbolism leads us to political propaganda. In this case, too, we will be using a term – unknown to the Greeks and Romans – in order to abstract. However they were familiar with the nature of the matter. In terms of content, form, and objective, Augustus, like few other statesmen, was a master of what we call propaganda. Both historians and philologists are in agreement on this, and I think they also agree that what mattered to Augustus was the legitimacy of his rule and the full acceptance by his subjects (which includes everyone, regardless of order or social strata). This aim is in accordance with the generally accepted views about legitimate rulership, such as the principle of ruling in such a manner that the subjects will show not only obedience but also trust, and that the values inherent in a community, as well as the ethical, judicial, and religious conceptions, especially of the leading and state-supporting social orders, will be visibly realized.

Taking this premise as a starting point, we have to understand parts of Augustus' 'political programme' as an answer to the expectations of his subjects. This is also true for every expression of *pietas* and *religio*. In monarchies, political propaganda serves the legitimization of rulers and their politics. In its contents it is the sum of all statements of legitimacy. In its form it is the sum of all media utilized for this purpose, be they material, pictorial or linguistic. In its function, political propaganda is the attempt to convince the subjects that the ruler is suited to rule and that to be ruled is for their own good.

The numerous expressions of *pietas* and *religio*, which are recorded for Augustus, gave visible evidence to all subjects, especially the population of Rome, of the correct worship of the gods within the cult in accordance with traditions and models. By these expressions we understand everything that Augustus proposed and realized: the restoration and resurrection of temples, the building of new temples and places of worship, religious sacrifices, games, celebrations and processions. Their purpose was the demonstration of legitimacy in the sense discussed above. Their representation was a part of political propaganda.

Political community and cult community
Of course the people were not simply confined to the role of spectators, but also took part in the religious cult. Thus the next step concerns the question of whom Augustus addressed with his religious politics. The answer is sweeping and simple: everybody. 'Everybody' includes first and foremost Roman citizens, who constitute that part of society which supports Roman rule. This union of citizens is made up of people of all orders and social strata. Just as it carried and guaranteed in its entirety the rule of the Roman people, so it also carried and guaranteed the worship of the gods through religious ceremonies and celebrations. In this the indispensable unity (in terms of the welfare of the state) between the political community and the cult community manifests itself.

Augustus accorded the highest significance to this fact. The functions within the cult were distributed according to the social conditions. Thus the ideal unity between political community and cult community corresponded with an actual division of responsibilities and duties within religious practice. The active and passive integration of the political community as cult community took place wherever the gods were worshipped publicly in the name and for the good of the common cause, but it received programmatical character under Augustus in connection with his efforts at reform. Prerequisite for the success of such a programme is, of course, a potential for consensus in religious views as well as the central political ideas of the ruler, or, as in a democracy for example, of the rulers. In this regard Augustus was not confronted with any difficulties. He was able to tackle his goals on the basis of the venerable and traditional contents of Roman religion and to make use of religious practice in order to build identity and consolidate his rule. If we take the political community in its original meaning as the community of the Roman citizens, then the senators and the lower orders of the city's population both acquire a special significance: the senators because priesthood and theological colleges were reserved solely for them, and the lower orders because of the varied diversions offered by the celebrations of the gods such as games, competitions, processions and celebrations, which took place on a regular basis. What status the senate had, especially with regard to religious practice, and how much Augustus was interested in emphasizing this, can be seen for example in the *res gestae Divi Augusti*. Velleius Paterculus in his *historia Romana* and Suetonius in his *vita Augusti* give a vivid account of the people of Rome in the Augustan era. The people took a lively part in all public events – peacefully or aggressively, depending on the circumstances and the occasion.[22]

Results and evaluations

1. I have defined *consensus, pax,* and *pietas* as condensation symbols. *Consensus, pax,* and *pietas* are awarded the same high status no matter whether we look at the emperor's programmatic statements or the responses of the subjects as they are mirrored in poetry. Two observations must be noted within this context:

a) Which ideas maintain the quality of condensation symbols depends on the one hand on the circumstances which cause rulers to declare certain needs and necessities as political and pedagogical aims, and also, on the other hand, on the fundamental positions of the rulers themselves.

b) Because condensation symbols receive the character of binding obligations, they cause strong repercussions on the subjects: they create emotions, expectations, and hopes; they may serve the remembrance of bygone greatness; they create trust. At the same time they are especially suited to create consensus regarding the aims to which the ruler aspires.

2. One expectation was especially emphasized by the Romans in the times of Augustus: the greatness of Rome. The prospect of future greatness was based on the memory of the greatness which Rome had won by many wars and recently by Julius Caesar's virtue. Defeats were incompatible with the *salus publica* or the *salva res Romana* – why else should Augustus have celebrated the return of the standards lost at Carrhae as a great success? Or again: the reconstruction of the Mater Magna temple destroyed by fire became a political necessity through the historical context. The cult of Magna Mater had been officially established in Rome during the Second Punic War. Moreover, it had been transferred from Asia Minor, alleged home of the Julian family.

Consensus, pax, and *pietas* were of course, besides *virtus*, preconditions for Rome's greatness and power. (*Pax* is taken here in the understanding which the Romans had about peace.) The values which were to guarantee the prosperous future of Rome are the same as those which had once founded the greatness of Rome and her rise to world power. Thus Augustus formed every memory of the past into an asset with regard to the future. The conviction that greatness and power are inconceivable without the help of the gods is part of this context. The gods as the guarantors of the *salva res publica* and the *salus rei publicae* require constant attention through correct cult service.

The setting down of the conditions necessary for the *salva res Romana* points to the future. The use of the past as evidence establishes a connection between past and future through the present and lets the living take part in shaping the future. This explains the strong pedagogical element in the religious politics of Augustus. The religious renewal under Augustus has no tendency towards restoration for its own sake but is orientated towards the future.

3. After the disaster of civil war Augustus headed the restoration and renewal. The time after disasters is a special phenomenon. The disaster which the Romans had experienced through civil war and which had spread like a smouldering fire under the continuous loss of *consensus*, internal *pax*, and *pietas*, was not characterized by a fundamental social, cultural or religious change, but nevertheless exhibited the explicit signs of a crisis. Therefore the crisis led to the formulation of certain condensation symbols.

4. We have just stated that the crisis was not characterized by fundamental social, cultural, and religious change. This also means that despite the general crisis of the state there was no crisis of the leading religious motives and structures. There was no radical change regarding gods and cults. There were no doubts about the guarantor gods; no crisis regarding the identity between state community and cult community.

I think it is very important that we emphasize this. I want to point out that Augustus' political aims and fundamental positions, which became the contents of his politics of renewal, were first of all the longstanding, tried and tested traditions, and second were able to create consensus on their own. Unlike Constantine – like Augustus an emperor of crisis – who had to form a new cult community, Augustus did not need to trouble himself about the potential for consensus. Augustus did not need to be afraid that the community of subjects would deny loyalty to cult; instead he could be certain of the unity of the cult community.

Something else should be noted: Jupiter protected the monarchy in the same way he had protected the republican order. But we must understand this differently: Jupiter was protecting the *res Romana*. It is the *res Romana* which forms the central point, not the constitutional order. It was enough to renew the formal religious elements, and it was important as always to focus on the *res Romana*. The time of Augustus had no need for reorientation in terms of religious content and forms. The gods remained the same as did the formal elements.

5. Augustus paid great attention to special gods such as Apollo and Mars Ultor, to whom he gave prominence either as supporters of his rule or as guarantors of Rome's continuous victories. Both aspects remained within the framework of the traditional worship. When Augustus personally turned to Apollo, worshipping him as his personal guarantor-god, this was really only one variable amongst many others. Everything remained within the traditional pantheon, the religious system was not changed in any way – unlike later, when Constantine the Great likewise commended an event of vital significance to the protection of a deity. From a structural point of view Constantine acted in the same manner as Augustus did and associated his rulership with a certain god as guarantor-god. However, he commended himself to a god who up to that point had not been a part of the traditional pantheon and whose cult community had not yet become a guarantor community in the sense of identity between state community and cult community.

6. In the field of religion as in other fields, the satisfaction of needs plays an important part. Augustus did not change the main principles and conditions. So we come to understand the religious renewal with its regular activities, celebrations and rituals, be that through their revival or their introduction, as a factor of social integration. In accordance with the existing traditions the religious renewal served, from a social point of view, the expectations of the orders and other social strata which were therefore established as a renewed cult community. The ritual aspects of *religio* concerned in particular the senatorial order, the visual and emotional aspects especially the lower classes.

As we know, the population of the Empire did not consist only of the *populus Romanus*, but also of the provincial people, who worshipped various other gods. For the Romans, politics and religion were inseparably connected. Wherever Roman influence was prevalent, the

Roman guarantor gods had to be present. Wherever the *res publica Romana* was represented, the Capitoline triad was present. The response of the subjects found direct expression in the imperial cult or rather the cult of Augustus and Roma. But the imperial cult is a different topic which need not be treated here.

7. Religion in the politics of Augustus served the re-formation of the *populus Romanus* as cult community and therefore as guarantor community regarding *pietas* and *religio*, which in turn were to ensure the care of the gods for the *res Romana*. It served the unity and formation of consensus and, through that, the realization of collective discipline. Religion in the politics of Augustus referred to the welfare of the *res Romana* and the *salus rei publicae*. The senatorial order which had the full backing of Augustus was the religious elite. Independent of the temporal context, the politics of Augustus had model character.

Notes

[1] Miss Alexandra Johne, alumna of the University of Augsburg, was very helpful in looking through my English manuscript and in correcting it. I owe her a great debt for doing this. I am grateful also to Mrs Riescher, now Professor at the University of Freiburg, Germany, for bibliographic advice on political science.

[2] Plb. 6.56.6–8.

[3] *Aen.* 12.838–40.

[4] Alföldy (1989) 56 f., 73, 99.

[5] Cic., *har. resp.* 19.

[6] Liv. 5.51.5.

[7] Mensching (1954) 12.

[8] Dihle (1989) 1 f.

[9] Cf. Dihle (1989) 1.

[10] Cic., *nat.deor.* 2.8 [...] *cum magno rei publicae vulnere*.

[11] Cod. Theod. 16.2.16 (AD 361).

[12] Barceló (1992) 153.

[13] On the controversy about the meaning of 'Trojan Caesar' cf. Stahl (1985) 340; O'Hara (1994) 72–82; Kraggerud (1994) 83–93.

[14] Cf. Strasburger (1931); Kienast (1982) 59, 67–9 and *passim*; Syme (1939), primarily as *consensus Italiae* and *concordia ordinum*, 276–93 and *passim*.

[15] Dihle (1989).

[16] Dihle (1989) 4.

[17] Liv. 5.52.2–7 and 54.4–7; Vell. 2.103.4 f.

[18] Liv. 39.15.2 f., on how important it is to worship the traditional gods; 39.15.11, strong measures against the *collegia illicita*.

[19] Cf. Cassirer (1994); Dörner (1995); Edelman (1972) and (1985); Pross (1974); Riescher (1994).

[20] Edelman (1985) 15.
[21] Edelman (1985) 6; cf. Introduction, 4–21.
[22] Vell. 2.103.4 f.; Suet., *Aug.* 41.2 and 42—43.4.

Bibliography

Alföldy, G.
   1989 'Die Krise des Imperium Romanum und die Religion Roms', in W. Eck (ed.) *Religion und Gesellschaft in der römischen Kaiserzeit. Kolloquium zu Ehren von Friedrich Vittinghoff*, Kölner Historische Abhandlungen 35, 53–102, Köln.
   1991 'Augustus und die Inschriften: Tradition und Innovation. Die Geburt der imperialen Epigraphik', *Gymnasium* 98, 289–324.

Ameling, W.
   1994 'Augustus und Agrippa. Bemerkungen zu PKöln VI 249', *Chiron* 24, 1–28.

Barceló, P.
   1992 'Zur Begegnung, Konfrontation und Symbiose von religio Romana und Christentum', in G. Gottlieb and P. Barceló (eds.) *Christen und Heiden in Staat und Gesellschaft des zweiten bis vierten Jahrhunderts. Gedanken und Thesen zu einem schwierigen Verhältnis*, Schriften der Philosophischen Fakultäten der Universität Augsburg 44, 151–210, München.

Becher, I.
   1985 'Augustus und der Kult der ägyptischen Götter', *Klio* 67, 61–4.
   1991 'Der Kult der Mater Magna in augusteischer Zeit', *Klio* 73, 157–70.

Berger, P. and Luckmann, T.
   1969 *Die gesellschaftliche Konstruktion der Wirklichkeit*, Stuttgart.

Birch, R.A.
   1981 'The correspondence of Augustus. Some notes on Suetonius', *CQ* 31, 155–61.

Burian, J.
   1985 'Die Vergangenheit Roms im Rahmen der Augusteischen Gegenwartspolitik', *Klio* 67, 29–34.

Cassirer, H.
   1994 *Philosophie der symbolischen Formen*, 3 vols., 9th edn, Darmstadt.

Castritius, H.
   1980 'Das römische Kaisertum als Struktur und Prozeß', *HZ* 230, 89–103.

Ceausescu, G.
   1987 'Augustus, der "Hellenisator" der Welt', *Klio* 69, 46–57.

Dihle, A.
   1989 'Die Religion im nachconstantinischen Staat', in W. Eck (ed.) *Religion und Gesellschaft in der römischen Kaiserzeit. Kolloquium zu Ehren von Friedrich Vittinghoff*, Kölner Historische Abhandlungen 35, 1–19, Köln.

Dörner, A.
   1995 *Politischer Mythos und symbolische Politik*, Opladen.

Edelman, M.
- 1972 *Politics as Symbolic Action: Mass Arousal and Quiescence*, 2nd edn, Chicago.
- 1985 *The Symbolic Uses of Politics*, 2nd edn, Urbana and Chicago.

Elsner, J.
- 1991 'Cult and sculpture: sacrifice in the Ara Pacis Augustae', *JRS* 81, 50–61.

Flach, D.
- 1972 'Die Dichtung im frühkaiserzeitlichen Befriedungsprozeß', *Klio* 54, 157–70.

Gagé, J.
- 1981 'Apollon impérial, Garant des "Fata Romana"', *ANRW* II 17.2, 561–630.

Galinsky, K.
- 1996 *Augustan Culture: An Interpretive Introduction*, Princeton.

Girardet, K.M.
- 1993 'Traditionalismus in der Politik des Oktavian/Augustus – mentalitätsgeschichtliche Aspekte', *Klio* 75, 202–18.

Gurval, R.A.
- 1995 *Actium and Augustus: The Politics and Emotions of Civil War*, Ann Arbor.

Hahn, I.
- 1985 'Augustus und das politische Vermächtnis Caesars', *Klio* 67, 12–28.

Herz, P.
- 1993 'Die Adoptivsöhne des Augustus und der Festkalender. Gedanken zu einer Inschrift aus Messene', *Klio* 75, 272–88.

Hölscher, T.
- 1985 'Denkmäler der Schlacht von Actium. Propaganda und Resonanz', *Klio* 67, 81–102.

Kienast, D.
- 1982 *Augustus. Prinzeps und Monarch*, Darmstadt.

Kirsch, W.
- 1985 'Die Augusteische Zeit. Epochenbewußtsein und Epochenbegriff', *Klio* 67, 43–55.

Kleiner, F.S.
- 1988 'The arch in honor of C. Octavius and the fathers of Augustus', *Historia* 37, 347–57.

Kraggerud, E.
- 1994 'Caesar versus Caesar again: a reply', *SO* 69, 83–93.

Liebeschuetz, J.H.W.G.
- 1979 *Continuity and Change in Roman Religion*, Oxford.

Linderski, J.
- 1984 'Rome, Aphrodisias and the *Res Gestae*: the *Genera Militiae* and the status of Octavian', *JRS* 74, 74–80.

Melte-Dittmann, A.
- 1991 *Die Ehegesetze des Augustus*, Stuttgart.

Mensching, G.
- 1954 'Wesen und Ursprung der Religion', in *Die grossen nichtchristlichen Religionen unserer Zeit: In Einzeldarstellungen*, 9–22, Stuttgart.

Ober, J.
- 1982 'Tiberius and the political testament of Augustus',*Historia* 31, 306–28.

O'Hara, J.J.
- 1994 'Temporal distortions. "Fatal" ambiguity, and *Iulius Caesar* at *Aeneid* 1.286–96', *SO* 69, 72–82.

Pöschl, V.
- 1979 'Virgil und Augustus. Dichtung im politischen Kampf', in W.-L. Liebermann (ed.) *Viktor Pöschl. Kunst und Wirklichkeitserfahrung in der Dichtung. Abhandlungen und Aufsätze zur Römischen Poesie*, Bibliothek der klassischen Altertumswissenschaften: N.F. 2, 66: 110–19, Heidelberg.

Pötscher, W.
- 1978 ' "Numen" und "numen Augusti" ', *ANRW* II 16.1, 355–92.

Price, S.R.F.
- 1980 'Between man and god: sacrifice in the Roman imperial cult', *JRS* 70, 28–43.

Pross, H.
- 1974 *Politische Symbolik*, Stuttgart.

Ramage, E.S.
- 1985 'Augustus' treatment of Julius Caesar', *Historia* 34, 223–45.

Riescher, G.
- 1994 *Zeit und Politik. Zur institutionellen Bedeutung von Zeitstrukturen in parlamentarischen und präsidentiellen Regierungssystemen*, Baden-Baden.

Rytlewski, R. and Sauer B.
- 1988 'Die Ritualisierung des Jahres. Zur Phänomenologie der Feste und Feiern in der DDR', in W. Luthardt and A. Waschkuhn (eds.)*Politik und Repräsentation. Beiträge zur Theorie und zum Wandel politischer und sozialer Institutionen*, 265–85, Marburg.

Schäfer, E.
- 1983 'Die Wende zur Augusteischen Literatur. Vergils Georgica und Octavian', *Gymnasium* 90, 77–101.

Speyer, W.
- 1986 'Das Verhältnis des Augustus zur Religion', *ANRW* II 16.3, 1777–1805.

Stahl, H.-P.
- 1985 *Propertius: 'Love' and 'War': Individual and State under Augustus*, Berkeley, Los Angeles and London.

Strasburger, H.
- 1931 *Concordia ordinum: Eine Untersuchung zur Politik Ciceros*, Borna. (Repr. Amsterdam, 1956) = *Studien zur Alten Geschichte I*, 1–82, Hildesheim and New York, 1982.
- 1983 'Vergil und Augustus', *Gymnasium* 90, 41–76.

Syme, R.
 1939 *The Roman Revolution*, Oxford.
Treinen, H.
 1965 'Symbolische Ortsbezogenheit. Eine soziologische Untersuchung zum Heimatproblem, Teil I und II', *Kölner Zeitschrift für Soziologie und Sozialpsychologie* 17: 73–97, 254–97.
Walbank, F.
 1987 'Könige als Götter. Überlegungen zum Herrscherkult von Alexander bis Augustus', *Chiron* 17, 365–82.
Wallace-Hadrill, A.
 1986 'Image and authority in the coinage of Augustus', *JRS* 76, 66–105.
Weber, E.
 1972 'Die trojanische Abstammung der Römer als politisches Argument', *WS* 85, 213–25.
Wlosok, A.
 1983 'Vergil als Theologe: *Iuppiter – pater omnipotens*', *Gymnasium* 90, 187–202.
Yuge, T.
 1980 'Die römische Kaiseridee. Zur Herrschaftsstruktur des Römischen Reiches', *Klio* 62, 439–49.

For Margaret Hubbard

3

POLITICAL STOP-OVERS ON A MYTHOLOGICAL TRAVEL ROUTE: FROM BATTLING HARPIES TO THE BATTLE OF ACTIUM
Aeneid 3.268–93*

Hans-Peter Stahl

Our discipline shows a tendency to interpret an author by comparing his work to its sources; especially so if the author himself confesses to practice the art of imitation. This is a valid approach – within limits.

The proem of the *Aeneid* combines features of *Homer*'s two proems. The opening words, *arma virumque cano*, announce both a new *Iliad* (*arma*, war) and a new *Odyssey* (*virum*, the man). Even in such minute details as the number of lines (seven) or in leaving the hero nameless and characterizing him in a relative clause, Vergil's proem emulates those of *Iliad* and *Odyssey*.[1]

But *imitatio* of poetic form does not necessarily entail agreement in the area of content and goals. Odysseus, homebound from Troy, pines to reach his island of Ithaca. Yet the opening lines of the *Aeneid* not only take Vergil's hero from sunken Troy to Italy, the homeland of his family, but they move beyond Aeneas himself, culminating in "the walls of high Rome", *altae moenia Romae*.

"High Rome": that is the imperial metropolis of the reader's day, adorned by Aeneas' descendant Augustus. An explanation is provided in Book 8. There the poet recalls the city's lowly beginnings, "which" – he adds – "*today* Roman power has raised equal to the sky", *quae* nunc *Romana potentia caelo | aequavit* (8.99 f.). In Book 8 Aeneas is being detoured for a stop-over at the site of future Rome. He is given a guided tour which takes him across three areas that will, more than a millenium later, in the twenties BC when Vergil will be writing his epic, represent three major high-rise construction sites of the Augustan building program.[2] Aeneas spends the night on the Palatine hill, setting a mythical precedent for the residence of his greater descendant.

In this case, then, verification of the topographical and architectural references in Book 8 can provide considerable help for today's interpreter of the proem. We now see that by the resounding climax of *altae moenia Romae* Vergil means the sky-scraping metropolis of *his own* day. None of the numerous Homeric features prepares the reader for the line of *political* development proclaimed in *Vergil*'s proem, viz. the success story of Rome and of the Julian family, from Trojan Aeneas to the imperial city of his descendant Augustus.[3]

Occasionally *Quellenforschung* can even mislead the interpreter. In the *Iliad*, Achilles' friend Patroclus is slain by Hector; so, bereft Achilles avenges his friend by slaying Hector. Vergil imitates the sequence: Pallas, young disciple of Aeneas (and son of Aeneas' ally), is killed by Turnus; ergo bereft Aeneas avenges his friend by slaying Turnus. Now one has argued that, since Turnus takes the place of Hector in the sequence of slayings and since Hector in Homer is a humanly attractive figure, dying a tragic death, so Turnus' death cannot but appear as tragic to the reader and affect us emotionally just in the way Hector's death affects us.[4]

Such source-oriented reasoning does not sufficiently account for the *changes* Vergil has superimposed on his source. In Homer, Patroclus is an experienced warrior, older than his stronger friend Achilles; he dies because he has allowed himself to be carried away by his ambition. In the *Aeneid*, Aeneas' friend Pallas is a *young* warrior (much younger than his *magister* (8.515), Aeneas; the poet even calls him a *puer* (12.943)), and the occasion is his first day in battle ever. In an encounter of unequal powers, *viribus imparibus* (10.459), Turnus *seeks out* Pallas as a lion goes after a bull (a fight which the bull always loses). It is hardly a compliment to Turnus' character that he wishes his victim's father could be present and watch his son die (10.443).

The concatenation reveals that the *Aeneid* competes with its source also in plot line sequence on the large scale. But only when one analyses Vergil's additions, especially of the moral accent (the murder of Pallas in due course entails capital punishment for Turnus), do we begin to understand the new role the sequence is to play in his own design.[5] Unlike Homer, Vergil even *doubles* the scene of the older, experienced warrior slaying a younger one: in the same Book 10 Aeneas kills Lausus, but only after trying to warn the young man away – unlike Turnus, who seeks out his victim in order to hurt the victim's father. Moreover, while Turnus despoils the young body, *pius Aeneas* (10.826) – his own words give *his* understanding of what he is about to do – *pius Aeneas* leaves dead Lausus his arms, even adds compassion to honor by addressing the corpse as *miserande puer* (825).

By metamorphosing Homer's mature warrior Patroclus into the two *pueri* Pallas and Lausus, Vergil not only adds another unattractive (and un-Hector-like) feature to the character of Turnus, the adversary of Aeneas; he also can, by way of contrast, throw into relief the compassion shown by the Julian ancestor, and so channel the reader's human sympathy in such a manner that we side with bereft Aeneas and understand his emotionally upset condition.

Though Homeric in origin (and, so, still challenging the *archipoeta*), the sequence of slayings has now acquired a new purpose which can no longer be established by reference to its former Homeric context. It certainly is not Vergil who tells us we should feel about Turnus' death as we feel about the death of Hector.

Two cautionary recommendations result from our methodological considerations. First, the literary critic should not despise the help which topographical and architectural references in our texts can occasionally provide in reducing the element of subjectivity inherent in our endeavour.

Second, while observing the changes the author imposes on his sources, our interpretation should above all try to respond to *his own* plot line and large-scale design. For, when selecting (or rejecting) source materials, he, in all likelihood, was looking at their potential as constitutive ingredients in his *own new* design context.

This may seem a long introduction to dealing with what, to the horror of A.W. Allen, has been called "the dullest Book of the *Aeneid*".[6] Allen replaced dullness with weariness, disappointment, frustration and grief. Drawing on Pöschl's then recent book (subtitled "Image and Symbol in the *Aeneid*"), Allen too saw the epic as an "interpretation of life that is not...merely Roman, but is of universal validity".[7]

Now it is certainly true that Vergil would indeed wish to win the reader's sympathy for the suffering of Aeneas and his men. This is what the poet's artful psychagogy aims at – but the epic also aims at making us share the Trojans' disdain for the "evil Greeks", the *mali Grai*, as Trojan seer Helenus calls them in the same Book (3.398). The prophecy hardly lends support to Pöschl's romanticising idea of the *Aeneid* being "mankind poetry".[8] The poem's alleged humanity may prove to be subject to certain restrictions, human empathy being dependent on political allegiance.

Others[9] have taken a comparative approach to access the leading ideas of Book 3. They compare the outline of Aeneas' travels given by Dionysius of Halicarnassus in his *Roman Antiquities*.[10] The first observation is that Vergil offers fewer stop-overs. But their alleged numerical groupings or prophetic meanings fail to reveal a consistent principle of composition.[11]

Another comparative result points to "careful selection and arrangement in order to avoid repetition and monotony", and also a desire to place "between the fall of Troy in II and the tragedy of Dido's death in IV" a less intense piece.[12] How about a travelogue?

This line of reasoning denies the poet *his own agenda* in selecting the stop-overs of Book 3, while his drive for economy is even said to lead to "geographical inaccuracy"[13] and similar defects: Vergil "simply was not writing in terms of conventional geography".[14] In one case he, we are told, even "telescoped three stops into one".[15] Much of this amounts to attempts to excuse Vergil for inconsistencies which modern hypotheses about his art and intentions run into when they are confronted with his text.

Even at the cost of not arriving at a symmetrically or numerically balanced organization, the present investigation would like to follow up on several aspects of the Greek phase of the travelogue, and, at one point, i.e., around the approach to Actium, it will go into greater detail.

First, a quick overview of the route taken by Aeneas and his men (the section this paper deals with may be traced on MAP 1): departure from Antandrus; founding Aenus (*Aeneadae*) in Thrace; a visit with King Anius and Apollo himself on Delos; then, via the Cyclades islands (several are mentioned by name), to Crete, where the Aeneadae found the city of Pergamon; from there, a storm takes the boats to the Strophades islands; now, in a few lines, another cluster of names signifying almost contiguous places (details on MAP 2): Zacynthus; Dulichium; Same; Neritos; Ithaca; Leucata (= Cape Ducato, southern tip and promontory of the island Leucas or Leucadia); landings at a nameless *parva urbs* and on the shores of Actium where they spend the winter; next spring, they sail along the coast of Epirus, past most of Corcyra, and pay a brief but intense visit to Trojan relatives at Buthrotum; at (Acro)Ceraunia a short stop before they cross over to southern Italy, where again all places are inhabited by *mali Grai* (3.398). After the forced detour (caused by Juno's storm) to Carthage, the ships in Book 7 finally enter the mouth of the Tiber river.

The first thing to take note of is that the stretch around Greece is

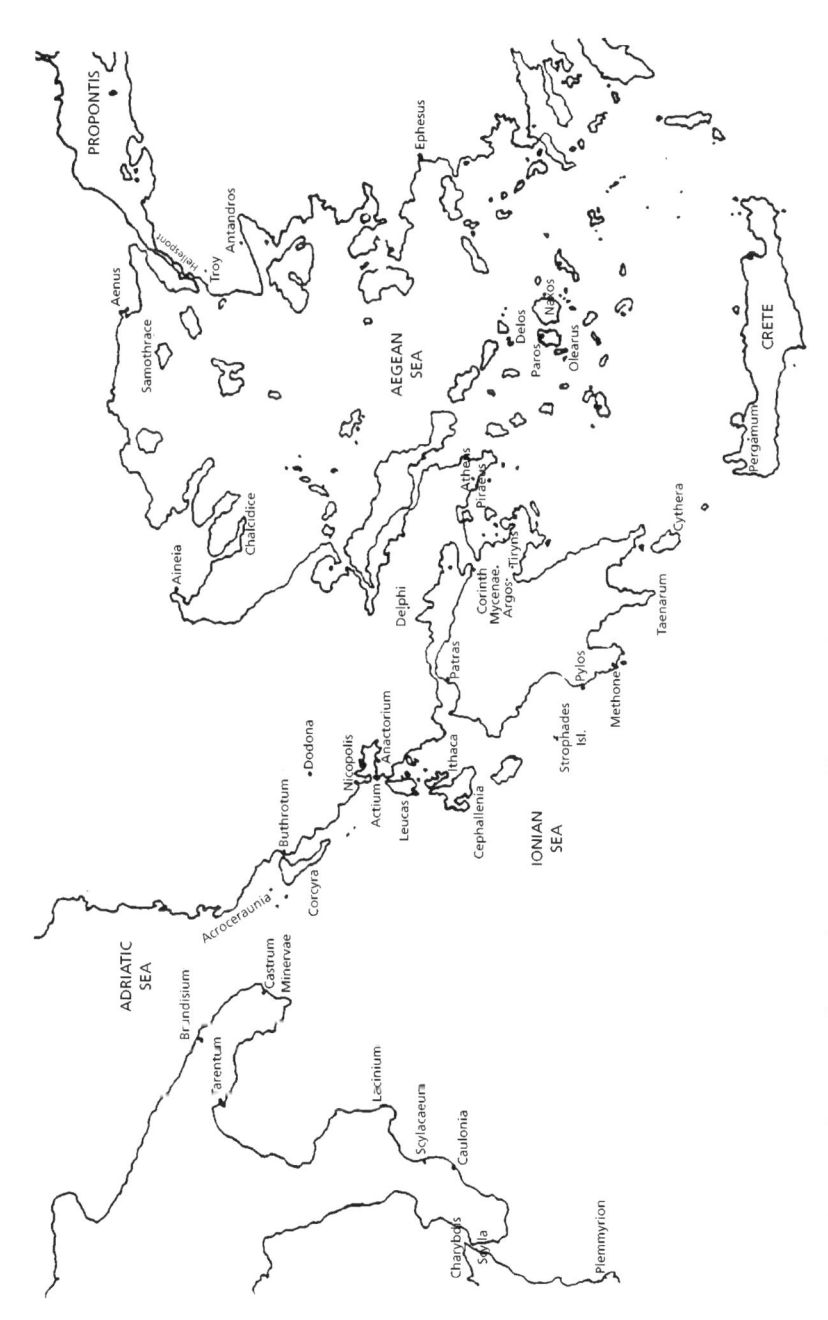

Political Stop-overs...from Battling Harpies to the Battle of Actium

Map 1. Overview map for tracing Aeneas' sailing route from Asia Minor around Greece as far as southern Italy.

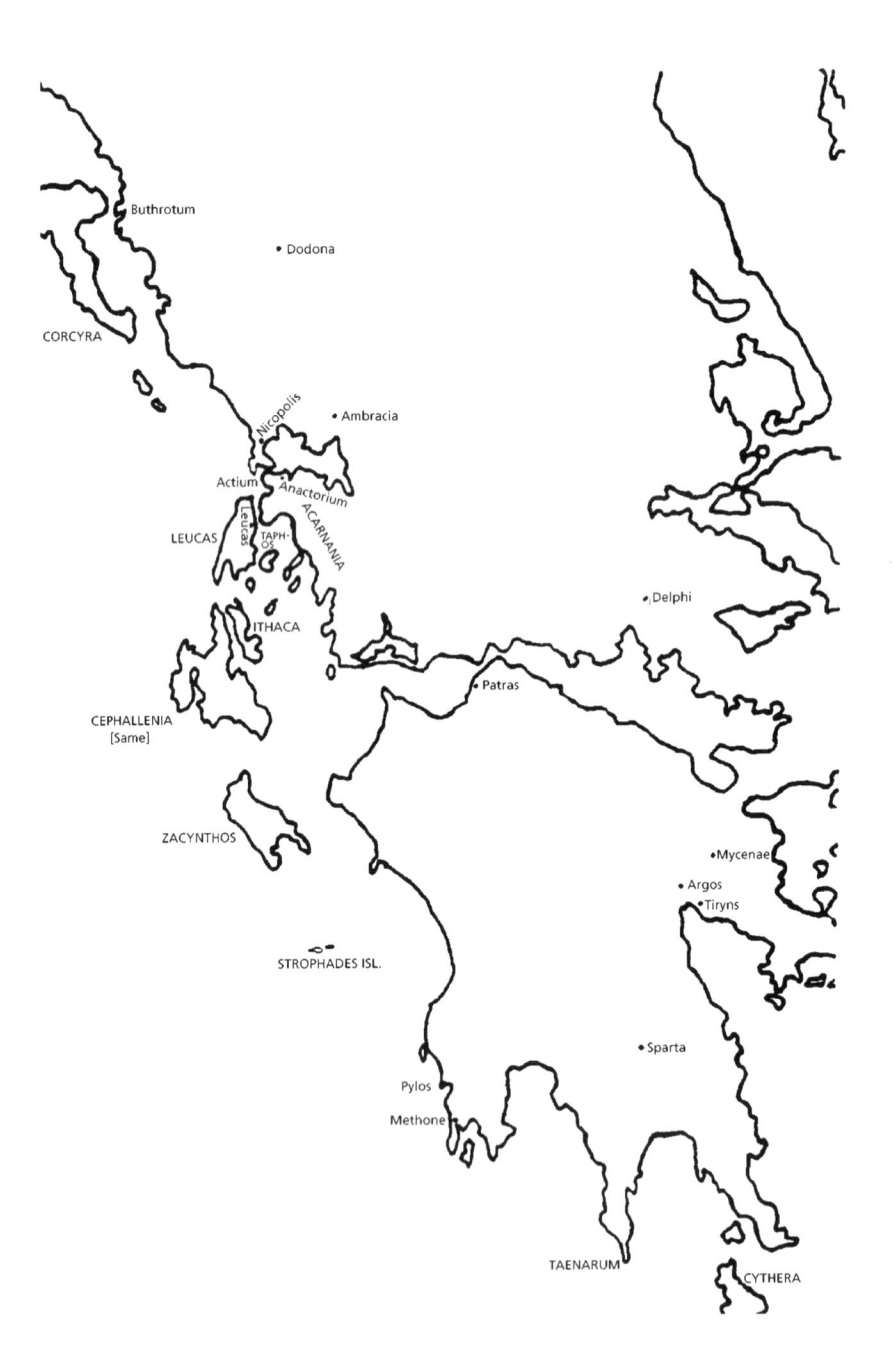

MAP 2. Western coast of Greece, comprising Aeneas' course from myth (Strophades Islands, Ithaca) to history (Actium).

only a section of Aeneas' travels. Nevertheless it has, it will turn out, its own literary climax.

Ever since the night of Troy's fall, supranatural revelations tell Aeneas to flee. In concrete terms, this guidance amounts to the ever-repeated injunction to flee a present location or imminent situation. The term *fuga* and the verbs *fugere*, *effugere*, *evadere*, often in imperative forms, appear eight times.[16]

There is every reason for the *Aeneadae* to get away from Greek-inhabited territory as quickly as possible, avoiding any risk of contact. Why then does Vergil allow them on occasion to get stuck and delayed, even to be detoured from the most direct route to their destination? By investigating these delays we appear to come closest to fathoming Vergil's own agenda.

A case in point is Aeneas' first stop. Leaving Antandrus, the Trojans give their sails not to the winds so much as to the fates (*dare fatis vela*, 3.9) – and land completely off course, far north, in Thrace (see MAP 1). Aeneas builds a city, naming the inhabitants *Aeneadae*, "after my own name" (*meo...de nomine*, 3.18). So the aetiological context is established: it was Aeneas who founded this city while on his way from Troy to Italy. But Vergil makes an addition completely his own here:[17] while duly preparing an offering to the divinities of good beginning for his new city, Aeneas finds the body of Priam's youngest son, Polydorus. He had once been entrusted for safety to the local Thracian king, who killed the boy for the money Priam had sent along with him. Pious Aeneas arranges for a worthy burial and leaves with his people.[18]

Certainly Vergil has raised our compassion for his hero: to the sorrowful experience of the downtrodden are added broken trust and even murder.

But the addition of the Polydorus-story also does something most important for Vergil's hero: it underlines Aeneas' legitimacy. Aeneas is, from Book 1 on, called *king* by the Trojan survivors (*rex erat Aeneas nobis*, says Ilioneus before Dido, 1.544), but we never hear how he acquired this title. If he acquired his position by default, it is highly desirable that the death of Priam's last surviving son is confirmed, of the son whom the king of Troy had spirited away when the city's situation began to turn hopeless.

Contemporaries would understand. Octavian the later Augustus faced a comparable problem when his adversary Antony claimed to have Caesar's rightful political heir and genuine son in his hands – Caesarion, son of Cleopatra and Divus Iulius. After the fall of

Alexandria, Octavian saw to it that the fugitive boy was tracked down and assassinated. Aeneas is placed in a more humane position: he only has to take care of a decent burial.

It would hardly be an objection that Aenus, historically an Aeolic foundation, is mentioned already in the *Iliad* (4.520), in a context long before Aeneas left Troy: as will be shown later, for ideological reasons even history may sometimes be overruled and rewritten by Augustan Vergil.[19]

One son of Priam did survive the Trojan War. He is Helenus, the seer. Aeneas encounters him on the penultimate stop-over that Vergil records on the east coast of the Ionian Sea, at Buthrotum (see MAP 2). This is the first time so far that Aeneas arrives at a *socia urbs* (352).

After an Odyssey of his own, Helenus has married Hector's widow, Andromache, and together they have built a nostalgic toy Troy, complete with Scaean gate. Clearly *rex* (353) Helenus lives in the past and does not aspire at all to rebuilding a real and strong kingdom of Troy here. The *parva Troia* (349) Buthrotum will never be in competition with the status of Troy Reborn which Augustus claims for Rome and which, Aeneas knows, will be in Latium (*"illic fas regna resurgere Troiae"*, Aeneas tells his shipwrecked men in Book 1, lines 205 f.).

The priest of Apollo and son of Troy's last king delivers the most detailed (though not complete) piece of oracular advice Aeneas receives in Book 3, preparing him for the trip around southern Italy and Sicily as far as Cumae and his encounter there with the vatic Sibyl. The clearest indication that the king of *Little* Troy is ceding the succession to the throne of Great Troy to the line of Anchises comes in his last words to Aeneas: "You by your feats do carry huge Troy up to the heavens", *ingentem factis fer ad aethera Troiam* (462). Aeneas' legitimacy is confirmed (and, implicitly, that of his descendant, Augustus, ruler of Troy Reborn today) by one who would well be able to question it.

But the poet's contemporary was bound to discover more in the passage than today's cursory reader finds. Let it first be stated that, in the orthodox version offered by Dionysius of Halicarnassus, Aeneas goes on a detour inland to Dodona (see MAP 2) in order to consult the oracle of Jupiter (D.H. 1.51.1). It is there that he meets Helenus and his Trojan followers. Why did Vergil transfer the encounter to Buthrotum? Sure, he did streamline the story by eliminating the stop-over at Dodona. But, then, he expanded again by turning the visit at Buthrotum into an affair of more than 200 lines. Poetic economy does not seem to have been on his mind. What is so special about Buthrotum?

In his parting words (500–5), Aeneas pronounces Buthrotum and his own people's future city in the Tiber vicinity and their populations relatives and neighbors: "We shall make both Troys one in spirit: let that be the concern waiting for our descendants." Vergil's readers think of their own time when they read of "relatives", Tiber-vicinity, and of *nepotes*: in their time, Buthrotum is a flourishing colony, where not long ago Caesar's veterans and, just recently, veterans of Octavian have settled. The names stated on coins are both *Colonia Iulia* and *Colonia Augusta Buthrotum*. Also among the surviving evidence is an aqueduct of the Augustan period.[20]

But "one Troy in spirit" points to an extraordinary closeness between the relatives. The puzzle can be solved with the help of epigraphical evidence from the site. In 1983 Franke published the following inscription which he found at today's Butrinto: "The colonists set this up as their gift to Lucius Domitius Ahenobarbus, son of Gnaeus, Pontifex and Consul, their patron."

> [L D]OMITIO CN F AHENOB
> PONTIF COS
> D D PATRON COLONEI

Franke identifies Ahenobarbus as the consul of 16 BC, and he dates the inscription to about 16 to 13 BC,[21] i.e., to a time three to six years after Vergil's death. But the connection of Ahenobarbus to Buthrotum and his representation of its colonists' interests in Rome may easily go back to Vergil's lifetime.

Another circumstance may prove more important for our *Aeneid* passage. Lucius Ahenobarbus was married to Antonia Maior, daughter of Antony and Augustus' sister, Octavia. Antonia was born in 39 BC, and, still an infant, engaged to Ahenobarbus in 37 BC. The occasion was the treaty of Tarentum, in which Antony and Octavian came to an agreement. Octavian's daughter Julia became betrothed to Antony's son, Marcus Antonius Antyllus. On the same occasion, Cn. Domitius Ahenobarbus, Antony's associate, had his son, Lucius Domitius Ahenobarbus, engaged to Antonia Maior. Before the Battle of Actium Ahenobarbus the father switched sides, going over to Octavian. The marriage of Antonia Maior and L. Domitius Ahenobarbus took place after the fall of Egypt in 30 BC. (Likewise after the fall of Egypt, Octavian had Marcus Antonius Antyllus, formerly his prospective son-in-law, killed.[22])

In emphasizing the close family ties between Aeneas and his

brother-in-law Helenus (Aeneas' wife Creusa was the sister of Helenus) as well as the ties between the cities deriving from these two founders, and by further letting Aeneas project these close ties onto the time of the *nepotes*, the *Aeneid* supplies a mythical precedent for conditions prevalent in the reader's day. Under Augustus, Buthrotum is again closely related, and the representative of its interests in New Troy, L. Domitius Ahenobarbus, is related to Aeneas' greater descendant by being married to his sister's daughter. Indeed, the *nepotes* can hardly be more closely related. L. Ahenobarbus has even been identified, together with his wife and their two children, among the members of Augustus' family that appear on the *Ara Pacis Augustae*,[23] and he later was appointed by Augustus executor of his will.

Now we are in a position to understand better why Vergil transferred the traditional encounter of Aeneas and Helenus from Dodona to Buthrotum; why he replaced a consultation with Jupiter with an oracular utterance by Priam's son Helenus; and why his Aeneas speaks of relatives and of one Troy in spirit. Just as we saw him do in the case of Aenus, Vergil rewrites recorded tradition by making the Trojans of Helenus antecede the historical founders of Buthrotum. In this way the veterans of Divus Iulius and of his greater son had settled on soil that not only was originally Trojan, but that also could be viewed by its population as subordinate to the leadership center in Italy by fate and by primeval agreement. The veterans fulfilled Aeneas' parting words about the two cities which would be one in spirit. History (historically, Buthrotum was founded by settlers from neighboring Corcyra) must not be allowed to interfere with the instruction given to the reader by the new national epic about the nation's fated Julian leadership.

The first and the last of Aeneas' detailed stop-overs on his way around Greece do, then, suggest that Vergil's principle in selecting landing sites was determined by an agenda of contemporary politics rather than by one of literary artistry. The stop-overs both at Aenus and at Buthrotum help to secure for Aeneas and Augustus the exclusive and rightful succession to Dardanus' heritage. Our result fits in well with the *Aeneid*'s overall idea that Dardanus, the earliest ancestor of *Troianus...Caesar* (as Augustus is called by Jupiter at 1.286),[24] left Corythus in Etruria and founded Troy; and that Dardanian Aeneas, in the words of river god Tiber, brings back home to Italy the Trojan city and here finds the seat for the Trojan Penates (8.36–9).

The next stop after Aenus is the island of Delos, where the Aeneadae are welcomed by Anchises' friend Anius, the priest of Apollo. Yet in spite of the availability of this *Phoebi...sacerdos* (80), Aeneas this time consults the god without an intermediary; and he is dignified by a direct personal answer, uttered by the divine voice (*vox*, 93; cf. *haec Phoebus*, 99); the divine presence makes itself felt by a sizeable earthquake. To Vergil's contemporaries, such intimacy between Apollo and the proto-Julian was hardly surprising. They could see every day up there on the Palatine hill the symbiotic collocation of Augustus' residence and the temple of his tutelary deity, connected even by a back entrance, a ramp that led from the Emperor's quarters to the quarters of his god.[25] No wonder, then, that Vergil represents the ancestor as communicating with Apollo in a comparable fashion.

It is interesting to note that Aeneas invokes the god not as "Delian" (or perhaps as "Pythian") Apollo but as *Thymbraee* (85), i.e., naming him after his temple at Thymbra near Troy. Clearly, we here can watch the process of the Greek seer god being recast into the guardian of the Trojan–Julian line.

Apollo's directive is: "Search out your ancient mother!", *antiquam exquirite matrem* (96). From that location, Apollo says, the house of Aeneas and the children of its children will exercise their rule over the world. But, although Apollo expressly addresses Aeneas and his followers as "Tough sons of Dardanus" (93; this would point to Dardanus' homeland in Italy), Anchises tells them the cradle of their race stands on Crete, because forefather Teucrus (as Anchises calls Teucer, 3.108) was coming from Crete when he founded his empire in the Trojan plain at the bottom of the valley (*vallibus imis*, 110). At that time, Anchises explains, the city of Ilium (i.e., Troy) and Pergamum, its citadel, were not yet standing.

Here we have to insert a *conclusio ex silentio*, which the Roman reader quite naturally performed; so it was left to Dardanus, Teucrus' son-in-law from Italy, and *his* line, to move up from the valley and build Troy city with its citadel, Pergamum.[26]

I cannot deal here with details about the ill-starred settlement on Crete, caused by forgetfulness on the part of old Anchises. His error is corrected by Apollo himself who accesses the mind of Aeneas at night via the *Penates* network.

The main point of the detour to Crete is that, by making Aeneas the founder of Pergamum on Crete, it prevents the reader from thinking that Cretan Teucer brought the name Pergamon with him to Troyland and, so, may have had a hand in founding Troy and its citadel,

Pergamon. When founding his Cretan city, Aeneas expressly asks his men (who are "happy" that he chooses a name recalling Pergamon) also to raise a *citadel*, *arcem* (3.134), and Vergil secures the city for Aeneas even beyond his personal presence by making him – in spite of disease and famine! – "leave a few behind", *paucisque relictis* (3.190). Thus a monopoly on Troy is being guaranteed to Italian Dardanus and his line. The detour to Crete, ill-motivated as it is through Anchises' forgetfulness, has the desirable political outcome of eliminating Teucrian (i.e. Cretan) competition.[27] In the reader's eyes, Aeneas is confirmed in his claim to represent, together with his followers, Troy's Pergamon, in the hero's own words, *altera Troiae Pergama* (3.86 f.). Augustan Rome owns the exclusive title to being Troy Reborn. The stop-over on Crete falls in line with those at Aenus and Buthrotum.[28]

How to get the Trojans back on track after a politically motivated detour which has taken them off their pre-defined geographical course around Greece toward Italy? Well, if no divine agent is easily claimed (like Juno or Aeolus in Book 1), there is always the possibility of high winds that happen to give their flight (*fugimus*, 268) the appropriate northwestern direction; the Homeric model passage is Zeus' punishing storm which Odysseus and his companions experience after leaving the island of the sungod with his cattle which they had expressly been forbidden to eat (*Aen.* 3.192–5 ≈ *Od.* 12.403–6).

But the Aeneadae had *not* been forbidden to eat the cattle of the Harpies (one can see that Apollonios' Harpies fit Vergil's scheme better than Homer's sungod-owned cattle); above all, before touching the objects of their hungry desire – it is worth quoting Aeneas' own account here – "we call on the gods and on Jupiter himself to share the booty" (3.222 f.). As always, *Aeneas* observes due religious process, even in adversity. Unlike Zeus in the *Odyssey*, Vergil's Jupiter has no reason to send a punishing (i.e., destructive) storm against the hero's crew.

Though the encounter with the Harpies is mythological in nature (and, so, fits the theme of Vergil's *Roman Odyssey*), the reader is already being pointed forward by being reminded of their geographical location in terms of his own time: "The Strophades...islands lie in the great *Ionian Sea*", *Strophades...insulae Ionio in magno* (3.210 f.). The (almost prosaic) geographical hint is not unimportant because it prepares us for the next leg of Aeneas' travels which will take him and us *from mythology to contemporary history, from battling Harpies to the battle of Actium*

Political Stop-overs...from Battling Harpies to the Battle of Actium

(cf. line 280), the name *Actia* evoking for contemporary readers Octavian's victory over Cleopatra and Antony in 31 BC.

It is hard for today's reader to realize the omnipresence of Actium all over the Empire. To picture the pounding of people's minds with Actium propaganda one may justifiably compare the all-pervasive influence of print and television media in our own time. So let it merely be stated that Aeneas' visit to and his activities on the shores of Actium can hardly have had anything exotic about them in the eyes of Vergil's contemporary readers.[29]

The group of lines 268–77, describing the last leg of the voyage on the hostile seas around Greece, is a compositional unit to itself, consisting of five sections of two complete lines each. Every time, the sections are marked grammatically and metrically by coincidence of sentence ending (period) and ending of the second line (ends of 269, 271, 273, 275, 277).

But not all of the five couplets fulfill similar functions. The first (268/269) generally characterizes the favorable navigational conditions during the flight across the waters. The second (introduced by *iam*, "already") describes the swift progress the Aeneadae are making in geographical terms; and so does the fourth (introduced by *mox*, "soon"). The third and fifth couplets, on the other hand, show the reader how they react (or what their attitude is) to the new situation each time outlined in the preceding couplet. The overall structure one arrives at, then, is a sequence of the form a-b-c-b-c.

> Already there appears on the waves of the high sea Zacynthos rich in forests
>
> > iam medio apparet fluctu nemorosa Zacynthos   (270)

Surprise about the swift sailing (*iam*) is joined to correct geography (see MAP 2): coming from the Strophades islands west of the Peloponnesus, they would, upon crossing open waters, first pass the island of Zacynthus, lying on their left. Behind it, again on the left, should appear Cephallenia (or Same; cf. Strabo 10.2.10); on their right (about opposite the *city* of Same) would begin the southern tip of Ithaca, island of Odysseus.

They are about to enter a channel about two and a half miles wide at narrow places (see *Fig.* 1), stretching for about fourteen miles between the northern half of Cephallenia and Ithaca.

The first b-element (270–1) offers the imitation of a Homeric line. It literally translates the words in which Odysseus describes to Alcinous, the Phaeacian king, some islands which lie around Ithaca, the center of his kingdom:

Dulichium and Same and, rich in forests, Zacynthos

Δουλίχιόν τε Σάμη τε καὶ ὑλήεσσα Ζάκυνθος (*Od.* 9.24)

Vergil has only reversed the order of names, adapting them to Aeneas' course, thus making huge Zacynthus in the south the first one to appear on the horizon:

...rich in forests, Zacynthus
and Dulichium and Same...

...nemorosa Zacynthos
Dulichiumque Sameque...   (*Aen.* 3.270 f.)

Lines 272–3 bring the reaction of the Aeneadae: we manage to avoid "the crags of Ithaca, realm of Laertes". The emphasis on the island's rocky nature possibly, as Servius thinks, contains a note of ridicule. It would fit well as a subjective reaction to a landscape vision prepared already by *ardua saxis*. At any rate, they "curse the land that nursed savage Ulixes". Any reader, mindful of (and who could forget?) the part played by "Ulixes, inventor of crimes" (2.164) in the story of Troy's fall so feelingly narrated by Aeneas in the preceding Book, will register the names of these islands and especially of Ithaca with the same sense of horror and of potential trouble as do the Aeneadae. R.D. Williams (ad loc.) points out the vehemence of line 273 with its spondaic movement: the crescendo of the couplet takes the reader from Ithaca to Laertes to (last word in the line) *Ulixi*.

Exiting from the strait (see MAP 2), they have to cross some seven further miles of open sea to reach the southern tip of Leucadia (the island also goes by the name of Leucas) with its steep and dangerous cape:

Soon, there comes into sight the top of Cape Leucata, surrounded by rain clouds, and Apollo, dreaded by sailors.

mox et Leucatae nimbosa cacumina montis
et formidatus nautis aperitur Apollo.   (274–5)

Again, there is no geographical problem in this description either. With the northern tips of Ithaca to the right (*Fig.* 2) and of Cephallenia to the left (*Fig.* 3) still in sight, the helmsman, facing the open sea and looking for guidance, already may (or may not) dimly discern the mass of Leucadia/Leucas in front (*Fig.* 4); he cannot yet realize that, what seems to stretch from left to right, from west to east, will soon reveal on its left a long promontory (*Fig.* 5) protruding from the island's western coast southward into the sea toward Cephallenia and toward his boat.

Political Stop-overs...from Battling Harpies to the Battle of Actium

Fig. 1. Channel between Cephallenia and Ithaca.

Fig. 2. Northern tip of Ithaca.

Fig. 3. Northern tip of Cephallenia.

Fig. 4. Island of Leucadia (also called Leucas) veiled by haze as viewed upon exiting the channel between Ithaca and Cephallenia in northern direction.

Fig. 5. Promontory Leucata (southern tip of Leucadia).

Hans-Peter Stahl

The precipitous cliff, of white color, rises on its western side about 200 feet vertically from the sea level (*Fig.* 6). In historical times, Apollo's temple stood on the second ridge of the cliff, one ridge up from today's lighthouse (*Fig.* 7), visible both from the open Ionian sea to its west and from the expanse of water to its east. Today, nothing but a few foundation blocks and the steps of a threshold are left, together with broken roof tiles.

Naturally, after the promontory's skyline has come into view (274), the temple will be the next feature to become visible (275), and it will serve as a confirmation that the course which is being sailed is correct. "Steep height, discernible to sailors from far away", is the way in which Philippus, while invoking Apollo, characterizes his promontory (*A.P.* 6.251.1). The Cape, famous for stories such as the lover's leap, was feared by sailors because it was dangerous to round. On coins, *Apollo Leucadius* (his Greek name being *Leukates Apollo*) was represented with a torch in his outstretched right hand – perhaps an indicator of an ancient lighthouse near his temple.[30]

Fig. 6. Promontory Leucata, western side: steep rise (200 feet) from sea level (sea appears black in picture).

Fig. 7. Promontory Leucata, western side: lighthouse and (one ridge closer to viewer) area where ancient temple of Apollo was located.

Political Stop-overs...from Battling Harpies to the Battle of Actium

The final couplet (276/277) of the section certainly takes the Aeneadae beyond this danger, thanks to their *active* response (*petimus*, 276, being said in sharp contrast with *effugimus*, 272):

> For this one we set our course and, tired, take shelter in a small city; the anchor is dropped from the prow, the sterns are standing on the shore.

> hunc petimus fessi et parvae succedimus urbi;
> ancora de prora iacitur, stant litore puppes.   (276/277)

Et is here used, as often,[31] in a postpositive fashion, allowing "tired" to go with "we enter for shelter". Of course they do not "try to reach" Apollo on the Cape but – a common nautical meaning of *petere* – they "set their course in direction of" the landmark to make sure they do not drift out west to the open sea.[32] Once near enough to make out clearly (but keeping a safe distance from) the dangerous promontory, they will (see MAP 2) turn to their right, then soon turn north again, and will enter the strait between Leucas and Taphos; the strait (on *Fig.* 8 viewed from the north) opens into an expanse stretching for more than five miles between the island of Leucas and the mainland, narrowing at its end. Should one expect an epic poet really to have filled in all these trivia? That he does know his geography and landmarks has become clear already. (And how should he not, being in a position to contact even leading participants in the events around Actium of 31 BC?)

Fig. 8. Strait between Leucadia and Taphos, viewed from the north (the strait is the narrow passage appearing above the two cypress trees).

Hans-Peter Stahl

So far, then, there is still no geographical problem. But what about the "little city"? Is it Leucas the city (of the same name as the island it was situated on, see MAP 3), situated directly at the isthmus at the northern end of the expanse, or is it Actium (the next name appearing in the text, at line 280 – but Actium is a peninsula and never was *polis*), or is it Ambracia beyond the Ambracian Gulf? Or is the "little city" at which the Trojans pull up their boats perhaps meant to be a precursor to Victory City (founded by Octavian five miles beyond the strait of Actium on the northern peninsula, in memory of the battle of 31 BC)?

All these suggestions have been made at one time or another, but all imply that Vergil "compressed" the geography. The "compression" most widely accepted requires us to assume that the poet "combines Leucas and Actium into a single stage apparently without reconciling the geographical facts."[33] In the view of Fordyce (ad 8.677), the geographical problem even is that Aeneas "lands at Leucate (274) and is at Actium".

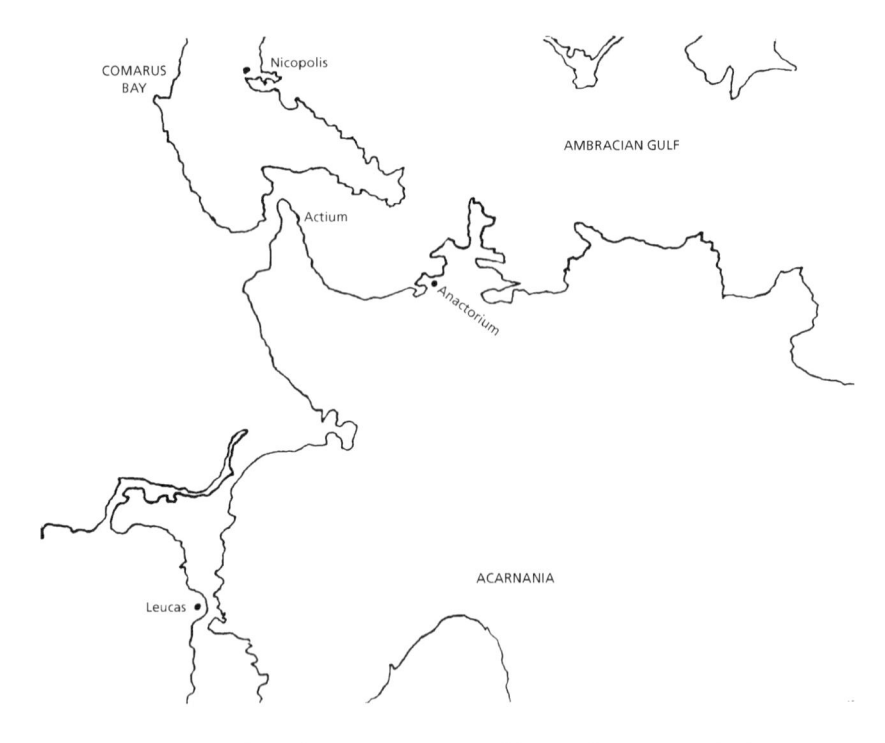

MAP 3. Actium and environment: areas of Aeneas' games and winter camp; of naval battle of 31 BC and of Octavian's camp as well as of his 'Victory City' (Nicopolis).

Political Stop-overs...from Battling Harpies to the Battle of Actium

There may be a more plausible way of reading line 276, if only one observes the composition of the section. The line opens a c-couplet of active response to a b-couplet situation: after Odysseus' kingdom, the next – and, as it will turn out, for this leg of their voyage final – landmark and potential cause for fear (*formidatus*) is Cape Ducato (the modern name) at the southern tip of Leucas. Once past the Cape, they are in for smooth sailing, staying within sight of the shore. Allowing *et* (276) to connect two successive stages of the itinerary, it is quite natural to understand that the "little city" indeed is Leucas near the northeastern end of the island.

But, today's reader may ask, how do shelter and boats pulled ashore at Leucas go together with the following line (278)?

Accordingly, having *finally* taken possession of the *unhoped-for land*,

Ergo *insperata* tandem *tellure* potiti,

The line definitely offers the emotional climax of relief after the preceding dangers and fears, emphasizing in a retrospective mode their despair (*insperata*) as well as their seemingly endless wait (*tandem*). Can these words of relief be spoken in reference to an island city still ten miles away (as the crow flies) from Actium?

The answer will have to be "yes". The "island" of Leucas/Leucadia has not always been an island in the strict sense. A narrow isthmus (see MAP 3) on its north-eastern side made Leucas part of the mainland i.e., of Acarnania. Immediately at the isthmus lay the ancient city of Leucas.[34]

The isthmus (*Fig.* 9; here viewed from the eastern shore: its remnants are today covered almost completely by the shallow lagoon)

Fig. 9. Partially submerged isthmus between Leucadia and Acarnania, viewed from Acarnanian side approximately in direction of the ancient city of Leucas.

was repeatedly dug through in historical times, but the canal apparently silted up easily, and boats were pulled over the isthmus. Actium and Leucas had long been regular stop-overs on the maritime route which connected Italy and Greece. Cicero, after a most uncomfortable boat ride from Brindisi and Corcyra, in 50 BC writes: "to round Cape Leucata seemed troublesome" (*ad Att.* 5.9.1) – and took the inshore route. So Vergil could count on his audience's notion that it was the natural thing to use the inshore water way and to approach Actium by crossing the isthmus at Leucas.[35] (After all, the Aeneadae had passed Cephallenia likewise by the in-shore water way opposite Ithaca, avoiding the open sea to the west.) Indeed, upon transporting their boats beyond the barrier, the Aeneadae would be considered to have hugged the shore, and that route hardly entailed any seafaring danger. The distance is so short that Cicero on the very same day wrote letters from both locations, one when "departing from Leucas" (*ad fam.* 16.5.2, Nov. 7, 50 BC), another from "Actium, in the evening" (*ad fam.* 16.6.2).

Since, once having reached the city of Leucas, the Aeneadae were practically done with any dangerous part of their sailing at least until they would depart from the area of Actium, their pulling up the boats (*Aen.* 3.277) at Leucas the city as well as taking hold of the land with great relief (278), then, are actions which are completely justified and natural in the situation as developed by the poet ever since he made the Trojans flee the islands of the monstrous Harpies under the guidance of a favorable wind. Consequently, line 278 can open a new action sequence (extending as far as 288) which pictures a situation of relief and celebration.

So it is really not surprising that the reader is not given any additional geographical information on the last leg to Actium. Why at all then make mention of the unnamed "little city" of Aeneas' landfall? Here, the *Vorgeschichte* of the battle is of interest. By the fall of 32, Antony had built his position at Actium; he secured his supply lines (see MAP 2) from Egypt by having bases around the Peloponnese at least at Taenaron, Methone, Patras (Patrae), Corinth; further north at Leucas (the city), this one safeguarding to the south also the strait between Ithaca and Cephallenia (passed through by fleeing Aeneas, *Aen.* 3.272) and the entrance to the Corinthian Gulf.[36]

Antony felt he could advantageously center the bulk of his own fleet inside the Gulf of Ambracia – precisely speaking, at the southern of the two peninsulae (with outposts on the northern shore) whose overlapping shape forms the strait granting entrance into the Gulf.

But Octavian disembarked his troops far north at the Ceraunian mountains (possibly at Panormus), ordering them to march quickly south along the coast of Chaonia and Thresprotia (Epirus) via Buthrotum, while the fleet likewise was moving south. This allowed him to establish his camp on the narrow neck of the northern peninsula, about five miles north from the strait of Actium (see MAP 3).

Over the summer of 31, Antony's situation deteriorated. The single most decisive event in this development seems to have been the capture of Leucas the city, including the ships in the harbor, by Agrippa. From now on the heavy supply vessels for Antony's camp had to take the seabound route around dangerous Cape Leucata, becoming an easy prey to Agrippa's fighting ships when sailing north and east toward Actium. In the end, Antony's actions in the Battle on Sept. 2 looked to Dio Cassius more like a breakout attempt than a bid for victory.

Now what could a contemporary public be expected to make of the feature that Vergil's hero, while in mythical time traveling across the present-day war theater, cannot find relief until reaching such historical places as Leucas, Actium, and, later, Buthrotum? Considering the fact that Octavian had declared the struggle a war against a *foreign* enemy (D.C. 50.4.3-5; cf. 26.3 f.), i.e., the Queen of Egypt, the reader is obviously asked to see that enemy territory and friendly territory here are the same for Romans led by Octavian as they had once been for Octavian's ancestor and his men. Again Vergil persuades the Roman people to view Octavian's involvement in the recent civil war not as ephemeral and arbitrary, but as the final act of his family's timeless, since fated, mission of world order and world domination. This is confirmed once more by the events at Buthrotum (3.293–505).

But why leave Leucas nameless? One reason is that all the emphasis is to go to Actium. Any reference to *Aphrodite Aineias*, as in Dionysius, might divert the reader's attention from the martial and imperial focus and its culmination in the victor god of Actium. A related motive would be that the poet wants to avoid assigning too much impact to Agrippa: on Vulcan's shield for Aeneas, Agrippa is duly given acknowledgement (8. 682–4), but he is clearly second by a long distance after the hallowed leadership appearance of "Augustus" (*sic*, 8.678–81). For those who know, enough will be said by Aeneas' deep sigh of relief (cf. *insperata*) at 3.278. His descendant may have felt similar relief when hearing that Leucas was no longer hostile territory.

Now we must not overlook that the relief experienced at Leucas, in spite of its emotional tone, in the final analysis concerns a subordinate aspect of their travels and of their mission. For at the end it is no longer the suffering at sea (and related worries) the poet wishes to dwell on. The main event opens a new perspective and a positive, celebratory aspect of the Trojans' experience, described in a new main clause connected by *-que* (280):

> Accordingly, after finally having taken possession of the unhoped-for land, we purify ourselves for Jove and set altars afire with offerings.
>
> And we crowd the shores of Actium with Trojan games.

> Ergo insperata tandem tellure potiti
> lustramurque Iovi votisque incendimus aras.
> Actiaque Iliacis celebramus litora ludis.   (3.278–80)

At 280, the Aeneadae definitely have reached Actium, as the first word in the line indicates. But what about line 279? For those hypothesizing that Vergil "compressed" the geography this is not a problem, since for them landing, lustration, and games take place at one and the same undetermined location.[37]

On one point one can easily agree with Lloyd (and Conington/Nettleship), viz., that "the devotional to Jupiter here is quite natural and appropriate",[38] considering his role in Book 3 and elsewhere as the principal ordainer (cf. 3.171, 251 f., 375 f.); in particular the dire prophecy of Celaeno, the Harpy, which, she claimed, ultimately derived from Jupiter (conveyed to her through Apollo, 3.251 f.), makes the lustration seem advisable. After all, Celaeno presents the famine which she predicts to the Trojans as a punishment for taking the Harpies' cattle (and, let us add, the taking of the cattle was done under invocations especially of *Jupiter*, 222 f.) and for attacking the monsters themselves.

Should one at all expect a lustration for Jupiter at *Actium*, the traditional sanctuary of *Apollo*?

A closer look suggests a distinction between lines 279 and 280, both on grounds of contents and of language. First, contents: in the context of the recent flight from the Harpies' islands, the landfall of the Aeneadae at Leucas results in a lustration for Jupiter whom, among other gods, they had invoked by name on the Harpies' island before seizing the cattle (222 f.). But at Actium, they will celebrate games (for Apollo, we may be sure), under a different perspective, viz., their escape from the danger which threatened from "so many Greek cities" (282 f.). One has to distinguish between the short-term chain of events since their adventure on the island of the Harpies and the larger context which has taken the Trojans around all of hostile Greece. In

Political Stop-overs...from Battling Harpies to the Battle of Actium

their first relief about having finally reached *land* (*tellure*, line 278), both strands come together. But their ensuing solemn and joyful (cf. *iuvat*, 282) activities are distinguished by divinities as well as by locales, according to the different sections they recall of their voyage.

Second, form: the two main clauses which deal with the devotional to Jupiter (279) are interconnected by coordinating *-que...-que*, which Roman epic likes to use in place of Homeric τε...τε (as happens on occasion with single *-que*, the relation of the two members is one of general and specific):

>lustramur*que* Iovi votis*que* incendimus aras.

Though a third *-que* is found at the opening of line 3.280, attached to *Actia*, it would be a misunderstanding to see this one as a mere continuation of the preceding pair, as if this were a triple connection on the same level of speaking. The new *-que* has a different function, setting the new metrical unit (280) off from the bipartite hexameter which precedes it (279). The *-que* found in line 280 is the one which is used, to quote *OLD*, (s.v., 4) "beginning a sentence, introducing a fresh event or situation," etc. (or, as Lewis and Short s.v., G.I., define the usage, "in transition to a new subject or thought").[39]

>But at Actium, we crowd the shores with Trojan games

>*Actia*que Iliacis celebramus litora ludis.   3.280

The new step takes the reader from Leucas to Actium. With the right emphasis (in Latin indicated by the first-word-in-line position), one can leave the translation "and" even in English: "And at *Actium*, we..."

With the idea of "games at Actium", Vergil has now *expressly* catapulted the Roman reader from myth to the political events following the victory at Actium. At newly founded Nicopolis, Victory City (see MAP 3), Octavian himself had set up games, clones of which were to be celebrated later almost empire-wide. We know of more than a dozen additional places that were home to periodic "Actian Games". Rome itself was among them.[40] So the Trojans' activities on the shore are hardly disorienting to the poet's contemporary readers. On the other hand, there was the age-old tradition of Greek games which took place directly at the Actian sanctuary of Apollo. For both perspectives, past as well as contemporary, a visit by forefather Aeneas might prove conducive to supplying the appropriate political perspective. So it is hardly a surprise that line 3.280 receives further elaboration:

>But at Actium, we crowd[41] the shores with *Trojan* games: naked (the oil is

slippery) the companions practice the wrestling matches *inherited from the forefathers*:

> Actiaque *Iliacis* celebramus litora ludis:
> exercent *patrias* oleo labente palaestras
> nudati socii: 3.280 ff.

The words *Iliacis* and *patriis* imply (as West has seen)[42] that Vergil here establishes a Trojan tradition *independent* from and potentially older than the local Greek games. (The playing field of the old Anactorian/Acarnanian games lies within a few hundred yards of the tongue of land that is Actium.) The juxtaposition of *Actia* and *Iliacis* may be designed to drive home what comes unexpectedly to the contemporary reader. There is something grotesque about the lines. For, when describing to Dido the games (performed, as Donatus puts it, *Iliaco more*), the only word the *Trojan* founder has available to name them is (as was also seen by West) a *Greek* one, *palaestra* (281). Rightly, the commentator Servius (ad loc.) shows himself perturbed by his author's use of the Greek word.

Apparently, the *poeta vates* defines his own function in exercising poetry's ability to establish a mythical precedent to the measures taken by his contemporary ruler and, so, to provide the legitimacy of Providence to the periodic celebration following the recent event which had raised Octavian to solitary power. By establishing a correspondence of mythical past and Augustan present, the vatic poet has lifted the veil somewhat from the fated course of history, allowing his contemporaries once more to view the Augustan age they live in as the glorious culmination of an age-old divinely-guided process.

Vergil achieved a double purpose. Not only do the Greeks now appear to be mere imitators of a foreign (Trojan) original. Also, the Greek games, at Actium before (and perhaps even now at Nicopolis), have been made to look like an aberrant, regional, and narrow perspective of an immeasurably wider potential. After all, Aeneas moved on to Italy, from where (as Vergil's Jupiter and Faunus inform us) his family was to subdue and rule the world (*Aen.* 7.98–101; cf. 1.278 f.), Greece included (1.283–5). So the *Aeneid* myth has laid the ground for empire-wide "Actian" games.

The foundation myth as told in the new national epic (bound to be distributed and read everywhere) would offer non-local and non-Greek (i.e. most) readers the only version available to them. Their conclusion must have been that Apollo granted victory at Actium in accordance with ancestor Aeneas' pious foundation of games in honor of the god; Augustus was right in reforming the games after his own victory.

Political Stop-overs...from Battling Harpies to the Battle of Actium

This leads us a step beyond the insight gained earlier. What Vergil on his part did, then, was not only once more to design a mythical precedent for a contemporary action undertaken by the Emperor (i.e., re-founding the games on a new scale and under an ideological perspective). In addition, the poet arranged the parameters of the foundation myth in such a way that the new story would supersede and even invalidate recorded history. The power of poetry can provide an unexpected dimension which makes even the well-known appear in a new light of being relative. The procedure employed here is comparable to the one we earlier saw Vergil employ concerning the original settlers of Buthrotum or to the one we see him use in Book 8 where he makes the Etruscans (masters of Rome during its early history) in prehistoric time place themselves under the military leadership of the Julian ancestor (cf. *subiungere*, 8.502 f.). The recurrence of this feature is a welcome methodological confirmation for our interpretation.

Once Vergil's contemporary political scene has been recognized as being the standard of reference for mythical Aeneas' visit at Actium, historical information is essential for today's reader of the epic. Let us in summary fashion visualize how, in the twenties BC, the visitor to Nicopolis was psychologically guided to appreciate the political message of the area.[43] Entering the strait (see MAP 3), one would find, on one's right, the precinct of Actian Apollo, with the temple, refurbished and enlarged by Augustus, rising from the flat, sea-level tongue of land (*Fig*. 10. Of the temple, only the raised foundation mound is visible today). In the adjacent docks, there was on permanent display, like a sort of maritime museum, Octavian's offering of ten complete, lifesize, enemy ships, one of each boat type. This (the local guide would inform the tourist) had been the area of Antony's camp.

Fig. 10. Middle ground: the long and narrow tip of the Actium peninsula, barely rising above sea level, with Acarnanian mountains in the distant background.

Hans-Peter Stahl

Having entered the Ambracian Gulf and turning northward for about five miles, the visitor would arrive at Nicopolis, the richly endowed and flourishing metropolis (cf. Strabo 7.7.6) of commercial transit and great regional influence: Octavian had endowed it as a member of the Delphic Amphictiony with six votes (Athens, for instance, had one). The city covered the site where Octavian's troops had had their camp before the battle (D.C. 50.12.2 f., 51.1.3). Remains of three edifices may help us today to visualize past glory: odeion; theater; western gate (the gate had three arches, a *nymphaeum* left and right of those passing through between its outer and inner openings, and the incoming aqueduct ran above it. See *Figs.* 11–13).

On an excursion to the northern suburb, the tourist's eyes would (provided he had not come for the special purpose of seeing the widely announced contests themselves) be impressed by the sumptuous space and facilities available for the Actian games.

On a hillside (see Map 3) still farther north and beyond the suburb, there was the site where Octavian had set up his tent (presumably, his *praetorium*)[44] and command post before the battle, and from where he is likely to have taken his auspices. And it was this same area which he, after the victory, turned into what Murray and Petsas in their trailblazing report call "the most important structure built by Octavian outside of Italy". He created a level rectangular platform with the help of a huge retaining wall, the length of which is stated to be 62 meters (about 200 feet; of the western and eastern returns there are lengths of 21 and 23 meters preserved).[45]

Fig. 11. *Odeion* at Nicopolis. (In the far distance: Mikhalitzi Hill, site of Augustus' Actium Memorial).

Political Stop-overs...from Battling Harpies to the Battle of Actium

On top of the terrace there was another rectangular structure, a three-sided stoa, about 40 m long, with its south-south-western side left open, affording the visitor a view (*Fig.* 14) towards that segment of the sea where the Battle of Actium had taken place, with the mountainous mass of Leucas in the background. (We have to discount today's salt lagoon in the left foreground.) The visitor could not miss the direction. The rams below him all looked toward the site where the ships whose prows they once adorned lost the battle.

The ground enclosed by the stoa must be assumed to have been that on which Octavian's tent had once stood, and so the location should be identified with the seat of Apollo's statue set up there by Octavian "under open sky", according to Dio (D.C. 51.1.3).[46] The succession

Fig. 12. View across the ruins of the theater at Nicopolis.

Fig. 13. Nicopolis: ruins of western gate (with integrated eastern *nymphaeum* on the right).

would resemble the collocation of residence and temple on the Palatine hill in Rome.

Two further statues were standing on the platform, viz., of Lucky the donkey driver and Victor, his ass. They could in popular fashion confirm the predestined character of Octavian's victory, because he had run into the ominously named pair of Eutychos and Nicon on the morning of the battle on his way down to the fleet (Plut., *Ant.* 65.3).

Before reaching the terrace, one faced the huge retaining wall (*Fig.* 15) into the face of which, resting on the first and reaching up into the third (and sometimes even fourth) course, thirty to thirty-five bronze rams had been mounted, taken from Antony's doomed fleet. Twenty-three sockets (like the ones shown in *Figs.* 16 and 17) are discernible still today, arranged in a rough order of rising sizes from right to left. The smallest of the "key-holes" must have held rams ten times larger than the smaller one of the two preserved from antiquity, i.e., the so-called Bremerhaven ram (the weight of which amounts to 53 kg; see *Figs.* 18 and 19).[47]

But the display of the trophies was (as was that of the Actian games) aiming not primarily at the local population. The new *rostra* set up in front of the *Divus Iulius* temple on the *forum Romanum* in Rome likewise were fruits harvested from Octavian's Actian victory. These, though being much smaller than the ones used in the Nicopolis exhibition, could nevertheless serve as reminders of the Great Battle.

Fig. 14. View from the Campsite Memorial looking south-west toward the area of the naval battle, across the campsite and the peninsula which lies north of the Actian strait. In the far distance, the mountainous mass of Leucadia is veiled in haze.

Political Stop-overs...from Battling Harpies to the Battle of Actium

Fig. 15. Retaining wall of the Campsite Memorial, showing sockets to anchor rams.

Fig. 16. 'Key-hole'-shaped socket for holding a ram.

Fig. 17. Sockets for holding rams.

Fig. 18: So-called Bremerhaven ram, front view.

Fig. 19. So-called Bremerhaven ram, close-up view from front.

Hans-Peter Stahl

There can be no doubt that the lay-out of the approach to the Campsite Memorial, stretching over many miles from the sanctuary of Actium onward, and combining geographical (landscape), architectural, and trophied elements, is orchestrated so as to produce a superb piece of psychological programming, consciously designed to impress upon the visitor (even the illiterate visitor) the inescapable and overwhelming experience of predestined historical greatness.

It is in the light of the post-Actium propaganda, displayed in the aftermath of the naval battle, that the Roman reader would view Aeneas' movements in the area of Actium.

Now: holding joyful games on hostile soil is a glorious provocation, even an insult to the victorious enemy. But spending the winter months (which allow no escape by ship from potential hostilities) on Greek territory (as Actium and Acarnania would be conceived to be also by the contemporary Roman reader) is a different matter. Conington/Nettleship wonder about Aeneas' safety (ad 3.287). Would the ancient reader?

Modern readers are likely to miss the caesura when the narrative moves on (*interea*) from games at Actium to Aeneas' winter camp (284 f.) and to his display of the shield there (286-8). That is, Actium was the last point on unfriendly Greek soil (unfriendly, then, to the ancestor in the new poetry as it proved unfriendly, being Antonian, to the descendant in recent history). Besides, the sea-level swampy tongue of land (see *Fig.* 10) that is Actium had proven conducive to causing disease among Antony's soldiers. Would Vergil quarter Aeneas there?

Vergil, it is true, does not use prosaic terms like "winter camp", "houses", or "shelters".[48] He only describes the forbidding season which "meanwhile" (*interea*, 284) has rolled in and during which (285) "the icy winter makes the seas rough with northern winds". The only clue (a solid one) is contained in the mention of Aeneas' *postes* (287): then (*tum*, 289), at the time of ordering departure (*linquere tum portus iubeo*, 289), i.e., in late spring, Aeneas affixes to his *postes* the shield of Abas (287).

A line-to-line interpretation yields four time periods: arrival on Actian shores and joyful games (probably in the fall, 280-3); harsh winter and rough seas (284/5); victory memorial with inscription (286-8); and, immediately following (*tum*, 289), orders (*iubeo*) for departure, presumably in late spring; this is followed by the actual departure (290; again set off by *asyndeton*). The spirit of the new sailing season (=

period 3) is stylistically separated from the winter (= period 2) by *asyndeton* between lines 285 and 286. Aeneas' dedication of Abas' shield must be understood as his first step towards resuming his travels, a sort of good-bye or sign-off he leaves behind for others to see: "Victorious Aeneas was here". A close reading of lines 280–90, then, takes the reader through four stages.

Where precisely did the Aeneadae have their winter quarters? The traditional answer, "at Actium, near the temple of Apollo", seems somewhat simplistic. Let us picture a reader and visitor to the area of Actium/Nicopolis (as Vergil himself probably was one, in the last stage of his life, and perhaps even earlier),[49] tracing the steps of his ruler's ancestor as adumbrated in *Aeneid* 3. Would Augustus' contemporaries not take a hint from Aeneas' dedication of the enemy's weapon? Would they not equate the harbor of their own landing at Nicopolis, admittedly the best natural harbor in the Gulf of Ambracia, with the *portus* (289, a poetic plural) from which Aeneas set out at winter's end?

The traveled reader, then, would locate Aeneas' *postes* right on that hillside where in his own time the raised terrace was being shown, i.e. the former site (meanwhile sanctified) of his ruler's tent. In Book 8, too, when staying for one night with King Evander on the Palatine in (future) Rome, Aeneas turns out to pre-occupy his greater descendant's residential grounds.[50] There, too, he sets a mythical precedent for something Vergil's contemporaries have seen come true in their own day. In the same way, the display of the shield which Aeneas dedicates will have been viewed by contemporary readers as determining precedent for Octavian's Campsite Memorial with its display of rams.

One cannot but ask the question: is it at all conceivable that Vergil could introduce Actian games (in recent memory relocated to the northern suburb of *Actia Nicopolis*) and *not* be thought to allude also to the victory monument on the hillside, at the foot of (and under the dominance of) which the games were being held in the poet's own day?

The problem, of course, was that Aeneas (unlike Octavian) could not claim any major victory or to have defeated any of the leading Greek heroes in the Trojan War. So, Vergil has his Aeneas set up the trophy of a victory of which no prominent record can be found:

> A shield of hollow bronze, weapon of huge Abas, I attach to the doorposts that face me...
>
> > aere cavo clipeum, magni gestamen Abantis,
> > postibus adversis figo...   (3.286 f.)

Hans-Peter Stahl

Of course, enemy Abas, too, had to be *huge* (*magni*, by no means a "transferred epithet") to be worthy of being overcome by the Julian ancestor (for the greatness of the latter) – but what was the occasion? Servius points to the night of Troy's fall as a likely possibility. What is the meaning? And who was Abas? A lot of effort has gone into answering these questions.[51] One thing is sure: in the narrative context of Book 3, Aeneas' act is (as Donatus points out) one of self-praise, in so far as the shield declares him the victor (*se procul dubio laudat quem constabat extitisse victorem*; ad 3.285). So, to anchor Octavian's Actian victory in destiny, a symbol of victory set up by his ancestor on "Actian shores" would once more remove any hint of chance from the emperor's predestined success.

The conclusion then is that, in making Aeneas set up a trophy at (or near) Actium, *Vergil seems to be reacting to the existing Campsite Memorial of his day*. It is not the historical moment of the Actium victory which is important to the poet here, but (as was already indicated by Aeneas' games) the way in which the victory is being memorialized and eternalized by the victor. The epic supports the official ideology and policies which propagandize the battle's outcome.

Are further details available to confirm this conclusion? Yes, it seems so. Vergilian Aeneas left behind also an *inscription* – a verse inscription, that is, which he calls *carmen*:

> and I mark my action[52] with a verse inscription: "It was Aeneas who dedicated these arms taken from the victorious Greeks."
>
> et rem carmine signo:
> 'Aeneas haec de Danais victoribus arma.'   (3.287 f.)

Needless to say that nowhere else in the epic does Aeneas leave behind an inscription, not to mention one commemorating a personal victory of his. Donatus remarks on the insults and ridicule contained in the wording; he even understands the emphasis on the "facing doorposts" (*postibus adversis*) as a way of making sure that no visitor to the site, even the one who is not searching for the shield, could overlook it.

Let us be guided by Donatus' emphasis on the adjective *adversis*, "directly facing so as not to be overlooked". Facing the visitor who, attracted by the spectacle of the rams, had walked up about a quarter of a mile from the stadium, was not only the huge retaining wall with its martial display. Over the length of about 185 feet, the wall was crowned by the inscription which began above the first ram, counting about 220 letters,[53] carved high up into the blocks of the wall's sixth course,[54] each letter being about a foot in height (a sample is shown in *Fig.* 20). Murray and Petsas see the eyes of the approaching visitor guided by the rising sizes of the rams (from right to left) to the beginning of the inscription.[55] The huge letters would secure the victor's intention that the monument's displays both down here on the retaining wall and on top of the terrace, including exhibits in the stoa and the view of the battle area, would be understood in *his* way. Determining the meaning of history must not be left to the individual; nor could the visitor be left to merely enjoying the vistas.[56]

The conclusion to be deduced by the reader of the *Aeneid* is that the poet expects him to make the connection, i.e., when reading Aeneas' inscription, to call to mind that of Octavian. Here an excerpt (from the translation given by Murray and Petsas): "Imperator Caesar, son of the divine Julius, following the victory in the war which he waged on behalf of the republic in this region, ...after peace had been secured on land and on sea, consecrated to Neptune and Mars the camp from which he set forth to attack the enemy now ornamented with naval spoils."[57]

Imperator Caesar, Divi filius, is a self-glorifying opening. At Rome, a similar, contemporaneous, inscription began as follows: "*Senate and people of Rome* for Imperator Caesar, son of the deified Julius, after the republic had been saved."[58] The difference is similar to that between the *rostra* displays: at Rome on the *forum*, Octavian showed 'republican' moderation, setting up in front of the Divus Iulius temple the lighter rams of Antony's smaller ships; the huge ones were set up at the Campsite Memorial outside Nicopolis.

Fig. 20. Sample of inscription at Campsite Memorial (fragment of IN HAC, sc. REGIONE).

Hans-Peter Stahl

Now Vergil could easily have had both shield and inscription for Aeneas set up by the Trojan nobles, the *proceres*, whom his hero on occasion consults.[59] But, loyal to his patron, he chose for the Julian ancestor the Nicopolitan version with its self-glorifying, more autocratic and less "republican" opening: <u>Aeneas</u> *haec de Danais victoribus arma*: "*Imperator Caesar, Divi filius*..." In defining the family's divinely guided political mission, Vergil seems to endorse a Julian independence from traditional political constraints.

So: if Octavian crowns his victory monument with an inscription, then Vergil feels occasioned to record a victory of Aeneas by means of a comparable inscription. In adjusting Aeneas' offering as well as his travel route to fit the newly created environment of Nicopolis, *Vergil supports the post-Actium propaganda of Octavian*.

In a necessary digression, our result may fruitfully be compared with the thesis of a recently published book on "Actium and Augustus". In it, R.A. Gurval attempts to downplay the immediate effect of the Actium victory (and of Actian Apollo) on Augustan propaganda and ideology. Four preliminary points may clarify the situation as far as the present chapter's purpose is concerned:

1. (a) Gurval, in accordance with his thesis, views Nicopolis and the Campsite Memorial predominantly in the context of the Empire's eastern parts rather than in relation to central Rome. This neglects that Nicopolis quickly became a highly frequented, well-known commercial center, situated right on the trade route to (and from) Rome from (and to) the East.

(b) The Campsite Memorial itself, far from displaying an 'eastern' perspective, is oriented toward Rome: its inscription is not written in Greek but in Latin, pointing to the war which Octavian "waged on behalf of the republic", *pro re publica*. Survival of the "republic" is hardly a matter of interest primarily to eastern subjects.

Work on the monument must have started almost immediately (probably within a few months) after the victory. The inscription (whose composition Murray and Petsas wish to date as late as early 29 BC) was cut when "the frieze course was already in place on the monument".[60]

(c) The smaller rams taken from Antony's ships were set up in Rome in front of the *Divus Iulius* temple (dedicated three days after Octavian's triple triumph of 29 BC, but work on this monument, too, must of course have started much earlier). The meaning of these Roman *rostra* cannot be exhausted if they are merely subsumed under Octavian's show of "debt and devotion to his adoptive father".[61] They constitute a political statement, as Zanker saw:[62] the old republican (Antiate) rams at the opposite end of the *forum Romanum* are complemented by the new Actian rams: the Actian victory by which "the republic had been saved" should be measured by the standard of an earlier key battle of the republic. Any traveler or guide could explain that, here in Rome, you saw on display only the miniaturized edition of the real threat to the republic averted by the Actian victory. Murray and Petsas point out that Octavian had an ax to grind here:[63] refurbishment of the Antiate rams had been left to Antony by C.J. Caesar. Octavian later even made Antony's structure *disappear* behind the new rectangular wall of his own *rostra Augusti*. If anything, the Actian *rostra* on the *forum Romanum* testify to the role of Actium in the Augustan ideology already during the early years.

2. Gurval admits that in *Aen.* 3 Vergil "alludes"[64] to Nicopolis and the Actian games. But the long-distance action line defines the joyful games at Actium, where Aeneas does the step from myth to historically marked territory, as the emotional climax and culmination of his wanderings up to this point. In terms of literary composition, the meaning of the Actian stop-over amounts to much more than a mere allusion. Above all the fact that Vergil makes his hero land and found games near Actium but does not record any visit to the area of Egyptian Nicopolis or to the founding of games there (after all, Octavian founded a Victory City and comparable games there, too, Dio 51.18.1), seems at least in the perspective of the *Aeneid* to take Octavian's arrangements at Actium out of any "eastern" context and to plant them firmly in an orientation towards Rome.

3. (a) Gurval, referring to the Palatine Apollo temple of 28 BC,[65] states that "the god in his acknowledged role as Apollo Actius makes his first appearance in extant Latin literature almost ten years after the temple's dedication, in the eighth book of Vergil's *Aeneid* (8.704-5)."

But work on the *Aeneid* started in 29 BC, even *before* the temple's dedication, and it was monitored along the way by the emperor. It is hardly admissible to isolate victory-granting Actian Apollo on Aeneas' shield in Book 8 from the rest of the work by arbitrarily assigning to his arrival in the *Aeneid* a date close to the posthumous publication. The god is firmly grounded in the epic as a guiding figure for Aeneas and the Julians' fated mission.[66] Augustus' ancestors, Aeneas and Ascanius-Iulus, even receive unmediated, direct communications from the god (3.93; 9.640). Apollo recognizes Ascanius as "descendant of gods" (i.e., Jupiter and Venus) and as "ancestor of gods" (i.e., Caesar and Augustus, 9.642). There is no reason to deny the god his place in the epic's original design and to make Actian Apollo a late ideological invention, added by Vergil to the epic's compositional skeleton ten years after the event.

(b) Besides, it is already *before* the *Aeneid* that Apollo is associated with Octavian in Vergil's poetry. The proem to *Georgics* 3, envisaging a temple to be built for Octavian by the poet (a projection which Kraggerud in this volume convincingly refers to the plan of the *Aeneid*), sets up a marble statue of "Troy's founder" Apollo (*Georg.* 3.36) together with statues of Octavian's Trojan ancestors. The line is left out in Gurval's discussion[67] (under the heading of "Apollo and the Poets"). One may compare, on the other hand, Kraggerud: "Apollo and Caesar are united in the same *templum*." Kraggerud even concludes, from Apollo's climactic final position in the decoration programme, "that Apollo Actius is behind and above it all".

(c) Again outside the *Aeneid*, there is evidence that even the act itself of founding Nicopolis was labeled an expression of Octavian's gratitude to Apollo: though not written in Latin but probably court-affiliated and certainly Augustan in spirit, an anonymous (Antipatros?) but obviously contemporary epigram of the *Anthologia Palatina* (9.553) maintains that "Lord Phoebus" accepts "divine Nicopolis" (which "Caesar set up and dedicated (εἴσατο)" to him) "in exchange for the Actian victory" (lines 5–6). It does not recommend Gurval's thesis that he, against our evidence (Dio 51.18.1), finds it "plausible" to switch around the founding dates of Actian Nicopolis and Egyptian Nicopolis so as to postpone the date of Actian Nicopolis' founding to a later year.[68]

4. Following Murray and Petsas, Gurval insists that the Nicopolitan Campsite Memorial, while mentioning Neptune and Mars, "surprisingly excludes the role of Apollo in the battle".[69]

Two pieces of information need reconsideration (further details cannot be discussed here): (a) Strabo's (7.7.6) testimony about the bipartite precinct, "the other part on the hill *sacred to Apollo* which lies above the grove;" and (b) Dio's information (51.1.3) that on the platform atop the memorial, where formerly Octavian had his tent, he set up a ἕδος (probably a statue, as was discussed earlier) of Apollo under open sky. Either fact is dangerous to Gurval's thesis, especially so if Apollo on the grounds of Octavian's tent is seen in parallel to his symbiosis with Octavian on the Palatine hill in Rome.

The poet's loyalty to his patron's ideology may also help to shed light on a final question which should at least be touched upon here: why dedicate a shield only and not a complete *tropaeum*? Admittedly, the Greeks seem (as Paschalis saw)[70] deprived of their main defensive weapon – a prophetic feature, symbolic of Greece in Vergil's day.

But shield dedications had a long tradition. Affixed to religious or private buildings, shields were among the signs of victory. A few examples from Vergil's own lifetime may suffice. At Oplontis on the Campanian coast, an imperial villa, perhaps the property of Nero's second wife Poppaea Sabina, shows in its older, original residential rooms Second Style murals. In the great hall, some painted shields are shown mounted between painted columns by means of unsightly holding bars (see *Fig.* 21). The bars are anchored in the shafts of the columns – a barbaric violation of a slender architectural form, but one obviously able to suggest the owner's trophies from a recent victory. Other shields and winged Victories on the door-valves complete the air of high social prestige, which is also known in the *Aeneid* (cf. 7.183–6). The eye-catching design is perhaps even topped by the center-piece of the triclinium mural which is focused on a golden round shield with starburst design, hanging from the lintel of a magnificent imaginary doorway and reflecting light coming from above.[71] In contrast with this tradition, Propertius praises his patron Maecenas for his modesty because he does not "burden your house with affixed arms", *onerare tuam fixa per arma domum* (3.9.24).

Augustus himself tells us in his *Res Gestae* (34.2) how he received from the senate a golden "shield of virtue", *clupeus virtutis*, for his manliness, piety, justice and clemency. This was in 27 BC. He had it set up in the senate house. Our best preserved copy, in marble, was found in Arles in southern France, and coins with the inscription "c.v." or "cl.v." were issued by mints as far away from Rome as France and Spain.

Fig. 21. Painted shields in Atrium, Villa of Oplontis.

Augustus loved the idea so much that he not only had a stone copy of the shield inserted in the facade, breaking up the architectural design, probably over the entrance, of the mausoleum which he had built for himself near the Tiber in the early twenties BC.[72] He also, still more than twenty years later, was pleased to report that his adopted sons and prospective political heirs, young Caius and Lucius, were, as *principes iuventutis*, given small round silver shields (*parmae*, *R.G.* 14.2); and upon their untimely deaths, shields were again inserted, *against* the architectural design, into the frieze of the same mausoleum.[73] By then the shield had advanced to being the emblem of the ruling family.

Must the ruler not have been extremely satisfied when his client poet set up a shield recording the virtue of his victorious ancestor near Actium? And could any reader, exposed as he was to the pounding Actium propaganda of the twenties BC, in his mind place the ancestor's doorposts and victory-offering anywhere else than precisely on the spot of that terrace atop the Campsite Memorial where in his own day Augustus himself had his *postes* at the time of the battle, and where now Apollo's statue was looking out from the three-sided stoa toward the site of the naval engagement?

Would the contemporary reader perhaps even rather assume that Aeneas had erected a triumphal arch? I *have* to mention this as a speculative possibility because we have coins[74] depicting the arch of the *forum Romanum* which the senate decreed for Octavian in honor of his Actian victory (see *Figs.* 22 and 23). They show a basic post-and-lintel construction, supported by an arch, with the triumphal chariot on top. The two *postes* appear to be decorated each with what looks like a shield, which squarely faces the onlooker, *postibus adversis*. So Vergil's Aeneas would set up at Actium the type of monument the victor of Actium set up at Rome.

In submitting its thesis concerning Aeneas' approach to and his actions around Actium, the paper presented here not only wishes to explain a difficult passage of the *Aeneid*. I also hope to have made a methodological contribution. Verification of Vergil's political agenda is not restricted to the three great prophecies issued by Jupiter, Anchises and Vulcan, all three of which culminate in Augustus. Sometimes these political prophecies have been said to be exceptional or perhaps even to stand in opposition to the true tendency that supposedly runs under the work's Augustan surface. In the case of Book 3, it has proved fruitful to verify the references the *Aeneid* makes to its contemporary political environment.

Political Stop-overs...from Battling Harpies to the Battle of Actium

Fig. 22. Silver denarius, showing Actian Arch of *forum Romanum* with triumphal chariot; shields (?) attached to posts.

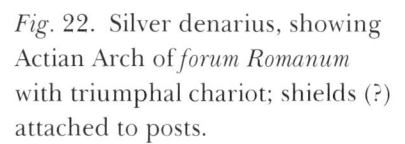

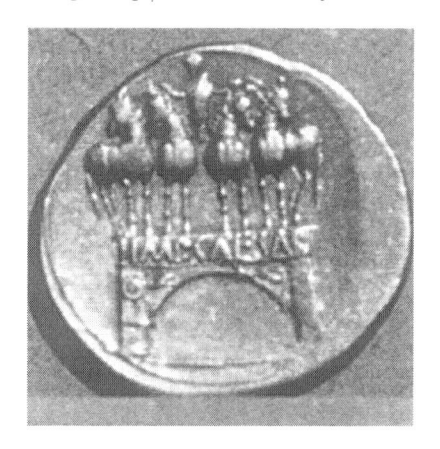

Fig. 23. Silver denarius, showing Actian Arch of *forum Romanum* with shield (?) affixed to left post.

The author was enabled to take these two photographs through the kindness of Dr Anne Kromann at the kgl. Mønt- og Medaillesamling, Copenhagen.

Such verification can be helpful in giving objectivity and support to one or the other of opposing interpretations which have been established by "literary" categories alone. This applies especially to sections of the work which to the present-day reader may appear politically less pronounced than the three great prophecies. For instance, the negative characteristic of Turnus in Book 10 and the positive evaluation of Aeneas in the same Book, resulting (as was explained in this paper's opening section) predominantly from Vergil's changes in the *Iliad*'s plot line, receive support from the thoroughly Augustan perspective of Book 3. Once more it seems then that Ovid was right when he, in addressing Augustus, called Vergil "the...author of *your Aeneid*", *tuae... Aeneidos auctor* (*Trist.* 2.533).

Notes

* The paper presented here is an abbreviated chapter taken from work-in-progress.

[1] For further details, see Buchheit (1963) 13–17; Austin ad 1.1–7.

[2] A detailed demonstration of the *Aeneid*'s architectural references cannot be given within the space available here and must be left to a separate publication.

[3] By no means should *altae* at 1.1.7 be taken as a transferred epithet, as if

75

logically belonging to *moenia*. Augustan Rome of "today" is higher than its walls. For another Julian reference in the epic's proem (i.e., the *Albani...patres* at 1.1.7), see West in this volume.

[4] Griffin (1985) 195.
[5] For details, see Stahl (1990) 199-205.
[6] Allen (1951/52) 119.
[7] Allen (1951/52) 120.
[8] "Die Aeneis ist eine Menschheitsdichtung und kein politisches Manifest." Pöschl (1964) 39. "Auch die Feinde des Aeneas sind Menschen" (op. cit. p. 175; followed by specific references to Turnus and Mezentius). On the *Aeneid*'s biased treatment of the Greeks, see H.P. Stahl, "Griechenhetze in Vergils *Aeneis*: Roms Rache für Troja" (contribution to conference on "Rezeption und Identität", ed. G. Vogt-Spira, forthcoming, Wiesbaden, 1997).
[9] Lloyd (1957) 138 ff. (immanent comparison); R.D. Williams (1981) 8-12. A different kind of comparison is tried by Hershkowitz who argues "that Book 3 can be read as a mini-epic which structurally reflects the *Aeneid* as a whole" (1991, 70). However, she fails to explain why and for what purpose Vergil would have gone through the trouble of setting up such an arrangement.
[10] D.H. 1.49.4—53.4.
[11] Both Lloyd and Williams follow Heinze (1965, 83 f.) who saw the Book's unity in the progressive revelation of the Trojans' final destination. But the number of supranatural revelations (Heinze counted six so-called "Etappen") is smaller than the number of stop-overs. Lloyd tried, not very convincingly, to assign oracular character also to the remaining three episodes of his own counting. Moreover, he himself admitted that his own number of nine episodes and its artistic as well as geographical subdivision "into a natural tripartite grouping" (1957, 138) is (in his own words, 1957, 136, note 17) "somewhat arbitrary" because of "the yoking of the stops in Northern Epirus and Castrum Minervae". And the chain of supranatural revelations starts, as Lloyd also admits (p. 147), long before Book 3, viz. in Book 2, when Hector's shade tells Aeneas to leave Troy and flee. Groupings by number may not have been a major concern when the author of Book 3 arranged his subject matter. Nor do revelations alone explain its composition.
[12] R.D. Williams (1981) 2.
[13] R.D. Williams (1981) 10 with note 2.
[14] Paschalis (1987) 63, note 32 (continued from preceding page).
[15] Lloyd (1954) 239 f.
[16] 2.289, 619; 3.44, 160, 268, 272, 282, 283. Other terms of avoidance and exodus are found at 2.704, 780; 3.688.
[17] Egan (1974) 40.
[18] As an aside let it be said that it is hard to verify in Aeneas, finder of Polydorus' corpse, "the symbolic cannibal" whom Putnam (1995, 52) found here. For one (and apart from a precise interpretation of the passage itself), would Polydorus' warning of "flee this land" then not be given to an unworthy person? And would this not inconsistently be the only instance of the recipient's unworthiness out of eight cases in which pious Aeneas is supranaturally

advised to flee? Long-range compositional consistency and plot coherence are factors not to be disregarded by the interpreter.

[19] The story of murderous king Polymestor is sometimes placed (MAP 1) in Aeneia in western Chalcidice. But Pliny (4.43) says Polydorus' grave was shown at Aenus near the mouth of the Hebrus river. If, as is then likely, Vergil means the latter by the ambiguous name *Aeneadae*, Aeneas would be made the founder of a city of great economic impact in Vergil's own time: via the Hebrus valley and its rich *hinterland* (rich in corn, fruit, and timber), the city also offered an alternative route to Odessus on the Black Sea/*Pontus Euxinus*, competing with the waterway of the Hellespontus.

[20] Franke (1983) 48 (with *Fig.* 93 on p. 46, showing an Augustan coin displaying the aqueduct), 49.

[21] Franke (1983) 49.

[22] See Bengtson (1977) 19, 183, 261 f.

[23] Coarelli (1988) 306 f. The close relationship between Rome and Buthrotum tends to get lost in Saylor's evaluation of "Toy Troy" (his term): "By miniaturizing Troy, however, Vergil conveys a change of spiritual perspective, *an intellectual distancing*, as it were, in the maturing Aeneas" (Saylor 1970, 26; italics mine).

[24] For the identity of *Troianus...Caesar* at *Aen.* 1.286 with Augustus (and not with his adoptive father), see Stahl (1985) 340, n. 46 (commenting on p. 126), and, with reference to recent discussion, Kraggerud (1994), whose result Harrison intends to "reinforce" (1996, 127). On the importance of understanding the compositional context (Jupiter adapts his revelation of the future to the fear and limited perspective of Venus) for identifying *Caesar*, see Stahl (1969) 353–6.

[25] See Carettoni (1983) 9, with *Plan 1* on p. 8, as well as the description of the ramp on p. 51 and the sketch of the restored view in *Abbildung* 6 on p. 48.

It is striking that Webb (1979, 45) should not list Apollo's *vox* (*Aen.* 3.93) among the direct contacts between the hero and the supernatural; it likewise comes unexpected that Putnam (1995, 53) should attribute the *vox* to King Anius.

[26] Cf. 8.134: *Dardanus, Iliacae primus pater urbis et auctor;* 6.650: *Troiae Dardanus auctor;* Servius ad 3.168 (*genus a quo principe nostrum* refers to Dardanus, not to the interposed Iasius: *anteriori respondit*).

[27] According to Servius Danielis (ad 3.167) there was even a version which called Dardanus himself a Cretan (*Cretensem*). Though alluding to *Iliad* 22.217 specifically, the *Aeneid* does not show as much interest in the *Baugeschichte* of Troy (its stages represented by Dardanus, Ilus, and Tros at *Iliad* 20.216 ff.), The question whether Dardanus arrived first in the Trojan plain (Servius ad *Aen.* 3.104) or Teucer (Servius Danielis ad 3.167) – the later one becoming the first-comer's son-in-law – is unproblematic for Vergil as long as the primary claim on founding Troy goes to the line of Italian Dardanus (*Dardania* in the *Aeneid* often stands for Troy: 2.281, 325; 8.120). Against Servius (ad 3.110) I am inclined to assume the subject of *habitabant* to be Teucer's not Dardanus' settlers. On *steterant* (3.110) see Williams, who compares 3.402 and Livy 8.32.12. There is no justification for maintaining that "Cretan civilization is seen as having primacy over the Trojan culture", and that Aeneas "cannot

Hans-Peter Stahl

return to the cradle of the race" (Day 1984, 26 and 27), Vergil's point being here that the "cradle of the race" is in Italy, not on Crete.

²⁸ Our result is in agreement with what Tib. Claud. Donatus (*prooemium*, p. 3, ed. Georgii) states about Vergil's method in delineating Aeneas' character: an unwelcome fact (in the present case, which does not directly refer to Aeneas, this would be the existence of Pergamon on Crete) is acknowledged but receives a favorable interpretation. For another instance (Aeneas seen in the company of warriors in Greek armour during the night of Troy's fall), see Stahl (1981) 167 with note 22 on page 176.

²⁹ For documentation of the Actium propaganda, see Hölscher (1985) 81–102.

Examples from coins are especially noteworthy. A denarius minted after Octavian's triumph in 29 BC would show himself in military habitus with scepter in one hand and globe in the other (see Giard 1988, *Plate 1, no. 1*). On the front of the coin appears Venus, the mother of Aeneas (and perhaps of C. Julius Caesar also). Octavian can also be viewed, naked like a god, holding a sceptre in one hand and an *aplustre* in the other. With one foot he is stepping on a globe. As if this is not clear enough an indication that the victory of Actium was propagated to mean rule over the world, the obverse displays a winged Victory (op. cit. *Plate 1, nos. 13–15*). Also, a sculpture of his winged Victoria, stepping on a globe, was set up in gold by Octavian inside the senate house. (One sees that Vergil hit the mark when, on Vulcan's shield for Aeneas, he pictured the victor of Actium accepting presents of homage sent by the most remote nations of the globe.)

³⁰ See Franke (1976) 162.

³¹ See, e.g., *Aen.* 2.383, 600; 3.430; 10.448; see also R.D. Williams ad 3.37, on "the postposition of particles".

³² By no means is it correct to translate, as Gurval (1995, 81) does, *mox* (274) with "thereafter" and *hunc petimus* (276) with "here we...seek" [sc., "the little town"]. In this way, Gurval contributes to "the particulars" which, he says (81) "scholars have been troubled by". He himself misunderstands the situation when saying "the escape [*sic*] from the stormy heights of Leucas [*sic*] belongs to the hurried flight [*sic*]" etc. And how Gurval understands the particulars when saying "the followers of Aeneas pass safely by the *Neritos ardua saxa* [*sic*] (271) and the *scopulos Ithacae*" is any Latinist's guess (1995, 82).

On Neritos see Lloyd (1954) 289–92; it must be said, however, that Neritos, in Homer a mountain on Ithaca, is later also understood to be another *insula* – e.g. by Pomponius Mela, *de Chor.* 2.7.110. Mela need not depend (as Lloyd 290 assumes) on Vergil: both may go back to a common source (*periplus* literature). Strabo's evidence-citing insistence on Neritos being the mountain (10.2.8) seems to point to the existence of a different opinion which would take Neritos to be an island.

³³ R.D. Williams (1962) ad 3.274. He proceeds to say that "the conclusion is really unavoidable that Virgil has combined Leucate and Actium in his mind without realizing the distances involved".

Aen. 8.677, mentioning Leucate in the context of the battle of Actium, does not necesssarily point to ignorance of geography either. Vergil may be speaking here in the same vein of riddling literary sophistication in which

Political Stop-overs...from Battling Harpies to the Battle of Actium

Ovid makes Jupiter, god of the *Capitolium,* occupy or inhabit the neighboring hilltop of "the Tarpeian citadel", *Tarpeias...arces (Met.* 15.866). Also, Heyne's argument from rhetoric may fit the encomiastic context: "locum ex vicinia posuit, ut tanto major rei esset species". The addition of *totum* to *Leucaten* at *Aen.* 8.677 lends support to Heyne's comment.

[34] For detailed physical maps, see Oberhummer (1887), facing title page; folding map and end of his volume.

[35] The route verified here differs from R.D. Williams' assumption that Vergil pictures Aeneas taking the outside route, rounding the west and north-west of the island. See Williams' map (1981, 9). The map also mistakenly assigns the name Actium to the northern instead of the southern shore of the strait that leads into the Ambracian Gulf.

[36] A good survey is found in Carter (1970) 200–14.

[37] Lloyd (1954, 295–6, referred to earlier) sees Leucas, Actium, and Ambracia collapsed into one, with Ambracia the likely location Vergil has in mind, because of the proximity to (and feeder-function for) Nicopolis, Octavian's foundation. Our preceding argument has rendered this choice improbable.

[38] Lloyd (1954) 297.

[39] Occasionally the progress from preceding to new development is one of time alone, indicated by *iam* in hexameters of Vergil (*Aen.* 3.521) and Horace (*S.* 1.5.20). Or it may, as in our case, be one prevalently of place (though a later time-stage is also involved): at Sallust, *Iug.* 104.5, two of King Bocchus' ambassadors return to him with good news, while three continue on to Rome: "But at Rome his ambassadors receive the following answer..." *Romaeque legatis eius...hoc modo respondetur.* Sometimes the new stage will be self-evident (e.g., Cicero, *Leg.* 2.12.30 and *Fin.* 3.20.67).

[40] Recently, Gurval (1995, 79) has questioned the spread of Actian Games for the Augustan period (as, for instance, maintained in Meyer Reinhold's Commentary on Cassius Dio: Appendix 10, p. 226). Even if Gurval's results on this point will, as seems possible, be confirmed and accepted by historians, there can be no doubt that Augustus' Nicopolitan games were well publicised at Rome. See below.

[41] Tib. Claudius Donatus (ed. Georgii, vol. 1, p. 303, line 25; p. 304, line 4), when paraphrasing, speaks just (as we would) of *ludos celebrare,* "celebrate games".

[42] West (1994) 58.

[43] A good overview over the monument itself is found in Murray and Petsas (1989) 85 f.

[44] Gagé (1936) 52.

[45] Murray and Petsas (1989) 23.

[46] The existence of Apollo's statue has been dismissed by Murray and Petsas (1989, 11, note 7), but their arguments have not convinced this interpreter; *hedos* at D.C. 51.1.3 certainly points to a statue base or socket (see already Gagé 1936, 55 f.). Publication of my detailed discussion must be postponed until later.

A curiously vacillating role is played in the scholarly debate by a denarius of the moneyer C. Antistius Vetus of 16 BC. Its reverse shows *Apollo Actius* with

Hans-Peter Stahl

cithara and *patera* next to an altar, standing on a raised platform; three ram-like objects (flanked by two anchors) are visible, affixed to the platform's side, facing the beholder.

Zanker (1983, 31 f. with note 40; cf. 1987, 90 f.), combining the coin with Propertius' elegy 2.31 (lines 5–8), identified the coin's *Apollo Actius* as the statue of the area in front of the temple of *Apollo Palatinus* (different from the cult statue inside the temple, Prop. 2.31.15 f.). Jucker (1982, 96–100) had denied the identity of the coin's *Apollo Actius* with Apollo's statue in front of the temple on the Palatine hill (his denial was accepted again recently by Gurval (1995, 285 f. with notes 20 and 22)); Jucker saw on the coin an abbreviated rendition of the actual monument at Nicopolis (denied by Murray and Petsas (1989, 91), both because of the unusual type of rams and because of the silence of authors other than Dio as well as because of lack of archaeological evidence). Trillmich (1988, 522 f.: "...passt nicht schlecht...") followed Zanker.

Sauron (1994, 503; his plate 55 offers a superb magnified photograph) again identifies Apollo on the coin as the statue in front of the Palatine temple, "installé sur les dépouilles d'Actium car la base de la statue était ornée d'ancres et de rostres", and he, like Zanker, identifies the statue on the coin with the one seen and described by Propertius (2.31.5 f.).

[47] On the measurement of the socket dimensions, see Murray and Petsas (1989) 34–51.

[48] At 1.266, when appearing in high style, *hiberna* is used metaphorically, as a time indicator, almost = "year". When Aeneas is introduced as building houses for his men, it is usually with an, albeit mistaken, purpose of permanence, and, so, a sense of symbolism. Cf. 3.18, 131; 4.260; 7.157–9.

[49] Donatus, *vita Vergili*, 35; Horace, *c.* 1.3. For doubts about this tradition: Horsfall (1995) 20 f.

[50] Details cannot be given here. They will be published separately.

[51] For a recent discussion, see J.F. Miller (1993) 445–50.

[52] Servius goes so far as to understand *rem* (3.287) as Aeneas' intention: "*rem*" *votum, id est voluntatem*.

[53] 220 is the number of letters in Murray's and Petsas' restoration (1989, 74).

[54] Murray and Petsas (1989) 59. The authors assume "at least another course" of stones above the inscription, crowning it.

[55] Murray and Petsas (1989) 85 f. They describe the first ram on the left as "a monster weighing over two tons". The rising order of ram sizes is observed also by the casual visitor even today, on the basis of the remaining sockets alone. See Jucker (1982) 98.

[56] It is worth noting that Donatus' emphasis on *adversis* is not derived from knowledge of the monument. He offers an independent linguistic interpretation which, it turns out, neatly matches the Actium monument as it is known again today. Methodologically speaking, if one sticks to the ancient interpreter's purely linguistic reading, one may be sure that one does not carry over into the *Aeneid* any of *our* recently enriched knowledge about Octavian's memorial. For *adversus* in the meaning of "facing the viewer, so it cannot be overlooked", cf. *Aen.* 1.166 and, especially, 6.755: Anchises places his son in

such a position that he can view *adversos* all who come.

[57] The most complete recent discussion of the Latin text is likewise found in Murray and Petsas (1989, 76 f.; translation on p. 86).

[58] The inscription certainly fits the time, though there is some mystery about where it was originally set up. Ehrenberg-Jones (1976, 57, no. 17 [= *ILS* 81]) listed it under "Rome, Forum".

[59] In Book 3, Aeneas consults the *delectos populi...proceres* in the matter of Polydorus' burial, 3. 58 f.

[60] Murray and Petsas (1989) 128.

[61] Gurval (1995) 33 f.

[62] Zanker (1987) 86 f.

[63] Murray and Petsas (1989) 120 f.

[64] Gurval (1995) 81.

[65] Gurval (1995) 130.

[66] The pervasive role of Apollo throughout the epic, once emphasized by Heinze (Apollo by Vergil "mit grossem Nachdruck in den Mittelpunkt gestellt", 1965, 84) has recently been evidenced again by Unte's investigation (1994).

[67] Gurval (1995) 103 f.

[68] Gurval (1995) 73 f. The argument that Octavian needed the booty of Egypt to found the city in Epirus (Murray and Petsas 1989, 127; Gurval 1995, 69) flies in the face of Strabo's testimony (7.7.6) according to which the city, endowed with wealth of land, was built from the booty – which in Strabo's context can only mean the booty from the Actium victory.

[69] Gurval (1995) 239.

[70] Paschalis (1987) 65.

[71] For a picture, see Ling (1992) 50, Fig. 50; Tybout (1989), *Tafel* 14.2. A similar arrangement is found in a bedroom of neighboring Boscoreale, now on display in the Metropolitan Museum of Art.

[72] See von Hesberg and Panciera (1994) 14 f. with *Tafel* 5, b; cf. p. 54.

[73] von Hesberg and Panciera (1994) 25 with *Tafel* 9a (showing the inscription C. CAESAR and, in the upper right corner, part of the shield circle; cf. the drawing in *Abbildung 34*); 43 with note 265 (where read *Parma* for *Palma*); 54; 98–108; *Tafel* 10, f.; *Abb.* 57; and, finally, the descriptions of *Dg* 1/VI and *Dg* 5 on p. 60.

[74] See *Figs*. 22 and 23. The author wishes to thank Dr Anne Kromann and the kgl. Mønt- og Medaillesamlingen, Kopenhagen, for providing him with the opportunity of taking the photographs and displaying them here. See also Nedergaard (1988), Fig. 114 on p. 225; for identification of the arch, ibid p. 225. Nedergaard thinks the round objects on the *postes* of the arch are *imagines clipeatae*.

Bibliography

Allen, A.W.
    1951-2 "The dullest book of the *Aeneid*", *CJ* 47, 119–123.

Austin, R.G.
    1971   *P. Vergili Maronis Aeneidos Liber Primus*, ed. with comm., Oxford.

Bengtson, H.
　1977　*Marcus Antonius: Triumvir und Herrscher des Orients*, Munich.
Buchheit, V.
　1963　"Vergil über die Sendung Roms. Untersuchungen zum Bellum Poenicum und zur Aeneis", *Gymnasium Beiheft* 3, Heidelberg.
Carter, J.M.
　1970　*The Battle of Actium: The Rise and Triumph of Augustus Caesar*, New York.
Carettoni, G.
　1983　*Das Haus des Augustus auf dem Palatin*, Mainz.
Coarelli, F.
　1988　*Roma*, Guide archeologiche Laterza 6, 5th edn, Bari.
Conington, J.
　1963　*The Works of Vergil with a Commentary*, Vols. 2, 3, revised by H. Nettleship, repr. Hildesheim.
Day, L.P.
　1984　"*Deceptum errore*: Images of Crete in the *Aeneid*", in D.F. Bright and E.S. Ramage (eds.) *Classical Texts and their Traditions: Studies in Honor of C.R. Trahman*, pp. 25–40, Chico, Calif.
Egan, R.B.
　1974　"Aeneas at Aineia and Vergil's *Aeneid*". *Pacific Coast Philology* 9, 37–47.
Ehrenberg, V. and Jones, A.H.M.
　1976　*Documents Illustrating the Reigns of Augustus and Tiberius*, 2nd edn, Oxford.
Fordyce, C.J.
　1977　*P. Vergili Maronis Aeneidos libri VII–VIII.* With a Commentary. Introduction by P.G. Walsh; ed. J.D. Christie. Oxford.
Franke, P.R.
　1976　"Apollo Leucadius und Octavianus?", *Chiron* 6, 159–63.
　1983　"Albanien im Altertum", *AW* (*Sondernummer*), 11–65.
Gagé, J.
　1936　"Actiaca", in École Française de Rome, *Mélanges d'Archéologie et d'Histoire* 53, 37–100.
Giard, J.B.
　1988　*Catalogue des Monnaies de l'Empire Romain. I: Auguste*, Paris.
Griffin, J.
　1985　*Latin Poets and Roman Life*, London.
Gurval, R.A.
　1995　*Actium and Augustus. The Politics and Emotions of Civil War*, Ann Arbor.
Harrison, S.J.
　1996　"*Aeneid* 1.286: Julius Caesar or Augustus?", Papers of the Leeds International Latin Seminar 9, 127–33.
Heinze, R.
　1965　*Virgils epische Technik*, 5th edn, Darmstadt.
Hershkowitz, D.
　1991　"The *Aeneid* in *Aeneid* 3", *Vergilius* 37, 69–76.

Hölscher, T.
   1985   "Denkmäler der Schlacht von Actium: Propaganda und Resonanz", *Klio* 67, 81–102.
Horsfall, N.
   1995   "Virgil: his life and times", in N. Horsfall (ed.) *A Companion to the Study of Virgil*, Mnemosyne, suppl. vol. 151, Leiden.
Jucker, H.
   1982   "Apollo Palatinus und Apollo Actius auf augusteischen Münzen", *MH* 39, 82–104.
Kraggerud, E.
   1994   "Caesar versus Caesar again: a reply." *SO* 69, 83–93.
Ling, R.
   1991   *Roman Painting*, (repr. 1992), Cambridge.
Lloyd, R.B.
   1954   "On *Aeneid* III, 270–78", *AJPh* 75, 288–99.
   1957   "*Aeneid* III: a new approach", *AJPh* 78, 133–51.
   1957   "*Aeneid* III and the Aeneas legend", *AJPh* 78, 382–400.
Miller, J.F.
   1993   "The shield of Argive Abas at *Aeneid* 3.286", *CQ* 43, 445–50.
Murray, W.M., and Petsas, P.M.
   1989   *Octavian's Campsite Memorial for the Actian War*, *TAPhS* 79, Part 4, Philadelphia.
Nedergaard, E.
   1988   "Zur Problematik der Augustusbögen auf dem Forum Romanum", in *Kaiser Augustus und die verlorene Republik* Exhibition catalogue, Antikenmuseum Berlin, Staatliche Museeen, Preussischer Kulturbesitz, 224–39, Berlin.
Oberhummer, E.
   1887   *Akarnanien, Ambrakia, Amphilochien, Leukas im Altertum*, Munich.
Paschalis, M.
   1987   "Virgil's Actium–Nicopolis", in A. Chrysos (ed.)*Nicopolis I: Proceedings of the 1st International Symposium on Nicopolis (23–29 September 1984)*, 57–69, Preveza.
Pöschl, V.
   1964   *Die Dichtkunst Virgils: Bild und Symbol in der Aeneis*, 2nd enlarged edn, Darmstadt.
Putnam, M.C.P.
   1980   "The Third Book of the *Aeneid*: from Homer to Rome", *Ramus* 9, 1–21. (Also in Putnam, M.C.J.,*Vergil's Aeneid: Interpretation and Influence*, 50–72, Chapel Hill, 1995.)
Reinhold, M.
   1988   *From Republic to Principate. A Historical Commentary on Cassius Dio's Roman History, Books 49–52 (36–29 BC)*, APA Monograph Series 34, Atlanta.
Sauron, G.
   1994   *Quis deum? L'expression plastique des idéologies politiques et religieuses à*

Rome à la fin de la république et au début du principat, Bibliothèque des écoles françaises d'Athènes et de Rome, vol. 285, Rome.

Saylor, C.F.
- 1970 "Toy Troy: the new perspective of the backward glance", *Vergilius* 16, 26–8.

Stahl, H.-P.
- 1969 " 'Verteidigung' des ersten Buches der Aeneis",*Hermes* 97, 346–61.
- 1985 Propertius: *"Love" and "War". Individual and State Under Augustus* Berkeley.
- 1981 "Aeneas – an 'unheroic' hero?", *Arethusa* 14, 157–77.
- 1990 "The death of Turnus: Augustan Vergil and the political rival", in K.A. Raaflaub and M. Toher (eds.) *Between Republic and Empire: Interpretations of Augustus and His Principate*, 174–211, Berkeley.

Trillmich, W.
- 1988 "Münzpropaganda", in *Kaiser Augustus und die verlorene Republik.* Exhibition catalogue, Antikenmuseum, Staatliche Museen, Preussischer Kulturbesitz, 474–528, Berlin.

Tybout, R.A.
- 1989 *Aedificiorum figurae. Untersuchungen zu den Architekturdarstellungen des frühen zweiten Stils*, Amsterdam.

Unte, W.
- 1994 "Die Gestalt Apollos im Handlungsablauf von Vergils Aeneis", *Gymnasium* 101, 204–57.

von Hesberg, H. and Panciera, S.
- 1994 *Das Mausoleum des Augustus: der Bau und seine Inschriften*, Munich.

West, D.
- 1994 "In the wake of Aeneas (*Aeneid* 3.274–88; 3.500–5; 8.200–3)", *G&R* 41, 57–61.
- 1997 "The end and the meaning: Vergil,*Aeneid* 12.791–842", in H.-P.Stahl (ed.) *Vergil's Aeneid: Augustan Epic and Political Context,* London.

Webb, N.C.
- 1978–80 "Direct contact between the hero and the supernatural in the Aeneid", *PVS* 17, 39–49.

Williams, R.D.
- 1962 *P. Vergili Maronis Aeneidos Liber Tertius.* Ed. with Comm., Oxford. (repr. Bristol 1981, 1990.)

Zanker, P.
- 1983 "Der Apollontempel auf dem Palatin. Ausstattung und politische Sinnbezüge nach der Schlacht von Actium",*ARID* Suppl. 10, 21–40.
- 1987 *Augustus und die Macht der Bilder*, Munich.

4

THE PEOPLING OF THE UNDERWORLD
Aeneid 6.608–27*

Anton Powell

Vergil's account of the underworld is more moralising, less for casual entertainment, than Homer's in *Odyssey* 11, the Νέκυια. Vergil has an undeniable interest in how certain Romans related to the underworld; in Book 8 (666–70) Catiline is portrayed in hell, Cato is in a better place. Augustus, his morality, and the prospects for his settlement were of great (and, we may think, of sympathetic) concern to Vergil, while for many Romans Octavian/Augustus was guilty of crimes on a massive scale against his own country. If Vergil, when portraying hell and heaven, Tartarus and Elysium, related the otherworld to Augustus, his friends, his allies and enemies, we may expect him to have proceeded with an unusual degree of delicacy, or at least of ingenuity. Vergil may even have seen himself as responding to earlier partisan imagery in this area: Cicero and Atticus in their correspondence had repeatedly referred to Julius Caesar's entourage of disreputable politicians as νέκυια (*ad Att.* 9.10.7, 11.2, 18.2).

Vergil's list in Book 6 of those in Tartarus begins with figures from Greek myth: the Titans, the Aloidae, Salmoneus, Tityos. Here are traditional denizens of the underworld, though they are presented with distinctly Vergilian slants. Then we may be lulled, or further lulled, when Vergil writes (601): 'Why should I mention the Lapiths, Ixion, Pirithous?', *quid memorem Lapithas, Ixiona, Pirithoumque?* After this *praeteritio*, we are awakened (605–7): 'The largest of the Furies rises...and bellows', *Furiarum maxima...exsurgit...intonat*. Then, fully awake, we move suddenly into the less traditional: from line 608 – our passage.

> Immured in this place and waiting for punishment are those who in life hated their brothers, or battered a parent or cheated a *cliens*, or those – an enormous mob – who kept treasure-trove to themselves, not sharing it with their families. Also those put to death for adultery, and those who had been followers in a wicked war, and had not hesitated to cheat their

master's hand. Do not ask to know what their punishments are, what form of pain or what misfortune has engulfed them. Some are rolling huge rocks, or hang spreadeagled on the spokes of wheels. Unhappy Theseus is sitting there, and there he will sit until the end of time, while Phlegyas, poor wretch, shouts this lesson for all men at the top of his voice in the darkness: 'Learn to be just and not to despise gods. You have been warned.' Here is the man who sold his own country for gold, imposed on it a mighty autocrat, made and unmade laws for a price. Here is the man who forced his way into his daughter's chamber and a forbidden union. All dared to undertake some monstrous wickedness, and achieved their aim. If I had a hundred tongues, a hundred mouths and a voice of iron, I could not encompass all their different crimes or speak the names of all their different punishments.' (David West's translation, much modified.)

>   hic, quibus inuisi fratres, dum uita manebat,
>   pulsatusue parens et fraus innexa clienti,
>   aut qui diuitiis soli incubuere repertis   610
>   nec partem posuere suis (quae maxima turba est),
>   quique ob adulterium caesi, quique arma secuti
>   impia nec ueriti dominorum fallere dextras,
>   inclusi poenam exspectant. ne quaere doceri
>   quam poenam, aut quae forma uiros fortunaue mersit.   615
>   saxum ingens uoluunt alii, radiisque rotarum
>   districti pendent; sedet aeternumque sedebit
>   infelix Theseus, Phlegyasque miserrimus omnis
>   admonet et magna testatur uoce per umbras:
>   'discite iustitiam moniti et non temnere diuos.'   620
>   uendidit hic auro patriam dominumque potentem
>   imposuit; fixit leges pretio atque refixit;
>   hic thalamum inuasit natae uetitosque hymenaeos:
>   ausi omnes immane nefas ausoque potiti.
>   non, mihi si linguae centum sint oraque centum,   625
>   ferrea uox, omnis scelerum comprendere formas,
>   omnia poenarum percurrere nomina possim.

Vergil would have expected here an unusual degree of attention in his audience, even by his own standards. Once his hearers or readers saw that what followed had a contemporary relevance, they would have asked, 'Which Romans of our own times is Vergil imagining in hell?'. Griffin has shown how apt were Romans of the time to identify characters presented from history or myth with eminentcontemporary politicians (1985, 191). Historical Roman individuals cannot be in the Tartarus of Book 6; here Vergil is giving, on the literal level, a picture of those who have died before Aeneas. The poet can, however, use types of sin as prophetic of Roman history. His apparent shift to Roman and contemporary interests is one which many scholars have noted, following Servius.[1]

First, to a brief (and in some cases preliminary) consideration of points which may establish this Romanness. It should be stressed: we are not claiming that Roman and contemporary references exhaust Vergil's meaning in this context, but that Roman affairs must have been part of what the poet had in mind.

Who is in hell?
'Those who hated their brothers', *quibus invisi fratres*, 608. On the face of it the reference of this could simply be universal. For Vergil in the *Georgics*, however, *invidia* between brothers is not just general 'hatred', 'resentment', but something political not less than domestic, which might involve bloodshed (2.510). At *Geo.* 2.499 *invidit* is used in a political context which involves (496) 'strife driving disloyal brothers', *infidos agitans discordia fratres*. (For the political context, note, for example, *populi fasces...purpura regum* at 495). Lucretius had linked *invidia* with ill-will between brothers, bloodshed within the citizen body, and envy of the powerful (3.70–5). At *Geo.*3.37–9 *invidia* itself, defeated, faces the Furies and other torments of the underworld at the end of a catalogue of scenes evoking the triumph of Octavian in war against foreigners. These points of course do not prove that Vergil had Roman civil strife at the front of his mind with the *invisi fratres* of Book 6. But they are suggestive, when taken with what follows.

'Those who battered a parent', *quibus...pulsatus...parens*, 608 f. Could a Greek have described this offence as leading to hell? Plato did, in the myth of the *Phaedo* (113e–14a). On the other hand, there may for Aristotle have been a comic aspect to father-beating. Of the very few elements of the *Nicomachean Ethics* susceptible of a humorous interpretation two are on this subject: for example, a young man who has dragged his father to the door of their house is told by the father, 'Stop. This is as far as I dragged *my* father!' (1149b).[2] There is no relaxation of tone here in Vergil: grimness, it may be, is part of the Roman message from an internecine age.

'Those who cheated a *cliens*', *quibus...fraus innexa clienti*, 608 f. The institution of *clientela* was distinctively Roman. Greek writers, when faced with the Latin term *patronus*, rather than translate it with some such word as προστάτης, at times transliterate as πάτρων, πατρώνης. Compare, with Vergil's phrase here, an expression which Servius (ad loc.) quotes from the Laws of the 12 Tables: *patronus si clienti fraudem fecerit, sacer esto*.

'Those who kept treasure-trove to themselves', *qui divitiis soli incubuere repertis*, 610. Pindar (*Nem.* 1.31) has gentle criticism of those who keep treasure hidden. It will be argued below that some Romans of Vergil's day had reason to be more intense.

'Those put to death for adultery', *qui...ob adulterium caesi*, 612. There were cases in Greek culture of people killed for illicit sexual affairs; we think for instance of Lysias' *On the Killing of Eratosthenes*. But in epic, as opposed to bourgeois legal text, the subject – albeit on a divine plane – could raise hilarity (in *Odyssey* 8, esp. 326). In Augustan, or rather pro-Augustan, Rome the subject was gravely topical. In 18 BC (probably), the death penalty for adultery was to be inscribed in law.[3]

'Those who had been followers in a wicked war, and had not hesitated to cheat their master's hand', *qui...arma secuti impia nec veriti dominorum fallere dextras*, 612–13. Here are distinctively, no doubt self-consciously, Roman ideas. *Pietas* had been the golden cant term of the recent civil wars.[4] Servius, though not infallible in these matters, as we shall see, was almost certainly right to think that Vergil here had in mind the forces of Sextus Pompeius, or – to give him his cognomen – Sextus Pompeius Pius. The cognomen would be bound to meet contradiction by Sextus' opponents in civil war; *impia* here may be such a case. The idea of runaway slaves was a favourite Augustan stick to beat Sextus, or at least his memory; we shall return to all this.

617 ff.: after the slaves who followed *impia arma*, Vergil reverts to individuals from Greek myth: Theseus and Phlegyas. These are not familiar villains: Theseus was an esteemed ruler; Phlegyas also was a ruler (*Hom. Hymn* 16.3). Theseus was punished for trying to drag off Persephone (cf. 397). Phlegyas seemingly was condemned for attempting revenge on a god, Apollo, after the latter had seduced then killed his daughter – a case of family-loyalty misapplied. Does *miserrimus* (618) imply that Phlegyas is to be pitied?[5] In the previous (38) lines on the torments of hell, there appears no hint of sympathy for any sufferer, save perhaps for Salmoneus paying *crudeles...poenas* (585). Theseus and Phlegyas are not merely an extension of the list which ended with Lapiths, Ixion and Pirithous. The two unhappy rulers may have been chosen to break down any sense that denizens of Tartarus were all remote figures, implausible in the simplicity and immensity of their crimes. These are mixed characters, like those Vergil's contemporaries knew best. Is the audience being prepared for the idea of a mixed, credible, contemporary figure? I shall have some claims to make about Mark Antony in a moment.

The sociology of Tartarus
Next it may help to look at the social rank of the various sinners. At 616 *alii* may mark a shift, with those who follow being of a higher social order than those in the preceding, somewhat Roman, list. In 624 are

mentioned those who 'dared to undertake some monstrous wickedness, and achieved their aim', *ausi...immane nefas ausoque potiti*. *Immane* may be purely a measure of moral excess; it may apply, for example, as much to incest in a hovel as in a palace. But *thalamum* at 623 hardly suggests a crowded cabin. Also we hear of making corrupt laws and selling one's country (621 f.), actions implying membership of a ruling group. The two individuals named in this section, Theseus and Phlegyas, were – to repeat – both rulers.

High social rank does not apply to all in the short, rather Roman, list (608–14) we looked at previously. The category of those who hoarded treasure-trove was surely not meant to exclude the digging class: small farmers or labourers, free or otherwise. The hoarders were *maxima turba*, 'an enormous mob'. The category of brothers who hated, while politically suggestive of civil war, sounds socially quite general. To be punished for adultery does not seem indicative of social class.

The battering of a parent does not suggest the wealthy; indeed, if such behaviour was likely to occur especially when father and adult son were living too close, the cramped housing of the poor might be its usual setting. The offence of cheating a client does admittedly catch the upper-class *patronus* and exclude the masses. A *patronus*, however, need not be quite of statesmanly rank. With *arma secuti impia* we deal explicitly with followers rather than leaders (cf. 3.54), and *dominorum fallere dextras* applies exclusively to slaves. To summarise: Vergil here tends to arrange his material by social class. The transition to the grander sinners is at 614–18. Before that, most of the categories point to the poor, or are socially neutral; after that come mostly leaders and the wealthy. In the lists of the blessed there will be a similar arrangement, with Trojan heroes and aristocratic ancestors (648–50) separated from a less socially-exclusive collection of public benefactors (660–5).

Contemporaries of Vergil foreshadowed in the Tartarus of Book VI?
Roman categories may be identified in the socially broader list of offenders; should we see Roman individuals behind Vergil's list of politically eminent villains? Line 621, according to Servius, refers to Curio – the bribed tribune of 50 BC. But consider the recurrence of *hic* (621, 623). This suggests, as Conington and Austin seem to have observed, that only two persons or types are involved; until the clause beginning with the second *hic*, every wicked action has been done by the first *hic*. That is, the selling of laws is done by the same person as imposes a *dominum potentem* on his country. If Curio had been meant, who would the *dominum potentem* have been? Julius Caesar. Could Vergil really consign Curio to hell for promoting the autocratic

schemes of Caesar, whose supernatural importance is asserted in the strongest colours at the end of *Georgics* 1, and whose son is to save the world? Again, as the agent of *divus Julius* could Curio be placed in hell, given that in the previous line Phlegyas has preached *non temnere divos* ('not to despise gods')? Curio's behaviour had arguably arisen from excessive compliance with the *divus*. Vergil can shift, as he does between the *Georgics* and the *Aeneid* on the political virtue of Julius Caesar.[6] He can be deliberately ambiguous. But did he here mean to problematise, to allude to Curio as a fact inconvenient to the Caesarian case? In this context of extremes, with Augustus' Trojan ancestors in bliss, to have consigned someone to hell for acts of assistance to Augustus' official father, would have suggested an awkward self-contradiction. It is better to assume that, if Vergil thought here of Curio at all, the portmanteau-category, 'selling his own country, imposing on it a mighty autocrat, making and unmaking laws for a price' was meant to exclude Curio, since not all elements of the category applied to him. We may shortly see other cases of Vergil in this context complicating, or otherwise contriving, his categories of wickedness so as to exclude a favoured person.

Did Vergil mean his audience here to think of Antony? Again the identification is found in Servius, this time in connection with the making and unmaking of laws for a price (622). But, perhaps unlike Servius, we should ask whether Antony would fit with all the terms in lines 621–2; can he discharge all the functions of the first *hic*? Did Antony sell his country – for Egyptian gold? He came close: the Donations of Alexandria (34 BC) involved giving to Cleopatra's family some Roman provincial territory. And Vergil has Antony at Actium using *ope barbarica*, 'alien wealth' (8.685). As for imposing on his country 'a mighty autocrat', the masculine *dominum* would surely not exclude thoughts of Cleopatra. But the point which most strongly supports Servius' interpretation is that Vergil here is consciously echoing a contemporary poem which – we have separate reason for thinking – referred to Antony in hostile terms. The words *fixit leges pretio atque refixit* (622) are an exact quotation from the *De Morte* of Lucius Varius Rufus, friend of Vergil and the rewarded associate of Octavian. Here is the relevant Varian fragment, of two lines; its subject is missing:

> vendidit hic Latium populis agrosque Quiritum
> eripuit, fixit leges pretio atque refixit.
> (quoted by Macrobius, *Saturnalia* 6.1.39)

This matches Vergil not just in most of the second line, but also in beginning the previous line with the words *vendidit hic. vendidit... Latium* is now interpreted as probably meaning sales of Latin rights.[7] For Antony's sale of citizenship, see Cic. *Phil*. 3.10; *ad Att*.14.12.1. The seizure of citizens' land also notoriously fitted Antony. For venality in making and unmaking laws Antony was repeatedly criticised by Cicero: *Phil*. 2.92, 3.30, 5.12; *ad Att*. 14.12.1 ('...*Antonius accepta grandi pecunia fixit legem*...'). In another fragment of the *De Morte* (Macrobius, *Saturnalia* 6.1.40) a reference to 'drinking from pure gold', *ex solido bibat auro*, ties in with Antony's gold vessels as described by later writers (Plut., *Ant*. 9.8; Plin., *N.H*. 33.50). It also resembles a phrase used by Vergil elsewhere in a polemic against futile conquest (*ut gemma bibat*, *Geo*. 2.506). Of the four verbs in Varius, Vergil repeats three but omits *eripuit*, which Varius had used of the seizure of land. Stealing citizens' land would have caught Octavian even more than Antony: in the Triumviral period Octavian, the partner who spent more time in Italy, was the main evictor (App., *B.C*. 5.3, 13 f.; Dio 48.6 f.). This is the first case within a pattern we shall be claiming: Vergil by omissions shaping Tartarus to exclude Octavian.

hic thalamum invasit natae vetitosque hymenaeos (623): we cannot confidently link this reference, to a father's incestuous crime against his daughter, with any prominent individual of Vergil's day.[8] However, attacks on the adultery of others were made by Augustus and his favoured contemporary writers. In choosing a sexual crime for his anthology of wickedness Vergil was appealing to a spirit of the times; in a less obvious way, the betrayal of daughter by father responded to contemporary fears (below, p. 98). To return to Antony: Vergil's possibly commiserative word for his associate in the list, Phlegyas, may suggest that Antony is owed a little sympathy. Antony was, after all, the former assistant of Julius Caesar, brother-in-law of Octavian, and effective comrade-in-arms of both. Vergil's picture of the liaison between Aeneas and an African queen suggests a certain ambivalence towards Antony. But any sympathy with the Antony-type here in Tartarus may be abruptly limited by the mention of incest and of the assorted criminals who follow. Each of the latter is no more than the embodiment of sin – and so fails to qualify for pity.

One wicked and eminent Roman individual may be meant here, but Vergil has no rogues' gallery for famous upper-class Romans – here or anywhere. The closest he comes elsewhere is in Book 8.666–70, where Catiline is in hell, and Cato presides over the *pii* – a singular villain contrasted with a group of indefinite size. Catiline there and Antony in our passage are plausible analogues. Both are exceptions, who have forfeited their membership of the Roman ruling class. It was against

Anton Powell

Catiline that the Roman upper-classes united: the consensus *bonorum omnium* (Cic., *Catil.* 4.22). And Antony by his eastern associations lent himself to similar exclusion, especially after his defeat. He was remembered much later for his 'un-Roman faults' (Sen., *Ep.* 83.25). Vergil worked to make a similar point, with the elaborate polarity in the portrayal of Antony at Actium in Book 8. Octavian there is attended by Roman people and gods; the message of inclusion could hardly be clearer:

> *Hinc Augustus agens Italos in proelia Caesar*
> *cum patribus populoque, penatibus et magnis dis,*
> ...   (678 f., cf. 698–700, 714 ff.)

For Antony no Roman support is mentioned, only eastern (esp. 685, 698–700, 705 f.). The mention of Catiline and Cato-with-the-*pii* immediately precedes the introduction of the Actium scene, with its similarly binary message. Hell, heaven and Actium are scenes on the supernatural shield. The Caesarians at Actium, loyal to their Roman gods, match the *pii* in the afterlife; isolated Antony with his alien gods is surely, like Catiline, *impius*.

The erasure of Sextus Pompeius
Vergil's choice of Antony, as (faintly sympathetic) arch-villain and arch-opponent of Octavian, was not as straightforward as it might seem today. The relative prominence of Antony – into our own time – is a product of Augustan, including Vergilian, propaganda. With his foreign associations, Antony was a gift, and a relief, for Augustus. Not so Sextus Pompeius; indeed, it was because of Octavian's experiences with Sextus that he had such need of an Antony-figure. For Augustus and Vergil the memory of Sextus was an intense embarrassment, best assailed implicitly and indirectly, as through the reference to his slave supporters.[9] Sextus had humiliated Octavian, lastingly. Augustan propaganda, as so often with political discourse, was shaped by the successes of the opponent while also being contrived to obscure those successes. However, much on the moral and military ascendancy of Sextus is clear to anyone willing to read Appian. On this we must summarise briefly, having dealt with the matter elsewhere.[10] Though Agrippa was to win the final naval battle for Octavian, off Naulochus in 36, Sextus' forces had five times beaten those of Octavian at sea. Twice an unseasonal storm seemed to intervene on Sextus' side; the gods, and especially Neptune, were thought to favour his cause. Octavian's military humiliation culminated in his abandoning his beaten fleet and fleeing in a small boat – appallingly rare desertion, by the standards of

a Republican general. This was at the battle of Tauromenium, in 36. Sextus' policies seemed to Romans to have more justice than those of Octavian, Appian tells us (*B.C.* 5.25, cf. 4.85). It was noted that Sextus refused to invade Italy (as his father had refused, in the late 60s). Most important of all was the contrast over proscriptions. Sextus offered double the Triumvirs' rewards – but, in his case, for anyone who *saved* the proscribed. In 39, with the support of riots from the plebs, Sextus extorted a surrender from the Triumvirs; most of the proscribed were to be guaranteed their lives, and one quarter of their property back. The mass of Romans celebrated (*B.C.* 5.74). Sextus' *pietas* was plausible indeed. There was even, associated with Sextus, a new Aeneas, a refugee who had physically carried his reluctant (though proscribed) father into exile. He fled from the death squads; the man who had saved him was Sextus. This new Aeneas was named M. Oppius; the plebs feted him for his *pietas* and made him aedile for 37 – to the chagrin of Aeneas' alleged descendant who, as part of the Triumvirate, had proscribed the father in the first place (*B.C.* 4.41; Dio 48.53.4–6).

A man who was *pius* could expect to be *felix*: *infelicitas* suggested lack of *pietas*, which in turn suggested that further *infelicitas* could be expected. Vergil is acutely aware of this link between good behaviour and worldly success; at the start of the *Aeneid* he defines his poetry as an explanation of how a man conspicuous for *pietas* could suffer so many mishaps (1.8–11). Sextus, far more than anyone, had insistently posed a question about the worldly success and the religious standing of Octavian. To consign Sextus' followers in fantasy to Tartarus, as Vergil almost certainly does, is a partisan act, an act almost of logical desperation. At all costs the relative merits of Sextus and Octavian, as for so long publicly perceived, had to be reversed.

A speculative point may be developed against the picture implied by Vergil, of Sextus supported by slaves who had defied their masters. When proscribed landowners fled from the Triumvirs' death squads, they mostly went to Sextus; so Appian tells us (*B.C.* 4.36, cf. 5.25, 59, cf. Dio 47.12). Would the proscribed always leave their able-bodied male slaves behind, for the benefit of their successors or out of respect for law? The successors would be seen as usurpers, the proscription as a violation both of formal law and of *salus populi*. Surely there were many slaves who were taken away by their outlawed masters (compare Cicero's last retinue), as bodyguards and to spite the Triumvirs. If the masters reached Sextus, it is likely that he, in return for the salvation and the sustenance he provided, would expect the slaves to fight for him (which might involve manumission), and that their masters concurred. (Compare the report of Suetonius that Octavian used 20,000 freed slaves in the forces which opposed Sextus: *D.A.* 16.1; cf. Dio 47.17.) In other cases, where proscribed refugees hoped to survive by escaping attention, slaves would of necessity be left behind. In some such cases it is likely that the able-bodied male slaves were urged to rally to the nearest point of military resistance to the Triumvirs: that would mean Sextus, and again might involve manumission. When ex-slaves were captured in arms by the Triumviral side, in the hope of postponing death the captives would surely claim that they had been manumitted; indeed this was probably their only defence, and it had the attraction of being irrefutable in many cases, since the masters had disappeared, and it might even be verified in cases where the masters could be found. But, precisely because this defence was available to so many and was so difficult to refute, for reasons of convenience it could not be accepted by the conquerors. The latter would anyway have a neat and obvious retort: 'The man who you claim manumitted you was in fact, as a result of the proscription, no longer your legal owner.' Vergil may have understood something similar: that, in the case of the very many slaves for whom the proscriptions brought a change of ownership, it was the *new* masters whom the slaves would have cheated. If so, the slave would be in hell for absconding from a master he had very likely never seen and whose title to ownership he was scarcely in a position to trust, especially if a long-established owner was present to deny its validity; in such cases to write of *dominorum fallere dextras* would have been at best partisan reductionism. Augustus himself was to claim that, after the war against Sextus, he had handed some 30,000 captured slaves back to their masters for punishment (*Res Gestae* 25.1). This is most easily taken to mean that, in the case of slaves from the estates of the proscribed, it was the new masters who received the men for punishment – and from whom they were deemed to have fled. There were no doubt genuine runaways among Sextus's men. But that was only part of the picture, the part which best suited Augustus – and Vergil. It was, in fact, a cliché of Augustan propaganda; compare Hor., *Epod.* 9.9 f; Velleius 2.73.3. In Vergil's poem, rather as Antony is marginalised through eastern allies, Sextus is damned by means of dissident slaves.

Selectivity among sins

We should now explore characters and possible identifications within the (largely) non-elite group. The first two lines (608–9), about brotherly hatred, battered parents and cheated *clientes*, seem general enough, within a Roman context, though the brothers have the hint of civil war. But then comes the curious inclusion in hell of those who

The Peopling of the Underworld

find and hoard treasure, not sharing it with their families (610 f.). Butler (ad loc.) observed gently that it was 'a little surprising to find the avaricious placed in this company'. *quae maxima turba est*: is this mere line-filling, as Butler suggested? Vergil is not usually otiose.[11] On principle we should assume that the words have some weight, that Vergil had some need to assert that this category, the misusers of treasure, really mattered. In what circumstances would it have been even plausible to claim that there was a serious amount of hidden treasure being recovered and sat on? Archaeologists tell us that hoards of treasure tend to be created in times when property is under general threat. We can imagine what happened when, from the late 40s, great numbers of wealthy Romans were evicted from lands and proscribed – for cash. (Dio describes the proscriptions as involving 'a general hostility towards the rich', κοινήν τινα κατὰ τῶν πλουσίων ἔχθραν, 47.6.5.) What were people to do with the family treasure in such circumstances? Who could be trusted to look after it, at a time of civil war when bounties were offered? Those who tried to flee incognito would know that to be found with much precious metal might be fatal. Burying it was a likely choice. And at what period would people have felt so passionately about the concealment of treasure-trove as to want to see the concealers in hell? A time perhaps when there was a perception of too little financial investment, when it suited the authorities to blame someone for the dereliction of the land – someone, that is, other than the instigators of the general conditions which had led to dereliction. Italy in the 30s must have suffered from planning blight. Why spend much on an estate when it might soon be confiscated? Indeed, conspicuous investment might increase the chance that an estate would be seized and its owner persecuted for his wealth (cf. App., *B.C.* 4.31, Dio 47.17). Neglect of land, lack of investment, probably helped to elicit the *Georgics*. Burying and sitting on gold are censured near the end of *Georgics* 2 (507), along with war and politicking, fratricidal strife and 'drinking from precious stones' – the context, in short, abounds in reflections of recent, lamentable events, and has explicit and unmistakable references to Rome (495, 498, 508f.; cf. 502). Horace, too, attacks hoarding (*Odes* 2.2.1). It is interesting that in the earlier work Vergil criticises those who *bury* the treasure and sit on it (*condit opes..defossoque incubat auro*), whereas in the later poem, the *Aeneid*, he blames those who *discover* the treasure (*divitiis...repertis*) and sit on it. This corresponds with the chronology of politics: at first, when the proscriptions and war are fresh, the burying is what matters; later, hoards are supposedly discovered, but finders are still, perhaps, afraid of admitting to wealth. Perpetrators of these secretive crimes-without-victims would not often come to light. Whence perhaps Vergil's need for the parenthetic assertion that they were numerous; his audience needed some persuading. Syme, without apparently meaning to refer to this passage, wrote felicitously: 'War and the threat of taxation or confiscation drives money underground.' He added: 'It must be lured out again.'[12]; it may be that Vergil's picture of hell for hoarders was meant in part to do just that.

The list of non-elite categories in hell is oddly selective. We might expect some quite general formula about how people qualified for damnation. Contrast the passage soon afterwards where the virtuous non-elite are described. That contains a very wide formulation: 'those who made some people remember them for good deeds', *qui...sui memores aliquos fecere merendo* (664). Among these good people there are also specified groups, including loyal seers, *pii vates* (662) and soldiers wounded for their fatherland (660). These in fact correspond to a degree with criteria of merit applied by one settled Greek society that we know: Sparta. Among the Spartans the only way for a male to acquire a named grave-marker was to die in war (Plut., *Lyc.* 27), and the only quality recorded as having led the Spartans to confer their citizenship on an outsider was excellence as a prophet (Hdt. 9.33-5). Vergil's positive list, then, is unremarkable, except perhaps in one respect. His list of virtuous categories, like that concerning vice, makes no clear reference to the activities of women;[13] this is one more sign that the poet here was interested in the public and political sphere above all.

Vergil's phrasing signals that he meant a degree of parallelism in presenting the sufferers in Tartarus and the blessed reposing elsewhere. He begins the list of villains with: *Hic genus antiquum Terrae, Titania pubes* (580); early in the list of the virtuous he has: *Hic genus antiquum Teucri, pulcherrima proles* (648).[14] Also, we have seen that in both there is a division between the socially more and less elevated. Why then does the Tartarus list, unlike the list of the virtuous, have such narrow and unfamiliar categories? Why is there not, in defining villains, a corresponding broad phrase such as 'those who made some people remember them for *bad* deeds'? There are not even some of the familiar sub-sets we might have expected. We have Phlegyas the temple-arsonist. But there are no temple-robbers, a more obvious category, relevant in Vergil's day. We have adulterers, but not adulterers in general; Butler (ad loc.) asks why not, and finds no clear answer. Why does the poet limit himself to those killed for adultery? This is the only time that Vergil makes earthly punishment a qualification for Tartarus. In Tartarus are those who sat on treasure-trove. Why not simply those who stole treasure? They were surely a more numerous and menacing group. Tartarus includes those who followed *impia arma;* why not, in the elite list, those who led *impia arma?*

If we now assemble the prima facie relevant categories of villainy which Vergil approaches but avoids, we may begin to trace the historical profile of someone. He is someone other citizens remembered for the harm he had done them. He is a leader, not a follower, of *impia arma;* he practised adultery and got away with it. He is a stealer of treasure; a snatcher of citizens' estates; a robber of temples. Could this be Octavian, the civil warrior, the proscriber of men formally accused of no crime, the seizer of estates, the man whose adulteries 'even his friends do not deny' (Suet., *D.A.* 69, cf. 71)? There is one discordant point. Surely Octavian/Augustus was a rebuilder of temples, not a robber of them? In fact he was both. At the time of the so-called Perusine War, when some of Octavian's men were expropriating Italian land, other agents of his were 'borrowing' sacred treasure from Italian temples. Italians reacted violently, expelling some of these 'borrowers', killing others (App. 5.13; 24). One can be sure how Octavian's opponents represented this attempt at fundraising.[15]

'Gentle Vergil' and the poetry of civil war

If the implicit peopling of Tartarus with (near-) contemporary Romans was such a delicate matter, actually recalling Augustan embarrassments to those with a political or an intertextual cast of mind, why did Vergil do it? If the poet's main interests in writing the *Aeneid* had been literary, to the exclusion of political apologia and prediction, he might have restricted himself to Homeric and other traditional imagery and omitted the contemporary references. That, moreover, would have been compatible with the forgiving, integrative policies which Augustus professed, and to some extent used, after Actium. Insistent moral distinctions are a recourse of the uneasy. From the public domain in our own day, two cases may illuminate. We recall how Mr Aldrich Ames, when interviewed in prison, distinguished repeatedly between ways of causing the deaths of western agents in the USSR: in identifying the latter to the Russians, he himself had not *intended* that they should be killed. He evidently drew comfort from conceiving a case worse than his own. If we look within the United Kingdom for a culture in which punishment is imposed with exceptional fervour and persistence, we may note H.M. Prisons. Here it is the prisoners themselves, those aware of having been cast out by society for misbehaviour, who define, and impose torments upon, a group within their own number: the 'nonces'. The pressure from the guilty against the more guilty is so intense as to oblige the authorities to arrange expensive segregation. In the prisons the nonces are defined largely as those convicted of sexual crime, especially against children. Why should this class, and sub-class, of offence be chosen? Official attempts to prevent the spread of HIV in prisons have generated extraordinary statistics about the extent of homosexual activity among male prisoners, working-class men who might be expected normally to regard such activity with contempt and as counter to an important part of their own self-image. One may imagine their unease, and their need to redirect contempt, in this area in particular. Vergil's Tartarus might be described, in British penal terms, as no mere Category A establishment: it is the isolation unit, imposed on one group of offenders by another, and in respect of offences which the two groups come close to sharing. I am suggesting that our poet's hell is the creation of some uneasy consciences; or – in terms of shame culture – of people with soiled reputations. Like the prisoners, Vergil combines convenient distinctions with a persecution, in fantasy, of those on the wrong side of the distinctions. He pursues even, or perhaps especially, when his quarry is dead. For the principle of civil warriors seeking out the deceased enemy, recall the story that the victorious Sulla dug out the remains of Marius and scattered them along the River Anio.[16]

In conclusion, let us observe the difference of tone between Vergil's account of Tartarus and the Homeric Νέκυια. Otos and Ephialtes, the Aloidae prominent in Vergil's list with their *immania corpora*, are described more positively by Homer: 'godlike' Otos and 'far-famed' Ephialtes are extremely handsome, πολὺ καλλίστους μετά γε…Ὠρίωνα (*Od.* 11.310). They are killed before they have down on their cheeks (11.318–20). They occur in the underworld not as receiving punishment, but as sons of a woman Odysseus meets at his trench. There may be pathos too in the vignette of Tantalos, which ends with tempting fruit blown by the wind beyond the reach of 'the old man' (11.588–92). Even the Tityos scene ends in pathos, with a gentle, comely adjective: διὰ καλλιχόρου Πανοπῆος (11.581). The Homeric underworld is less austere than Vergil's Tartarus. Perennial Roman exposure to mass execution may be relevant here. But Vergil has, for his severity, a reason particular to his own age. In contrast to our contemporary preoccupation with the dangerous outsider – the stranger at the school gate, the loner with firearms – Vergil is chiefly concerned to punish in Tartarus the trusted person who does harm. Every category in the first, mainly non-elite, list involves betrayal of someone who had reason to trust. Reading from line 608, we have betrayal of brother, parent, client, family, spouse, (state and) master. In the second list, from 616, Theseus and Phlegyas sin against divinity, to whom reverence is owed; then come cases of betrayal of country, of fellow citizens, of daughters. Tartarus, for Vergil, is actually defined by the concept of disloyalty: he calls it *impia Tartara*, twice (5.733 f., 6.543). From various cultures we meet, as a main element in civil strife, the pain of not knowing whom to trust. We read of it concerning Greece in 1967, when democrats saw among supporters of the colonels' coup people whom they would never have expected to betray democracy. Thucydides (8.66) writes that the Athenian democrats during the revolution of 411 all mistrusted each other, because in the new regime were 'some men who no one would ever have thought would turn to oligarchy'. Prominent among the many tales of betrayal during the Proscriptions of the late 40s are accounts of treachery within the family.[17] If Vergil's fantasies seem vindictive, we should make some attempt to imagine the bewildering terror caused by civil war, the insecurity as well as the guilt which arises most from the enemy within.

Notes

* This paper was first presented at Pittsburgh in September 1995. I am grateful for the suggestions made on that occasion, notably by Professors A.G. McKay and R.F. Thomas; above all I owe thanks to Professor H.-P.Stahl for the invitation to participate in the Pittsburgh conference.

[1] e.g. Norden (1926) 287, 289; Butler (1920) 208–9; Austin (1977) 193, writes: 'The background [of lines 608 ff.] is largely Greek...; but its application is to aspects of contemporary Rome.' On Servius, see especially the commentary on lines 609, 612, 622.

[2] The same chapter contains an account of a man on trial for father-beating, who defended himself with the claim that his father had beaten his grandfather and the grandfather had beaten *his* father; the defendant added, pointing to his little son, 'and he will beat me when he has grown υρσυγγενὲς γὰρ ἡμῖν.

[3] *Dig.* 48.5.23 (22) (Papinian); ibid. 48.5.24 (23) (Ulpian). Badian (1985) has challenged the long-held view that Propertius 2.7 refers to an unsuccessful attempt at legislation on marriage in the early 20s. (Cf. Ferrero Raditsa, 1980, 205 f.) But in any case it remains likely that the marriage legislation of 18 BC, given the sensitivity of the matter, reflected public concern apparent long enough to have been known in Vergil's lifetime.

[4] e.g. Syme (1939) 157; cf. Powell (1992) 157–9.

[5] *infelix* of Theseus in the same line seems more dispassionate; Vergil uses it of the consul Brutus at 6.822, but of *invidia* at G. 3.37.

[6] Powell (1992) 145–6.

[7] Courtney (1993) 272, citing *OLD* s.v. 2.

[8] For a rhetorical accusation concerning Cicero's relations with his daughter, [Sallust] *In M.Tullium Ciceronem Invectiva* 2.

[9] I have argued elsewhere (1992, *passim*) that much of the *Aeneid* is an attempt implicitly to vindicate Octavian's record against that of Sextus.
[10] Powell (1992); for the military references, ibid. 156.
[11] For a possible example, 6.441.
[12] (1939) 194.
[13] Contrast Sparta, where there was special recognition, in the form of grave-markers, for women who died in the service of the community, as there was for men who died in war: Plut. *Lyc.* 27, *IG* V.1.713–4. See also, on Vergil's silence here about women, Habinek (1989) 233 n. 17.
[14] There is further parallelism with the phrase *dum vita manebat* used of Tartarus (608) and of Elysium (661).
[15] See now, on Octavian's appropriation of sacred treasure, Scheer (1995).
[16] Val. Max. 9.2.1.
[17] References at Powell (1992) 169 (n. 98).

Bibliography
Austin, R.G.
   1977   *P. Vergili Maronis Aeneidos Liber Sextus*, Oxford.
Badian, E.
   1985   'A phantom marriage law', *Philologus* 129, 82–98.
Butler, H.E.
   1920   *The Sixth Book of the* Aeneid, Oxford.
Conington, J.
   1884   *P. Vergili Maronis Opera*, vol. 2, London.
Courtney, E.
   1993   *The Fragmentary Latin Poets*, Oxford.
Ferrero Raditsa, L.
   1980   'Augustus' legislation concerning marriage, procreation, love affairs and adultery', *ANRW* II.13, 278–339.
Griffin, J.
   1985   *Latin Poets and Roman Life*, Oxford.
Habinek, T.N.
   1989   'Science and tradition in *Aeneid 6*', *HSCP* 92, 223–55.
Norden, E.,
   1926   *P. Vergilius Maro Aeneis Buch VI*^{3}, Leipzig.
Powell, A.
   1992   'The *Aeneid* and the embarrassments of Augustus', in A. Powell (ed.) *Roman Poetry and Propaganda in the Age of Augustus*, 141–74, London.
Scheer, T.S.
   1995   '*Res Gestae Divi Augusti* 24: Die Restituierung göttlichen Eigentums in Kleinasien durch Augustus',' in C. Schubert, K. Brodersen and U. Huttner (eds.) *Rom und der Griechische Osten. Festschrift für Hatto H. Schmitt*, 209–23, Stuttgart.
Syme, R.
   1939   *The Roman Revolution*, Oxford.

5

VERGIL AS A REPUBLICAN
Aeneid 6.815–35*

Eckard Lefèvre

Even the most important works of world literature are subject to misinterpretation. As regards Vergil's three great poems, the aim both of the *Bucolics* and the *Georgics* has always been debated. However, it was assumed that one could be sure with respect to the *Aeneid*: Vergil was considered to be an adherent of the emperor Augustus, since in the *Divina Commedia* he is presented saying that he had lived *sotto il buon Augusto*.[1] After Vergil and Augustus had been thought to have spoken *una voce* for almost two thousand years, people suddenly seemed to hear 'two voices' and additionally even 'further voices'.[2] During the past twenty-five years the political significance of Vergil's *Aeneid* has been discussed with greater force than ever. As often happens, everything is reduced to black and white in this debate. In addressing this problem today, I will try to keep between the two extreme views which label Vergil either a court poet or a member of the opposition. And I do not want to let myself be distracted too much by the vast amount of secondary literature either, as it could not be properly dealt with here anyway.

The question to what extent Vergil was a Republican certainly is of great interest.[3] The pageant of heroes in *Aeneid* 6 is remarkably full of allusions to a 'Republican' point of view. Wherever possible, it is advisable to compare the description of early Rome there with Livy's account written slightly earlier. Thus the view current at Vergil's time will emerge.

After dealing with Augustus in lines 788–807, Vergil continues with the kings, who were Romulus' successors, starting with Numa Pompilius and Tullus Hostilius. He then goes on to say (815–35):

> Hard on him follows over-boastful Ancus, even now rejoicing overmuch in the people's breath. Wilt thou see, too, the Tarquin kings, and the proud soul of avenging Brutus, and the fasces regained? He shall be first

Eckard Lefèvre

to win a consul's power and cruel axes, and when his sons stir up new war, the father, for fair freedom's sake, shall call them to their doom – unhappy he, howe'er posterity extol that deed! Yet love of country shall prevail, and boundless passion for renown. Nay, see apart the Decii and Drusi, and Torquatus of the cruel axe, and Camillus bringing home the standards. But they whom thou seest gleaming in equal arms, souls harmonious now, while wrapped in night, alas! if they but reach the light of life, what mutual war, what battles and carnage shall they arouse! the father coming down from Alpine ramparts, and the fortress of Monoecus, his daughter's spouse arrayed against him with the armies of the East. O my sons, make not a home within your hearts for such warfare, nor upon your country's very vitals turn her vigour and valour! And do thou first forbear, thou who drawest thy race from heaven; cast from thy hand the sword, thou blood of mine![4]

>   815   quem iuxta sequitur iactantior Ancus
>   nunc quoque iam nimium gaudens popularibus auris.
>   vis et Tarquinios reges animamque superbam
>   ultoris Bruti fascisque videre receptos?
>   consulis imperium hic primus saevasque securis
>   820   accipiet, natosque pater nova bella moventis
>   ad poenam pulchra pro libertate vocabit,
>   infelix, utcumque ferent ea facta minores:
>   vincet amor patriae laudumque immensa cupido.
>   quin Decios Drusosque procul saevumque securi
>   825   aspice Torquatum et referentem signa Camillum.
>   illae autem paribus quas fulgere cernis in armis,
>   concordes animae nunc et dum nocte prementur,
>   heu quantum inter se bellum, si lumina vitae
>   attigerint, quantas acies stragemque ciebunt,
>   830   aggeribus socer Alpinis atque arce Monoeci
>   descendens, gener adversis instructus Eois!
>   ne, pueri, ne tanta animis adsuescite bella
>   neu patriae validas in viscera vertite viris;
>   tuque prior, tu parce, genus qui ducis Olympo,
>   835   proice tela manu, sanguis meus!

These lines obviously show the writer's distance from Caesar. Therefore closer inspection is justified. It will be of special interest whether the analysis leads to any consequences relating to the Princeps himself.

Aura popularis

The characterization of Ancus Marcius in lines 815–16 is not very favourable. There is no parallel to the remark that he was *iactantior* and *nimium gaudens popularibus auris*. Livy applies this metaphor to Appius Claudius in a negative sense. He says that Appius Claudius had taken on a new character in 452 BC, since he had suddenly become a friend of the people and started courting their favour (*novum sibi ingenium induerat, ut plebicola repente omnisque aurae popularis captator evaderet*).[5] Horace uses this metaphor in the same way when he talks about the swaying politician, who *sumit aut ponit securis | arbitrio popularis aurae*.[6] One can either follow Norden's suggestion that this behaviour was a characteristic of Servius Tullius, who is not mentioned by Vergil, but said to δημαγωγεῖν and θεραπεύειν τοὺς ἀπόρους τῶν πολιτῶν by Dionysius of Halicarnassus,[7] or Skutsch's suggestion[8] that the king is equated with Ancus Poplicius mentioned by Dionysius,[9] or Austin's suggestion[10] that this expression points to a family story. In each case[11] Vergil must have had a special reason for characterizing this king in a negative way; after all, Caesar claimed to be a descendant of him by way of his aunt Julia.[12] In his *laudatio funebris* he had said according to Suetonius: *amitae meae Iuliae maternum genus ab regibus ortum… nam ab Anco Marcio sunt Marcii Reges, quo nomine fuit mater… est ergo in genere…sanctitas regum, qui plurimum inter homines pollent*.[13] Binder called it a 'diskreten Hieb gegen Caesar'.[14] That is the least thing to be admitted. Did Caesar raise himself above the senate with the help of the people? Was Augustus about to do the same? His 'ständige[s] Bemühen um das Wohlwollen der *plebs urbana* gerade in den Jahren nach 27'[15] is strange at any rate.

Libertas

In antiquity already it was being discussed whether *anima superba* in line 817 refers to Brutus or to Tarquinius Superbus. The former possibility would be in line with the natural flow of the text, the latter involves assuming that the particle *-que* in line 818 occupies an unusual third place in the phrase. Servius explained the sentence thus: *unus enim de Tarquiniis fuit superbus*, Tiberius Donatus thus: *superbiae vitium Tarquinio applicatur secundum veterum fabulas, non Bruto*. Following Leo[16] and Norden[17] one could prefer this explanation from late antiquity in contrast to the modern *communis opinio*.[18] However, if *anima superba* should refer to Brutus, the epithet *superba* certainly is positive, as it is in the rare cases of *Aeneid* 2.556 with reference to Priam (*superbum | regnatorem Asiae*) and of *Aeneid* 3.475 with reference to Anchises' marriage with Venus (*coniugio, Anchisa, Veneris dignate superbo*). At any rate, Vergil does not show himself distanced from Brutus![19] On the contrary!

Lines 818–23 are in praise of the Brutus[20] who killed the tyrant in 510 BC; the Brutus who killed Caesar in 44 BC points to his relationship to him. Thus the parallel is clear enough. The elder Brutus is called *infelix* (822). In Vergil this epithet is mainly used for poor Dido. Brutus is being praised, since he was the first consul, i.e., the founder of the Republic. Augustine noticed that Vergil praised the *infelix* man with great sympathy. He says: *quod factum Vergilius postea quam laudabiliter commemoravit, continuo clementer exhorruit. cum enim dixisset:* natosque pater nova bella moventes | ad poenam pulchra pro libertate vocabit, *mox deinde exclamavit et ait:* infelix, utcumque ferent ea facta minores. *quomodolibet, inquit, ea facta posteri ferant, id est praeferant et extollant, qui filios occidit, infelix est. et tamquam ad consolandum infelicem subiunxit:* vincit amor patriae laudumque inmensa cupido.[21] One could assume that the deed of the elder Brutus was used to justify that of the younger. Can one go further? Was it possible for anyone living in 23 BC not to notice that someone was said to have made personal sacrifices *pulchra pro libertate*?[22] Was this statement made, not only with reference to Caesar, but also to Augustus? In the description of Aeneas' shield the notion of *libertas* is also very important (8.646–51):

> There, too, was Porsenna, bidding them admit the banished Tarquin, and hemming the city with mighty siege: the sons of Aeneas rushed on the sword for freedom's sake. Him thou mightest have seen like one in wrath, like one who threats, for that Cocles dared to tear down the bridge, and Cloelia broke her bonds and swam the river.

> nec non Tarquinium eiectum Porsenna iubebat
> accipere ingentique urbem obsidione premebat:
> Aeneadae in ferrum *pro libertate* ruebant,
> illum indignanti similem similemque minanti
> aspiceres, pontem auderet quia vellere Cocles
> et fluvium vinclis innaret Cloelia ruptis.

The descendants of Aeneas rush into battle for the sake of liberty. Cocles and Cloelia opposed Porsenna who was threatening liberty. And what about Vergil's own time? What associations were there at that time? In his *Res gestae* Augustus had presented himself as a man providing liberty.[23] In fact, however, he had deprived the citizens of it. The only difficulty is to find out what people thought about this process. Syme was of the following opinion: 'There is something more important than political liberty; and political rights are a means, not an end in themselves. That end is security of life and property: it could not be guaranteed by the constitution of Republican Rome. Worn and broken by civil war and disorder, the Roman people was ready to surrender the ruinous privilege of freedom and submit to strict government.'[24] In his review Momigliano fiercely contradicted this view. He said: 'In our opinion, the truth is different; if we take the whole of the movement 80–27 BC, it may scarcely be doubted that in the Roman

Revolution leaders of a majority, who had no real political rights, dispossessed the senatorial class and the Roman People as a voting class. The Italians, who had obtained the Roman franchise, were destitute of real rights for lack of a representative system. The Romans lost their freedom because they had not shared it. They did not surrender their freedom for their own advantage: they were deprived of it.'[25]

I do not want to interfere in a quarrel between scholars of ancient history, I would rather like to look at Livy, a contemporary of Vergil. In his description of the origin and growth of the Roman Republic (2.1–15) he uses the idea of *libertas* as a *leitmotif*. This fact rightly led Burck to speak of '*libertas*-Erleben'.[26] In Livy just as in Vergil, Brutus is an admirable and tragic figure, the representative of *libertas par excellence*. The expression of *pater liberator* (2.5.7) shows the tragedy in an especially obvious way. The following remark by H. Tränkle is true both for Vergil and for Livy: 'Dieses Wissen, daß jemand nicht nur in voller Übereinstimmung mit sich handeln, sondern auch zu einem Tun geführt werden kann, das ihn in Widerstreit mit seiner Neigung bringt, mag er es noch so sehr für unausweichlich halten, ist für Livius recht bezeichnend. ...die überlegene Macht des Schicksals läßt aus dem unerbittlich Handelnden einen tief Leidenden werden.'[27] Brutus is most similar to Aeneas, who has overcome himself.[28] Did Vergil have the impression that Caesar and Augustus did not overcome themselves for the sake of the people's *libertas*?

Livy's account is written slightly earlier than that of Vergil. He is quite likely to have still believed in Octavian's promise to restore *libertas*. Von Haehling thought that the use of the phrase *vindex libertatis* with reference to Brutus (2.1.8) was a direct allusion to Octavian/Augustus, since he is referred to by this title on a Cistophorus minted in Asia Minor in 28 BC.[29] But he also says that Brutus, called *deinde custos* [sc. *libertatis*] in the same context by Livy, is not to be equated with Augustus. Additionally, von Haehling closely analysed the passage 3,66–70, dealing with the war against the Volsci and Aequi in 446 BC. In this war the consul Agrippa Furius temporarily entrusted absolute power to T. Quinctius Capitolinus, his more experienced colleague. This analysis led von Haehling to the following interpretation: 'Brutus befreite das von der tyrannischen Willkür des letzten Königs unterdrückte Volk, durch seine einzigartige Tat legte er den Grundstein für die libera res publica. Auch Augustus' Wirken bildet einen Eckstein in der Entwicklung der römischen Geschichte, ihm ist es offensichtlich vorbehalten, die durch Parteienkämpfe und Bürgerkriege zerrüttete res publica wieder aufzurichten, auch wenn bei der

Eckard Lefèvre

Wiederherstellung der *maiestas populi Romani* die Prinzipien der libera res publica *vorübergehend* außer Kraft gesetzt werden müssen. Nichts vermag den politischen Standort des Livius besser zu beschreiben als die Tatsache, daß er sich dagegen wehrt, Oktavian/Augustus auf eine Stufe mit Brutus zu stellen. ...Sein Urteil über den mächtigsten Mann seiner Zeit ist von einer gewissen Reserve geprägt. Bei aller Anerkennung seiner politischen Leistungen, der vorläufigen Beendigung der Bürgerkriege, bewahrt sich Livius eine innere Unabhängigkeit. Er sieht in Oktavian/Augustus nicht den alleinverantwortlichen Zerstörer der Freiheit, aber er *erhofft* sich von ihm – zum Zeitpunkt der Abfassung von III.66–70 – die langfristige Wiederherstellung der libera res publica.'[30]

Livy still hoped for the restoration of *libertas*. Was Vergil calling for the fulfilment of this promise a few years later? We know today that his calling was in vain. 'Man konnte...von Oktavian kein Verständnis für die aristokratische *libertas* erwarten und konnte von ihm nicht verlangen, daß er sich für eine *libera res publica* einsetzte, die er niemals selbst erlebt hat.'[31]

Pro re publica

Before dealing with Caesar directly, Anchises mentions outstanding representatives of the early Republic in lines 824–5, starting with the two Decii. *hi duo fuerunt, qui Mures dicti sunt, pater et filius. horum alter se bello Gallico, alter Samnitico vovit pro re publica.*[32] These actions in 340 BC and 295 BC respectively were examples of self-sacrifice with great implications for posterity. The Decii are worthy companions of Brutus in this respect. The Drusi follow next in Anchises' account. According to Servius the main focus is on M. Livius Salinator (an ancestor of this family), who defeated Hasdrubal near the river Metaurus in 207 BC,[33] and additionally on Drusus, Livia's son, of whom Augustus expected a lot. Vergil is likely to be somewhat vague here on purpose. In Salinator's case Vergil could have thought of the following story transmitted by Suetonius: when Salinator was censor, he reproached all the tribes for their thoughtlessness in electing him consul a second time and also censor, although they had made him pay a penalty after his first consulship.[34] He, too, considered his personal affairs less important than the dignity of the state.[35] The next man pointed out by Anchises is Manlius Torquatus, whose mention recalls the war against the Latini in 340 BC. Like Brutus, he is an outstanding example of unselfishness. A single glance at Livy's account shows that this episode could make a strong appeal to the readers. *Disciplina militaris, qua stetit ad hanc diem Romana res*,[36] was important for the consul Torquatus (as it was for the Great Elector) although his son (like the Prince of Homburg) was victorious after having set out contrary to commands. The father was brought into a dilemma (*necessitas*) and thus sentenced his son to death. Confirmation of the consuls' power was at stake (*sancienda...consulum imperia*, 8.7.19). For the sake of this the father made a great sacrifice. And what did Augustus do?

Finally Camillus appears in the pageant of heroes. It was well known that he recovered the gold offered to the Galli in 390 BC, because he decided on starting battle again.[37] What does *signa* refer to? Servius seems to be right who (maybe following Vergil) supplemented as follows: *Gallos iam abeuntes secutus est: quibus interemptis aurum omne recepit et signa*.[38] By reading Livy (and that is what Vergil perhaps did) one finds out that Camillus was about to resign from the dictatorship after his triumph and that he did not carry out his plan for the only reason that the senate implored him not to do so in the present unsafe situation, as the people were willing to move the capital to Veii.[39] He was able to prevent them from doing so by taking vigorous action. Even then he was allowed to resign only after he had completed his year in office: *ceterum primo* [sc. *urbs renata*], *quo adminiculo erecta erat, eodem innixa M. Furio principe stetit, neque eum abdicare se dictatura nisi anno circumacto passi sunt*.[40] Livy here calls Camillus *princeps*. As in other passages, the allusion to Augustus is very obvious. Being *diligentissimus religionum cultor*,[41] he is *pius*, like Aeneas and Augustus.[42] In his triumph he is praised by receiving the title *Romulus ac parens patriae conditorque alter urbis*,[43] thus 'a Roman reader of the 20's would be bound to feel their contemporary force'.[44] After Camillus has finally saved the city, he finally is 'allowed' to resign from dictatorship. And what did Augustus do? Was he a second Caesar?

Patriae in viscera

Then – with greatest frankness – Caesar and Pompey are mentioned as being representative of, even responsible for, terrible civil wars (826–35). The contrast with Brutus is most obvious. Brutus put up with personal disaster because his sons were about to start civil war (*nova bella*); Caesar and Pompey carry out what was prevented by Brutus. They are examples showing the opposite behaviour. One has to infer that the younger Brutus killed Caesar with full justice.

There are evil undertones in this passage. Caesar and Pompey are called *socer* and *gener*. Thereby 'Virgil has given Epic cachet to what was originally a gibe of the lampoonists.'[45] Comparable is the use of these expressions by Catullus[46] and the author of the *Catalepton*[47] in the same negative context. These phrases were also used by Lucan[48] and Martial.[49] Austin put it very well by saying: 'the marriage-relationship between Caesar and Pompey added a special family *impietas* to the wider *impietas* of civil war'.[50] When Vergil talks about Caesar's route from Gaul to the civil war in Italy, he mentions the crossing of the Alps. Because of the accounts of Petronius[51] and Lucan,[52] Norden[53] arrived at the conclusion that this description was a topic of declamatory speeches and thus 'ein Seitenstück zu Hannibals Alpenübergang'.[54] What was appreciated by the orators for the sake of creating a good point for their story, was of political significance for Vergil: like Hannibal, Caesar was Italy's enemy![55]

Syme said about Anchises' direct address to Caesar in lines 834–5: 'Save for that veiled rebuke, no word of Caesar in all the epic record of Rome's glorious past.'[56] It is well known that Pompey was considered a representative of *libera res publica*. This fact probably is the reason why Vergil's Anchises does not ask both rivals to put down their weapons at the same time, but addresses Caesar first.[57] Perhaps one can go even further. Servius commented on *adsuescite bella* (832) in a remarkable way:

> mire dictum: ab ipsis enim quasi consuetudinem fecit populus Romanus bellorum civilium. septies enim gesta sunt: ter a Caesare, contra Pompeium in Thessalia, contra eius filium Magnum in Hispania, item contra Iubam et Catonem in Africa: mortuo Caesare ab Augusto contra Cassium et Brutum in Philippis, civitate Thessaliae; Lucium Antonium in Perusia, Tusciae civitate; Sextum Pompeium in Sicilia; Antonium et Cleopatram in Epiro.[58]

Norden had firmly rejected the view 'daß die Rezitation dieser Verse den Kaiser verletzt haben könnte wegen des von ihm selbst gegen Antonius geführten Bürgerkriegs'.[59] How could Augustus have reacted differently? Was he not bound to be annoyed about being connected with the 'destroyer of the Republic'? Was it even intended that he was annoyed?

'Republicanism'

The pageant of heroes as a whole demonstrates 'outspoken republicanism'.[60] It manifests itself in praise of the old Republic on the one hand and distance from Caesar, threatening the Republic in more recent times, on the other. Like Livy, Vergil was a 'Republican'.[61] A brief analysis of the structure of Anchises' prophecy will make clear that the extract dealt with here has not been chosen at random. In lines 756–816 the pre-republican time is described, with lines 781–807

Vergil as a Republican

looking forward to later Rome and Augustus. (It certainly is tempting to think of Augustus as a second founder in the manner of the first king. However, is it of greater significance that he appears – as *'rex'* – among the *reges*?[62]) In lines 817–35 and lines 836–46 heroes of the Republic are presented, outstanding in 'internal affairs' and 'external affairs' respectively.[63] Lines 826–35 (separated by *autem*) are looking forward to the time of the degenerate representatives Pompey and Caesar. It is worth noting that Caesar and Pompey, who were also very successful in external affairs, appear as sinners with regard to internal affairs.[64]

As soon as one has introduced the term 'Republican' as referring to Vergil, the mention of Cato of Utica, the 'Republican *par excellence*', as judge of the dead in the description of Aeneas' shield gains special significance. For it is he of all people who is contrasted with the revolutionary Catilina in his capacity as a positive figure (with assonance of their names) (8.666–70):

> Away from these he adds also the abodes of Hell, the high gates of Dis, the penalties of sin, and thee, Catiline, hanging on a frowning cliff, and trembling at the faces of the Furies; far apart, the good, and Cato giving them laws.

> hinc procul addit
> Tartareas etiam sedes, alta ostia Ditis,
> et scelerum poenas, et te, Catilina, minaci
> pendentem scopulo Furiarumque ora trementem,
> secretosque pios, his dantem iura Catonem.

Cato becomes even more important, since he and Catilina are the only people to be mentioned of those who lived between early Rome and the time of Augustus. And Cato is 'the implacable opponent of Julius Caesar and the uncompromising champion of the lost cause of the Republic'.[65] How many levels of meaning are contained in these lines? The following ways of understanding them are all possible:

1. Catilina is being used as a negative example. Why is it he of all people who is being mentioned? For it is known that Caesar was sympathetic with the movement started by him although Sallust tried very hard to conceal it.

2. Servius says about this passage that *hoc quasi in Ciceronis gratiam dictum videtur*. But during the last phase Cicero was a firm opponent of Caesar.[66]

3. Binder recognized 'diskrete Kritik an Caesar'[67] because Cato won the debate in the senate about the punishment of the Catilinarians and Caesar's opponent now sees his demands fulfilled in Tartarus.

4. The mention of the Republican *par excellence* speaks for itself.
5. Vergil makes Cato *iura dare*,[68] an activity which is carried out by outstanding figures only.[69]

In the section of Anchises' speech dealt with here Vergil has mentioned both positive and negative aspects. Norden explained this remarkable circumstance by rhetorical theories, which demand both ἐγκώμιον and ψόγος,[70] as well as by the 'antike Schicklichkeitsgefühl'. Thus he played its importance down: 'Wir werden also schon aus diesem allgemeinen Grunde die Ansicht einzelner Kritiker nicht teilen, die die Erwähnung des Bürgerkriegs 826 ff. nicht passend finden, und dem Dichter unsere Anerkennung zollen, daß er von König Ancus lieber eine entlegene, diesem abgünstige Legende benutzt (815 f.), statt sich mit einem wohlfeilen Lob zu begnügen, und daß er die Tat des Brutus (822 f.) nicht im Fanfarenstil der Rhetorik gepriesen hat.'[71] One gets the impression that a certain helplessness manifests itself when the use of rhetorical devices is approved of at one time and their omission is commended at another.

It is appropriate to ask what follows from Vergil's distance from Caesar and his praise of Cato with regard to his relationship to Augustus. In Lucan, Vergil's most important successor in epic poetry, distance from Caesar and praise of Cato reappear, greatly intensified. Lucan's rejection of Caesar doubtless implies the rejection of Nero. Does Vergil's distance from Caesar imply distance from Augustus? Was it consistent with Augustus' wishes that Vergil wrote poetry in a 'Republican' manner and that he declared himself a 'Republican'?

In 36 BC Octavian had promised *rem publicam restituere*. As *princeps*, he had propagated that he had kept his promise by talking of the *res publica restituta* as a matter of course. Forced by political necessity, Augustus presented himself as a Republican. In overcoming the Republic he had to keep largely to its formal organisation. Due to this way of proceeding he had to keep his distance from Caesar and to praise Cato. Syme said that in his youth Augustus overthrew the Republic, in his mature years the statesman stole its heroes and its vocabulary.[72] He even claimed to have brought the country to freedom: *rem publicam a dominatione factionis oppressam in libertatem vindicavi*.[73] The idea of *rem publicam in libertatem vindicare* could also have been a maxim of Cato, but in a sense different from the sense it had with Augustus.[74] The meaning of *libertas* in Cato's, Livy's and Vergil's minds was different from what Augustus thought it to be.

Topicality

Vergil was not able to publish the *Aeneid*, but he wrote the sixth Book (like all the others) believing that he would do so. However, he made slow progress because he was very precise and always mindful of corrections when writing. It had taken him very long to finish the *Georgics*; Servius says that it was seven years, and if he is right in assuming that the *laudes Galli* at the end of *Georgics* 4 were eliminated, it will be even more than ten years. So Vergil can hardly ever have hoped to finish the *Aeneid* in a shorter period of time. It is not speculative to say that Vergil, when writing *Aeneid* 6, did not think of finishing the *Aeneid* as a whole until, let's say, 15 BC. Supposing that Anchises' prophecy in *Aeneid* 6 was 'eine Mahnung für die Gegenwart', as Norden put it:[75] what points would there be on account of which Vergil could admonish Augustus? Would Augustus still be alive, would he be willing to change anything? Would it not be too late? But the situation is different if one takes into account recitations during the process of composition. In the *vita* by Suetonius and Donatus recitations are mentioned several times, particularly with reference to *Aeneid* 6: *cui* [sc. Augusto]...*tres omnino libros recitavit, secundum quartum sextum, sed hunc notabili Octaviae adfectione, quae, cum recitationi interesset, ad illos de filio suo versus: 'tu Marcellus eris'* [Aen. 6.883] *defecisse fertur atque aegre focilata <esse>*.[76] This allusion is relevant to the year 23 BC. Vergil did not only recite parts of his works quite often, but also very well: *pronuntiabat autem cum suavitate, cum lenociniis miris*, as Suetonius[77] says; *nam recitavit voce optima*, as Servius[78] says. Anchises' prophecy was a piece especially appropriate for being recited on its own. Norden, influenced by Tiberius Donatus, has pointed out the rhetorical character of this passage and said 'daß die Helden Vergils die typischen der Rhetorenschule sind'.[79] He also thought about the effect the recitation might have had on Augustus.[80] Goold was of the opinion that 'the Pageant, that is the speech of Anchises 756–853', was especially appropriate for recitation.[81]

Horace's *Odes* are also thought to have been recited.[82] Among the odes recited there probably were not only poems addressed to friends, but also poems of political significance. The 'Roman Odes' are very likely to have become widely known before 23 BC. These odes, too, are not really in praise of the monarch, but rather an attempt to place him under an obligation in public. *Ode* 2.10, probably recited in the same year as *Aeneid* 6, is an especially remarkable example if the Licinius addressed is Licinius Murena, consul in 23 BC.[83] A recitation of this poem among the appropriate people did not only imply an appeal to

Augustus to be merciful, but also to Licinius to be moderate.[84]

A 'Mahnung für die Gegenwart' (in Norden's words) had its greatest impact when the poem was recited. Because of the present situation in 23 BC a special reason was offered: Augustus' government had entered a state of crisis because – among other things – Murena's conspiracy was discovered. That year 'certainly' was 'the most critical, in all the long Principate of Augustus'.[85] In 27 BC Octavian had resigned from his special powers and Republican rule could have started again. But the senate did not allow Octavian to resign, just as it had once done in Camillus' case. In 23 BC there was a comparable situation: Augustus resigned from the consulship after he had held this office continuously since 31 BC (however, he got *tribunicia potestas annua et perpetua* and *imperium proconsulare maius* in exchange). This period was a 'Republican phase'. L. Sestius became the successor to the consul Augustus; he was 'ein alter Republikaner, der einst an der Seite des Brutus gekämpft hatte und noch immer dessen Andenken in Ehren hielt'.[86] Gn. Calpurnius Piso became the successor to the consul Murena; he was 'a Republican of independent and recalcitrant temper'.[87] Augustus' aim was 'die Meinung der republikanischen Kreise des Senats zu gewinnen'.[88] Who knows whether the senate would have allowed him to resign this time, just as it once did in Camillus' case?

I do not want to argue that Vergil wished something like that; I would simply like to suggest that the passage analysed contains a 'personal voice' against the background of discussions about the 'Republic' in 23 BC. For at that time many people were asking for more Republican elements in Rome's political organisation than Augustus claimed to offer.

Notes

* I wish to express my gratitude to Gesine Manuwald for her kind help with translating this article.

[1] Dante, *Inf.* 1.71.

[2] Lyne (1987).

[3] The following remarks are a new version of a passage in an older article of mine (1983a, 29–33), the present article being more comprehensive and taking recent research into account.

[4] This translation and the following ones of 8.646–51 and of 8.666–70 are taken from the Loeb edition. In this edition, however, *animam superbam* in lines 8.817–18 is construed in a way different from that of the present author.

[5] Livy 3.33.7.

[6] Horace, *Carm.* 3. 2.19–20.

[7] Dionysius, *Ant. Rom.* 4.8.3.

[8] Skutsch (1972) 14–16.

[9] Dionysius, *Ant. Rom.* 3.34.3.

[10] Austin ad loc.

[11] Cf. Feeney (1986) 9–10, for other suggestions. Horsfall (1995) 149, thinks of an 'error'.

[12] By the way, Augustus was also related to Ancus Marcius: L. Marcius Philippus (consul in 56 BC) was his mother's second husband.

[13] *Div. Iul.* 6.1. Cf. Grimal (1954) 47.

[14] Binder (1971) 207. 'Le vers ne pouvait manquer d'évoquer les Lupercales de 44 et la démagogie césarienne, qui se complaisait aux acclamations de la populace.' (Grimal (1954) 47).

[15] Kienast (1982) 86 (with bibliography).

[16] Leo (1895) 429 n. 3.

[17] Norden ad 812 f.

[18] According to Austin (1977) 251, Sabbadini and Geymonat also prefer the explanation from antiquity.

[19] Knight's (1932) interpretation of this passage is completely wrong. He says that Brutus has a 'tyrant soul' (Conway (1932) basically agrees); therefore it is 'the extreme republicans, the enemies of Aeneas and Augustus, who are *superbi*'. Zetzel's interpretation (1989, 282) also misses the point. He terms it a 'failure' that 'Brutus is overcome by *laudum immensa cupido*'.

[20] Cf. Kraggerud's important interpretation (1995, 62–7). His result is as follows: 'die Rechtmässigkeit der Tat des Brutus' (Norden) 'is in no way questioned or undermined' (66).

[21] Augustine, *C.D.* 3.16.

[22] Brutus 'stellt die Freiheit der Republik über sein persönliches Glück', Glei (1991) 172.

[23] See below.

[24] Syme (1939) 513.

[25] Momigliano (1940) 80.

[26] Burck (1934) 52; cf. 53: he says that Livy puts 'in bewußter Bindung an seinen thematischen Leitsatz den Nachdruck auf die Gefühle der Zuschauer, die den Verrat der Patrizier an der *libertas* nicht begreifen können (5, 7).'

[27] Tränkle (1965) 329.

[28] Cf. Lefèvre (1983b) 39. Glei (1991, 172) notices a 'typologische Verbindung' between Vergil's Brutus and Aeneas.

[29] Von Haehling (1989) 209.

[30] Von Haehling (1989) 209–10 (italics mine).

[31] Kienast (1982) 18.

[32] Servius on 822.

[33] It is plausible that the main focus is on this man since all the others mentioned besides are heroes of the early Republic.

[34] *Salinator universas tribus in censura notavit levitatis nomine, quod, cum se post priorem consulatum multa inrogata condemnassent, consulem iterum censoremque fecissent* (Suet., *Tib.* 3.2). After his triumph *de Illyriis* Salinator was convicted of having distributed the booty unjustly.

[35] Austin (ad loc.) assumes that 'primary reference' is made to M. Livius Drusus, the famous tribunus plebis of 91 BC, who became 'Gracchus der

Aristokratie' according to Mommsen (*Röm. Gesch.* 2.217). If this suggestion is true, another person who has set himself 'uneigennützige' tasks (domestic affairs and the problem of how to deal with the allies) is mentioned here (H.G. Gundel, *Der Kleine Pauly*, II (1975) 169). His being murdered in his own house was a source for topics in the schools of rhetoric. The Auctor ad Herennium mentions one of them (4.31): *tuus, o Druse, sanguis domesticos parietes et voltum parentis aspersit.* Feeney's interpretation (1986, 11–12) is unconventional.

[36] Livy 8.7.16.
[37] Cf. Livy 5.49.
[38] Servius on 825.
[39] Livy 5.49.8–9.
[40] Livy 6.1.4.
[41] Livy 5.50.1.
[42] Cf. Burck (1934) 134.
[43] Livy 5.49.7.
[44] Ogilvie (1965) 739.
[45] Austin ad 830 f.
[46] *socer generque, perdidistis omnia?* (Catullus 29.24).
[47] *gener socerque, perdidistis omnia?* (6.6).
[48] *socerum depellere regno | decretum genero est* (Lucan 1.289–90); *gener atque socer bello contendere iussi* (Lucan 4.802); *non in soceri generique favorem | discedunt populi* (Lucan 10.417–18).
[49] *cum gener atque socer diris concurreret armis* (Martial 9.70.3).
[50] Austin ad 830 f.
[51] Petronius 122.144–55.
[52] Lucan 1.183.
[53] Norden ad 826 ff.
[54] According to Juvenal 10.166, Hannibal's crossing of the Alps was a topic of declamatory speeches.
[55] Perhaps his strange route via the Western regions of the Alps can be explained by an allusion to Hannibal's crossing?
[56] Syme (1939) 317.
[57] Incorrectly, this passage has widely been connected with Caesar's *clementia* towards the Pompeians since Servius' times (Norden: amnesty after the battle of Thapsus). The right interpretation is Feeney's (1986, 12): 'here Anchises is begging his descendant to lay down his arms first, before Pompey does.'
[58] Cf. Strasburger ((1983) 1990, 290): '...Octavian, der sich vom privaten Erben zum politischen Nachfolger hochstilisierte und Caesars Machtkampf gegen den eigenen Staat mit äußerster Härte und Verschlagenheit erneuerte.'
[59] Norden ad 826 ff.
[60] Frank (1938) 93.
[61] 'Livy, like Virgil, was a Pompeian.' 'The term "Pompeianus", however, need not denote an adherent of Pompeius. The Romans lacked a word for "Republican"' (Syme 1939, 464 with n. 2, with reference to Tac. *Ann.* 4.34).
[62] Cf. Feeney (1986) 9: 'note that Augustus, by this arrangement, is one of the *reges*'.

[63] It is obvious that in connection with Mummius, Aemilius Paullus, Cato, Cossus, Scipio maior and minor, Fabricius, Serranus and Fabius Maximus Cunctator, *Gracchi* (842) (as well as *Fabii* (845)) denote representatives of this family in general and not the two reformers: Tiberius Sempronius Gracchus (consul in 238 BC) fought in Sardinia, his son (consul in 215 and 213 BC) against Hannibal and Hanno, the father of the reformers (consul in 177 BC) in Spain and Sardinia (his achievements in war were praised by a eulogy in the Forum of Augustus; cf. Norden ad 842 f.). Cf. also Austin ad 842; Feeney (1986) 13.

[64] Maybe the perversion from external to internal wars is suggested by mentioning that Caesar came from Gaul and Pompey from the East (830–1).

[65] Fordyce ad 666 ff.

[66] Cf. Strasburger (1990).

[67] Binder (1971) 208.

[68] *Aeneid*: Dido (1.507), Jupiter (1.731), Aeneas (3.137), Acestes (5.758), Priamus (7.246–7); *Georgics*: Octavian (4.562). Cf. Binder (1971) 210–11.

[69] Vergil has created a unique picture. It inspired Dante to make Cato the guardian of the penitent in the first canto of his *Purgatorio*, even if he owes individual traits to Lucan (cf. Dante Alighieri, *Die göttliche Komödie*, Kommentar von H. Gmelin, II. Teil: Der Läuterungsberg, Stuttgart (1955) 33). Vergil presents Dante to the guardian Cato, who is characterized on this occasion (70–4):
>Or ti piaccia gradir la sua venuta:
>Libertà va cercando, ch' è si cara,
>Come sa chi per lei vita rifiuta.
>Tu il sai, chè non ti fu per lei amara
>In Utica la morte.

[70] Cf. Horsfall (1995) 146.

[71] Norden ad 752 ff.

[72] 'In his youth Caesar's heir, the revolutionary adventurer, won Pompeian support by guile and coolly betrayed his allies, overthrowing the Republic and proscribing the Republicans: in his mature years the statesman stole their heroes and their vocabulary.' (Syme 1939, 317). Cf. also Norden ((1901) 1966, 372): 'Wohl niemals ist mit größerer Virtuosität als von Augustus die (übrigens für den römischen Nationalcharakter bezeichnende) Kunst geübt worden, unter dem Schein konstitutioneller, ja reaktionärer Formen eine faktische Neuordnung der Verhältnisse zu begründen, so daß die Umwandlung des Freistaats in den Prinzipat der Wiederherstellung der ältesten Einrichtungen eben dieses Freistaates glich.'

[73] *Res gestae* 1.1.

[74] It would be in line with Vergil's high esteem for Cato if he did allude to Cato in the simile in *Aen.* 1.148–52. Cf. Pöschl (1977) 20–1.

[75] Norden ad 752 ff.

[76] § 32. Cf. Servius on 6.861: *et constat hunc librum tanta pronuntiatione Augusto et Octaviae esse recitatum, ut fletu nimio imperarent silentium, nisi Vergilius finem esse dixisset.*

[77] Suetonius/Donatus § 28.

[78] Servius on *Aen.* 4.323.
[79] Norden ad 752 ff.
[80] Norden ad 826 ff.
[81] Goold (1992) 118: 'The variety of intonation, tempo, and delivery called for would provide a gifted reader with abundant scope to move an audience.'
[82] Cf. Lefèvre (1993) in general.
[83] Cf. Hanslik (1953) 282–7; Nisbet/Hubbard (1978) 151–8.
[84] Cf. Lefèvre (1993), 151-153.
[85] Syme (1939) 333.
[86] Kienast (1982) 88; cf. Syme (1939) 335.
[87] Syme (1939) 335; cf. Kienast (1982) 87: 'ein alter Republikaner'.
[88] Kienast (1982) 88.

Bibliography

Austin, R.G.
    1977   *P. Vergili Maronis Aeneidos Liber Sextus, with a commentary*, Oxford.
Binder, G.
    1971   *Aeneas und Augustus. Interpretationen zum 8. Buch der Aeneis*, Beiträge zur Klassischen Philologie 38.
Burck, E.
    1934   *Die Erzählungskunst des T. Livius*, Problemata 11.
Conway, R.S.
    1932   'Vergil and Octavian', *CR* 46, 199–202.
Feeney, D.C.
    1986   'History and revelation in Vergil's underworld',*PCPhS* n.s. 32, 1–24.
Fordyce, C.J.
    1977   *P. Vergili Maronis Aeneidos libri VII–VIII, with a commentary*, ed. J.D. Christie, Oxford.
Frank, T.
    1938   'Augustus, Vergil, and the Augustan Elogia', *AJPh* 59, 91–4.
Glei, R. F.
    1991   *Der Vater der Dinge. Interpretationen zur politischen, literarischen und kulturellen Dimension des Krieges bei Vergil*. Bochumer Altertumswissenschaftliches Colloquium 7, Trier.
Goold, G.P.
    1992   'The voice of Virgil. The pageant of Rome in *Aeneid* 6', in T. Woodman and J. Powell (eds.) *Author and audience in Latin literature*, 110–23, 241–5, Cambridge.
Grimal, P.
    1954   'Le livre VI de l'Énéide et son actualité en 23 av. J.-C.'*REA* 56, 40–60.
Haehling, R. v.
    1989   *Zeitbezüge des T. Livius in der ersten Dekade seines Geschichtswerkes: nec vitia nostra nec remedia pati possumus*, Historia Einzelschr. 61.
Hanslik, R.
    1953   'Horaz und Varro Murena' *RhM* 96, 282–7.

Horsfall, N. (ed.)
  1995 *A Companion to the Study of Virgil*, Mnemosyne Supplement 151, Leiden, New York and Köln.
Kienast, D.
  1982 *Augustus. Prinzeps und Monarch*, Darmstadt.
Knight, W.F.J.
  1932 'Animamque superbam', *CR* 46, 55–7.
Kraggerud, E.
  1995 'Notes on Anchises' Speech in Vergil's *Aeneid*, Book VI', in M. Asztalos and C. Gejrot (eds.) *Symbolae Septentrionales. Latin Studies Presented to Jan Öberg*, 59–71, Stockholm.
Lefèvre, E.
  1983a 'Vergil: Propheta retroversus', *Gymnasium* 90, 17–40.
  1983b 'Argumentation und Struktur der moralischen Geschichtsschreibung der Römer am Beispiel von Livius' Darstellung des Beginns des römischen Freistaats (2, 1–2, 15)', in E. Lefèvre and E. Olshausen (eds.) *Livius – Werk und Rezeption, Festschr. E. Burck*: 31–57, München.
  1993 'Waren horazische Gedichte zum "öffentlichen" Vortrag bestimmt?' in G. Vogt-Spira (ed.) *Beiträge zur mündlichen Kultur der Römer*, ScriptOralia 47, Reihe A: Altertumswiss. Reihe 11: 143–57, Tübingen.
Leo, F.
  1895 'Bemerkungen über plautinische Wortstellung und Wortgruppen', *NGG*, 415–33.
Lyne, R.O.A.M.
  1987 *Further Voices in Vergil's* Aeneid, Oxford.
Momigliano, A.
  1940 Review of Syme 1939, *JRS* 30, 75–80.
Nisbet, R.G.M. and Hubbard, M.
  1978 *A Commentary on Horace: Odes. Book II*, Oxford.
Norden, E.
  1901 'Vergils Aeneis im Lichte ihrer Zeit', *NJbb* 7, 249–82, 313–34 = *Kleine Schriften zum Klassischen Altertum*, 358–421, Berlin, 1966.
  1927 *P. Vergilius Maro Aeneis Buch VI*, 3rd edn, Leipzig.
Ogilvie, R.M.
  1965 *A Commentary on Livy Books 1–5*, Oxford
Pöschl, V.
  1977 *Die Dichtkunst Virgils. Bild und Symbol in der Äneis*, 3rd edn, Berlin.
Skutsch, O.
  1972 'Readings and interpretations in the Annals', *Entretiens* 17, 3–29.
Syme, R.
  1939 *The Roman Revolution*, Oxford.
Strasburger, H.
  1938 'Vergil und Augustus', *Gymnasium* 90, 41–76 = *Studien zur Alten Geschichte III*, 281–316, Hildesheim and New York, 1990.
  1990 *Ciceros philosophisches Spätwerk als Aufruf gegen die Herrschaft Caesars*,

Spudasmata 45 = *Studien zur Alten Geschichte III*, 407–98, Hildesheim and New York, 1990.

Tränkle, H.
1965 'Der Anfang des römischen Freistaats in der Darstellung des Livius', *Hermes* 93, 311–37.

Zetzel, J.E.G.
1989 '*Romane memento:* justice and judgment in *Aeneid* 6', *TAPhA* 119, 263–84.

Dedicated to Gerhard Binder on the occasion of his 60th birthday

6

THE SHOW MUST GO ON:
THE DEATH OF MARCELLUS AND THE
FUTURE OF THE AUGUSTAN PRINCIPATE
Aeneid 6.860–86

Reinhold F. Glei

Preliminary remarks

On the last day of his life he asked every now and then whether there was any disturbance without on his account; then calling for a mirror, he had his hair combed and his falling jaws set straight. After that, calling in his friends and asking whether it seemed to them that he had played the comedy of life fitly, he added the tag:
        'Since well I've played my part, all clap your hands
        And from the stage dismiss me with applause.

Supremo die identidem exquirens, an iam de se tumultus foris esset, petito speculo capillum sibi comi ac malas labantes corrigi praecepit et admissos amicos percontatus, ecquid iis videretur mimum vitae commode transegisse, adiecit et clausulam:
        ἐπεὶ δὲ πάνυ καλῶς πέπαισται, δότε κρότον
        καὶ πάντες ἡμᾶς μετὰ χαρᾶς προπέμψατε.[1]

Suetonius reports this in his biography of Augustus. The first emperor was indeed a master actor throughout his life, a master at stage-managing, a master at illusionism. It will suffice at this point to recall a few well-known stages on Octavian's way to power. When, at the funeral ceremonies for C. Iulius Caesar in July 44 BC, a comet appeared, Octavian interpreted it as the soul of the deified dictator and, skilfully taking advantage of Roman superstition, displayed the *sidus Iulium* on his coins and called himself *Divi filius* from then on. Further, he disguised the civil war against Antony as a *bellum externum* against Cleopatra and in 32 BC declared war on her in person, dressed up as a fetial priest, – naturally a *bellum iustum* for which he invoked the *Di patrii* against the dog-headed idols of the whore of the Nile. Eventually, in January of 27 BC, Octavian stage-managed a 'comedy of abdication',[2] renouncing all extraordinary legal powers and 'restoring the republic' (the famous *restitutio rei publicae*). His statement in the *Res Gestae* that, from then on, although outshining all others by his *auctoritas*, he did not have more *potestas* than his official colleagues,[3] may be constitutionally correct but is completely illusory in terms of *Realpolitik*.

I cannot and will not give an overall appreciation of the Augustan principate; my topic is a far more modest one: it relates to the events surrounding the death of Marcellus, Augustus' nephew and son-in-law, in the autumn of 23 BC, and its reflection in Vergil's *Aeneid*. I would like to show how and why Vergil incorporated these political events into his epic and simultaneously commented on them. To this end I would like to proceed as follows: first and by way of introduction, the events of the twenties will be related to the degree they are relevant to our topic; second, the Vergilian Marcellus passage will be interpreted in the context of a) the pageant of heroes, b) Book 6 in general, and c) the *Aeneid* as a whole; in the third place, the consequences for Vergil's overall historical and philosophical concept will be analysed; and finally, as a corollary, early evidence will be presented concerning the reception of the Marcellus passage.

I. Historical introduction[4]

C. Claudius Marcellus, born in 42 BC as the son of Octavia, sister of Caesar Octavianus, was given exceptional honours by his uncle very early on. At the triple triumph of 29 BC Marcellus was allowed, together with Tiberius, Livia's son of roughly the same age, to ride next to the victor,[5] and Octavian donated large sums of money to the public in Marcellus' name to make him popular. In the Cantabrian campaign in 26/25 BC Marcellus accompanied Augustus and gained his first military honours which were celebrated not only by Vergil but also by the Greek poet Crinagoras in an epigram.[6] After his return from Spain, Marcellus, only seventeen years old, married the fifteen-year-old Julia, only child of Augustus, an event which Horace alludes to in his Ode 1.12 in a panegyric context.[7] After Augustus himself had returned from Spain in 24 BC, in not particularly good health, he had further honours bestowed on his new son-in-law: Marcellus was given a seat in the senate with praetorian rank, was designated to the aedileship for the year 23 BC, and received permission to apply for the consulship ten years before the legal minimum age.[8]

All this indicates that Augustus wanted to 'build up' Marcellus as his long-term successor. One should, however, not introduce the possibility of a dynastic line of succession in this early, by no means unchallenged, phase of the principate: Augustus could pass on to Marcellus his name and fortune but not his personal powers – they were not defined in the 'restored' republic's constitution but were based on privileges passed *ad hominem*, which were by no means hereditary.[9] It was therefore an exceptionally clever political move that Augustus, when he became severely ill in the spring of 23 BC, did not officially involve Marcellus at all, but instead handed over his powers in a painfully correct way to his then co-consul and entrusted his signet ring, symbol of the right of disposal of his fortune, not to Marcellus but to Agrippa: only he, the right-hand man of Augustus, would be able, if anyone at this time, to gain a position comparable to that of Augustus himself. However, these measures had no practical consequences: Augustus recovered soon, and the successful water-cure prescribed by his personal doctor, Antonius Musa, became so fashionable that it was used as a universal remedy from then on[10] – a fact that would prove fatal for Marcellus. Despite the deliberate non-recognition of Marcellus in the crisis of 23 BC, persistent rumours remained that Augustus would really have liked to appoint him his heir,[11] and even the offer of Augustus to have his will read in the senate did not alleviate doubts, being of course a sham offer and consequently turned down. Agrippa, annoyed about what appeared (at least in retrospect) a staged performance on the death-bed,[12] withdrew from Rome to Mytilene,[13] and Augustus had to calm down the 'republican' circles of the senate with his resignation from the consulship, a position he had occupied uninterruptedly from 31 BC onwards, – this being of course another 'comedy of abdication'.

In the autumn of 23 BC Marcellus himself, the nineteen-year-old hopeful, became severely ill and succumbed soon after to the medical skills of Antonius Musa. The death of Marcellus was certainly a severe blow for Augustus and his long-term dynastic plans. On the other hand, further developments show that Augustus was by no means consumed with grief (as reported about Octavia, Marcellus' mother[14]), but exploited the death of his nephew for propaganda purposes. He staged a grandiose state funeral, personally gave the *laudatio funebris* for Marcellus, and had the corpse buried in his own colossal mausoleum on the *campus Martius*, which was finished just recently.[15] After an appropriate period of time, assumed to be mid-21 BC, Augustus married off his daughter Julia again, this time to none less than the recalled Agrippa himself, forcing him to get a divorce from his wife. As early as 20 BC the first grandchild was born, in 17 BC the second, both gradually assuming the role that had been held by Marcellus.[16]

So much for the historical context. In those years, Vergil was working on the *Aeneid*, the completion of which was impatiently awaited by Augustus. Even from Spain, while on the previously-mentioned Cantabrian campaign, he wrote letters, asking Vergil to send him a part of the *Aeneid*.[17] The poet, however, refused, claiming that he still had research to do[18] – presumably he was at this time still working on the prose draft of his work. Only much later, in 22 or even in 21 BC, did he recite to Augustus and his family Books 2, 4, and 6, which were obviously the first ones to reach an acceptable degree of completion. At line 883 of Book 6: *tu Marcellus eris*,[19] Octavia fainted and could only be revived with some effort;[20] but she would not have missed much, because the remaining lines, concerning the return of Aeneas to the world of the living through the so-called Gate of False Dreams, have not been understood to this day.[21]

II. The Marcellus passage in Vergil

In interpreting the Marcellus passage, I am not going to emphasize the links with the tradition of the funeral speech and the burial epigram, as has been done by Eduard Norden[22] and, in our times, by Frederick Brenk,[23] but shall instead endeavour to stress the passage's function in the context of the pageant of heroes, the sixth Book in general, and the *Aeneid* as a whole. I assume, in accordance with most scholars, that the Marcellus episode is not a later addition but an integral part of the *Heldenschau*.[24] Its function obviously is to let the revelational speech of Anchises end not like a thunderbolt with the famous imperial promise: *Tu regere imperio populos, Romane, memento...* (*Aen.* 6.851), but on a quieter note: 'For he did not wish to close on a note of triumph and exultation', as Brooks Otis[25] says (and has been quoted more or less literally by many others since).[26] In this interpretation, however, the panegyric tones of the passage remain a problem; they do not seem to match the sad mood most noticeable at the beginning and the end of the passage. Panegyric are, for example, the mention of the *pompa funebris*[27] and of the newly built Augustan mausoleum (*Aen.* 6.872–4), the strongly emphasized virtues of Marcellus, his *pietas*, his *prisca fides* and, particularly, his courage in war (*Aen.* 6.878–9) – all this reminds one of the *clupeus virtutis* –, finally the extreme hopes for the future, to which the young Marcellus gave rise (*Aen.* 6.875–7) – passages which Vergil probably borrowed from Augustus' own funeral speech together with the reference to the great ancestor of the Marcelli, the famous commander in the war with Hannibal and conqueror of Syracuse (*Aen.* 6.854–9). No wonder: Vergil and

Augustus had both studied the textbooks of the rhetors closely,[28] which recommend in the case of the prematurely deceased, if they themselves lacked deeds of their own, to praise their ancestors and put the emphasis on the hope the deceased had given rise to instead.[29]

With this juxtaposition of panegyric and melancholy, of triumph and grief, of hope and despair, the Marcellus passage can be seen as a touchstone for any interpretation of the *Aeneid*; depending on the school of thought, the one or other aspect will of course be emphasized more strongly. The different schools of Vergilian interpretation will be mentioned later – for the time being, I would like to concentrate on some generally accepted aspects of the Marcellus passage. Central in all cases is the idea of the victim. Otis rightly pointed out that Marcellus prefigures similar characters in the second half of the *Aeneid* – Pallas, Lausus, Nisus and Euryalus, Camilla. 'The ordeal of empire is based on sacrifice, especially sacrifice of the young.'[30] One could add further sacrifices, especially from Book 6 itself – Palinurus and Misenus – who will, however, not be dealt with in detail here; Alexander McKay has commented conclusively on these cases.[31] Even Icarus' tragic death, which opens the sixth Book, clearly belongs here; his importance, too, will be shown later. The question at hand concerns the legitimacy and purpose of these sacrifices.[32]

In the case of Marcellus a plausible answer is, in my opinion, possible. To this purpose one has to stress another aspect of the Marcellus passage far more than has hitherto been done: the aspect of *hybris* or *superbia*. After Anchises has formulated the famous line, *parcere subiectis et debellare superbos* (*Aen.* 6.853) as a maxim of Roman foreign policy, the following passage contains a definite warning against one's own, that is Roman (or more precisely, Augustan) *superbia*:

> Too mighty, O gods, ye deemed the Roman stock would be, were these gifts lasting.[33]

> ...nimium vobis Romana propago
> visa potens, superi, propria haec si dona fuissent.
> (*Aen.* 6.870–1)[34]

If the uniquely talented Marcellus[35] had lived, already taken to their hearts by the populace as their crown prince, this could have aroused the envy of the gods[36] and so led to a far more serious threat to the Augustan rule than the death of Marcellus could ever have been. Viewed rationally and in political terms, the premature death of his nephew saved Augustus from several difficulties: from a serious disagreement with Agrippa who was suspicious of the young rival,[37] from trouble with Livia who resented the rejection of her own son, Tiberius,[38] and also from a republican-minded opposition in the senate which would not have tolerated steps towards a hereditary monarchy.[39] Not without reason did Augustus hasten to deny the statements of a certain M. Primus, the proconsul of Macedonia, who had justified his own high-handed activities by referring to instructions from Augustus and – even more scandalous – his son-in-law Marcellus. The princeps could keep the situation under control only by acting with extreme determination, when faced with the conspiracy started by the Primus affair, in which even his fellow consul played a leading part and in which Maecenas did not exactly distinguish himself either.[40]

Vergil wrapped these solid political arguments in the religious padding of a warning against too much power, which could provoke the wrath of the gods; and with hindsight (that is at the time of recitation of the sixth Book of the *Aeneid* in the year 22 or 21 BC) Augustus can only have shared Vergil's view. The question of a possible succession to Augustus was in any case postponed indefinitely, as a likely new carrier of hope, Augustus' grandson, was only at the pre-embryonic stage at that time.[41]

The interpretation of the Marcellus passage presented here can be supported by the evident parallel of Icarus. Charles Segal especially has pointed out that the death of Icarus and the death of Marcellus frame the sixth Book and are therefore structurally related; a parallel Segal saw enacted primarily in the role of the *pietas* which Daedalus and Anchises use to honour the dead.[42] The reference can be expanded typologically even further (I shall return to typology later on): while Daedalus, stricken with grief, cannot construct an adequate artistic monument to his son (*Aen.* 6.30–3) and Anchises can only carry out an *inane munus*[43] (*Aen.* 6.885–6), a short-term floral offering,[44] Augustus has far exceeded both by staging a grand funeral for Marcellus and putting him to rest in his mausoleum, destined for eternity. And so did Vergil – by composing a eulogy on Marcellus and giving him a prominent place in his everlasting poem.[45] Finally, we must remind ourselves that Icarus died because, in his *hybris*, he ignored the limitations set by the gods to humans, and rose too high into the sky; Marcellus' death was also, as we have seen, meant to be understood as a warning of the gods against such *hybris*. That this warning typologically refers to Augustus, becomes clear from the fact that it intrinsically refers to Aeneas, Augustus' forerunner: it is Aeneas who is forced to react to the fate of young Marcellus, it is Aeneas who asks his father about that sad young man,[46] and it is Aeneas who, to quote Otis, 'avoids the sin of *hybris* and feels the sadness of success'.[47]

At the end of Part Two, let us ask about the function of the Marcellus passage in the general structure of the *Aeneid*. Wendell Clausen has rightly pointed to the significance of that part in the context of the final scene of the *Aeneid*.[48] I shall, however, not repeat the well-known discussion on the final scene, but only point to a structural parallel between both halves of the work: both halves are open-ended. Beyond the death of Marcellus, Vergil does not give any explicit references to the future of the Augustan principate, which is nevertheless not completely indefinite; at the time of reciting Book 6 it was already easy to see that Augustus would set his hopes on the marriage of Agrippa and Julia. Correspondingly, Vergil gives no description of events beyond the death of Turnus, and the future of Aeneas' rule remains open, but not completely uncertain; there are prophecies, hopes, and allusions, and it is not inconsistent that there exists a thirteenth Book of the *Aeneid*, unfolding the 'implicit future' of the Vergilian epic.[49] And from that we can maybe draw the conclusion that the future of the Augustan principate, too, had not come to an end in Vergil's time.

III. Vergil's concept of history

In general, it is assumed that Vergil's teleological understanding of history views the Augustan principate as the high point and end of Roman history, understanding it as a kind of timeless eternal condition, i.e., a condition in which the dynamic flow of history has been superseded by the static condition of a heavenly Golden Age. There is admittedly little doubt that for Vergil Augustus is the *telos*, that is, the *aim* of history; nobody, however, would have claimed that in fact the *end* of history had been reached with him: Vergil and his readers were not naive enough to believe that history would not continue. But even in the *Aeneid* itself we find a definite statement to this effect. In the prophecy of Book 1 Jupiter says:

> For these (i.e., the Romans) I set neither bounds nor periods of empire; dominion without end have I bestowed
>
> > his ego nec metas rerum nec tempora pono:
> > imperium sine fine dedi.   (*Aen.* 1.278–9)

History under Augustus therefore does not lead to a timeless eternity, but is perpetuated beyond the actual point in time. The post-Augustan course of history is open, but there *is* definitely some kind of history. When Vergil in his *Aeneid* left the future mainly open, this is simply due to the fact that – despite widely held prejudices to the contrary – even he, though being the greatest Roman *vates*, could *not* predict the future.

What, then, can nevertheless be said about that future? I would like to try to answer this question by offering a typological interpretation. Although the concept of typology is well known in Vergilian scholarship, it is perhaps not worthless to reconsider that term here. A typological relationship is present when a person or event on the (fictitious) narrative level is put into relation to a person or event on the (real) historical time level in such a way that the fictitious person or event can be understood as a kind of precursor to the real person or event.[50]

One of the main typological relations in the *Aeneid* is obviously the one between Aeneas and Augustus. The future of the (fictitious) hero Aeneas can therefore be related to the future of the (real) Augustus. About the future of Aeneas we learn, to our surprise (or not to our surprise any more?), very little, and what little we learn is very vague. The early death of Aeneas and his elevation to god-like status are only hinted at (*Aen.* 12.794–5); there was the fear that Augustus, too, might die prematurely due to his delicate health, his deification was certainly to be expected and even foretold by Vergil himself at a different point (*Georg.* 1.24–5). Aeneas' hopes rest on his son Iulus, who can be observed growing up in the *Aeneid*; he was the son of Aeneas' first wife Creusa, who had stayed in Troy and had died there. Is it a coincidence that Augustus' hopes rested on Julia, his daughter from his first marriage? But maybe it *is* a coincidence, and we are in danger of overinterpretation. Let us therefore keep to more concrete indicators.

A key term for the future, reaching beyond the epic plot, is the word *nepotes*. It always denotes, at any rate in the plural, the offspring of people in the epic, usually of the Trojans, and occurs as a rule in prophecies, or similar passages. In the *Heldenschau*, the future Romans are twice (*Aen.* 6.683, 757) called *nepotes*, and the young Marcellus is called *aliquis magna de stirpe nepotum* (*Aen.* 6.864). In *Aen.* 4.629 Dido conjures up the Punic Wars, which the *nepotes* would wage, and similarly in *Aen.* 2.194 Sinon the Greek talks about the conquest of Greece by the *nepotes* of the Trojans. At the end of Book 8 Aeneas shoulders Vulcan's shield and the poet comments on this in the last line, saying:

uplifting on his shoulder the fame and fortunes of his children's children

attollens umero famamque et fata nepotum.   (*Aen.* 8.731)

In all these cases the term refers to individuals who are future from the point of view of Aeneas, and to individuals past or present from the point of view of poet and reader. There are, however, sections where the term refers to people who are in the future even from Vergil's perspective, or which at least could be so interpreted: three times in Book 3 (158, 409, 505) *nepotes* are mentioned, alluding to an unknown faraway future. If one assumes with Heinze[51] that Book 3 is one of the last books completed by Vergil, then one would presumably reach a time where there were already hopes for genuine *nepotes*. One should recall again that Augustus' first grandchild, son of Agrippa[52] and Julia, was born in 20 BC, which means in Vergil's lifetime.

To summarize: the situations at the end of the *Aeneid* and in the poet's time are typologically related. The future is in every case indefinite, but one can be certain that the *imperium sine fine* as prophesied by Jupiter will last and that the *nepotes* (whoever they will turn out to be) will continue the work of Aeneas *and* Augustus.

Let us finally return to the Marcellus passage. It is surprising that here the schools of interpretation, which have been differing in their opinions for thirty-five years,[53] are closer to each other than expected. In the sixties, the statements of scholars as widely different as Clausen[54] and Segal[55] on the one hand, and Otis[56] and Klingner[57] on the other, were still relatively similar; it was only in the seventies and eighties that opinions grew wider apart and produced extreme interpretations, as, for instance, that of Stephen Tracy: 'His (i.e., Marcellus') death pointedly symbolizes the death of the future',[58] or of Gordon Williams: 'The future beyond Augustus has collapsed.'[59] Recent interpretations, which mostly deal with the Marcellus passage *en passant* only, seem to tend towards more careful judgements,[60] while others keep on walking in the footsteps of the pessimistic interpretation, especially James O'Hara: 'With the lament for Marcellus the possibility is raised that the *gens* of the emperor will not carry on, that Augustus will not be like Aeneas, the Silvii, the Bruti, the Drusi, the Scipiones ...'[61] This is, as we have seen, an unhistorical view.

So what can be said in the end about Vergil and Augustus? Maybe one could reach agreement about *Vergil* by using the unifying words of Galinsky: 'Vergil, however, does not end on that note (sc., of triumph and exultation). ...Rome is not a nation of supermen; Rome has had and will continue to have her share of grief and losses... The depiction of Rome and her glory is complemented by the evocation of the purely human feeling of loss and helplessness.'[62] But *Augustus* the power politician certainly did not have much time for such profundity: Marcellus had left the stage of the Augustan world theatre suddenly and unexpectedly – but the show had to go on, and it did!

Reinhold F. Glei

IV. How the show did go on

Marcellus was dead but Augustus was not. It may be permitted, therefore, to add a little digression which shows how the show went on, how, so to speak, a satyr play followed the tragedy of Marcellus. The extraordinary honours for Marcellus had angered not only Agrippa, but also Livia, whose son Tiberius had been neglected in favour of the only slightly older Marcellus. Now, after the death of Marcellus, Livia could hope that Tiberius (and her second son Drusus, born in 38 BC) would play a more prominent role, and, as a matter of fact, both became the most glorious Augustan commanders, whose victories Horace could (or had to) celebrate in Pindaric odes.[63] In the meantime, however, the grandsons were growing up, and, as on a hydra one head, when struck off, is replaced by two new ones, so C. and L. Caesar became a twin-headed 'new edition' of Marcellus. But good fortune[64] – supposedly helped along a little by Livia[65] – carried off the two grandsons in AD 2 and 4, and Tiberius finally became Augustus' adoptive son and designated successor.

Presumably in this ambience of courtly intrigues is rooted a literary epilogue of the Marcellus episode, a parody of Vergil disguised as a youthful work of Vergil himself, the *Culex*. The small poem to a mosquito, handed down in the *Appendix Vergiliana*, has been shown by more recent philological research to be a forgery, written during the reign of Tiberius.[66] Taking up this line of interpretation in a recent study, Wolfram Ax has put forward and substantiated the thesis that the *Culex* poet intended to suggest an allegorical identification of the mosquito with Marcellus.[67]

Let us recall the contents of the *Culex*. The dead mosquito appears to a shepherd in his dream and reports its adventures in the underworld – including clear allusions to the Vergilian *Heldenschau*. At the end of the poem, the shepherd builds a grandiose monument for the mosquito which, in its architectural outline, its planting and other details clearly represents the Augustan mausoleum. The tiresome dead insect is buried in a gigantic tomb, following a parody of lines from Vergil's *Heldenschau*, at the end of which the death of an irksome rival put to rest in the mausoleum is lamented. And what does the reader of the *Culex* infer from all of this? Nothing else than this: *tu Marcellus eris!* It springs to the eyes that this malicious parody was written by a poet who was close to Tiberius, and it even cannot be ruled out that Tiberius himself was the author. Whatever the case may be, the author must have drawn an impish enjoyment out of foisting the work on to the same poet who sang Marcellus' praises.

The Show must go on: the Death of Marcellus and...the Augustan Principate

As can be seen, in antiquity one was definitely able to make fun of Vergil and his political partisanship, despite all the esteem in which the divine poet was held; we should follow this relaxed attitude and not persist in our Vergil-worship, no matter how many voices we think he is speaking with.

Notes

[1] Sueton. *Aug.* 99; translation by J.C. Rolfe (London/Cambridge, Mass., 2nd edn, 1951).

[2] Gardthausen (1896) 726, 'Komödie der Abdankung'.

[3] *R.G. Divi Augusti* 34: 'Post id tempus auctoritate omnibus praestiti, potestatis autem nihilo amplius habui quam ceteri, qui mihi quoque in magistratu conlegae fuerunt.'

[4] I am following, in general, Syme (1939) 341–8; for detailed references, see Kienast (1982) 84–92.

[5] Cf. Sueton. *Tib.* 6.4.

[6] *Anth. Pal.* 6.161. Another epigram of Crinagoras is found in *Anth. Pal.* 9.945.

[7] Hor., *Carm.* 1.12.45–9: 'Crescit occulto velut arbor aevo | fama Marcelli: micat inter omnis | Iulium sidus velut inter ignis | luna minores.'

[8] Cf. Cass. Dio 53.28.3 f.

[9] See, especially, Syme (1939) 341.

[10] Cf. Hor., *Epist.* 1.15.2.

[11] Cf. Tacitus, *Ann.* 2.41.5 and Seneca, *Cons. ad Marciam* 2.3; on the mausoleum, see now Hesberg/Panciera (1994) 54.

[12] See also Gardthausen (1896) 724.

[13] Cf. Suet., *Tib.* 10.1 and *Aug.* 66.3.

[14] Cf. Seneca, *Cons. ad Marciam* 2.3–5.

[15] Cf. Cass. Dio 53.30.5; Plut., *Marc.* 30; *Comp. Pelop. et Marc.* 1.

[16] See Grimal (1954) 58 and 48, n. 2.

[17] Cf. *Vita Donati* 31.

[18] The letter is cited in Macrobius, *Sat.* 1.24.11.

[19] On the exact meaning of that phrase, see now Shackleton Bailey (1986).

[20] Cf. *Vita Donati* 32.

[21] Scholarship on the 'Gates of Dreams' in Homer and Vergil has been examined in detail by Pollmann (1993).

[22] Sc. in his monumental commentary on Book 6 (1903, 4th edn, 1957), 338–46.

[23] Brenk (1986) 218–28.

[24] So already Norden (1903, 4th edn, 1957) 338–9; more recently, only Goold (1992, 118–22) votes for a 'Marcellus addition' to the *Heldenschau*.

[25] Otis (1964) 303.

[26] See, e.g., Klingner (1967) 494; Williams (1987) 40; Galinsky (1992) 82.

[27] The thesis of Skard (1965), taken up again by Burke (1979), that the whole *Heldenschau* resembled the historical *pompa funebris* for Marcellus, the

heroes being the *imagines* carried along in the *pompa*, is not convincing, because Vergil clearly does not describe a *pompa*, but rather a precursor of Mme Tussaud's.

[28] That Augustus' funeral speech was in a rhetorical sense 'conventional', is stated by Cassius Dio 53.30.5; on rhetorical convention in general, see Kierdorf (1980).

[29] The older and the younger Marcellus are 'balanced' (*instar*: *Aen*. 6.865); see Kraggerud (1996) 109–12.

[30] Otis (1964) 303.

[31] McKay (1984) 121–37.

[32] The *Opferthese* is overemphasized by Dupont/Neraudau (1970); their view that 'la mort de Marcellus, quelque cruelle qu'elle soit, est l'annonce, pour Rome, d'une proche renaissance' (259) is cynical. On the other hand, Mellinghoff-Bourgerie (1990) denies any justification of the sacrifices at all: 'Comment trouver une justification réelle à la mort de Marcellus? La résignation est la seule attitude sage' (110).

[33] All translations of the *Aeneid* are by H. Rushton Fairclough (London/Cambridge, Mass., 2nd edn, 1934/5).

[34] Brugnoli (1988) suggests that these lines are borrowed from Augustus' funeral speech, but would Augustus have warned himself against too much *superbia*?

[35] Horsfall (1989) is going too far in referring the famous lines *Aen*. 6.847 ff. *excudent alii...* to Marcellus' education in Greek arts and science.

[36] See, e.g., von Albrecht (1967) 181.

[37] See above, n. 13.

[38] There were even rumours of Livia having caused the death of Marcellus: Cass. Dio 53.33.4.

[39] See Syme (1939) 343.

[40] For detailed information, see Kienast (1982) 86–7.

[41] Agrippa was called back from Lesbos and married to Augustus' daughter Julia in the summer of 21 BC. As soon as possible, in 20 BC, C. Caesar began his earthly life.

[42] Segal (1966) 50–6.

[43] Scholars were puzzled with the epithet *inane*, but Servius gives the simple explanation: 'inani munere] secundum Epicureos, non profuturo' (ad *Aen*. 6.885).

[44] For the motif, see Brenk (1990) 218–23.

[45] Of course, this is not the view of the 'pessimistic' school; see, especially, Putnam (1987 (1995)) and my review in *Gymnasium* 103 (1996), 470–2.

[46] This is rightly pointed out by Lyne (1987) 208; Henry (1989) 141; and O'Hara (1990) 168–9.

[47] Otis (1964) 315.

[48] Clausen (1964) 145.

[49] Written in AD 1428 by the young Maffeo Vegio (1407–58) from Lodi: see Schneider (1985).

[50] For a more detailed discussion, see Glei (1991) 24-8. The 'fathers' of Vergilian typological interpretation are Knauer (1964) 353-6; Binder (1971)

1–4; and Buchheit (1973) 23–50.

[51] Heinze (3rd edn, 1915) 82.

[52] One should also consider the important role Agrippa is playing on Aeneas' shield (*Aen.* 8.682).

[53] On the history of the two schools, see Glei (1991) 11–24 and my forthcoming *Forschungsbericht* in CTA, Vol. 6.

[54] Clausen (1964) 146: 'The book might have ended – were Virgil not Virgil – with the praise of Augustus, which occurs earlier, and an optimistic view of the shining future. But the book ends rather with a somber and pathetic laudation of the younger Marcellus, Augustus' nephew and destined successor, who had excited such high hopes, but who was dead when these lines were written.'

[55] Segal (1966) 55: 'He (i.e. Marcellus) exemplifies the persistence in history of an element which negates the possibility for total happiness, a degree of suffering built into the structure of things.'

[56] See the quotations given above in section II of this paper.

[57] Klingner (1967) 494: 'Es liegt nun aber nicht in Virgils Art, die Offenbarung des Anchises und dieses Buch seines Gedichts mit verherrlichenden Worten stolz zu beschließen. ...Es kommt zu einem gedämpften Schluß.'

[58] Tracy (1975) 38; for another extremely pessimistic view, see Mack (1978) 71: 'In any case, the prophecy that has so often been assumed to proclaim a glorious future ends with death, not with life, and Marcellus' death casts a shadow back over what has gone before.' There is, on the other hand, a rather moderate ambiguity in the statement of Johnson (1976) 107: 'They (i.e., the lines on Marcellus) also suggest a tragedy, indeed a bitterness, that threatens to overwhelm the magnificence of Roman achievement.'

[59] Williams (1983) 214; see also 149: 'The great hope for the future has been totally destroyed'. Similarly, Boyle (1986, 146) is speaking of 'the failure of the ideology of empire.'

[60] See, e.g., Lyne (1987, 208 n. 1), who stresses the 'heavy emphasis throughout on pain, cost, and suffering', but does not declare the Roman future 'collapsed'. Henry (1989, 141) gives a statement very similar to Lyne's, but without citing him. See further Feeney (1986, 15): 'Augustus' designated heir receives high praise, but waste and futility are the ruling tones.'

[61] O'Hara (1990) 169.

[62] Galinsky (1992) 82, widely following Otis

[63] See Glei (1995) 333–50.

[64] Suetonius is citing the testament of Augustus which begins as follows: 'Quoniam atrox fortuna Gaium et Lucium filios mihi eripuit...' (*Tib.* 23). Cf. also Augustus himself in the *Res Gestae* (14): 'Filios meos, quos iuvenes mihi eripuit fortuna, Gaium et Lucium Caesares...'

[65] Cf. Tacitus, *Ann.* 1.3.3 and 1.10.5.

[66] See Güntzschel (1972) and especially Ax (1984).

[67] Ax (1992) 89–129, with full references.

Bibliography

Albrecht, M. von
- 1967 'Vergils Geschichtsauffassung in der Heldenschau', *WS* 80, 156–82.

Ax, W.
- 1984 'Die pseudovergilische 'Mücke' – ein Beispiel römischer Literaturparodie?', *Philologus* 128, 230–49.
- 1992 'Marcellus, die Mücke. Politische Allegorien im Culex?', *Philologus* 136, 89–129.

Binder, G.
- 1971 *Aeneas und Augustus. Interpretationen zum 8. Buch der Aeneis*, Meisenheim am Glan.

Boyle, A.J.
- 1986 *The Chaonian Dove. Studies in the* Eclogues, Georgics, *and* Aeneid *of Virgil*, Leiden.

Brenk, F.E.
- 1986 '*Avorum spes et purpurei flores*: the eulogy for Marcellus in *Aeneid* VI', *AJPh* 107, 218–28.
- 1990 '*Purpureos spargam flores*: a Greek motif in the *Aeneid*?', *CQ* n.s. 40, 218–23.

Brugnoli, G.
- 1988 'Verg. Aen. 6, 871', *GIF* 40, 229–30.

Buchheit, V.
- 1973 'Vergilische Geschichtsdeutung', *GB* 1, 23–50.

Burke, P.F.
- 1979 'Roman rites for the dead and *Aeneid* 6', *CJ* 74, 220–8.

Clausen, W.
- 1964 'An interpretation of the *Aeneid*', *HSCP* 68, 139–47.

Dupont, F. and Neraudau, J.-P.
- 1970 'Marcellus dans le chant VI de l'Énéide', *REL* 48, 259–76.

Feeney, D.C.
- 1986 'History and revelation in Vergil's underworld', *PCPhS* 212, 1–24.

Galinsky, K.
- 1992 *Classical and Modern Interactions. Postmodern Architecture, Multiculturalism, Decline, and Other Issues*, Austin, Tex.

Gardthausen, V.
- 1896 *Augustus und seine Zeit (Teil 1, Bd. 2; Teil 2, Bd. 2)*, Leipzig. (Repr. Aalen, 1964.)

Glei, R.F.
- 1991 *Der Vater der Dinge. Interpretationen zur politischen, literarischen und kulturellen Dimension des Krieges bei Vergil*, Trier.
- 1995 'Ein Paradigma höfischer Kommunikation: Horaz' viertes Odenbuch als Spiegel dynastischer Politik', in G. Binder and K. Ehlich (eds.) *Kommunikation durch Zeichen und Wort*: 333–50. Trier.
- Forthcoming 'American Scholarship on Vergil', in J.R. Fears, W. Haase and M. Reinhold (eds.) *The Classical Tradition and the Americas* Vol. 6, Berlin and New York.

Goold, G.P.
- 1992 'The voice of Virgil. The pageant of Rome in *Aeneid* 6', in T. Woodman and J. Powell (eds.) *Author and Audience in Latin Literature*, 110-23, Cambridge.

Grimal, P.
- 1954 'Le livre VI de l' 'Énéide' et son actualité en 23 av. J.-C.', *REA* 56, 40-60.

Güntzschel, D.
- 1972 *Beiträge zur Datierung des Culex*, Münster.

Heinze, R.
- 1915 *Virgils epische Technik*, 3rd edn, Leipzig and Berlin. (Repr. Darmstadt, 1976.)

Henry, E.
- 1989 *The Vigour of Prophecy. A Study of Virgil's* Aeneid. Carbondale and Edwardsville.

Hesberg, H. von and Panciera, S.
- 1994 *Das Mausoleum des Augustus. Der Bau und seine Inschriften*, München.

Horsfall, N.
- 1989 'Virgil and Marcellus' education', *CQ* n.s. 39, 266-7.

Johnson, W.R.
- 1976 *Darkness Visible. A Study of Vergil's* Aeneid, Berkeley, Los Angeles and London.

Kienast, D.
- 1982 *Augustus. Prinzeps und Monarch*, Darmstadt.

Kierdorf, W.
- 1980 *Laudatio Funebris. Interpretationen und Untersuchungen zur Entwicklung der römischen Leichenrede*, Meisenheim am Glan.

Klingner, F.
- 1967 *Virgil. Bucolica, Georgica, Aeneis*, Zürich and Stuttgart.

Knauer, G.N.
- 1964 *Die Aeneis und Homer. Studien zur poetischen Technik Vergils mit Listen der Homerzitate in der Aeneis*, Göttingen. (2nd edn, 1979.)

Kraggerud, E.
- 1996 'Against the consensus. Some problems of text and interpretation in Vergil', *SO* 71, 102-14.

Lyne, R.O.A.M.
- 1987 *Further Voices in Vergil's Aeneid*, Oxford.

Mack (Amis), S.
- 1978 *Patterns of Time in Vergil*, Hamden, Conn.

McKay, A.G.
- 1984 'Vergilian heroes and toponymy', in H.D. Evjen (ed.) *Mnemai. Classical Studies in Memory of Karl K. Hulley*, 121-37, Chico, Calif.

Mellinghoff-Bourgerie, V.
- 1990 *Les incertitudes de Virgile. Contributions épicuriennes à la théologie de l'Énéide*, Bruxelles.

Norden, E.
- 1903 *P. Vergilius Maro, Aeneis Buch VI*, Leipzig. (4th edn, 1957.)

O'Hara, J.J.
  1990 *Death and the Optimistic Prophecy in Vergil's Aeneid*, Princeton, N.J.
Otis, B.
  1964 *Virgil. A Study in Civilized Poetry*, Oxford.
Pollmann, K.
  1993 'Etymologie, Allegorese und epische Struktur. Zu den Toren der Träume bei Homer und Vergil', *Philologus* 137, 232–51.
Putnam, M.C.J.
  1987 'Daedalus, Virgil, and the end of art', *AJPh* 108, 173–98. (Repr. in M.C.J. Putnam, *Virgil's Aeneid. Interpretation and Influence*, 73–99, Chapel Hill/London, 1995.)
Schneider, B.
  1985 *Das Aeneissupplement des Maffeo Vegio. Eingeleitet, nach den Handschriften herausgegeben, übersetzt und mit einem Index versehen*, Weinheim.
Segal, C.P.
  1966 '*Aeternum per saecula nomen*. The Golden Bough and the tragedy of history: Part II', *Arion* 5, 34–72.
Shackleton Bailey, D.R.
  1986 'Tu Marcellus eris', *HSCP* 90, 199–205.
Skard, E.
  1965 'Die Heldenschau in Vergils Aeneis', *SO* 40, 53–65.
Syme, R.
  1939 *The Roman Revolution*, Oxford.
Tracy, S.V.
  1975 'The Marcellus passage (*Aeneid* 6.860–86) and *Aeneid* 9–12', *CJ* 70, 37–42.
Williams, G.
  1983 *Technique and Ideas in the* Aeneid, New Haven and London.
Williams, R.D.
  1987 *The* Aeneid, London.

Not available to me was:
Yamasawa, T.
  1990 'Virgil's lamentation over Marcellus (*Aen.* 6.860–86)', *Classical Studies* 7, 77–98 (in Japanese, with English summary, p. 141), Kyoto.

7

ALLECTO'S FIRST VICTIM: A STUDY OF VERGIL'S AMATA
Aeneid 7.341–405 and 12.1–80

Elaine Fantham

I. Before Vergil: the record of an evil queen

For most students of Latin literature Vergil has so shaped their conception of the early society of Latium that they see the poet's epic invention if not as history, yet as the authentic Roman tradition. Certainly few readers of Vergil's dense moral and psychological narrative would fault his choices on dramatic grounds; but we sometimes forget how bold his innovations were, whether in relation to the historical tradition or to ancient drama and epic.

The reader seeking to understand Vergil's Amata as a literary creation might start by considering the precedents for her social and familial role. Here is a married woman, old enough to be mother of a girl whose marriage is the focus of the dramatic action. In comedy such a woman is either foolish or obstructive; if she features in tragedy she is more likely to be destructive like Clytemnestra. Such obstruction is to be expected when the marriageable daughter's life is demanded by the gods, as with Iphigeneia; the pious queen Praxithea in Euripides' *Erechtheus*, who gladly sacrifices her daughters for Athens in a long and edifying speech is truly – and perhaps fortunately – exceptional.[1] But surely the dominant model in epic and tragedy for the aging mother is Hecuba, whether we think of her as beseeching her best son Hector not to risk his life before his final combat, or mourning his death, or as a captive widow, grieving for and avenging her children in Euripides' *Hecuba* and *Trojan Women*, or again as Vergil's Hecuba, rebuking and trying to protect her old husband in his death scene at Troy's fall.[2]

We should keep these possible literary models in mind, while reviewing the various legends of Aeneas' arrival in Latium. It is well known that Vergil transformed the traditional account of the coming of the Trojans to Latium in order to align Aeneas with the lawful king Latinus and represent his marriage to Latinus' daughter as intended and achieved by the King himself. What traces of Amata could he have found?

In Cato's *Origines*, according to Servius,[3] Aeneas first fought against both Latinus and Turnus; then after Latinus died in battle, Aeneas fought Turnus and Mezentius in a second campaign where both Aeneas and Turnus met their deaths. In another citation Servius reports Cato as saying that after Aeneas' marriage to Lavinia Turnus embarked on war in anger against both Aeneas and Latinus.[4] Both of Livy's alternative versions secure an early alliance of Aeneas and Latinus and report Turnus' war on Trojans and Latins alike.[5] But Latinus' queen *Amata* is found only in a different tradition, incompatible with Cato's lost narrative, and one which is particularly important because it gives her an obstructive and indeed destructive role.

When Vergil introduces Latinus, he stresses his age and lack of an heir (7.50–1): "He had no son or male offspring, which had been snatched away rising in first youth", *filius huic...prolesque virilis | nulla fuit, primaque oriens erepta iuventa est*. Here Servius' commentary shows that offspring (*proles*) refers to two sons, not one, and the pathetic *erepta*[6] substitutes for a hideous palace intrigue; "Amata had killed in a partisan plot Latinus' two sons who were betrothing Lavinia to Aeneas according to their father's will."[7] Servius Auctus offers the variant that these sons were blinded by their mother when Aeneas was betrothed to Lavinia after Turnus' death.[8] Where does this story come from? Should it be related to Servius' last comment on Amata, the note on her death by hanging in Vergil's twelfth book? He notes that she suffered a different manner of death, by starvation, according to another tradition – indefinite *"alii"* in the later Servian manuscripts, but Fabius Pictor, Rome's first historian, earlier even than Cato – in the superior Floriacensis.[9]

With one slight modification of Servius Auctus these references offer a coherent narrative of palace conflict, in which Amata plays the role of murderous kingmaker, a precursor of Tanaquil or Tullia – or, according to some, Livia – eliminating stepsons to secure power for her favorite.[10] But Servius' comment only makes sense if Latinus' sons acted to betroth Lavinia to Aeneas after his death, and Amata had the power to kill (or blind) them to prevent it.[11] Ovid too seems to reflect a dominant role for Amata in his introduction at *Fasti* 4.879 to Mezentius' demand of the Latin *primitiae* which rightly belonged to Jupiter: the war, he says, was fought to decide whether Turnus or Aeneas should be Amata's son-in-law.[12] The absence of Latinus from

Ovid's account may also imply his death, leaving Amata as dowager and arbiter of Lavinia's marriage.

In this version, discarded by Vergil, Amata outlives Latinus and tries to steer the succession away from Aeneas, the dead king's appointed heir. In the earliest annalistic tradition the villainous queen either starved herself, or was perhaps starved to death when Aeneas killed Turnus and besieged and captured the city. Dionysius of Halicarnassus also introduces Amata in association with her cousin Turnus (ἀνέψιον...Τυρρηνόν): according to his account she instigated Turnus to put himself at the head of a Rutulian rebellion against Latinus, because he "blamed Latinus over Lavinia's marriage".[13] The significant difference is that Turnus is identified only through his kinship with Amata, and far from being chief of the Rutuli, seems to be an aggrieved Latin deserter who wages war on Latinus. Nothing more is said of Amata in this version; Latinus and Turnus both fall in battle, thus leaving Aeneas as unchallenged ruler, beyond the reach of conspiracy.

It seems that here too Amata is only mentioned in her role as partisan of Turnus, though Dionysius includes no hints at the murder plot. Whatever the full narrative, before Vergil's adaptation Amata and Turnus belonged together by blood[14] and in their opposition to Aeneas, and their dooms were interconnected.

These variants may be confusing but they cast light on the directions and motives of Vergil's remodeling. Book Seven of the *Aeneid* opens with a tranquil community and an apparently harmonious family. Latinus' daughter at first goes unnamed (52–5) and so does his royal wife (*regia coniunx*), introduced only in her subordinate role as partisan of the chief suitor Turnus, eager "with a strange passion" (*miro...amore*) to link him to her family as son-in-law. Nothing is seen of the queen in the ensuing account of the portents that cluster around Lavinia and Latinus' consultations of Faunus' oracle. She is forgotten until Juno summons Allecto from hell to create havoc in Latinus' house and community. Juno's appeal to Allecto stresses the Fury's special power to destroy family loyalties – "you can arm loving brothers for battle against each other, and overthrow a family with feuding" (*atque odiis versare domos*, 7.335–6) – and the Fury moves from the private to the public realm in implementing her task. She first uses Amata to overthrow Latinus' family, then drives Turnus, and after him the Laurentine countryfolk, to arm for battle.

II. Allecto's assault on the queen

For Vergil's first readers Allecto was a gruesome innovation; they could hardly have guessed where she would aim her assault. Indeed her presence in this epic has seemed to many a generic intrusion, all the stranger because the tragic function of Furies and Erinyes had been to harry those already guilty of crimes, usually blood crimes, against their family. Only Lyssa, the madness sent by Hera/Juno to Heracles, can be seen as a precedent for madness inflicted on one innocent of family crime. When the Fury makes for Latinus' palace, the *tecta tyranni* (342), she makes for "the quiet doorway of Amata" (343). But although Vergil mentions the queen's name here for the first time, he does not identify her. Does this mean that she was a familiar figure of the myth to most readers?

Would they also recall her previous reputation and the offences she would commit? Perhaps this goes too far: in the time-frame of the *Aeneid* Amata will never reach the phase in her career when tradition assigned her these family crimes; indeed Vergil will bring about her death before that of Latinus. Even so it may be her murderous record that originally prompted the poet to introduce the Fury.

Scholars have reacted very differently to Allecto's infection of the queen, as indeed of Turnus. Heinze rightly noted Vergil's representation of Allecto as a personification of discord rather than simply of madness. Hence his focus on the secondary, social, phase of Amata's frenzy, when she rouses up the other married women to abandon their homes in Bacchic rioting. Heinze notes the impact of this collective madness "making the mad lust for war spread all over Latium; the women, who are more susceptible to this infectious mania, are the agents whereby the men, who are slower to be moved *en masse*, are all individually inflamed to resist Latinus' plans".[15] Otis, developing Heinze's discussion of Allecto in relation to Lyssa, cites Fraenkel to argue the same point, "Allecto's visits to Amata and Turnus are each carefully divided into two parts in such a way that the emotional feeling of the first is intensified and made public in the second."[16] Certainly each immediate victim of Allecto is associated with a group uprising – Amata arouses the wives, Turnus calls out the warriors, and the royal shepherd whose daughter's pet deer is killed leads a rising of the countryfolk – but I would like to pass over the undeniable instrumentality of each victim in generating the war and focus, instead, on the psychological depiction of the individual Amata until the moment of her death.

More recent scholars have naturally found Allecto herself significant of a wider change in ancient attitudes to the supernatural. Ralph Johnson felt that with Vergil's introduction of Allecto and the Dira,

Allecto's first Victim: a Study of Vergil's Amata

Roman culture was "passing from the world of Graeco-Roman rationalism into the worlds of Seneca's tragedies, of Lucan, of Apuleius", and adds:

> the ministers of darkness are not new creations in the sense that they have no models in Greek *mimesis* but they are new in their revelling in evil, their pleasure in mindless destruction...their ability to dominate the *muthos* of a poem and in their ability to threaten to dominate the *praxis* of a poem.[17]

The growing dominance of these supernatural embodiments of evil in post-Vergilian epic is one of the most powerfully treated themes of Philip Hardie's superb study of Vergil's influence on post-Augustan epic. For Hardie "The fury is like a virus that replicates itself in her victim, often in multiple copies... Allecto finally leaves the upper world when she has created versions of herself in Amata, Turnus and the Italian shepherds."[18] For Johnson, Allecto's attack on Amata is "a description of how the human soul is sapped of its reason", but he affirms the simultaneous externality and subjectivity of this F/fury:

> All of these agents of evil become states of mind for those whose minds and volition they have perverted; but they nevertheless remain realities that exist in the space and time of the poem which they inhabit together with the human figures.

To offer a verdict, as Johnson and Hardie have done, on the objective reality or unreality of these forces of evil, does not affect the question of Amata's and Turnus' moral responsibility for the madness with which Allecto infects them. Against the considered view of other scholars I would like to argue that the issue of moral responsibility is in one sense irrelevant, and in another it is beyond determination. It is more helpful to consider how both Amata and Turnus are psychologically predisposed for the Fury's assault. Since so much more attention has been paid to the infection of Turnus in the succeeding episode, his behavior may provide a measure by which to assess Amata. Here is the description of the Fury's unseen infection of the queen.

> Then Allecto, saturated with the Gorgon's poison, went first to Latium and the lofty palace of the ruler of the Laurentines, and beset the quiet door of Amata's chamber, Amata seething with womanly concerns and resentment about the coming of the Trojans and the marriage with Turnus. The goddess hurled at her a serpent from her murky locks and set it inside her breast to reach her innermost heart, so that frenzied by this horror she would throw the whole household into confusion.
> Slipping between her garments and her smooth breasts he glided without contact and instilled his venomous breath unknown to the

woman he was maddening: the massive serpent turns into the gold twisted round her neck, turns into the tapes of her long fillet, entwines her hair, and oozing strays over her body. (341–53)

As the evocative *tacitum* of 343 suggests, Amata is alone and outwardly calm, but seething with the suppressed resentment of a woman over the coming of the Trojans and *Turni...hymenaeis*, – not Lavinia's marriage, but that of Turnus. Why? Because the marriage is needed to guarantee Turnus' future as heir and successor to Latinus's throne. The Ennian metaphor of Amata's cares and passion "stewing" the burning woman (*femineae ardentem curaeque iraeque coquebant*)[19] will find its developed counterpart in the full simile of 462–6 when Turnus, stricken by Allecto's torch with raging love of battle, seethes like a cauldron whose boiling waters threaten to spill over its rim. Unlike the sleeping Turnus in the following scene, Amata is conscious, like Turnus she is *ardens* (a word not usually applied to a woman),[20] but through the unseen and even unfelt influence of the serpent as it glides without physical contact (*attactu nullo*) under her clothing, Amata is infected with a slow-acting frenzy. At this stage, unlike Turnus, to whom the "priestess" Allecto openly reveals her fiendish nature in word and deed, Amata seems untroubled, only potentially *furens* (350). Unlike Turnus, who leaps out of bed shouting for arms, Amata is next seen pleading in emotional, but still rational, terms with her husband. The reader is left to deduce the occasion, since neither time nor place are given for her speech, and the addressee must be inferred from *O genitor* (361).

At 354 the temporal adverbs of the opening sentence both mark Amata's initial calm (*dum prima*) and mark it as a lull (*necdum*) before the oncoming emotional storm:

> And *as long as the first phase* of the scourge gliding in with sticky poison assails her feelings and weaves fire into her bones, but her spirit has *not yet* caught fire with all her heart, she spoke gently, rather like a mother, with many tears over the marriage of her daughter and the Trojan: (354–8)
>
> "Is Lavinia being handed over to these exiled Trojans in marriage, father, and have you no pity for your daughter or yourself, or of her mother, whom the treacherous brigand will abandon, carrying the girl away as he seeks the high seas with the first wind from the north? But isn't this how the Phrygian shepherd broke into Sparta to carry off Leda's daughter Helen to the cities of the Trojans? What of your holy pledge? What of your former concern for your family and the right hand you so often gave to your kinsman Turnus?" (359–70)

Already Vergil has begun to insinuate the tragic affinity between Amata and Dido, in the form taken by the supernatural furor – call it passion or madness – which determines each woman's loss of control and ultimate downfall. Of the many scholars who have noted this, La Penna's article and contribution to the *Enciclopedia* are the most powerful,[21] yet each new analysis discovers more evidence of Vergil's modelling of the later and less important queen upon his tragic heroine. Verbal reminiscences from the beginning of Allecto's attack look back to the moment in *Aeneid* 1 that first foreshadows Dido's lovesickness. The first reference to her poisoning (*fallitque furentem... inspirans* 7.350–1, and cf. *veneno* 354) uses verbs of concealed infection that draw on Venus' instruction to Cupid (*occultum inspires ignem fallasque veneno*, 1.688); the recapitulation (*atque ossibus implicat ignem*, 7.355) echoes the language of Vergil's narrative in 1.660 (*atque ossibus implicet ignem*). Twice, then, the account of Amata's infection recalls the way in which another goddess, Venus, sets out to infect Dido with another kind of mad passion.

Only with the failure of her appeal to Latinus (373–4) does Amata reach the breaking point, descending into the tragic phase of her affliction; yet the echoes of Dido in her language subliminally alert the reader to anticipate the crisis. La Penna has noted the formulation common to the first part of this appeal (7.359–66) and Dido's appeal to the departing Aeneas. Amata's accusation that Latinus feels no pity (*nec te miseret*, 7.360–1) recalls Dido's accusation that Aeneas feels no love, and her appeal for pity (*nec te noster amor...tenet*, 4.307–8; *miserere domus labentis*, 318). If these echoes seem too commonplace, note instead how Amata foresees Aeneas' departure "at the onset of the north wind" (*primo Aquilone*, 7.361) in words that echo both language and event from Dido's reproach: "and you hasten to cross the deep sea in the full onslaught of the north winds", *et mediis properas Aquilonibus ire per altum* (4.310). (It does not affect the verbal recall that the wind which is obstructive for sailors from North Africa or Italy is here seen as favourable.)

Leaving aside the common pathos of the two women's appeals, it is worth pausing to examine Amata's arguments by the standards of masculine rationality. Here, and to a lesser extent in Book 12 also, she has ordinary secular reason on her side. Marrying the princess to a stranger is the stuff of myth, not social practice. A father will usually betroth his daughter to a man of known parentage and status from his own community, if not for her sake, then for the sake of the family's descent. Only when political alliance enters the picture will he contemplate marriage to an outsider, perhaps to avoid jealousy between internal suitors, perhaps for the political asset of new foreign support. Thus Augustus himself betrothed his daughter to his sister's son Marcellus in 23, and Livia would later encourage the widow's marriage to her own son Tiberius. It is true that according to Suetonius Mark Antony claimed that Augustus betrothed Julia first to his son Iullus Antonius, then to Cotison the king of the Getae, but Suetonius himself does not endorse this unlikely tale.[22]

From the point of view of the Italian queen the outsider Aeneas has nothing going for him but the reported favour of the gods; he has arrived from a ruined city without land, and Vergil's readers know, if Amata does not, that his previous sexual relationship resulted in the desertion of a queen and near-collapse of her city.[23] If this freebooter leaves with Lavinia, Latinus will not only lose his daughter: he will have no heir – hence "and you do not take pity on your daughter or yourself, nor on her mother", *nec te miseret nataeque tuique | nec matris miseret* (360–1).[24] Both Latinus and Amata will speak to Turnus as a dear kinsman and see the risk of his death as a loss equally to family and community at the opening of Book 12 – to which we will return. What differentiates Amata from Latinus is her refusal to accept his understanding of the will of the gods, shown by her persistent attempt to reinterpret the oracle of Faunus to fit her candidate, Turnus. Call it self-deception, even willful blindness to a higher "categorical imperative", she is acting in what she sees as the best interests of the family and its continuity.[25] As Dido begs Aeneas to take pity on a failing family (one without children) so Amata in Book 12 will invoke the endangered family of Latinus.[26]

III. The poison takes effect

It is Latinus' persistent refusal that provokes the second phase of Amata's affliction, when the poison penetrates her entrails (374–5).[27] The serpent's infection and the effects of its poison are kept distinct. The crisis is signalled by line 376: "only then does the unhappy woman, driven by overwhelming supernatural manifestations...rave," *tum vero infelix ingentibus excita monstris | ...furit*.[28] Vergil marks with the simile of the whirling top (378–84) the delayed onset of madness which will be immediate in Allecto's assault on Turnus. Amata's public loss of control seems to grow during the simile of the top, returning in the form of hyperbolic plurals converting the single vast city (*immensam... per urbem*, 377) into whole "cities and warlike peoples" (384).

> Then at last, driven by enormous horrors, the unhappy queen raves frenzied and out of control through the vast city, like a top at times spinning under the twist of the whip, which boys intent on sport whirl in

a huge spiral around the empty halls – driven by the lash it is swept in its curved trajectory, and the childish band, unaware, gapes amazed at the whirling toy of boxwood: their blows give it life; just as swiftly as its racing is Amata driven through the centre of cities and warlike peoples.

As David West has shown, this simile is integrated by many correspondences with elements of the narrative, extending as far as the *stimuli* of 405 which correspond to the boys' lashing of the top.[29] Robert Rabel notes how its power is increased by crossreference with the other *turbo*, the storm generated by Juno through Aeolus (*Aen.* 1.83), and by the echo of Chrysippus' Stoic analogy between a top or hoop (whose mobility is inherent and merely intensified by whipping) and humans, whose natural predisposition to anger or passion is merely intensified by external stimuli.[30]

Amata's public madness has its closest equivalent in Dido's shock at the news of Aeneas' departure.[31] The Carthaginian queen's public frenzy through the streets has always defied literal understanding and been easier to read within the simile of the Bacchante, and Amata's doubly signalled frenzy also goes beyond the physically possible in its second version. The rhetorical plural "through whole cities and warlike peoples" finds more credibility as it expands into the Bacchic excitement of her *thiasos* in 385–405.

As editors since Heinze have pointed out, the allusion to "the feigned possession of Bacchus" (*simulato numine Bacchi*) at 385 seems to cast doubt on Amata's condition, and openly jars with 405 where Allecto is said to "drive [Amata] from every direction in turn with Bacchus' goads", *stimulis agit undique Bacchi*. We have to allow for the obvious articulation in stages which Vergil has given to this narrative, as Amata's wildness is increased by the women's collective *enthousiasmos* after 394.[32] Yet given the final, summary, position of 405 and its consistency with the driving causality of Allecto that readers have been experiencing, *simulato* must attribute Amata's appearance of *enthousiasmos*, less to her wilful pretence, than to the imposing of this delusion upon her; her "false" condition originates not with Bacchus but with Allecto.[33]

Interpreters of this ambiguous phrase have taken into account the precedent of Helen's false and destructive behavior as reported in *Aeneid* 6. "Feigning a dance (*chorum simulans*) she was leading the jubilant Trojan women around the sacred objects; in the center she held up the huge flame" (517–19). Yet they are not comparable. Helen certainly acts in deliberate deception of the Trojans, exploiting her Bacchic rites to brandish the signal torch that will let in the Greek invaders. Like Helen's dance, Amata's revels serve a different, non-religious, purpose, and like Helen she holds aloft a torch, but Vergil himself shows us her confusion of purpose. At one moment she vows her daughter as a votary to Bacchus (387–90) in order to prevent the Trojan union, at another (397–402) she claims a mother's right to preside over Lavinia's union with Turnus.

The frequency of similes comparing frantic women such as Dido to Bacchantes, even when there is no literal development of Bacchic worship,[34] suggests that Bacchic *enthousiasmos* was the only kind of female frenzy recognized in ancient Greece and Rome. As Friedrich points out,[35] Ovid clearly construed Amata's Bacchic behavior as pretence, in his imitative description of the frenzy of Procne at*Met*. 6.594–8: "Frenzied in the woods, accompanied by a crowd of her maids, the dreadful Procne, driven by furies of vengeful grief, feigns your furies, Bacchus; at length she comes to the remote stalls, and wails and cries Evoe…snatches her sister and puts the costume of Bacchus upon her."[36]

But Procne, like Helen, is sane and purposeful, and the occasion is an actual festival of Bacchus (*Met*. 6.587–9). Amata in her madness cannot control the boundaries between pretence and reality, and this is paralleled by Vergil's passage from the queen's apostrophe in direct speech to the poet's own apostrophe, first in reporting her speech ("shouting that you alone are worthy of the maid", 389) then in his expansive account of her behavior: "For (she claims) that Lavinia is taking up the wanton thyrsus for you, moving around you in ritual dance and growing her hair for you" (390–1).[37] Like Dido's love madness, Amata's frenzy resembles Bacchic madness but it lacks the god's inspiration or consent. It comes from another source, the incessant goading (*stimuli*, 405) of Allecto. In the same way the feminine singular adjective "fraught with fury" (*furibunda*, 348) and participles "attempting evil…beginning frenzy" (*adorta…orsa*, 386) without expressed subject permit misreadings that assign Amata's earlier destructive behavior to Allecto.

Fama takes a part in swelling the contagion, here as in Book Four,[38] drawing the other wives, equally inflamed by fury (the Furies? *furiis accensas*, 7.392) from their homes, impelled by the queen's authority.[39] The scene where Amata leads the revels brandishing her torch brings new cross-references to Turnus and to Dido. The echo of Helen brandishing her torch also anticipates the behavior of Turnus; both epithets in 7.397–8, "inflamed, she holds aloft a blazing torch" (*flagrantem fervida pinum | sustinet*), recur in his attack on the Trojan ships at 9.72 "inflamed, he fills his hand with a blazing torch" (*manum pinu flagranti fervidus implet*). As she rolls her bloodshot gaze (*sanguineam torquens aciem*, 7.399) Amata recalls Dido turning her bloodshot gaze around her at her death (*sanguineam volvens aciem*, 4.643).

The entire Bacchic episode has provoked some of the most interesting and speculative writing on the role of Amata. Friedrich has rightly stressed Roman horror of Bacchic rioting, with the clear precedent of the Bacchanalian "conspiracy" and its Italian setting as reported by Livy in Book 39. There too the women are represented as instigators, whose chief offence in Roman eyes is their role in corrupting and involving young men and women in participation. For Friedrich Amata's behavior is more than *impotentia muliebris*, it is treasonous in creating civil discord, and so impious. His discussion illustrates from Roman political writings the blurring of the lines between what seem to us the different discourses of politics, ethics and religion, used interchangeably to condemn the same dangerous behavior.

The substitution of an alien passion for civic loyalty goes far to explain why in both Greek and Latin poetry Bacchic frenzy is always distanced by being marked as foreign; in the Euripidean tragedy it occurs at Thebes, with a thiasos from Asia; in Roman poetry Bacchantes are usually imagined as Thracian, and even the simile applied to Dido at *Aen.* 4.300–2 associates her with the Greek festival on Mount Cithaeron.[10]

The beauty of Vergil's description in 7.393–405, close to that of Euripides' wondering messenger in the *Bacchae*, could more easily be associated with a positive interpretation of Bacchic enthusiasm than with the obvious harm caused to Latinus and his community, or with traditional Roman horror of the orgiastic, but this conflict of incompatibles – of beauty and horror, of calculation and frenzy, – may itself reflect the polymorphous perversity of Allecto, conveying the bewildering impact of the supernatural. Neither the women nor their menfolk can understand what has happened, because it comes from powers beyond their, or our, understanding.

Considered as Bacchic madness, Amata's frenzy and that of the women can be expected to return to an exhausted calm (*debacchari*) when it has played itself out. Indeed when they reappear in the narrative in Book 11, there is no trace of their past frenzy. Like Homer's *Hecuba* (*Il.* 6.293–311) the queen is seen proceeding in decorous supplication with a great crowd of women (*magna matrum... caterva*, 11.478) to appeal in vain to Pallas.

IV. The departure of Turnus and Amata's self-destruction
Only the last book shows Amata with all her family; one short scene

Elaine Fantham

(12.1–80) reveals through the speeches of Latinus and Amata to Turnus and through Lavinia's famous blush – her sole action during the epic – the complex relationship between king, queen, and the kinsman who aims to be son-in-law. It is vital to look carefully at this scene step by step, not least because in recent years post-Freudian scholars have taken a cue from *miro properabat amore* in 7.55 and from Lavinia's embarrassment in this scene to treat Amata as a kind of Latin Phaedra, incestuously infatuated with Turnus.[41]

The opening of *Aeneid* 12 reflects both Turnus' passion and the defeat of the Latins which he has caused. In the dialogue with Lavinia's parents Turnus shows the same obsession as Amata, impatient for the single combat with Aeneas that will assign rule over the Latins and Lavinia's hand as the double reward of the victor. While Turnus speaks intimately, addressing Latinus and Amata as *pater* (13) and *mater* (74), Latinus himself is more distant, beginning with a warning that as the young man excels in spirit Latinus surpasses him in counsel. Affirming that it is not *fas* to unite his daughter with any Italian suitor, as he has been warned by gods and men, the old king voices his shame and regret: "Overcome by love for you, overcome by your kindred blood and the tears of my grieving wife, I violated all these bonds: I snatched Lavinia, promised as she was, from my son-in-law, and took up impious warfare."[42] Neither here nor in his oath before the truce does he promise Lavinia to Turnus, since he is not free to do so. He allows only the unacceptable alternative that Turnus admit defeat and save his life by renouncing his claim.

It is only when Turnus, unmoved, insists on his right to risk death for glory, that Amata breaks in, terrified by the new danger of the battle, and holds back her passionate son-in-law (*ardentem generum*, 12.55).[43] She is already *moritura*. We may read this at first only as "destined to die" but it can also mean "resolved on dying".[44] Gradually the harsher meaning emerges. Latinus has spoken of his love for Turnus; Amata now voices her complete dependence on him: "Turnus, by these tears, by any respect for Amata that moves your heart, you are now my only hope, the repose of my old age, the glory and dominion of Latinus is in your hands, on you the whole sinking house now leans" (12.56–9).

Is Amata speaking out of turn? The modern reader feels discomfort that in front of her royal husband Amata should declare him the only champion and hope of their family, yet the reality is that Latinus is too old to fight, and relinquished all attempt to govern at the outbreak of the war.[45]

Allecto's first Victim: a Study of Vergil's Amata

In begging Turnus not to fight, Amata uses terms that recall Dido's appeal to Aeneas and so assimilates herself once more to a doomed model. Dido too begged her chosen champion not to depart, if he felt any gratitude or affection for her, for the sake of her endangered family and household (*miserere domus labentis*, 4.317–8). The ominous echo is confirmed by Amata's last words: "Whatever outcome of this combat awaits you, Turnus, awaits me in turn: at this same time I shall leave this hated light and never as a captive see Aeneas my son-in-law" (12.61–3). These words mark a new level of desperation: *moritura* reveals its meaning not as "destined to die", but as "resolved" in the event of an increasingly certain condition. The queen's obsessive dependence on Turnus is revealed in the logical conflict between her words and her desire. Though he may survive, Turnus will never be her son-in-law if he refuses to fight. And since Aeneas will swear to leave Latinus in command (12.192–3) the reader is soon disabused of Amata's extravagant fear that Latinus will lose *imperium* or his queen be taken captive.

Then comes Lavinia's blush. She blushes, surely, not at her mother's behavior, but to face her lover and know she is the prize of this contest; if it is an ill omen that Amata should imply Turnus' death (as he affirms in 72) it is a worse embarrassment that he must decide in front of Lavinia whether to risk his life for her. Stepping back just a little the reader can see this colloquy of father, mother and suitor in the daughter's presence as a final negotiation in which the father tries to release Turnus from his suit, the mother cannot resolve herself to face either outcome, and Turnus commits himself to risk his life as Lavinia's suitor.

But the ancient reader would have measured the behavior of Latinus and Amata in this scene by other standards and precedents. Vergil has constructed the last four books of the *Aeneid* in close relationship to the tragic climax of the *Iliad*, and we should not neglect the Homeric model for this scene. I suggested earlier that Hecuba is the natural model for Amata as tragic mother-figure; this is not perhaps apparent until *Aen.* 11.477–85, where the queen performs the same act of supplication in defeat that Vergil and Homer assign to Hecuba.[46] In *Iliad* 22 when Hector departs for the last time to face death at the hands of Achilles, both Priam (himself too old to fight) and Hecuba beseech him not to go; first Priam invokes the image of his own future abasement if Hector is killed (22.59–76) then Hecuba, baring her breasts and weeping, begs him not to meet the challenge but to stay within the city (22.82–9). Homer gives Hector no reply, since none would be possible, but voices instead Hector's thoughts in relation to his fellow warriors and Achilles himself.

Surely as Turnus is now the doomed Hector, his aunt and uncle Amata and Latinus have also to fill the roles of Priam and Hecuba. Then indeed both Latinus' and Amata's pleas seem less extravagant as parallels to the Trojan anticipation of the captivity and degradation that will follow defeat.

But there is another couple to whom we should at least partly assimilate Latinus and Amata. However weak a representative of Jupiter Latinus may be, the King does correspond to the King of the gods in lawful authority and knowledge of and respect for what is fated. And Juno even more closely corresponds to Amata in her conflict with her husband over the choice of favored hero, and her desperate attempts to protect Turnus. Amata has only words to plead with, but Juno has supernatural powers that will twice postpone Turnus' duel, first through Juturna's violation of the truce, then through her impersonation of Turnus' charioteer, as she drives him from the field, twisting and turning to carry him away from Aeneas.

It is now that Aeneas in frustration is prompted by Venus to besiege Latinus' city, and announce to his men that he will sack it and raze it to the ground as *causa belli* (567). As he attacks, Amata's suicide is the fatal blow from within that causes the city's collapse. Shocked by the mistaken conviction that Turnus is dead, she takes on herself the responsibility and guilt of all that has happened.[47] Remorse doubling her grief strengthens her resolve to die.[48] When Amata hangs herself, no special explanation is needed for her means of death. In Greece at least hanging was a recognized choice of suicide for men and women, but especially for women, who had neither a sword nor the strength to drive it in. Fraenkel showed this in his brief *Selbstmordwege*, and Nicole Loraux has argued at considerably greater length[49] how common it was for the woman to hang herself, whether in shame, like Epicaste/Jocasta or Phaedra, or in despair. In early Rome such a death disqualified the corpse from burial,[50] and this prospect adds horror to Amata's precipitate death; but Vergil's discretion moves away from this hazard, just as he ultimately leaves open the assumption that Turnus will receive burial – beyond the epic.

Amata's death is of more consequence, since it brings about the overthrow of the city in a tableau of female lament and despair that echoes the fall of Priam's palace (*Aen.* 2.486–8) and the collapse of Carthage at the news of Dido's death (*Aen.* 4.666–8). Latinus is no Macbeth, but like an uncomprehending Creon mourning his Eurydice, he is stricken by his wife's death to defile himself with the ashes of mourning.

Amata's madness, repeatedly signaled since it was induced by Allecto,[51] has played itself out with the last allusion (*furorem*, 12.601) at her death, tragic even in its basis on delusion. Dido's *furor*, induced by Venus and Cupid (*furentem*, 1.659) was slower to betray itself publicly, but took root in 4.65 and 69, to be called *furor* for the first time at 4.91; it too is held responsible by the poet himself for her death.[52] That both women made their survival depend on a man does not commit them to the same kind of passion: it is simply a corollary of the ancient view of the dependency of women; for Dido depended on Aeneas' love, not his survival or the achievement of his own goals, whereas Amata wanted only what Turnus sought for himself.

I have tried to argue that Vergil inherited a villainess and refined his narrative, so that without falsely sentimentalizing Amata or softening her imperious nature, he made her an object of tragic pity. Her passionate partisanship is contrary to destiny; her decline is horrifying; her death is necessary but grievous – a last blow before the necessary death of the man she saw as her champion.

Notes

[1] Eur., *Erechtheus*, fr. 50 Austin = 360 Nauck, cited with approval by Lycurgus, *Against Leocrates* 100.

[2] Cf. Homer, *Iliad* 6.251–62, 22.79–89: after his death 22.405–28. She is protagonist of Euripides' *Hecuba*, and dominates three episodes of *Troades*. Hecuba appears in the *Aeneid* only at 2.515–25.

[3] Cf. Servius on *Aen*. 1.267 = Cato, fr. 9 Peter, and on *Aen*. 4.620 = Cato, fr. 10 Peter.

[4] *Laviniam accepit uxorem. propter quod Turnus iratus tam in Latinum quam in Aenean bella suscepit* Cato fr. 11, ap. Servius on *Aen*. 6.760.

[5] Livy 1.1.6–7.

[6] One thinks of Creusa (2.738) or Lausus (10.878); the word can, but need not, denote an unnatural death (*OLD*, s.v. *eripere*, 3a)

[7] *Amata enim duos filios voluntate patris Aeneae spondentes Laviniam sororem factione interemit, unde et "erepta" dixit, quasi per vim.*

[8] Serv. Auct. on *Aen*. 7.51: *hos alii caecatos a matre tradunt, postquam amisso Turno Lavinia Aeneae iuncta est.*

[9] Serv. on *Aen*. 12.603 = Fab. Pictor, *Latini Annales* fr. 1 HRR Fabius Pictor dicit quod <Amata> inedia se interemerit. Cf. Ps. Aurelius Victor, *Origo gentis Romanae*, 13.8: *Piso quidem Turnum matruelem Amatae fuisse tradit, interfectoque Latino mortem ipsam sibi conscivisse.*

[10] According to Livy 1. 46–7 Tanaquil secures the kingship for her protégé Servius Tullus after Tarquin's natural death; then in Tullus' old age his evil

Elaine Fantham

daughter Tullia instigates young Tarquin to murder her father so as to obtain the succession. The variant accounts of Amata seem to oscillate between the two models.

[11] For this interpretation cf. La Penna (1984) 1.125-8. The variant in Servius Auctus also makes better sense if Amata is supposed to have blinded these young men (not necessarily her own sons) after the death of Latinus rather than of Turnus; the confusion could easily have arisen from misunderstanding *quo* or *eo amisso* in the commentator's source.

[12] *Turnus an Aeneas Latiae gener esset Amatae | bellum erat.*

[13] D.H. 1.64, where she is called Amita, a variant which seems to have no warrant.

[14] I pass over here conflicting evidence for the exact degree of kinship – Amata's nephew in Vergil, he is cited in Ps.-Aurelius Victor 13 as both Lavinia's cousin (*consobrinus*) and maternal cousin (*matruelis*) of Amata herself.

[15] Heinze tr. (1994) 152 = Heinze (1915) 187.

[16] Otis (1963) 324 citing Fraenkel (1945) 1-14.

[17] Johnson (1976) 144 and 148.

[18] Hardie (1992) 41. It is not clear to what extent Hardie would apply to Amata the status of "living dead": this suggests something more remote from her original personality, and closer to a zombie.

[19] On *coquere* as Ennian see Friedrich (1948) 227-301.

[20] For *ardens* of Turnus compare 12.55 below. *Ardere, ardens, ardor* are applied to Dido, from 1.713 *ardescitque tuendo*, to 4.101 *ardet amens Dido*, to 6.467 *ardentem et torva tuentem*, all moments of passion; it describes Cassandra's gaze as she is raped by Ajax; 2.405 *tollens ardentia lumina frustra*, and the warrior women Penthesilea 1.491 and Camilla 11.782 represented in battle.

[21] La Penna (1967) 309-18, also (1987) 125-9; see also Putnam (1965) 158-62, 176-9.

[22] Suet., *Aug.* 63. Antonius adds that at the same time Augustus was seeking king Cotison's daughter for himself.

[23] Here my assessment differs from the orthodox interpretation of Cairns (1989) 121.

[24] The odd phrase *matris | quam...relinquet* surely is shorthand for "he will leave her childless", *orbam relinquet*.

[25] Turnus too rejects the right interpretation of the portent at 9.128-39, but his language in 134-5 leaves open the possibility that he has recognized the validity of the portents.

[26] 12.59 "The whole tottering house rests upon you", *in te omnis domus inclinata recumbit*.

[27] Simon (1978, 244-51) notes that women often succumb to hysteria when they are refused something important to them by their husbands or fathers. This seems to be a classic instance.

[28] It is difficult to do justice to *monstra*: here (like the singular at 348) a manifestation of the power of supernatural evil, it has been used already in Book 7 to designate Circe's transformed victims (7.21), and the three portents (cf. *portenta, portendere* 7.58, 81, 256) sent by the gods to Latinus, 7.80 and 270. Latent in events designated as *monstra* is the sense of demonstrating power, as

Allecto's first Victim: a Study of Vergil's Amata

well as of showing or warning men the divine purpose they should obey. Compare 9.120 (the transformation of the ships as *mirabile monstrum*, interpreted negatively by Turnus (*haec monstra*, 128) as aimed against the Trojans.

[29] West (1969) 49.

[30] Rabel (1981) 27-31. See now Bleisch (1996) 453-71 who argues from the Callimachean Epigram (54 Gow-Page) that Vergil has adopted the top simile not only for its Bacchic associations but also for the Callimachean citation of Pittacus' apophthegm on choosing a familiar rather than an alien marriage. From this she infers (469-71) a possible extension of Callimachus' tactful allusion to Ptolemaic brother-sister marriage to contrast Turnus' quasi-incestuous claim with Aeneas' exogamy.

[31] *Aen.* 4.69: "Unhappy Dido is consumed with fire and wanders raving through the whole city", *uritur infelix Dido totaque vagatur | urbe furens*, and 300-2 "she rages, out of control, and riots inflamed through the whole city, like a Bacchante aroused when the rites are started up", *saevit inops animi totamque incensa per urbem | bacchatur, qualis commotis excita sacris | Thyias*.

[32] Simon (1978) discusses group hysteria (118, 119 and 251-7) and notes that persons affected by mania generate exaltation and progressively lose control in the process of forming themselves into a group.

[33] Servius on 3.385 rejects the idea of real pretence; contrast Heinze (tr. 1996) 150-1.

[34] Compare e.g. Prop. 3.8.14; Ov., *A.A.* 1.312; 3.710; *Her.* 10.48; *Fast.* 4.458; Sen., Med. 849.

[35] Friedrich (1940) 142-9.

[36] "Concita per silvas, turba comitante suarum | terribilis Procne *furiis agitata doloris* Bacche *tuas simulat*: venit ad stabula avia tandem | exululat euhoeque... | germanamque rapit raptaeque insignia Bacchi |induit.'

[37] "euhoe *Bacche*" fremens, solum *te* virgine dignum | vociferans; etenim molles *tibi* sumere thyrsos, | *te* lustrare choro, sacrum *tibi* pascere crinem. Cf. Williams (1983) 185 "here the apostrophe can be seen taking its origin in the vocatives shouted by Amata and then being carried on by the vocatives that follow, now from the mouth of the poet acting...on behalf of Amata." But Williams' concern is primarily with the function of the apostrophe in enabling the poet "to make his presence felt in the text", rather than with the way the apostrophe absorbs him into the obsessive devotion of the queen.

[38] *Fama* operates twice in Book 4, after Dido's surrender to Aeneas (4.173-97), and again to spread the news of her suicide. There the Maenad simile is transferred from Dido herself: "Rumor revels like a Maenad through the shattered city", 4.666 *concussam bacchatur Fama per urbem*.

[39] There is a certain irony in 393 "the same passion drives them all on to seek new homes", *idem omnes ardor agit nova quaerere tecta*. This both attributes to the women of this settled community the passion of the colonizing Trojans, and contrasts their rebellion with that of the Trojan women in *Aeneid* 5, whose offence it was *not* to share the Trojan men's quest for new homes.

[40] *Aen.* 4.302-3 "when the triennial festival goads them on at Bacchus' call, and Cithaeron resounds with shouting by night", *ubi audito stimulant trieterica Baccho | orgia nocturnusque vocat clamore Cithaeron*.

Elaine Fantham

[41] For the Amata/Phaedra analogy and a Freudian reading of *Aeneid* 7–12 see especially Mitchell (1991) 231; more generally Lyne (1987) 114–22, (1989) 80–1. See also Lyne (1983) 60–1 = (1990) 163–4, for a spectrum of interpretations of Lavinia's blush.

[42] 12.29–31 *victus amore tui, cognato sanguine victus, | coniugis et maestae lacrimis, vincla omnia rupi: | promissam eripui genero, arma impia sumpsi.*

[43] As Aeneas is son-in-law in Latinus' speech (12.31 *promissam eripui genero*) so Turnus is son-in-law, even in the poet's narrative, where Amata in concerned.

[44] As repeatedly of Dido: *Aen.* 4.519, 604, and of Euryalus *Aen.* 9.400.

[45] Cf. *Aen.* 7.591–600 *rerumque reliquit habenas*, 616–7 *et caecis se condidit umbris.*

[46] *Aen.* 11.477–81 = *Aen.* 1.479–82, where the scene of supplication on Dido's temple frieze reproduces *Il.* 6.297–311.

[47] 12.599–600 *subito mentem turbata dolore | se causam clamat crimenque caputque malorum.*

[48] *Moritura* (602) recalls 12.55, while both instances parallel Dido's resolve to die; similarly Amata speaks at 12.62 of leaving the hated light (of day/life: *simul haec invisa relinquam | lumina*) as Dido dies in 4.631 "longing to break off the hated light of life", *invisam quaerens quam primum abrumpere lucem.*

[49] Fraenkel (1932) 470–73 = (1960) 1.465–7: Loraux (1985).

[50] The source is Servius on *Aen.* 12.603, probably citing Varro: "There was a stipulation in the pontifical books that anyone who committed suicide by hanging should be cast away unburied", *cautum fuerat in pontificalibus libris ut qui laqueo vitam finisset insepultus abiceretur.*

[51] Cf. *furibunda*, 7.348; *furentem*, 350; *furiale*, 375; *furit*, 377; *furo rem*, 386.

[52] Compare Amata "distraught with sudden grief" (*subito mentem turbata dolore*, 12.599) and "sad frenzy" (*maestum...furorem*, 601) with Dido "inflamed by sudden madness" (*subito accensa furore*, 4.697).

Bibliography

Bleisch, P.
    1996   "On choosing a spouse: *Aen.* 7.378–84 and Callimachus' Epigram 1", *AJP* 117, 453–72.

Buchheit, V.
    1963   *Vergil über die Sendung Roms*, Heidelberg.

Cairns, F.
    1989   *Virgil's Augustan Epic*, Cambridge.

Fraenkel, E.D.M.
    1932   "Selbstmordwege", *Philol.* 87, 470–3 = *Kleine Beitrage* I, 465–7, (Rome 1964).
    1945   "Some aspects of the structure of *Aeneid* VII", *JRS* 35, 1–14 = *Kleine Beitrage* II, 145–72.

Friedrich, W.H.
    1940   "Excurse zur Aeneis: Amatas Raserei", *Philol.* 94.
    1948   "Ennius – Erklärungen", *Philol.* 97, 297–301.

Hardie, P.
    1993   *The Epic Successors of Virgil*, Cambridge.
Heinze, R.
    1915   *Virgils Epische Technik*, edn 2, = (1993) *Virgil's Epic Technique*, tr. H. and D. Harvey, F. Robertson, Berkeley, Calif.
Johnson, W.R.
    1976   *Darkness Visible: A Study of Vergil's* Aeneid, Berkeley, Calif.
La Penna, A.
    1967   "Amata e Didone", *Maia* 19, 309–18.
    1987   "Amata", in *Enciclopedia Virgiliana*.
Lyne, R.O.A.M.
    1983   "Lavinia's Blush", *Greece and Rome* 30, 55–64 = (1990) *Greece and Rome Studies: Virgil*, ed. McAuslan/Walcot, 157–66, Oxford.
    1987   *Further Voices in Virgil's* Aeneid, Oxford.
    1989   *Words and the Poet*, Oxford.
Mitchell, R.N.
    1991   "The violence of virginity", *Arethusa* 24, 219–38.
Norden, E.
    1916   *Vergilius: Aeneis VI*, Stuttgart.
Otis, B.
    1963   *Virgil: A Study in Civilized Poetry*, Oxford.
Pichon, R.
    1913   "L'episode d'Amata", *REA* XX, 161–6.
Pöschl, V.
    1962   *The Art of Vergil: Image and Symbol*, tr. G. Seligsen, Ann Arbor.
Putnam, M.
    1965   *The Poetry of the* Aeneid, Cambridge, Mass.
Rabel, R.J.
    1981   "Vergil, tops and the Stoic view of fate," *CJ* 77, 27–31.
Schweizer, H.J.
    1967   *Vergil und Italien*, Aarau.
Simon, B.
    1978   *Mind and Madness in Ancient Greece*, Ithaca.
Voisin, J.L.
    1979   "Le suicide d'Amata", *REL* 57, 254–71.
West, D.
    1969   "Multiple correspondence similes in the *Aeneid*", *JRS* 59, 40–9.
Williams, G.
    1983   *Technique and Ideas in the* Aeneid, New Haven.
Zarker, J.W.
    1969   "Amata: Vergil's other tragic queen", *Vergilius* 15, 2–24.

8

OPENING THE GATES OF WAR
Aeneid 7.601–40

Don Fowler

'Vergil and the monuments' has become as popular a rubric for contemporary Vergilian scholarship as 'Homer and the monuments' was for an earlier generation of Homerists. Art historians are as varied as literary scholars, as can be seen from the very different ways that a monument like the *Ara Pacis* has been handled by Jas Elsner and Karl Galinsky.[1] But there is no doubt that many, in framing the *Aeneid* with the public monuments of Augustan Rome, seek literally to ground interpretation in something concrete – to establish sure foundations on which interpretation may build, as an escape from the shifting sands of textuality. It will come as no surprise to learn that I do not think this can be done. There is no 'outside' that can frame the text, if by 'outside' we mean something outside the act of interpretation, not itself subject to the hazards and indeterminacies of textuality. I want to examine a passage in the *Aeneid* which has a clear Augustan reference, but I do not want to use that reference to determine the meaning of the passage. Rather, to put it tendentiously, as my title suggests I am here to open things up, to argue that the *Aeneid* resists the closure of its time and place as much as it resists the closure of ours – at least if we let it. And though I didn't realise it when I originally gave the title, there is a third meaning potentially there – to open the gates of war amongst the Augustanising Vergilians assembled in this volume, to arouse conflict and discord amongst us. I shall try not to disappoint.

I do not believe that disputes about the *Aeneid* can be settled by reference to their Augustan context, for two reasons that I have given elsewhere:[2] because there is no stable context, no frame which itself is not a contestable construct, and because, even if there were, the relationship between text and context is always a matter of interpretative choice. Since the rest of this paper is going to be largely about ancient detail, let me offer you for a moment a modern example of how context and intertextuality function in the political sphere.[3] An indisputable part of the propaganda of President Clinton, from his earliest days as a presidential candidate, has been the use of the model of Jack Kennedy. His supporters think he is like the Kennedy of Camelot and what Robert Frost famously prophesied would be a 'golden age of poetry and power'; his detractors think he is the Kennedy who was Marilyn's boyfriend, or who launched the Bay of Pigs. All sides – and there are many more than two – agree that intertextuality with Kennedy's doings and sayings is an inescapable part of reading Clinton, but how exactly the context is delineated, and what one does with the parallels once one has them, depend on what one wants to do with them. The intertextuality is of course reversible – our readings of Kennedy have been altered by our readings of Clinton; and there are more and less sophisticated ways to do things. A sophisticated supporter, for instance, might not wish to deny, say, Kennedy's and Clinton's (alleged) womanising, but would vector this into a view of the potency of power. But how to read Clinton is not fixed by the Kennedyan context: that only complicates our attempts. There is no neutral, ideology-free 'context' to the relationship between Kennedy and Clinton which can help us to know what to think about him. We have to make up our own minds, being the people we are. So it is with Augustanism.

The passage that I want to talk about is the description in Book Seven of the opening of the Gates of War by Juno:[4]

> There was a custom in Hesperian Latium, which next the Alban cities practised as sacred, and now Rome the most powerful practises, when they move Mars for the beginnings of war, whether they prepare to take with their own hands tearful war to the Getae, or the Hyrcani or the Arabs, or to make for the Indians, follow the dawn and seek the return of the standards from the Parthians. There are twin gates of war (so called), sacred for the religious awe they inspire and the terror of savage Mars: a hundred bronze bars close them, and eternal strong points of iron, nor is Janus absent from the threshold as a guard. These, when the senators are set in a decision to fight, the consul himself, distinguished in the Quirinal gown and girded in the Gabinan fashion, unbars, their thresholds screeching: he himself calls for fighting, and then the rest of the manhood of Rome follows, and the bronze horns blow in raucous agreement.
>
> This was the custom by which then also Latinus was being urged to declare war on the followers of Aeneas, and open the sad gates. The father drew back from their touch, and turning away fled the foul action, burying himself in blind shadows. Then the very queen of the gods herself, gliding down from the sky, pushed with her hand at the delaying gates, and as the hinge turned the Saturnian one broke the iron posts of

Opening the Gates of War

war. Ausonia, previously unexcited and unmoved, blazed: some made ready to go forth over the plains as infantry, others riding tall horses raged, covered in dust: all call for arms. Some clean shields smooth and spears bright with rich fat, and work axes on the whetstone; men find pleasure in bearing standards and hearing the sound of trumpets. Five great cities, no less, set up anvils and make new their weapons: powerful Atina, proud Tibur, Ardea, Crustumerium, and tower-bearing Antemnae. They hollow out safe coverings for their heads and curve willow shield frames; others draw out bronze breast-plates or smooth greaves in pliant silver; this is where respect of plough and sickle, this is where all love of the plough ends up – they cook again their fathers' swords in the furnaces.

Already the trumpets sound, the word goes round as a sign for war; this man anxiously snatches the helmet from his house, this man forces into harness the trembling horses, and takes on his shield and the chainmail triple threaded with gold, and puts around him the faithful sword.

> *M*os erat Hesperio in Latio, quem protinus urbes
> *A*lbanae coluere sacrum, nunc maxima rerum
> *R*oma colit, cum prima mouent in proelia *Martem*,
> *s*iue Getis inferre manu lacrimabile bellum
> Hyrcanisue Arabisue parant, seu tendere ad Indos
> Auroramque sequi Parthosque reposcere signa.
> sunt geminae belli portae (sic nomine dicunt)
> religione sacrae et saeui formidine Martis;
> centum aerei claudunt uectes aeternaque ferri
> robora, nec custos absistit limine Ianus.
> has, ubi certa sedet patribus sententia pugnae,
> ipse Quirinali trabea cinctuque Gabino
> insignis reserat stridentia limina consul,
> ipse uocat pugnas; sequitur tum cetera pubes,
> aereaque adsensu conspirant cornua rauco.
> hoc et tum Aeneadis indicere bella Latinus
> more iubebatur tristisque recludere portas.
> abstinuit tactu pater auersusque refugit
> foeda ministeria, et caecis se condidit umbris.
> tum regina deum caelo delapsa morantis
> impulit ipsa manu portas, et cardine uerso
> belli ferratos rumpit Saturnia postis.
> ardet inexcita Ausonia atque immobilis ante;
> pars pedes ire parat campis, pars arduus altis
> puluerulentus equis furit; omnes arma requirunt.
> pars leuis clipeos et spicula lucida tergent
> aruina pingui subiguntque in cote securis;
> signaque ferre iuuat sonitusque audire tubarum.
> quinque adeo magnae positis incudibus urbes

> tela nouant, Atina potens Tiburque superbum,
> Ardea Crustumerique et turrigerae Antemnae.
> tegmina tuta cauant capitum flectuntque salignas
> umbonum cratis; alii thoracas aënos
> aut leuis ocreas lento ducunt argento;
> uomeris huc et falcis honos, huc omnis aratri
> cessit amor; recoquunt patrios fornacibus ensis.
> classica iamque sonant, it bello tessera signum;
> hic galeam tectis trepidus rapit, ille trementis
> ad iuga cogit equos, clipeumque auroque trilicem
> loricam induitur fidoque accingitur ense.

This is one of the places where there is an explicit prolepsis of future Roman practice (607–15), and a clear allusion to Augustus' closing of the doors after Actium, as well as to his foreign campaigns, and in particular the actual or anticipated recovery in 20 BCE from the Parthians of the standards lost by Crassus and others. Servius on *Aen.* 7.607 and 610 tells us about the temple where this took place:

7.607: *there are two gates of war*: this shrine, that is the 'gates of war' Numa Pompilius constructed at the bottom of the Argiletum near the Theatre of Marcellus. It consisted of two very short temples: two, because Janus is double-headed. Later, after the capture of the Etruscan city of Falerii, an image of Janus was found with four faces. Hence the shrine instituted by Numa was moved to the Forum Transitorium and a single temple with four gates was instituted. It is not surprising that Janus is in some authors double-headed, in others with four heads: for some want him to be the lord of the day, in which there is sunrise and sunset (as in Horace *Satires* 2.6.20 'father of the morning, or Janus if you prefer'), others of the whole year, which it is agreed is divided into four seasons. That he is the god of the year is proved by his name, because the first part of the year is named after him: for January is named after Janus.

7.607: *svnt geminae belli portae*: sacrarium hoc, id est belli portas Numa Pompilius fecerat circa imum Argiletum iuxta theatrum Marcelli. quod fuit in duobus brevissimis templis: duobus autem propter Ianum bifrontem. postea captis Faleriis, civitate Tusciae, inventum est simulacrum Iani cum frontibus quattuor. unde quod Numa instituerat translatum est ad forum transitorium et quattuor portarum unum templum est institutum. Ianum sane apud aliquos bifrontem, apud aliquos quadrifrontem esse non mirum est: nam alii eum diei dominum volunt, in quo ortus est et occasus (Horatius 'matutine pater, seu Iane libentius audis'), alii anni totius, quem in quattuor tempora constat esse divisum. anni autem esse deum illa res probat, quod ab eo prima pars anni nominatur: nam ab Iano Ianuarius dictus est.

7.610: *Janus*: some call Janus 'Eanus' from *eo*, 'to go', and say that he is Mars, and that because he has the greatest power amongst the Romans, for that reason he is honoured first in cult. Others hold that Janus is air, and because he is the begetter of the voice, for that reason he is entrusted with taking our prayers to the gods. Others say that Janus is the world-system, whose passages are closed in time of peace because the world-system is closed on all sides, and are opened in time of war in order that they might lie open to seek help. As the world, they gave him two faces, the rising east and the setting west, as explained before: others gave him four faces as representing the four parts of the world. Others call him 'Clusivius', others 'Patulcius', because he has the power to open gates. Again, he is called 'Iunonius', and it is for this reason a fine touch that Juno is brought in to open the gates. He is also called Quirinus, whence they say that the consul opens the gates 'trabeatus', in the costume worn by Quirinus.

7.610: **Ianvs**: quidam Ianum Eanum dicunt ab eundo; eumque esse Martem; et quod apud Romanos plurimum potest, ideo primum in veneratione nominari. alii Ianum aërem credunt; et quia vocis genitor habeatur, idcirco mandari ei preces nostras ad deos perferendas. alii Ianum mundum accipiunt, cuius caulae ideo in pace clausae sunt, quod mundus undique clausus est, belli tempore aperiuntur, ad auxilium petendum ut pateant. nam quasi mundo ei duas facies dederunt, orientis et occidentis, quod iam supra dictum est: alii quattuor secundum quattuor partes mundi. alii Clusivium dicunt, alii Patulcium, quod patendarum portarum habeat potestatem. idem Iunonius; inde pulchre Iuno portas aperire inducitur. idem Quirinus, unde trabeatum consulem aperire portas dicunt, eo habitu quo Quirinus fuit.

The Temple of Janus Geminus stood at the heart of the city, at the point where the Argiletum joins the Forum Romanum at its north-east corner; we do not know the exact spot, because the temple was later moved by Domitian.[5] It is represented on a coin of Nero,[6] who also closed the gates, and was rectangular in shape with two long walls with a window with a grating; the doors are shown as on the short wall. Inside the temple was the famous statue of Janus with two heads, holding a staff in his right hand and a key in his left. His fingers were arranged to indicate the days of the year.[7] Various foundation stories were current, but the most prominent connected the temple's foundation with Numa Pompilius. This is the version given by Livy (1.19.1–3):

> Having in this way obtained the crown, Numa prepared to found anew, by laws and customs, that City which had so recently been founded by force of arms. He saw that this was impossible whilst a state of war lasted, for war brutalised men. Thinking that the ferocity of his subjects should be mitigated by the disuse of arms, he built the temple of Janus at the bottom of the Argiletum as an index of peace and war, to signify when it

was open that the State was under arms, and when it was shut that all the surrounding nations were at peace. Twice since Numa's reign has it been shut, once after the conclusion of the first Punic war in the consulship of T. Manlius, the second time, which heaven has allowed our generation to witness, after the battle of Actium, when peace on land and sea was secured by the emperor Caesar Augustus.

qui regno ita potitus urbem nouam conditam ui et armis, iure eam legibusque ac moribus de integro condere parat. quibus cum inter bella adsuescere uideret non posse, quippe efferari militia animos, mitigandum ferocem populum armorum desuetudine ratus, Ianum ad infimum Argiletum indicem pacis bellique fecit, apertus ut in armis esse ciuitatem, clausus pacatos circa omnes populos significaret. bis deinde post Numae regnum clausus fuit, semel T. Manlio consule post Punicum primum perfectum bellum, iterum, quod nostrae aetati di dederunt ut uideremus, post bellum Actiacum ab imperatore Caesare Augusto pace terra marique parta.

Karl Galinsky has recently stressed the importance of Numan elements in Augustan propaganda,[8] and a temple of peace obviously fits in with the image of the king who succeeded Romulus and matched his expertise in war with the arts of peace, setting the pattern for the alternation of war and peace in the immediately succeeding kings.[9]

The gates of the temple had been closed only twice before his own time, according to Augustus in the *Res Gestae* (2.42–5):

Our ancestors wished the temple of Janus Quirinus to be closed when peace had been achieved through victories throughout the whole sway of the Roman people. Before my time it was said to have been closed only twice from the foundation of the city: three times while I was *princeps* the senate decreed that it was to be closed.

[Ianum] Quirin[um, quem cl]aussum ess[e maiores nostri voluer]unt, [cum p]er totum i[mperium po]puli Roma[ni terra marique es]set parta vic[torii]s pax, cum priu[s qua]m nascerer a condita urbe bis omnino clausum [f]uisse prodatur m[emori]ae, ter me princi[pe senat]us claudendum esse censui[t].[10]

The earlier closures had taken place once under Numa Pompilius himself, and once in 235 BCE after the first Punic War and its aftermath, although they were opened again in the same year according to Varro, *Ling.* 5.165:

The third gate is the Ianualis, so-called from Janus, and for this reason the statue of Janus was placed there and the custom instituted by Pompilius, as Piso writes in his *Annales*, that it should always be open, except when there is nowhere war. It is said to have been closed in the time of King Pompilius, and again when Titus Manlius was consul after

Opening the Gates of War

the end of the first Punic War - but then opened the same year.

tertia est Ianualis, dicta ab Iano, et ideo ibi positum Iani signum et ius institutum a Pompilio, ut scribit in annalibus Piso,[11] ut sit aperta semper, nisi cum bellum sit nusquam. traditum est memoriae Pompilio rege fuisse opertam et post Tit[i]o Man[i]lio consule bello Cart<h>aginiensi primo confecto et eodem anno apertam.

It is this last opening that is alluded to by Ennius in the celebrated and controversial lines (*Annales* fr. 225–6 Skutsch) which are the principal model for the Vergilian scene, whether we take them to be literal or metaphorical:

after foul Discord broke open the iron gateposts and gates of war

postquam Discordia taetra
belli ferratos postes portasque refregit.

Under Augustus the gates were closed in 29, reopened in 27, reclosed in 25, and reopened and reclosed one further time at some later date which is controversial. The closures are alluded to in Book One (286–96) in the reassurance speech of Jupiter, when he tells Venus that there will come a time, after the assumption of Caesar into heaven, when Furor will be shut inside the temple with the doors firmly shut, chained but still roaring defiance (the temple looks a bit like a cage on the coin of Nero):

From this noble stock there will be born a Trojan Caesar to bound his empire by Oceanus at the limits of the world, and his fame by the stars. He will be called Julius, a name passed down to him from the great Iulus. In time to come, have no fear, you will receive him in the sky, laden with the spoils of the East. He too will be called upon in prayer. Then wars will be laid aside and the years of bitterness will be over. Silver-haired Truth and Vesta, and Romulus Quirinus with his brother Remus will sit dispensing justice. The dread Gates of War with their tight fastenings of steel will then be closed, and godless Strife will sit inside them on his murderous armour roaring hideously from bloody mouth, hands shackled behind his back with a hundred bands of bronze.

nascetur pulchra Troianus origine Caesar,
imperium Oceano, famam qui terminet astris,
Iulius, a magno demissum nomen Iulo.
hunc tu olim caelo spoliis Orientis onustum
accipies secura; uocabitur hic quoque uotis.
aspera tum positis mitescent saecula bellis:
cana Fides et Vesta, Remo cum fratre Quirinus
iura dabunt; dirae ferro et compagibus artis
claudentur Belli portae; Furor impius intus

>   saeua sedens super arma et centum uinctus aënis
>   post tergum nodis fremet horridus ore cruento.

The notorious ambiguities of *Caesar* there make the reader not entirely sure whether this closing of the gates has already happened or is in the future, but the reference to the Augustan closures is clear.[12] So too, I take it, is an Augustan reading of the Book Seven passage. Juno's opening of the gates is the mirror of Augustus' closure: the action parallels the unleashing of the winds by Aeolus in Book One, and represents an irruption of furious discord into the ordered worlds of the cosmos and the state. Instead of the due performance of ritual by a consul *Quirinali trabea cinctuque Gabino | insignis* (612), we have a woman taking matters into her own hands, in an act whose sexual perversion is plain. Juno is the goddess whose sphere is the appropriate opening of the female body, in defloration, childbirth or menstruation:[13] but here her breaking of the gates is more like a rape, albeit a rape which turns on its victim: in 623 *ardet*[14] *inexcita Ausonia atque immobilis ante*. Under her influence, we get the familiar topos of war-fever striking a people, as the love of the plough gives way to enthusiasm for war, and the *Aeneid* takes over from the *Georgics*. In the end, however, she will come to know her place; peace and order will be restored, the gates of war will be closed for all time.

There is, however, a complication here. If it is good to close the gates, why is the allusion in 603–6 not to their closure but to Augustus' reopening of them for his foreign wars? More generally, if it is good to close the doors, is it not bad to open them? But what would it mean to have a Rome permanently at peace, the gates forever closed? We should remember that the gates have nothing to do with civil war, but with any kind of war, domestic or foreign. How could a Roman possibly see himself other than as a warrior? These lines begin with that most Roman of words *mos*, and in 601–4 we have the acrostic Mars to which I drew attention a few years ago.[15] Michael Hendry has subsequently pointed out[16] that the initial letters of the opening of one of Ennius's most famous lines, *moribus antiquis res stat Romana virisque*, also spells out the name of the Roman god. Servius points out that the phrase in 603, *cum prima movent in proelia Martem*, may be seen as an allusion to the moving in time of war of the *ancilia*, the shields copied from the one that fell to earth in the time of Numa which were kept in the temple of Mars outside the city on the Via Appia:

> 7.603: *they move Mars to war*: for it was customary when war was declared to move the *ancilia* in the shrine of Mars, hence in Book Eight (3) 'and when he moved arms'

7.603: *mouent in proelia Martem*: nam moris fuerat indicto bello in Martis sacrario ancilia commouere, unde est in octauo 'utque inpulit arma'.

8.664: *the ancilia that fell from the sky*: when Numa Pompilius was king, a small round shield fell from the sky; and when the haruspices gave a response that where that was would be the lordship of the world, through the diligence of Numa, to prevent any enemy ever carrying it off, many similar shields were made with the help of a smith Mamurius, and placed in the temple of Mars. When Vergil says *ancilia*, he is using the plural for the singular: for only one fell to earth.

8.664: *lapsa ancilia caelo*: regnante Numa Pompilio scutum breue et rotundum caelo lapsum est. et cum haruspices respondissent illic fore orbis imperium, ubi illud fuisset, diligentia Numae, ne quandoque ab hostibus posset auferri, adhibito Mamurio fabro multa similia facta sunt et in templo Martis locata. quod autem dicit ancilia, plurali utitur numero pro singulari: nam unum lapsum est.

Servius also points out that it was at this temple that the armies gathered in answer to the consul's *euocatio*[17] – a Roman act if ever there was one. Mars is encoded not only in the letters of this passage but like *mos* and *manus* in those of the word *Romanus* itself, and the identity of being a Roman. The excitement caused by Juno recalls the description in Book Six (808–15) of how Tullus Hostilius had to break the *otia* created by Numa and make proper Roman soldiers again of the Romans (a fact recalled by Servius on the passage in Book Seven):

> But who is this at a distance resplendent in his crown of olive and carrying holy emblems? I know that white hair and beard. This is the man who will first found our city on laws, the Roman king called from the little town of Cures and the poor land of the Sabines into a mighty empire. Hard on his heels will come Tullus to shatter the leisure of his native land and rouse to battle men that have settled into idleness and armies that have lost the habit of triumph.

> quis procul ille autem ramis insignis oliuae
> sacra ferens? nosco crinis incanaque menta
> regis Romani primam qui legibus urbem
> fundabit, Curibus paruis et paupere terra
> missus in imperium magnum. cui deinde subibit
> *otia qui rumpet patriae residesque mouebit*
> *Tullus in arma uiros* et iam desueta triumphis
> agmina.

7.601: *in Hesperian Latium*: that is, in the ancient Latium: for, as I remarked in the first book (on 1.6), there were two Latia, hence the addition of 'Hesperian' is not redundant. It is not however true that this custom was ancient, because it was begun by Numa Pompilius, but Vergil as usual mixes history into his poem. It is to be noted that this passage is out of order, if one looks at the construction of the whole book: for just before he said 'he was ruling peaceful cities in long peace' (7.46), and he is going on to say 'Ausonia was ablaze that was previously unaroused and immobile' (7.623), and now he says 'it was the custom in Hesperia' (7.601), and before he also remarked 'the captured chariots were on display' (7.184) and 'go now and lay waste the Etruscan battle lines' (7.426). To prevent the inconsistency, we may suppose that Italy at first blazed hot with wars, then in the middle period was quiet, and now is being recalled to its old profession, just as the Romans blazed in war under Romulus, were quiet under Numa, and sought their old ways again under Tullus Hostilius. Hence Vergil says 'he was ruling peaceful cities in *long* peace', not 'eternal peace', and 'he [= Messapus] calls the troops unused to war to arms suddenly and handles again the iron sword' (7.693–4), because 'to handle again' means to seek again what you have given up.

7.601: *Hesperio in Latio*: hoc est in antiquo: nam, ut in primo diximus, duo Latia fuerunt, unde non frustra 'Hesperio' addidit. quod autem dicit hanc consuetudinem antiquam fuisse, falsum est; nam a Numa Pompilio primum instituta est. sed carmini suo, ut solet, miscet historiam. notandum sane inconexum esse hunc locum, si quis totius libri consideret textum; nam supra ait 'longa placidas in pace regebat', item dicturus est 'ardet inexcita Ausonia atque inmobilis ante', et nunc dicit 'mos erat Hesperio in Latio', supra etiam dixit 'captivi pendent currus', item 'Tyrrhenas, i, sterne acies'. quae ne sint contraria, accipiamus Italiam primo caluisse bellis, medio tempore quievisse, et ad antiquum studium nunc reverti, *sicut Romani bello flagravere sub Romulo, quievere sub Numa, sub Tullo Hostilio pristina studia repetiverunt.* hinc est quod et ipse Vergilius ait 'longa placidas in pace regebat', non perpetua, item 'desuetaque[18] bello | agmina in arma vocat subito ferrumque retractat': nam retractare est repetere quod omiseras.

It is natural in the light of this that the emphasis in accounts should fall on the act of closure, rather than the fact of the gates being closed, despite the prophecy of eternal closure in Book One. So Augustus in the *Res Gestae* says that the gates were closed *[cum p]er totum i[mperium po]puli Roma[ni terra marique es]set* parta vic[torii]s pax, that is, stressing the warlike acts which brought about the closing as much as the closure itself.

We have then here a contradiction, reminiscent of Plato's attack on pleasure in the *Philebus*. We can only pursue the closure of the gates if they have previously been opened; more generally, pacification requires a preceding state of war. If *furor* is to be shut inside the temple, he must sometimes be let out: the implications of the passage in Book

One, if it is taken literally, are that *furor* is only under control when the Romans are not fighting anywhere, in which case they are scarcely Romans at all. To be a Roman is to be a son of Mars, a soldier, and this is not consistent with universal peace. Now I do not want to deny that there is more than one thing we can do with this contradiction. We can open it out, and see in it a problem that Rome could never solve, an irresolvable opposition at the heart of the culture, or we can close it down, and join (some of) the Romans in their attempt to forge an ideology which combines the perspectives of Romulus and Numa, war and peace. What I would stress is that neither of these approaches is any more historicist or objective than the other. Which way we choose to jump is determined by which way we want to jump.

One aspect of this passage that has received considerable attention in recent Latin criticism is its metapoetics.[19] Jupiter is the male god of closure, whose cue for entry into the poem is notoriously *et iam finis erat*, 'already it was the end' (1.223); his attempts to bring things to an end are frustrated, at least for a time, by the female excess and energy of Juno, who keeps wanting to keep on going. Book Seven represents a turning point in the epic, and it is Juno who turns things around when it looked as if they were going to come to a happy end. The turning or overturning of the hinge of the gate in 621 *cardine verso* represents her contribution to getting the second half of the epic under way; we may note that Venus had used the metaphor of the *cardo* at an earlier nodal point in Book One (670–3):

> Now he is in the hands of the Phoenician Dido, who is delaying him with honeyed words, and I am afraid of Juno's hospitality and what it may bring. She will not stand idle when the gate of the future is turning.
>
> > nunc Phoenissa tenet Dido blandisque moratur
> > uocibus, et uereor quo se Iunonia uertant
> > hospitia: haud tanto cessabit *cardine* rerum.[20]

One of the ways in which the opposition between male control and female disorder is deconstructed in the *Aeneid* is through the notion of energy. Male power when manifested as control becomes a lack of power, in that it stops things happening, it shuts the gates, whereas female *furor* opens the gates and starts things up: it lets the genius out of the bottle, and inspires the poet to further poetry. This energy is a Roman energy, the energy that created Rome and creates the epic; the act of control itself is not possible without the previous existence of that energy. It has often been noted that in the description of the closure of the gates of war in Book One, *furor* is not lulled to sleep or killed but remains within the temple roaring despite its chains, and that indeed the picture ends with the roars of defiance rather than their containment. In part this is a reminder that *furor* is always there, that on Vergil's pessimistically (un/)Platonic view of the soul appetite and passion can never be eradicated by reason. But it also provides a way of giving the closure of the gates a Roman dynamism: because *furor* is always there, the need to control it is a constant one, and an element of forceful action can be inserted into what otherwise might be a picture without that most Roman of all properties, *vis*.

Another aspect of the mutual implicature of closure and opening is the question of repetition, so very persuasively made a central topic of Roman epic by Philip Hardie.[21] Juno's action occurred once and is narrated once, but it is aligned with the regular opening of the gates which occurs many times; that at least is the implication of 601–15, although we know from Augustus' own words that the gates had only twice been closed before his time. Juno has opened things up before, and will do so again; as Denis Feeney pointed out,[22] her refusal to stop will not stop with the end of the epic, and there will come another time when it will be possible *certare odiis*, as Jupiter remarks in 10.14. We know that things don't stop with Augustus, whether we are talking about civil war or Roman epic. These are not the first doors or gates that we have met in the *Aeneid*, nor the first time that they have been linked with Juno. The passage in Book Seven recalls the gates to her temple in Book One[23] – as well, of course, as those of the temple of Apollo in Book Six – and in the revelation of divine activity that Aeneas is given by his mother in Book Two (612–13), *Juno Scaeas saevissima portas | prima tenet*. We have already noted the doors to Aeolus' cave of the winds, the instrument of Juno's vengeance in Book One.[24] The fall of Troy began when it opened its gates and walls,[25] and later in Book Two Pyrrhus will smash his way into Priam's palace;[26] in the second half of the epic, the opening and closing of the gates both of the Trojan camp and of the city of Latinus will figure prominently in the action. In particular, when in Book Nine (722–30) Pandarus shuts Turnus into the camp by mistake, it is like the imprisonment of *furor* in Book One, except that this time Turnus is unchained and wreaks havoc:

> When Pandarus saw his brother stretched out in death and knew how his fortunes stood and the turn events were taking, he put his broad shoulder to the gate with all his force and heaved it shut on its hinges, leaving many of his own people cut off outside the walls with a hard battle to fight, but taking in those who came running and shutting them in with himself. Fool that he was! He did not see the Rutulian king bursting into the city in the middle of the press. By his own act he penned him in like a great tiger among helpless cattle.

Opening the Gates of War

> Pandarus, ut fuso germanum corpore cernit
> et quo sit fortuna loco, qui casus agat res,
> portam ui multa *conuerso cardine* torquet
> obnixus latis umeris, multosque suorum
> moenibus exclusos duro in certamine linquit;
> ast alios secum includit recipitque ruentis,
> demens, qui Rutulum in medio non agmine regem
> uiderit inrumpentem ultroque incluserit urbi,
> immanem ueluti pecora inter inertia tigrim.

Beyond the *Aeneid* itself,[27] there are many more gates to take into consideration, but I foreground just one: the gates of nature which Epicurus assaults in Book One (66–78) of the *De rerum natura*, itself, as Buchheit argued,[28] using the imagery of Alexander and his conquests:

> A Greek man first dared to lift mortal eyes against religion, first took stand against her. Neither stories of the gods, nor thunderbolts, nor the sky with threatening noise held him back, but all the more they aroused the fierce manliness of his soul, and thus brought him to desire, first of all men, to shatter the tight bars of nature's gates. Therefore the lively power of his mind won through, and he made an expedition far beyond the flaming walls of the world, traversing the immense universe in thought and imagination; from where victorious he brings back to us knowledge of what can come into being, and what cannot, in a word, how each thing has a finite power and deep-set boundary mark. Therefore religion is now in turn cast down and trampled underfoot, but victory brings us level with the sky.

> primum Graius homo mortalis tollere contra
> est oculos ausus primusque obsistere contra;
> quem neque fama deum nec fulmina nec minitanti
> murmure compressit caelum, sed eo magis acrem
> inritat animi virtutem, effringere ut arta
> naturae primus portarum claustra cupiret.
> ergo vivida vis animi pervicit et extra
> processit longe flammantia moenia mundi
> atque omne immensum peragravit mente animoque,
> unde refert nobis victor quid possit oriri,
> quid nequeat, finita potestas denique cuique
> qua nam sit ratione atque alte terminus haerens.
> quare religio pedibus subiecta vicissim
> opteritur, nos exaequat victoria caelo.

This shares with the *Aeneid* a use of sexual imagery for the opening of the gates,[29] but of course in the Epicurean context there is also a sense of the freeing of nature from her bonds and of a liberation from containment for humanity.[30] It is noteworthy in the *Aeneid* passage that the result of Juno's opening of the gates is described in terms of intense cultural activity as old weapons are reforged and new weapons made. Agriculture is abandoned for a later stage of civilisation, mass warfare; Italy is recalled from its Saturnian slumber to a Jovian sense of struggle and cultural progress. The military-industrial complex kicks in and technology makes a great leap forward. One reading of this is obviously as a parody of the Epicurean celebration of the triumph of reason, with madness rather the motivating force within society. But it is difficult not to read the parallel another way, in which Juno's action is another example precisely of that human drive towards action rather than stasis, however motivated. Juno as culture-hero in her opening of the gates is not simply a matter of parody: there is a sense in which this is the way progress really is made in human societies.

Latinus in the passage is urged to act constitutionally, to open the gates *hoc...more* and declare war on the Aeneadae:[31] but he refuses and hides himself in the shadows.[32] Juno has to come down to release the gates and help give birth to war, just as she sent Iris down to allow Dido to die at the end of Book Four (693–5):

> All-powerful Juno then took pity on her long anguish and difficult death and sent Iris down from Olympus to free her struggling spirit and loosen the fastenings of her limbs.
>
> > tum Iuno omnipotens longum miserata dolorem
> > difficilisque obitus Irim demisit Olympo
> > quae luctantem animam nexosque resolueret artus.

In times of difficulty, one may have to cut the Gordian knot,[33] and take direct action, as Aeneas does earlier in Book 4 (579–83) when he makes his escape:

> As he spoke he drew his sword from its scabbard like a flash of lightning and struck the mooring cables with the naked steel. In that instant they were all seized by the same ardour and set to, hauling and hustling. The shore was emptied. The sea could not be seen for ships. Bending to the oars they whipped up the foam and swept the blue surface of the sea.
>
> > dixit uaginaque eripit ensem
> > fulmineum strictoque ferit retinacula ferro.
> > *idem omnis simul ardor habet*,[34] rapiuntque ruuntque;
> > litora deseruere, latet sub classibus aequor,
> > adnixi torquent spumas et caerula uerrunt.

It is difficult not to feel that another dimension to this act is what had happened at Rome in the last thirty years, what T. Habinek and A. Schiesaro call in a forthcoming volume the 'Roman Cultural Revolution' – the destruction of the republic and the birth of a new polity.

Clearly that is not how Augustus represents his acts: he fashions himself not as creating something new but as restoring the old, not as breaking with the past and opening things up but as keeping everything under tight control. But the Roman civil wars had begun when Caesar had refused to brook with delay and had broken with constitutional rule; a century later Lucan will of course find it easy to use this imagery of Caesar. To see not just the Roman spirit but Caesar and Augustus in Juno in the *Aeneid* passage may seem the height of perversity, and I do not want to press the point, but if we do look back from Lucan there is one episode which it is again difficult to keep out of one's mind: the scene in Book Three where Caesar attempts to break into the Aerarium Saturni and L. Metellus tries to stop him:

> Stubborn Metellus, when he saw the Saturnian temples being burst open with huge force, quickly ran there and, breaking through the ranks of Caesar, took his stand at the gates which had not yet been forced open.

>> pugnaxque Metellus,
>> ut uidet ingenti Saturnia templa reuelli
>> mole, rapit gressus et Caesaris agmina rumpens
>> ante fores nondum reseratae constitit aedis.   (114–17)

> Straightway Metellus was taken aside and the temple laid bare. Then the Tarpeian rock sounded, and with loud screeching bore witness to the opening of the doors; then the wealth of the Roman people, stored in the depths of the temple and untouched for many a year, was dragged out.

>> protinus abducto patuerunt templa Metello.
>> tunc rupes Tarpeia sonat magnoque reclusas
>> testatur stridore fores; tum conditus imo
>> eruitur templo multis non tactus ab annis
>> Romani census populi.   (153–7)

Caesar's dynamic defiance of custom makes the scene a popular one in the historians, and all emphasise the moment when Caesar breaks open (or orders to be broken open) the treasury:

> Caesar hurried to Rome. The people, remembering what had happened under Sulla and Marius, were terrified, but Caesar tried to reassure them with many hopes and promises, and as a signal of his clemency to his enemies, he said that even if he captured Lucius Domitius he would release him unharmed and let him keep his money. But he cut open the fastenings of the public treasury, and threatened Metellus, one of the tribunes, with death when he tried to stop him.

> ὁ δὲ Καῖσαρ ἐς Ῥώμην ἐπειχθεὶς τόν τε δῆμον, ἐκ μνήμης τῶν ἐπὶ Σύλλα καὶ Μαρίου κακῶν πεφρικότα, ἐλπίσι καὶ ὑποσχέσεσι πολλαῖς ἀνελάμβανε καὶ

τοῖς ἐχθροῖς ἐνσημαινόμενος φιλανθρωπίαν εἶπεν, ὅτι καὶ Λεύκιον Δομίτιον ἑλὼν ἀπαθῆ μεθείη μετὰ τῶν χρημάτων. τὰ δὲ κλεῖθρα τῶν δημοσίων ταμιείων ἐξέκοπτε καὶ τῶν δημάρχων ἑνὶ Μετέλλῳ κωλύοντι θάνατον ἠπείλει.
(Appian *BC* 2.41).

One Lucius Metellus, a tribune, spoke out against the proposal about the money, and when he got nowhere, he went to the treasury and placed its doors under guard. But the soldiers paid as little heed to his guard as to his outspokenness, and they cut through the bolt (the consuls having the key) as it was not possible to use any axes instead of it, and carried off all the money.

ἀντεῖπε μὲν οὖν πρὸς τὴν περὶ τῶν χρημάτων ἐσήγησιν Λούκιός τις Μέτελλος δήμαρχος, καὶ ἐπειδὴ μηδὲν ἐπέρανε, πρός τε τοὺς θησαυροὺς ἦλθε καὶ τὰς θύρας αὐτῶν ἐν τηρήσει ἐποιήσατο· σμικρὸν δὲ δὴ καὶ τῆς φυλακῆς αὐτοῦ, ὥσπερ που καὶ τῆς παρρησίας, οἱ στρατιῶται φροντίσαντες τήν τε βαλανάγραν διέκοψαν, τὴν γὰρ κλεῖν οἱ ὕπατοι εἶχον, ὥσπερ οὐκ ἐξόν τισι πελέκεσιν ἀντ᾽ αὐτῆς χρήσασθαι, καὶ πάντα τὰ χρήματα ἐξεφόρησαν.
(Dio Cassius 41.17.2)

When the tribune Metellus tried to prevent Caesar taking money from the reserve funds of the state, and cited certain laws, Caesar said that arms and law had not the same season. 'But if you are unhappy at what is going on, for the present get out of the way, since war has no use for free speech; when, however, I have come to terms, and laid down my arms, then you can come forward and address the people. And in saying this I waive my own just rights; for you are mine, you and all of the faction hostile to me whom I have caught.' After this speech to Metellus, Caesar walked towards the door of the treasury, and when the keys were not to be found, he sent for smiths and ordered them to break in the door. Metellus once more opposed him, and was commended by some for so doing; but Caesar raising his voice, threatened to kill him if he did not cease his troublesome interference. 'And you must know, young man,' said he, 'that it is more unpleasant for me to say this than to do it.' Then Metellus, in consequence of this speech, went off in a fright, and everything else was speedily and easily furnished to Caesar for the war.

Τοῦ δὲ δημάρχου Μετέλλου κωλύοντος αὐτὸν ἐκ τῶν ἀποθέτων χρήματα λαμβάνειν καὶ νόμους τινὰς προφέροντος, οὐκ ἔφη τὸν αὐτὸν ὅπλων καὶ νόμων καιρὸν εἶναι· σὺ δ᾽ εἰ τοῖς πραττομένοις δυσκολαίνεις, νῦν μὲν ἐκποδὼν ἄπιθι· παρρησίας γὰρ οὐ δεῖται πόλεμος· ὅταν δὲ καταθῶμαι τὰ ὅπλα συμβάσεων γενομένων, τότε παριὼν δημαγωγήσεις. καὶ ταῦτ᾽ ἔφη λέγω τῶν ἐμαυτοῦ δικαίων ὑφιέμενος· ἐμὸς γὰρ εἶ καὶ σὺ καὶ πάντες ὅσους εἴληφα τῶν πρὸς ἐμὲ στασιασάντων. ταῦτα πρὸς τὸν Μέτελλον εἰπών, ἐβάδιζε πρὸς τὰς θύρας τοῦ ταμιείου. μὴ φαινομένων δὲ τῶν κλειδῶν, χαλκεῖς μεταπεμψάμενος ἐκκόπτειν ἐκέλευεν. αὖθις δ᾽ ἐνισταμένου τοῦ Μετέλλου καί τινων ἐπαινούντων, διατεινάμενος ἠπείλησεν ἀποκτενεῖν αὐτόν, εἰ μὴ παύσαιτο παρενοχλῶν· καὶ τοῦτ᾽ ἔφη μειράκιον οὐκ ἀγνοεῖς ὅτι μοι δυσκολώτερον ἦν εἰπεῖν ἢ πρᾶξαι. οὗτος ὁ λόγος τότε καὶ Μέτελλον ἀπελθεῖν ἐποίησε καταδείσαντα, καὶ τὰ ἄλλα ῥᾳδίως αὐτῷ καὶ ταχέως ὑπηρετεῖσθαι πρὸς τὸν πόλεμον. (Plutarch, *Caesar* 35.6–11)

I do not, as I say, press the point, but for those who wanted to recall the act, *Saturnia* in *Aen.* 7.622,[35] though there are other reasons for calling Juno that at this point where she is at her least Saturnian – there is a tension here with *ferratos*, the sign of the iron age – might call to mind that Caesar's act took place in the *Aerarium Saturni*.

The custodian of the gates of war was Janus, a figure who has played an important part in recent criticism of Ovid as a symbol of the necessarily two-faced nature of reading.[36] He is therefore a welcome figure on which I too might conclude, might try once more to close the gates. I have no quarrel at all with those who wish to contextualise the *Aeneid* within the surviving literary and figurative remains from the period. But I repeat that to do so is not going to settle anything, is not going to solve any puzzles or enable us to reach any agreement, because we are not going to agree on what the relevant context is and if we did we would not agree on what to do with it. If you want your Augustan monuments, then I shall have my pillaging of the Central Bank. We are however bound together in mutual dependence, in that unless the one side closes the gates the other cannot open them, and vice versa. However much we might think we do, we really do not want to close those gates for good – at least if we want our successors still to have a job.[37]

Notes

[1] Elsner (1991), Galinsky (1992). Cf. Castriota (1995), Gurval (1995) 125 n. 95.

[2] Cf. Fowler (forthcoming 2).

[3] I expand here on some brief remarks in Fowler (forthcoming 3).

[4] My translation; other translations from the *Aeneid* are taken from David West's Penguin translation (London 1990); except where noted, translations from other authors are my own.

[5] Richardson (1992) 207–8.

[6] Hill (1989) 10. The coins date from 66 CE

[7] Cf. Ovid, *Fasti* 1.99, 259: for the arrangement of the fingers, cf. Pliny, *NH* 34.33, *Ianus Geminus a Numa rege dicatus, qui pacis bellique argumento colitur digitis ita figuratis, ut CCCLV dierum nota [aut per significationem anni temporis] et aevi esse deum indicent.*

[8] Galinsky (1996) 34–7, 84, 282, 346.

[9] Cf also Fox (1996) 25–6, 113–15.

[10] Cf. Suetonius, *Aug.* 22 *Ianum Quirinum semel atque iterum a condita urbe ante memoriam suam clausum in multo breuiore temporis spatio terra marique pace parta ter clusit.*

[11] L. Calpurnius Piso, *Annales* fr. 9. For Piso's topographical interests, see Rawson 1991.

[12] Cf. most recently O'Hara (1990), Kraggerud (1992), O'Hara (1994), Dobbin (1995), Harrison (1996). I personally find it impossible to separate *olim* from *tum*, and conclude therefore that the Golden Age comes to be after the assumption of Caesar – whoever he is – into heaven (cf. Lucan 1.60). For a different view, see Stahl (1985) 340 n. 46.

[13] Cf. Isidore, *Orig.* 8.11.69: *Iunonem dicunt quasi ianonem, id est ianuam, pro purgationibus feminarum, eo quod quasi portas matrum natis pandat, et nubentum maritis;* Hershkowitz (forthcoming).

[14] Cf. O'Hara (1996) 192 for etymological intensification of the name *Ardea* (631).

[15] Fowler (1983).

[16] Hendry (1996).

[17] Cf. Servius on 7.614, Berger (1953), s.v. *evocati*, 'persons who in case of emergency assumed military service for as long a time as the state remained in danger'.

[18] Cf. 1.722, 2.509, 6.814.

[19] Cf. D. Feeney (1991) 137; Hershkowitz (forthcoming).

[20] Cf. D. Servius on 1.672: *quidam sic intellegunt: cum in incerto statutae res sunt, in cardine esse dicuntur, et translationem verbi a ianua tractam volunt, quae motu cardinis hac atque illac inpelli potest.* Compare the similar metapoetic use of *cardo* in the Argonauts' prayer to Apollo at the beginning of the second half (?) of Valerius Flaccus' *Argonautica*, 5.18–21 *hoc, pater, hoc nobis refove caput, ulla laboris | si nostri te cura movet, qui* cardine summo *| vertitur atque omnis manibus nunc pendet ab unis!'* Valerius' poem, as well as the Argonauts' enterprise, turns at this point on its *cardo*, dependent on the hands of the reader as s/he turns the new scroll.

[21] Hardie (1993).

[22] Feeney (1984).

[23] 1.446–9 *hic templum Iunoni ingens Sidonia Dido | condebat, donis opulentum et numine diuae, | aerea cui gradibus surgebant limina nexaeque |aere trabes,* foribus cardo stridebat aënis.

[24] 1.81–3, *haec ubi dicta, cauum conuersa cuspide montem | impulit in latus; ac uenti uelut agmine facto, | qua data* porta, *ruunt et terras turbine perflant.*

[25] Cf. 2.27–8, 242–5.

[26] Cf. 2. 479–85, 291–3.

[27] Cf. also 3.455–52 (Sibyl's cave), 6.573–5 (doors of Tartarus).

[28] Buchheit (1971); cf. Hardie (1986) 194.

[29] Cf. Nugent (1994).

[30] Cf. Fowler (forthcoming 3).

[31] 7.616: *hoc et tum Aeneadis indicere bella Latinus| more iubebatur.* That 'the Latin' is urged to declare war on the Aeneadae is obviously pointed (cf. 7.284).

[32] Latinus' quasi-sexual revulsion at the *foeda ministeria* of touching the gates and his retreat into blind oblivion suggests perhaps an implicit myth of Oedipus.

[33] Cf. Buchheit (1971); e.g. Plutarch, *Alex.* 18.2 ff.; Curtius Rufus 3.1.15 ff. Compare the decisive Roman breaking of constraints by Cocles and Cloelia on

the shield in Book Eight (650–1): *pontem auderet...vellere Cocles | et fluvium vinclis innaret Cloelia ruptis.*

[34] Expanding on Apollonius, *Arg.* 1.878: σπερχόμενοι.

[35] On the epithet in general, cf. Anderson (1958); J. O'Hara (1996) 69, 270.

[36] Cf. Barchiesi (1991), Hardie (1991). Note that Latinus swears by *Latonaeque genus duplex Ianumque bifrontem* (12.198) when he attempts to close down the epic a little (but not much) prematurely in the oath-taking scene in Book 12: you would think that he would have noticed that the subsequent description of his sceptre came from *Iliad* Book 1 (234 ff.), not Book 24, and that as Servius remarks on 1.449, *Iano consecratum est omne principium*, given that his own palace prominently displays *Saturnusque senex Ianique bifrontis imago* precisely in its *vestibulum* (7.180–1: on *vestibulum* there, cf. Aulus Gellius 16.5). Latinus' choice of Janus in Book 12 recalls one of the explanations given by Servius on 1.291 for the latter's double nature: *alii dicunt Tatium et Romulum facto foedere hoc templum aedificasse, unde et Ianus ipse duas facies habet, quasi ut ostendat duorum regum coitionem* (repeated on 12.198), but Vergilian ambiguity here celebrates Latin duplicity. On the shield, the treaty between Romulus and Tatius concludes the Sabine section (8.639–41), but Tatius was going to come to a bad end (Livy 1.14), in another of those messy Roman closural beginnings.

[37] I am grateful for comments to the participants at the Oxford conference, and especially to Peta Fowler and John Henderson.

Bibliography

Anderson, W. S.
   1958   'Juno and Saturn in the *Aeneid*', *SP* 60, 519–32.

Barchiesi, A.
   1991   'Discordant Muses', *PCPhS* 37, 1–21.

Berger, A.
   1953   *Encyclopedic Dictionary of Roman Law*, Philadelphia.

Buchheit, V.
   1971   'Epikurs Triumph des Geistes (Lucr. 1.62–79)',*Hermes* 99, 303–23.

Castriota, D.
   1995   *The Ara Pacis Augustae and the Imagery of Abundance in Later Greek and Early Imperial Art*, Princeton.

Dobbin, R.F.
   1995   'Julius Caesar in Jupiter's prophecy, *Aeneid* Book I', *CA* 14, 5–40.

Elsner, J.
   1991   'Cult and sculpture: sacrifice in the*Ara Pacis Augustae*', *JRS* 81, 50–61.

Feeney, D.C.
   1984   'The reconciliations of Juno', *CQ* 34, 179–94.
   1991   *The Gods in Epic*, Oxford.

Fowler, D.P.
   1983   'An acrostic in Vergil (*Aeneid* 7. 601–604)?' *CQ* 33, 298.
   Forthcoming (1)   'The feminine principle: gender in the *De rerum natura*',

in the proceedings of the Naples conference on Epicureanism in honour of Marcello Gigante.

Forthcoming (2) 1997 'Epicurean anger', in S.M. Braund and C.Gill, *The Passions in Roman Thought and Literature*, Cambridge.

Forthcoming (3) 'Standing on the shoulders of giants: intertextuality and classical studies', in a special issue of *MD*, ed. D.P. Fowler and S.J. Hinds.

Fox, M.
  1996 *Roman Historical Myths*, Oxford.
Galinsky, G.K.
  1992 'Venus, Polysemy, and the Ara Pacis Augustae', *AJA* 96, 457–75.
  1996 *Augustan Culture*, Princeton.
Gurval, R.A.
  1995 *Actium and Augustus*, Ann Arbor.
Hardie, P.R.
  1986 *Virgil's Aeneid: Cosmos and Imperium*, Oxford.
  1991 'The Janus episode in Ovid's *Fasti*', *MD* 26, 47–64.
  1993 *The Epic Successors of Virgil*, Cambridge.
Harrison, S.J.
  1996 '*Aeneid* 1.286: Julius Caesar or Augustus?', in *Papers of the Leeds international Latin seminar* 9, 127–33.
Hendry, M.
  1993/96 'A Martial acronym in Ennius?', *LCM* 19, 108–9.
Hershkowitz, D.
  Forthcoming 1998 *Madness in Greek and Roman Epic*, Oxford.
Hill, P.
  1989 *The Monuments of Ancient Rome as Coin Types*, London.
Kraggerud, E.
  1992 'Which Julius Caesar? On *Aen.* 1. 286–96', *SO* 67, 103–12.
Nugent, S.G.
  1994 'Matter matters: the female in Lucretius' *De Rerum Natura*', *Colby Quarterly* 30, 179–205.
O'Hara, J.J.
  1990 *Death and the Optimistic Prophecy in Vergil's Aeneid*, Princeton.
  1994 'Temporal distortions, "fatal" ambiguity, and Iulius Caesar at *Aeneid* 1.286–96', *SO* 69, 72–82.
  1996 *True Names, Vergil and the Alexandrian Tradition of Etymological Wordplay*, Ann Arbor.
Rawson, E.
  1991 'The first Roman annalists', in *Roman Culture and Society*, 245–71, Oxford.
Richardson, L. jr.
  1992 *A New Topographical Dictionary of Ancient Rome*, Baltimore and London.
Stahl, H.-P.
  1985 *Propertius: 'Love' and 'War', Individual and State under Augustus*, Berkeley.

9

ASSIMILATION AND CIVIL WAR: HERCULES AND CACUS*
Aeneid 8

Llewelyn Morgan

I. Hercules v. Cacus
This paper addresses Vergil's account of the struggle between Hercules and Cacus in *Aeneid* 8. There are few passages in the whole poem which are more familiar or have been analysed more thoroughly. It is as a consequence hard to say anything very original about *Hercules and Cacus*, and as far as detailed interpretation of the passage goes this paper will make little attempt to. Rather, what it will suggest is a different way of organizing and interpreting those details, and indeed I have chosen an episode with which everybody is reasonably familiar deliberately so as to create a kind of test case. In addition I have tried, for clarity's sake, to keep references to secondary literature to a minimum, aiming to illustrate general trends in scholarship of the episode, and nothing more.

The question this paper will consider is how *Hercules and Cacus*, and the *Aeneid* more generally, could operate as the politically directed product of the Augustan regime which the external evidence about its creation would lead us to expect it to be. I feel strengthened in posing this somewhat unfashionable question by the rubric of this collection of papers, since this is another way of asking how we can make sense of *Hercules and Cacus* in its political context.

Let us start from a position widely held in Vergilian scholarship: namely, that the *Aeneid* – and the *Hercules and Cacus* episode which has such a central symbolic role in the *Aeneid*[1] – was originally designed in essence to comprise fairly straightforward panegyric of Augustus, the view that Vergil *praises* Augustus *simpliciter*.[2] Now as it is generally formulated I do not think this view stands too much investigation, but scholars who have argued this position have found evidence for it in this passage, and this material would seem an appropriate place to start.

To a certain extent, then, what we are dealing with in this passage is – as these scholars have pointed out – a series of fairly stark polar oppositions constructed about and between the two combatants. Much of Vergil's colouring implies that in the struggle between Hercules and Cacus we are witnessing a battle between good and evil. Cacus' very name establishes a moral contrast: Κάκος is κακός, 'wicked'.[3] And much of the imagery of the passage works to develop this dualism; the Hercules *versus* Cacus opposition yields a series of further, interrelated oppositions: besides good v. bad, there is light v. darkness (195, 198, 211), revelation v. concealment (241), day v. night (255), heaven v. hell (241–6), divine (201, 275, 301) v. bestial (194, 267), reason v. unreason (299), height v. depth (221, 241–6), West v. East,[4] and so on. It is not hard to see that many of these oppositions will recur in the description of Actium at the end of Book 8,[5] and there are thus immediately certain things which can be said about *Hercules and Cacus*' resonance with contemporary politics. Buchheit, Galinsky and Gransden, building upon this basic dualism, establish the typological links between a series of heroes exemplified in this passage by the figure of Hercules, and a corresponding series of villains epitomized by Cacus. Thus Gransden, representatively:[6]

> Vergil emphasises typological parallels between Cacus, Turnus and Antony as enemies of civilisation, and between Hercules, Aeneas and Augustus as defenders of it, so that the exploit (sc. Hercules' defeat of Cacus) becomes a model of the 'heroic encounter' with evil.

The good Hercules thus parallels the good Aeneas and of course the good Augustus, who towards the end of the book, like Hercules in this passage, arrives at Rome victorious: the triple triumph celebrated by Augustus on August the 13th, 14th and 15th, 29 BC, followed immediately after the festival of Hercules at the Ara Maxima (August the 12th), of which *Hercules and Cacus* is the aetiological myth.[7] Aeneas also arrives at the same time, and Galinsky points out that the 'god' whose arrival at Rome is referred to at lines 200–1 could be Augustus as much as Hercules.[8] An equally ingenious reference to contemporary events is the emphasis on the chief priest of the Ara Maxima cult, Potitius (*primusque Potitius auctor*, 269; *primusque Potitius*, 281), a member of one of the two families which according to tradition had originally established the cult (Livy 1.7.12–14). Potitius prefigures the suffect consul of 29 BC, Octavian's colleague Potitus Valerius Messalla, who performed sacrifices in celebration of Octavian's arrival in Rome in 29 BC, just as his remote ancestor had performed them to celebrate Hercules' visitation.[9]

Hercules mirrors Aeneas; and his opponents correspondingly mirror Aeneas' and Augustus' opponents; so behind Cacus we can discern (amongst others) Turnus the enemy of Aeneas,[10] and Mark Antony, the enemy confronted by Augustus at the end of Book 8.[11] An apparent innovation on Vergil's part regarding the location of Cacus' home – the pre-Vergilian tradition would seem to have located it on the Palatine (where a track known as the 'Scalae Caci' was to be found),[12] in which case Vergil relocated it to the Aventine (231) – activates, as Gransden notes, another, highly significant, set of associations for *Hercules and Cacus*: the Aventine lay outside the sacred Roman *pomerium* and was – according to the dominant tradition – the augural station of Remus, who trespassed on the Palatine and was slain for it by Romulus.[13] Thus, according to Livy (1.6.4), 'Romulus took the Palatine and Remus the Aventine for their inaugural quarters', *Palatium Romulus, Remus Auentinum ad inaugurandum templa capiunt*; Propertius refers simply to 'Aventine Remus',*Auentinus Remus* (4.1.50).[14] Romulus, the founder of Rome, must underlie much of the ktistic imagery of this passage and of this book, and we will be returning to him and his twin brother later in this paper.[15]

There is of course much more to be said on the opposition between Hercules and Cacus. Hardie, in particular, brings out the cosmic dimension of the struggle: the Olympian Hercules against the monstrous, gigantic Cacus reflects the original imposition of order on chaos in the battles of the Olympian gods against the Giants, Titans and Typhoeus. *Hercules and Cacus* is thus in one aspect a creation myth.[16] But the general picture is clear enough. Suffice it to say with Galinsky that 'the poet was anxious to impress on the reader the analogy between Herakles and Aeneas, and between Cacus and Turnus even at the risk of seeming tedious.'[17]

II. Types and anti-types

Gransden has a useful term for all this: the wicked partner in each pair – Cacus, Turnus, Antony – is an 'anti-type' of the good. It is worth analysing this term briefly. Gransden uses the word to emphasize the *difference* between the members of each pair, but it also clearly implies some kind of similarity between them: *type* and *anti-type* are at least of the same *type*. As Gransden well appreciates, one of the most striking features of the *Aeneid* is how very similar to one another each hero and villain is. Gransden employs the term 'anti-type', for example, at 196–7 describing the trophies at the entrance to Cacus' cave:

> pinned to its proud doors faces of men hung pale with grim decay
>
> foribusque adfixa superbis
> ora uirum tristi pendebant pallida tabo

Cacus' trophies here, as Galinsky points out, foreshadow the heads hung from Turnus' chariot (12.511–2),[18] but are also 'anti-types' both of the spoils on the doors of Latinus' temple (7.183–6) and of the gifts which Augustus *affixes to the doorposts* of the temple of Apollo (8.721–2):

> he reviews the gifts of the peoples and fixes them to the proud door-posts
>
> dona recognoscit populorum *aptatque superbis postibus*

The presentations of the good Augustus and the bad Cacus are thus in some respects extremely similar. Not only that, Cacus is also very comparable to his immediate adversary, Hercules, who at 202 is

> proud with slaughter and spoils of threefold Geryon
>
> tergemini nece Geryonae spoliisque *superbus*

This – the similitude of the adversaries – is an insight which Lyne makes the basis of his interpretation of the passage.[19] As Lyne shows, there are a number of other details in the Hercules and Cacus episode which have the effect of *assimilating* the combatants or their analogues. Lyne begins with the striking metaphor used of the light beaming from Augustus' temples at 8.680–1:

> his joyful temples vomit twin flames
>
> geminas cui tempora flammas
> laeta uomunt

As Lyne says, the expression occurs five other times in the *Aeneid*, four of those times in Book 8. Aeneas' new helmet 'vomits flames' (8.620), as does the boss of his shield at 10.271. But in addition Cacus is depicted three times 'vomiting fire', *vel sim.*:

> vomiting Vulcan's black fires from his mouth
>
> illius atros
> ore uomens ignis   (8.198–9)

> he vomits out great smoke (wondrous to relate) from his jaws
>
> faucibus ingentem fumum (mirabile dictu)
> euomit   (8.252–3)

Hercules seizes Cacus as he vomits futile fires in the darkness

> hic Cacum in tenebris incendia uana uomentem
> corripit   (8.259–60).

Such closely related imagery, as Lyne argues, cannot help but make us associate Cacus and Augustus; there can, as far as I can see, be no ignoring it. But, if so, this obviously poses problems for the *Aeneid*-as-pure-panegyric view, and we can discern a certain anxiety. A recent translation of the poem, for example, which states in the introduction that 'the *Aeneid* is successful panegyric', translates the expression 'vomit', 'vomit', and 'belch', when it is used of Cacus, but 'spurt' when we reach Aeneas' helmet and 'stream' of Augustus' temples. It takes the highly malevolent colouring of 10.270–5 to exact the translation 'belch' again.[20] Well, we should be clear that the word *is* 'vomit', and that it is hard to ignore its pejorative associations.[21] Lyne, interpreting the image as (amongst other things) symbolizing *uis*, 'power' or 'force', concludes – reasonably enough – that 'force on the 'right' side may not only be as passionate as the enemy's, but monstrous like an enemy's.'[22]

Lyne must be right in this. Yet I still consider that *Hercules and Cacus* is capable of yielding a significance which we could reasonably call propagandistic. The challenge is to show that these 'negative' elements do not preclude a propagandistic function for the poem as a whole. What is clear is that we cannot ignore them: the spoils attached to the doors and the *uomo*-motif are far from the only examples of this assimilation of Hercules and Cacus and the other combatants. The floor of Cacus' cave (195–6), for example, 'was always warm with fresh slaughter', *semperque recenti | caede tepebat humus*, foreshadowing the battle of Actium, where (695) 'the fields of Neptune redden with fresh slaughter', *arua noua Neptunia caede rubescunt*. By the term 'foreshadow' here I mean: when Vergil's account of Augustus' glorious victory at Actium is read, can it be free of associations with Cacus' cave?

Augustus and Cacus here seem to resemble each other not only in their *uis* but also in their killing. Lyne shows also how Hercules and Cacus resemble each other in their *fury*. 'The mind of Cacus is wild with frenzy' (*at furis Caci mens effera*, 205),[23] whilst the wrath of Hercules 'had blazed forth with frenzy' (*furiis exarserat*, 219). And we can compare 228, 'behold! the Tirynthian was at hand, frenzied with anger', *ecce furens animis aderat Tirynthius*.[24] I could continue in this vein, but it should be clear that, whilst it is true that Vergil establishes associations between his heroes (Hercules–Aeneas–Augustus) and his villains (Cacus–Turnus–Antony), he also takes great pains to assimilate each member of a pair to his opposite number, and to the opposite numbers of his analogues. Cacus is, in a manner of speaking, Hercules' twin. Why?

For Lyne, of course, the assimilation of hero to villain is symptomatic of the tendency of Vergilian narrative to 'comment on, question, and occasionally subvert' the panegyric superficially voiced by the text. 'Why,' he asks, 'should our heroes be equipped with imagery that recalls the monstrous Cacus? How do we interpret the pattern? A further voice is jogging us to questions.'[25]

We have thus sketched (in the broadest terms) two methodologies in Vergilian criticism, or strictly in the study of Vergilian politics: first, the interpretation exemplified (in this paper) by Buchheit, Galinsky and Gransden, that the *Aeneid* is more or less straightforward panegyric; and secondly the 'pessimistic' (or however we would like to refer to it) position of a scholar like Lyne. But in fact these superficially antithetical positions are related: Lyne builds upon the Buchheit–Galinsky–Gransden position. He accepts that a first reading of *Hercules and Cacus* would yield a simple panegyrical significance:

> The exemplary Hercules appears to prefigure the exemplary Aeneas, who prefigures the exemplary Augustus: Hercules (and Aeneas) are mythical paradigms for an idealized Augustus. Such, I think, may well be the way in which the episode first appears to us.[26]

This, he says elsewhere,[27] is how Vergil wished it initially to seem, until the niggling doubts he sows in the shape of the *uomo*-motif, etc. set about undermining the superficial praise.

III. The requirements of Augustan propaganda

So we are in danger of finding ourselves back at the rather tedious debate between 'optimists' and 'pessimists'. A typical contemporary approach to this debate is to forget it, 'move beyond it' to more interesting approaches to a reading or readings of the text. Hardie talks of the 'monotonously reductive debate about whether Vergil was really for or against Augustus'.[28] He is certainly right that it was monotonous, but 'reductive' is less fair. Hardie believes that a reading which seeks to establish the political design underlying the poem will necessarily involve a quite arbitrary decision as to which elements of the text are significant for an interpretation and which are not. I remain unconvinced by this argument, which is to say that such a choice does not seem to me necessarily arbitrary. The optimism/pessimism issue occupied attentions for so long because the political circumstances of this poem and this poet continued to be felt to be important and continued to be unclear. There was a sense that the framework for interpretation provided by authorial design had a fundamental role to play in any understanding of the text, a sense I remain far from convinced was misguided.

Hardie's 'reductive' implies that any satisfactory solution of the optimism/pessimism dilemma is inherently impossible, requiring as it does arbitrary suppression of half the evidence. Part of the grounds for his position is the seemingly irresoluble nature of the debate, as it was typically conducted; there are, as we have seen, unquestionably 'positive' elements to the depiction of Hercules, but these are consistently balanced by 'negative' elements. A positive reading of the text, it is suggested, can only be constructed by (arbitrarily) ignoring these negative elements. This, I am now going to suggest, need not be the case. I grant that the optimism/pessimism debate, as it tended to be framed, was inherently irresoluble, but this need not mean that the *Aeneid* is incapable of yielding a 'positive', 'Augustan' (etc.) meaning. What I am going to spend the rest of this paper doing is showing how Vergil's depiction of Hercules and Cacus as so similar to each other might serve a propagandistic end. And where I think we need to start is by clarifying the notion of 'propaganda' which has repeatedly cropped up in this paper.

The solution to the problem lies, I think, in a clearer understanding of the nature of literary propaganda. That 'monotonous', irresoluble debate as to whether the *Aeneid* was pro- or anti-Augustan was largely built on certain assumptions as to the sort of things an 'Augustan' epic would say. It was assumed that it would offer a certain amount of propaganda, of course, but also that that propaganda would be direct, categorical, panegyrical. There is a tendency to think of propaganda as a strident and unsubtle mode of communication. Lyne rather exemplifies this assumption when he talks about the 'further voices' which in his view undercut the superficially Augustan message of *Hercules and Cacus*. As we have seen, Lyne postulates a superficially panegyrical message – at its most basic, 'Augustus = the heroic Hercules' – which is undercut by these extra details. 'Vergil tempts us into thinking he will give us propaganda,' Lyne writes, 'but in fact delivers truth.'[29] 'Propaganda' here is assumed to be the same as 'praise', but this is at best a partial picture. Simply stated, if propaganda is blatant, or blatantly misleading, it does not work as propaganda. Effective propaganda is subtle, acceptable; it 'coalesces unnoticed with the existing values of a society';[30] it is propaganda which 'succeeds in engaging us directly as participants in its communicative systems.'[31] In other words, effective propaganda does not depart blatantly from the beliefs, attitudes, language and experience of its public. If it does so, it is blatantly unconvincing and fails to be compelling, which is of course its entire point. So the first step to answering my question is asking what overriding public experience Vergil might have been obliged to confront at this time; and the short answer, I would suggest, is *civil war*. If we can assume for a moment that one of the aims of the *Aeneid* was to reconcile Rome to its new leader, Augustus, then an Augustan propagandist's most pressing problem in the 20s BC was this: as far as his readership – the Roman elite – was concerned, Augustus was irretrievably tainted by his involvement in the Civil Wars. Yavetz, for example, in connection with Augustus' apologetical autobiography, the *De Vita Sua*, composed in the 20s BC, writes:

> To survive five civil wars, he (sc. Augustus) had had to be firm and ruthless, but he must have found out to his distress that he had acquired a reputation as a cruel, vengeful, selfish, and treacherous youth. This image had to be changed. It was not easy to alter public opinion, and he could not become a 'clementissimus' overnight...[32]

An ancient author says something rather similar. Seneca, in his *De Clementia*, contrasts the mildness and clemency of the mature Augustus with the behaviour of his youth (1.11.1):

> Such were the actions of Augustus when an old man, or just on the verge of old age. When young he was hot-headed, he burned with anger, and he did many things which he looked back on with regret. No one will dare to compare the divine Augustus to your (sc. Nero's) mildness, even if he brings youthful years into competition with an old age more than mature. Granted he was restrained and merciful – to be sure, after the sea at Actium had been stained by Roman blood, after his own and others' fleets had been wrecked in Sicily, after the altars of Perusia and the proscriptions.
>
> Haec Augustus senex aut iam in senectutem annis uergentibus; in adulescentia caluit, arsit ira, multa fecit, ad quae inuitus oculos retorquebat. comparare nemo mansuetudini tuae audebit diuum Augustum, etiam si in certamen iuuenilium annorum deduxerit senectutem plus quam maturam; fuerit moderatus et clemens, nempe post mare Actiacum Romano cruore infectum, nempe post fractas in Sicilia classes et suas et alienas, nempe post Perusinas aras et proscriptiones.[33]

The later reputation of the *princeps* tends to obscure this fact, but the Augustus of the 20s was a man deeply implicated in the horror of the Civil Wars.[34] If indeed one of Vergil's aims was to reconcile the Roman elite to its new ruler (and this has been thought plausible), then he could not simply brush the Civil Wars under the carpet. Earlier in his reign, at any rate, we have to assume that Augustus and internecine conflict were inseparable in people's minds. A good propagandist seeking to manipulate the attitudes of his readership could not ignore their preoccupation with the Civil Wars. He had to do something much harder: that is, simply put, take the dreadful destruction that the Civil Wars represented and negotiate its potential for good.

IV. *Hercules and Cacus* as civil war

Vergil did not ignore the Civil Wars, of course. The *Aeneid*, like its readership, is preoccupied by them. Johnson, for instance, writes that

> It is the clear terrible truth of civil war and the fact of uncertainty about anything in human affairs that shape this poem and stick in the mind when we put the poem aside.[35]

And, as he says, the 'war that fills the last half of the *Aeneid* is, unequivocally, a civil war'[36] between the two peoples – Trojans and Latins – who would subsequently make up the city of Rome. It hardly needs to be said that this is particularly the case with Book 8, ending as it does with the battle at Actium and its aftermath. It is in a sense hardly surprising, then, that conflict as it is presented in the *Aeneid* is an extremely uncompromising affair – on both sides. Civil war is now, and was for the Romans, proverbially ghastly. Cicero, for example, describes his pleas for peace in January 49 (*ad fam.* 16.12.2):

> As for myself since I came to Rome I have not stopped doing everything in thought word and deed for the furtherance of peace. But a strange madness had possessed not only the unrespectable but also those regarded as respectable which made them eager to fight, despite my cries that nothing is more dreadful than civil war.
>
> equidem ut ueni ad urbem, non destiti omnia et sentire et dicere et facere quae ad concordiam pertinerent; sed mirus inuaserat furor non solum improbis sed etiam his qui boni habentur ut pugnare cuperent, me clamante nihil esse bello ciuili miserius.

The civil wars which had just started as Cicero wrote in 49 and ended with Octavian's triumphs in 29 are described epigrammatically by Tacitus (*Ann.* 3.28.1) as 'twenty relentless years of upheaval, no morality, no law: villainy never punished, decency often a cause of death', *continua per uiginti annos discordia, non mos, non ius; deterrima quaeque impune ac multa honesta exitio fuere*. The Civil Wars represented for the Romans total cultural breakdown (*non mos, non ius*). Rome in fact, it could be claimed, ceased to exist: hence Augustus could later claim to be refounding it. Classically, the Romans expressed the catastrophic effects of civil war in terms of intra-familial conflict. What made civil war so perverse was that it was war between intimates, members of the tiny Roman elite set against one another. Memorable expression is given to this in the description of the aftermath of Pistoria at the end of Sallust's *Bellum Catilinae* (61.7–9):

> The army of the Roman people had won no joyful or bloodless victory, however, either: all the most vigorous men had either died in battle or come away seriously wounded. Moreover many who went out from the camp to have a look or to pillage on turning over the enemy corpses found a friend or a guest or a relative; others, similarly, recognized their own enemies. Thus throughout the whole army was variously provoked joy and grief, lamentation and rejoicing.

> neque tamen exercitus populi Romani laetam aut incruentam uictoriam adeptus erat. nam strenuissumus quisque aut occiderat in proelio aut grauiter uolneratus discesserat. multi autem, qui e castris uisundi aut spoliandi gratia processerant, uoluentes hostilia cadauera amicum alii pars hospitem aut cognatum reperiebant; fuere item qui inimicos suos cognoscerent. ita uarie per omnem exercitum laetitia maeror luctus atque gaudia agitabantur.

Caesar and Pompey, again, were *socer generque*, 'father- and son-in-law';[37] their conflict was the more shocking for the marital tie between them. Similarly, civil war was often conceived of in terms of fraternal conflict, conflict between brothers, a transgression of the most basic taboos.[38] In each case mythological precedents were found. When Ovid describes the rape of the Sabine women as a struggle between *gener* and *socer* (*Met.* 14.800–2) he is clearly relating the rape of the Sabines (another future element of the Roman polity) to the civil war between Pompey and Caesar.[39] For the *fratricidal* nature of civil war the Romans found a precedent in Romulus' killing of his twin brother Remus,[40] the best example of this being Horace's seventh *Epode*. Horace questions why the Romans are so eager to destroy their own city in civil war (*Epod.* 7.17–20):

> This is the reason: bitter fate pursues the Romans, and the crime of a brother's murder, from the time when the blood of undeserving Remus flowed onto the ground, a curse for posterity.

> sic est: acerba fata Romanos agunt
>   scelusque fraternae necis,
> ut immerentis fluxit in terram Remi
>   sacer nepotibus cruor.

I have already suggested that Romulus' conflict with Remus is one of the analogous conflicts underlying the conflict of *Hercules and Cacus*;

and this might well be counted as another of the disturbing 'further voices' of the kind Lyne discovered in the passage. Hercules is equated (subtly, but nonetheless) with Romulus at the moment of his commission of this dreadful crime, the slaying of his own twin brother; Hercules, Aeneas, and Augustus are being brought into close proximity with a fratricide. By this connection, too, and also through the similarity of the combatants to each other – a characteristic feature of civil war, as we have seen – the struggle of Hercules with Cacus becomes a kind of mythical model for the Civil Wars.

V. Constructive destruction

The crucial point here, I think, is that Vergil does not soft-peddle on the violence involved in Hercules' defeat of Cacus, in fact quite the contrary. The violence of the encounter is his main emphasis. Galinsky points out that:

> whereas all other writers – notably Dionysius, Livy, Propertius and Ovid – describe the actual combat between Herakles and Cacus in a few words or, at most, ten lines, it is Vergil's central concern. Vergil spends almost fifty lines depicting Herakles' hard struggle and his conquest of the Underworld monster.[41]

Vergil emphasizes the violence, I would suggest, because it is with violence that he is centrally concerned. The violence of Hercules is not played down in the slightest. Consider 259–61:

> Hercules seizes Cacus as he vomits futile fires in the darkness in a knotlike embrace and throttles him hard till his eyes pop out and his throat is dry of blood.
>
> > hic Cacum in tenebris incendia uana uomentem
> > corripit in nodum complexus, et angit inhaerens
> > elisos oculos et siccum sanguine guttur.[42]

This is violent in the extreme. But what I want to suggest Vergil does with this violence is argue that it is, in a paradoxical way, constructive; in fact he seems to imply that the more unqualified the violence the more constructive it is. If we look at the Romulus and Remus myth we will get an idea of what I would suggest he is trying to do. Romulus committed fratricide, an appalling act, an act terrible enough to foreshadow civil war; yet this act was also, paradoxically, a constructive act, quite literally: the death of Remus allowed the foundation of the city of Rome. It was in fact a prerequisite of it. Propertius' terms, 'the walls made firm by the slaughter of Remus', *caeso moenia firma Remo* (3.9.50), or 'the land to be sanctified by Aventine Remus', *Auentino rura pianda*

Remo (4.1.50), even imply, as Wiseman suggests, a foundation sacrifice.[43] Florus (1.1.8) speaks of Remus as the 'first victim' who 'hallowed the fortifications of the new city with his blood', *munitionemque urbis nouae sanguine suo consecrauit*.

Remus, considered from this perspective, *had* to die for Rome to exist. The parallel with Hercules' slaying of Cacus is close. Romulus kills Remus to found Rome; Hercules kills Cacus to save the *Ur*-Rome of Evander (188–9). Each is a *conditor* in the same sense that Augustus was, who some senators thought should be offered the name Romulus 'inasmuch as he was himself founder of Rome', *quasi et ipsum conditorem urbis*, by virtue of his actions – his salvation of the city – in the Civil Wars (Suet., *Aug.* 7.2).[44] In Romulus' case the killing/destruction and the creation are indivisible; Tertullian (*De Spec.* 5.6) felicitously terms Romulus the 'fratricide founder', *fratricida institutor*. It is in this way, I think, that the emphatic violence of the Hercules and Cacus episode was meant to be interpreted: the brutality of the conflict and the similarity of the combatants recalls civil war, but the struggle is described in terms which assimilate it to instances of violent destruction which are paradoxically constructive. Underlying the case of Remus is the notion of sacrifice, which Bandera investigates with particular reference to the struggle between Aeneas and Turnus.[45] Bandera makes much of the interchangeability of Aeneas and Turnus. 'Vergil', he says, 'is making Aeneas fight his own double, his enemy twin'.[46] Vergil's stroke of brilliance here is that the very thing which makes an analogy with civil war possible – the similarity and interchangeability of the combatants – also allows an analogy with blood sacrifice: the victim of sacrifice, as Bandera says, 'is a stand-in, a substitute' for the sacrificer.[47] He must necessarily resemble him. Nicoll shows how it is precisely the similarities between Aeneas and the *gubernator* Palinurus which make the latter an appropriate, effective sacrificial substitute for Aeneas.[48]

Sacrifice, the myth of Romulus and Remus, and also the gigantomachic imagery elucidated by Hardie[49] all embody the mystical notion that destruction is constructive. The *mysteriousness* of Vergil's scheme is an essential element of it, but one that by its very nature tends to be lost in interpretation. Hardie is right to emphasize the religious tone of the Cacus myth.[50] As he says, 'Evander's opening words (185 ff.) place the Cacus story within a liturgical setting'; and the pointed departures from Lucretius in the passage which Hardie discusses, such as Vergil's mention of Hercules' most recent escapade, Geryon, dismissed as insignificant by Lucretius in very similar language,[51] signify a more general departure from the Lucretian tenet *non est mirandum*: the mysterious and paradoxical is at the very heart of the Vergilian scheme.

VI. The gladiatorial *munus*

But there is one more form of institutionalized violence which I think is of particular relevance to the *Hercules and Cacus* episode, and that is gladiatorial combat. Hardie notes the presence of gladiatorial imagery in the *Aeneid*. He cites the gladiatorial expression *habet* or *hoc habet*, 'he's got it', which was used of wounded gladiators by spectators, at *Aen*. 12.296, and the similarly gladiatorial term *harena* used of the dust of the battlefield in the same book.[52] But the gladiatorial arena is a particularly relevant analogy for *Hercules and Cacus*. As Ahl has pointed out, the first gladiatorial *munus* at Rome took place in the Forum Boarium, the location of the Ara Maxima and the focus of the struggle between Hercules and Cacus.[53] In 264 BC the funeral of Decimus Iunius Brutus Pera was marked by his sons with three pairs of gladiators fighting to the death in this location.[54] The connection is strengthened by the fact that, as Wiedemann says, 'the Roman Hercules was closely associated with gladiators'.[55] When they were lucky enough to be able to retire, for example, gladiators dedicated their weapons to Hercules.[56] A shrine of Hercules was found in the amphitheatre on the site of the Guildhall in London in 1988, and this accords with Vitruvius' precepts for the location of temples (*De arch*. 1.7.1):

> Temples to Mercury, however, in the forum, or also, as to Isis and Serapis, in the business centre; temples to Apollo and father Liber beside the theatre; to Hercules, in cities without gymnasia or amphitheatres, at the circus.
>
> Mercurio autem in foro, aut etiam ut Isidi et Serapi in emporio; Apollini Patrique Libero secundum theatrum; Herculi, in quibus ciuitatibus non sunt gymnasia neque amphitheatra, ad circum.

In Seneca's tragedy *Hercules Oetaeus* it is, appropriately enough, Hercules himself who employs the gladiatorial expression on the point of death (1472 f.):

> That's it. Finished. My fate unfolds. This is my last day.
>
> habet. peractum est. fata se nostra explicant.
> lux ista summa est.

Hercules' association with gladiators shades into an association with the other activities which took place in the arena. Martial's *Liber Spectaculorum* 6b, 15, 16b and 27 all compare the achievements of *bestiarii*, wild beast fighters who performed on the morning of an afternoon gladiatorial display, to the labours of Hercules.[57] The figure of Cacus clearly contains elements of the wild beast: he is semihuman (194) or alternatively semibestial (267), he lives in a cave (193, etc.), he has a hairy chest (*uillosa...saetis | pectora*, 266–7) – all the standard signs. But the public display of Cacus' corpse at 264–5,

> the hideous corpse is dragged out by the feet. Hearts cannot be satisfied with gazing on the terrible eyes...

> pedibusque informe cadauer
> protrahitur. nequeunt expleri corda tuendo
> terribilis oculos...

is also reminiscent of the treatment of executed criminals – criminals in general, such as Sejanus at Juv. 10.66–7:

> Sejanus is drawn by a hook, in public: everyone rejoices

> Seianus ducitur unco
> spectandus: gaudent omnes[58] –

and those criminals killed in the arena during the lunch-break between *uenationes*, wild beast hunts, and the gladiatorial *munera*.[59] Seneca (*Ira* 3.3.6) talks of 'the hook which drags the corpses', *cadauera ...trahens uncus*, through the arena; presumably an element of public display (with a view to deterrence) was present. Cacus of course was a criminal (206, 263); his name practically tells us as much, and 205, depending on the text adopted,[60] may explicitly call him a thief.

The slaughter of animals and criminals in the arena tends to strike moderns as sadistic, but Wiedemann is clear that as far as the audiences were concerned these bloodthirsty displays were (like sacrifice) an acceptable, necessary form of killing. 'The arena,' according to Wiedemann,

> was where Roman society dealt...with the chaos represented by wild beasts and of crime... It was a symbol of an ordered world, the cosmos; it was the place where the civilized world confronted lawless nature.[61]

Hence partly, perhaps, the association of the civilizing hero Hercules with the arena. The cosmic and gigantomachic imagery which Hardie reads into the passage dovetails tidily with these elements from the arena. Hercules violently imposes order on chaos, in the shape (or rather unshape)[62] of the monstrous, criminal Cacus.

But let me return specifically to the gladiatorial. This institution would seem to suit Vergil's purposes – as I have presented them – closely. Equality between the combatants was obviously of the very nature of the sport: the two gladiators were called a *par* (a 'match' would be a fair translation) and we find other indications of the fundamental importance of this equivalence. Seneca (*Prov.* 3.4), for example, says that 'a gladiator considers it a disgrace to be matched with an inferior', *ignominiam iudicat gladiator cum inferiore componi*. Again, the similarity between the combatants – along with the extreme violence of the institution – made gladiatorial combat an obvious metaphor for internecine conflict, one widely exploited.[63] But gladiatorial combat, like sacrifice, was obviously a culturally sanctioned form of violence. It was indeed related – or at any rate was understood by the Roman elite to be related – to human sacrifice, of which sources treat it as a substitute or development.[64] It was originally associated with funeral ceremonies (as we have seen), and this association continued.[65] Tertullian in the second century even suggests that the gladiatorial display originated in human sacrifice to the ghosts of the dead (*De Spec.* 12.1–3):

> It remains to examine the most important and most popular spectacle. It was called a *munus* from being a service: *munus* and *officium* mean the same thing. The ancients thought that by this spectacle they were rendering a service to the dead, after they had modified it with a more civilized form of cruelty. For at one time, since it was believed that the souls of the dead were propitiated by human blood, they used to buy prisoners-of-war or slaves of low status and sacrifice them at funerals. Later they decided to conceal their impiety behind pleasure. So those they had procured were trained – to the point of learning how to be killed – in the weapons available and to the best of their ability, and were then killed on the appointed day of the funeral at the tombs. In this way they found comfort for death in murder. This was the origin of the *munus*.

> Superest illius insignissimi spectaculi ac receptissimi recognitio. munus dictum est ab officio, quoniam officium etiam muneris nomen est. officium autem mortuis hoc spectaculo facere se ueteres arbitrabantur, posteaquam illud humaniore atrocitate temperauerunt. nam olim, quoniam animas defunctorum humano sanguine propitiari creditum erat, captiuos uel mali status seruos mercati in exequiis immolabant. postea placuit impietatem uoluptate adumbrare. itaque quos parauerant, armis quibus tunc et qualiter poterant eruditos, tantum ut occidi discerent, mox edicto die inferiarum apud tumulos erogabant. ita mortem homicidiis consolabantur. haec muneri origo.[66]

Augustus seems to have recognized some kind of sacral dimension to the gladiatorial games. Wiedemann explains that 'when Augustus institutionalised them as annual ceremonies, they took place at the two times of the year that correspond to Christian Easter and Christmas.[67] They were, in other words, symbols of spring regeneration and of the ending of one year and beginning of the next at the period of the winter solstice.'[68] The emperor Julian says something rather similar (*Or.* 4. 156b–c):

> Before the beginning of the year, immediately after the final month of Kronos, we celebrate the most famous games in honour of the Sun, dedicating the festival to the Invincible Sun. After this it is not permitted to perform any of the grim but necessary shows which belong to the final month.
>
> πρὸ τῆς νουμηνίας, εὐθέως μετὰ τὸν τελευταῖον τοῦ Κρόνου μῆνα, ποιοῦμεν Ἡλίῳ τὸν περιφανέστατον ἀγῶνα, τὴν ἑορτὴν Ἡλίῳ καταφημίσαντες ἀνικήτῳ, μεθ' ὃν οὐδὲν θέμις ὧν ὁ τελευταῖος μὴν ἔχει σκυθρωπῶν μέν, ἀναγκαίων δ' ὅμως, ἐπιτελεσθῆναι θεαμάτων.

The 'grim but necessary' displays are the gladiatorial displays at the time of the Saturnalia which, according to Julian, mark the death of the old year before the joyful rebirth of the new.[69] Other sources relate the gladiatorial games to the worship of Jupiter Latiaris or to Nemesis,[70] but whether in fact correct or not as accounts of the historical origins of the *munus*,[71] there is a clear consensus in the sources that the *munus* had a ritualistic, and paradoxically life-*affirming* dimension for its audience.

VII. The ambivalence of fire

What I have been trying to suggest is that Vergil's object was not in any way to elide the violence exhibited by Hercules. Unqualified violence had been the common experience of Romans for decades, and it was this violence that Vergil was attempting to present as ultimately meaningful and purposeful. As Bandera says, glossing violence as sacrificial confers *meaning* on otherwise arbitrary destruction.[72] The paradoxical nature of the scheme, which causes modern critics so much difficulty (hence the endless optimism/pessimism controversy), is quite deliberate. The problems critics have with it result from a failure to appreciate quite how radical a project Vergil is engaged upon. He must establish that utter catastrophe such as the Civil Wars had a power for good. The much-touted 'ambivalence' of Vergilian poetry is perhaps just a partial view of a complex attempt to assert the paradox – familiar, above all, from religious practice – that destruction is creative. As Bandera puts it,

> he [sc. Vergil] discovered that even the most respectable sacrificial order is not only grounded on violence, but in fact made possible through violence. In other words, the social order arises originally out of the same thing that can also annihilate it.[73]

Assimilation and Civil War: Hercules and Cacus

Out of civil war, for example. I shall conclude by trying to clarify what is to a certain extent, as I have suggested, a deliberately obscure scheme – and one undoubtedly much more subtly developed than I can do justice to – through the language and imagery of fire which pervades the *Hercules and Cacus* passage and in which the paradox can perhaps be seen in its least embroidered form.[74]

One of the respects, as we have seen, in which Cacus and Augustus resemble each other was the 'vomiting fire' motif which was applied to both of them. Cacus' nature is above all fiery (198 f., 252–9, 267). He is in fact the son of the fire god, a Vergilian innovation (198 f.):[75]

> The father of this portentous creature was Vulcan. It was *his* black fires he belched from his mouth...

>> huic monstro Volcanus erat pater: illius atros
>> ore uomens ignis...

But language which is used more or less 'literally' of Cacus is also applied (more metaphorically) to Hercules. Thus at 219 f. we read:

> At this the indignation of Hercules had blazed forth furiously with black bile

>> hic uero Alcidae furiis exarserat atro
>> felle dolor

Later (230–1) Hercules

> three times, blazing with anger, traverses the whole Aventine

>> ter totum feruidus ira
>> lustrat Auentini montem

Emphasis is also placed on the role of fire in the ceremonies in honour of Hercules led by Potitius (281 f.):

> and now the priests went forth, Potitius first, clad in skins as was their habit, and brought the flames

>> iamque sacerdotes primusque Potitius ibant,
>> pellibus in morem cincti, flammasque ferebant.

At 542 f., again, Aeneas pointedly 'rouses the dormant altars with *Herculean* fires', Herculeis *sopitas* ignibus *aras | excitat*. Hercules also is fiery, then. We may further recall that the fire vomited by Cacus is Vulcan's fire. Later in the book this same fire is of course put to very constructive purposes. *Ignipotens* (414, 423) visits his smithy under Etna (419, 440),[76]

> the home of Vulcan and Vulcan's land by name

Volcani domus et Volcania nomine tellus

and the result is the shield, *Volcania arma* (8.535; cf. *arma dei ad Volcania*, 12.739).

As Gransden says, 'Vulcan was an ambiguous deity, as was the element, fire, which he personified.'[77] Vulcan's fire is destructive, 'negative'; but that very same fire creates the shield, a very obvious parallel to the creation of Rome which is itself analogous to Hercules' annihilation of Cacus. The craftsman or demiurge – of the shield, of the *urbs* or of the *orbis* – in the very process of destroying mysteriously creates. Lyne considers the same material, and concludes,[78]

> Vulcan forges Aeneas' weapons for him; but Vulcan, according to Vergil, is also Cacus' father.

A further voice. But we might profitably try turning this around: 'Vulcan is Cacus' father; but Vulcan also forges Aeneas' weapons for him.' Follow Lyne and we have the liberal, ambivalent Vergil of the orthodoxy; take it the other way and what we have is a rather brilliant propagandist engaging with the traumatic political conditions of his time – no less complex, mind, and no less subtle, though undoubtedly less liberal. I must leave it up to my reader. As we are often reminded, a text is in no position to force us to read it one way or another. But if we sense a difference between these Vergils – if we feel that one is somehow more satisfactory than the other – then we are, like it or not, recognizing the relevance to interpretation of political intent and authorial design.

Notes

* I am grateful to Professor Hans-Peter Stahl for letting me participate in the conference organized by him at Oxford in July 1996, and for criticism of an earlier version of this paper. The contents of the paper originated in lectures given to my students at University College Dublin.

[1] For the paradigmatic status of *Hercules and Cacus* within the *Aeneid* see, for example, Hardie (1986) 110 f., Lyne (1987) 28, n. 55.

[2] The view will be represented in this paper by Galinsky (1966), Buchheit (1963) 116–33, and Gransden (1976).

[3] See, for example, Ogilvie (1965) 56, Fordyce (1977) 224.

[4] West is the direction from which Hercules is travelling, Geryon tending to be located in Spain (e.g. Plin., *HN* 4.120). At 223 Cacus is compared in flight to the Eurus, the East wind: 'Eurus' commonly denotes the East in general. The same expression describes Turnus at 12.733.

[5] See Hardie (1986) 97–110.

[6] Gransden (1976), ad *Aen.* 8.190–305.

Assimilation and Civil War: Hercules and Cacus

[7] Gransden (1976) 16.

[8] Galinsky (1966) 22 (*attulit et nobis aliquando optantibus aetas | auxilium aduentumque dei*).

[9] Dio 51.21.1 (τοῦ δὲ δὴ θέρους ἔς τε τὴν Ἑλλάδα καὶ ἐς τὴν Ἰταλίαν ὁ Καῖσαρ ἐπεραιώθη, καὶ αὐτοῦ ἐς τὴν πόλιν ἐσελθόντος οἵ τε ἄλλοι ἔθυσαν, ὥσπερ εἴρηται, καὶ ὁ ὕπατος Οὐαλέριος Ποτῖτος). See Reinhold (1988) ad loc., Gordon (1954), and Syme's review of Gordon, *JRS* 45 (1955) 155–60.

[10] Buchheit (1963) 126–31; Galinsky (1966) 26 ff.

[11] In connection with Mark Antony Richmond (1958, 181) offers a particular contemporary parallel to the Cacus myth: he suggests that the Hercules and Cacus episode provides a precedent for the 'cleansing of the Palatine from evil influence' represented by the burning down of Antony's house on the Palatine. According to Richmond the destruction of the house was deliberate, a 'Reichstag fire' which was a prerequisite of Augustus' building programme on the hill. This is an attractive suggestion, but the evidence in Dio (53.27.5) for the fire is too meagre for any very firm conclusions as to the cause or the nature of the fire; even the precise whereabouts of Antony's house is unclear. See Roddaz (1984) 236, n. 32.

[12] Gransden (1976) 31. For a discussion of the tradition regarding Cacus' home, and for the intimate association between the legends about Cacus and Roman foundation myth, see Small (1982) 16–36.

[13] Gransden (1976) 108.

[14] Cf. Ov., *Fast.* 4.816 ff.; Sen., *De Brev. Vitae* 13.8.

[15] On the dominant foundational imagery of Book 8, and Romulus' role in it, see Gransden (1976) 15–17. For a typological connection between Augustus and Romulus see Gransden (1976), ad 680–1.

[16] Hardie (1986) 110–18.

[17] Galinsky (1972) 145.

[18] Galinsky (1966) 35.

[19] Lyne (1987) 27–35. Much of the remainder of this paper consists of criticism of Lyne's reading of *Hercules and Cacus*. I concentrate on Lyne because his approach is representative of many recent interpretations of Vergil, but also because his scholarship is a model of clarity.

[20] West (1991) pp. 195, 197 (*bis*), 209, 211 and 250.

[21] As Lyne (1987) 27 n. 52 points out, 'in pre-Vergilian uses the phrase 'ignem uomere', *vel. sim.*, is confined to fire-breathing monsters and volcanoes'. When Ovid retells the story of Cacus (*Fast.* 1.543–78), and reuses the 'ignem uomere' expression (572, cf. 577), he renders the comparison with monsters and volcanoes explicit: Cacus' vomiting of fire is like the breath of Typhoeus, i.e. the eruptions of Mt. Etna, under which Typhoeus was imprisoned. Ovid also by these means brings out the 'gigantomachic' colouring of Vergil's *Hercules and Cacus*. See Buchheit (1963) 128–30; Hardie (1986) 112.

[22] Lyne (1987) 32.

[23] See Gransden (1976), ad loc.: the majority of the MSS read 'furiis'; others read 'furis'. Cf. Prop. 4.9.13–14.

[24] For the translation see Fordyce (1977) ad loc.

[25] Lyne (1987) 28.

[26] Ibid. 28–9.
[27] Ibid. 28.
[28] Hardie (1993) 2.
[29] Lyne (1987) 31.
[30] Wallace-Hadrill (1987) 222.
[31] Foulkes (1983) 107.
[32] Yavetz (1984) 2.
[33] Seneca refers to salient events of the triumviral period in reverse chronological order: the battle of Actium (31), naval engagements between Octavian and Sextus Pompey (38 and 36), the siege and capture of Perusia (41–40), and the proscriptions (43). In the expression 'Perusinae arae' Seneca is referring specifically to a presumably apocryphal but nevertheless persistent story that Octavian sacrificed some of his aristocratic opponents at Perusia before an altar of Divus Julius: see, e.g. Suet., *Aug.* 15. The siege anyway became a 'byword for cruelty': Woodman (1983), ad Vell. 2.74.4.
[34] For Augustus' poor reputation as a consequence of his behaviour during the Civil Wars cf. Sen., *Clem.* 1.9.1; Dio 56.44.1; Stat., *Silv.* 4.1.31-2.
[35] Johnson (1976) 137–8.
[36] Ibid. 138.
[37] Catull. 29.24; Cic., *Tusc.*1.86, *Off.* 3.82; Verg., *Aen.* 6.830–1; Luc. 1.114 ff., 9.1038–43; Mart. 9.70.3.
[38] Lucr. 3.70–3; Verg., *Geo.* 2.496, 510; Luc. 1.93–5.
[39] Cf. Ov. *Fast.* 3.202; Luc. 1.118.
[40] Verg., *Geo.* 2.533 and Thomas (1988) ad loc.; Luc. 1.93–5.
[41] Galinsky (1972) 143.
[42] There is some evidence that the tradition considered Hercules' killing of Cacus potentially criminal in its violence, and thus comparable to Romulus' morally ambivalent killing of Remus. In Livy Cacus' fellow shepherds accuse Hercules of *manifesta caedes*, 'flagrant murder' (1.7.9).
[43] Wiseman (1995) 125.
[44] Evander is another *conditor*: the word is used of him at 8.313 (*Romanae conditor arcis*), its only appearance in the poem. See Gransden (1976) ad loc.
[45] Bandera (1981).
[46] Ibid., 233.
[47] Ibid., 234.
[48] Nicoll (1988) 460–5.
[49] See p. 177 and n. 16 above.
[50] Hardie (1986) 213–19.
[51] *Aen.* 8.202; Lucr. 5.28.
[52] Hardie (1986) 152, n. 80: *harena*, *Aen.* 12.276, 340, 382, 741; Hardie (1993) 20; Donatus ad Terence, *Andria* 1,1.56.
[53] Ahl (1976) 86 and n. 8; Val. Max. 2.4.7 (*nam gladiatorium munus primum Romae datum est in foro boario App. Claudio Q. Fuluio consulibus. dederunt Marcus et Decimus filii Bruti* Perae *funebri memoria patris cineres honorando*); Livy, *Per.* 16; Servius ad *Aen.* 3.67; Ausonius, *Gryph.* 2.36 f.
[54] Wiedemann (1992) 5.
[55] Ibid., 178.

[56] See Hor., *Ep.* 1.1.4–5: *Veianius armis | Herculis ad postem fixis latet abditus agro*
[57] On such *uenationes* see Wiedemann (1992) 55–67.
[58] See Friedländer (1895) ad loc. For the emphatically *public* nature of such punishments see Wiedemann (1992) 72; Coleman (1990) 48–9.
[59] Wiedemann (1992) 68–97.
[60] See n. 23 above.
[61] Wiedemann (1992) 179.
[62] See 264, *informe cadauer*.
[63] Jal (1963) 341 ff.; Ahl (1976) 84–8; Nisbet and Hubbard (1970), ad Hor., *Carm.* 1.28.17.
[64] Wiedemann (1992) 33 f.; Schwenn (1915) 172–5. For an association between human sacrifice and the Forum Boarium see also Livy 22.57.6; Pliny, *HN* 28.12; Plut., *Marcell.* 3.4, *Quaest. Rom.* 283 f.; Orosius 4.13.3.
[65] See, for example, Dio 55.8.5 on Augustus' funeral displays for M. Agrippa in 7 BC.
[66] Cf. Ahl (1976) 86.
[67] That is, at the times of the *Saturnalia* and the *Quinquatrus* of 19–23 March.
[68] Wiedemann (1992) 47.
[69] Cf. Ausonius, *Ecl.* 23.33–7; and Prudentius, *Symm.* 2. 1116 (*tam triste sacrum*) and 1124–5.
[70] Ville (1960).
[71] Ville argues forcibly, not.
[72] See, for example, Bandera (1981) 236 ('by openly presenting the destruction of Troy as a process of victimization, literally and symbolically, Virgil confers on such a destruction the same meaning that sacrifice confers on the destruction of the victim').
[73] Ibid., 230.
[74] Gransden (1976) 39–41 covers similar territory.
[75] Fordyce (1977) 224.
[76] Cf. Hardie (1986) 110–18 and Buchheit (1963) 128–30 on the 'volcanic' nature of Cacus, and his similarity to Typhoeus, denizen of Etna. In the creation of the shield the violence of Typhoeus-Cacus is thus put to paradoxically constructive use.
[77] Gransden (1976) 39.
[78] Lyne (1987) 31.

Bibliography
Ahl, F.M.
   1976   *Lucan: An Introduction*, Ithaca and London.
Bandera, C.
   1981   'Sacrificial levels in Virgil's *Aeneid*', *Arethusa* 14, 217–39.
Buchheit, V.
   1963   'Vergil über die Sendung Roms: Untersuchungen zum Bellum Poenicum und zur Aeneis', *Gymnasium*, Beiheft 3, Heidelberg.

Coleman, K.M.
- 1990 'Fatal charades: Roman executions staged as mythological enactments', *JRS* 80, 44–73.

Fordyce, C.J.
- 1977 *P. Vergili Maronis* Aeneidos *Libri VII–VIII, with a commentary*, Oxford.

Foulkes, A.P.
- 1983 *Literature and Propaganda*, London.

Friedländer, L.
- 1895 *D. Junii Juvenalis Saturarum Libri V*, 2 vols., Leipzig.

Galinsky, G.K.
- 1966 'The Hercules–Cacus episode in *Aeneid* VIII', *AJPh* 87, 18–51.
- 1972 *The Herakles theme: The Adaptations of the Hero in Literature from Homer to the Twentieth Century*, Oxford.

Gordon, A.E.
- 1954 *Potitus Valerius Messalla Consul Suffect 29* BC, University of California Publications in Classical Archaeology 3.2, Berkeley.

Gransden, K.W.
- 1976 *Virgil:* Aeneid *Book VIII*, Cambridge.

Hardie, P.R.
- 1986 *Virgil's* Aeneid: *Cosmos and Imperium*, Oxford.
- 1993 *The Epic Successors of Virgil*, Cambridge.

Jal, P.
- 1963 *La guerre civile à Rome: étude littéraire et morale*, Paris.

Johnson, W.R.
- 1976 *Darkness Visible: A Study of Vergil's* Aeneid, California.

Lyne, R.O.A.M.
- 1987 *Further Voices in Vergil's* Aeneid, Oxford.

Nicoll, W.S.M.
- 1988 'The sacrifice of Palinurus', *CQ* n.s. 38, 459–72.

Nisbet, R.G.M. and Hubbard, M.
- 1970 *A Commentary on Horace*, Odes *Book I*, Oxford.

Ogilvie, R.M.
- 1965 *A Commentary on Livy Books I–V*, Oxford.

Reinhold, M.
- 1988 *From Republic to Principate: An Historical Commentary on Cassius Dio's* Roman History *Books 49–52 (36–29* BC*)*, Atlanta.

Richmond, O.
- 1958 'Palatine Apollo again', *CQ* n.s. 8, 180–4.

Roddaz, J.-M.
- 1984 *Marcus Agrippa*, Paris.

Schwenn, F.
- 1915 *Die Menschenopfer bei den Griechen und Römern*, Giessen.

Small, J.P.
- 1982 *Cacus and Marsyas in Etrusco-Roman Legend*, Princeton Monographs in Art and Archaeology 44, Princeton.

Thomas, R.F.
   1988   *Virgil*, Georgics, 2 vols., Cambridge.
Ville, G.
   19960 'Les jeux de gladiateurs dans l'Empire chrétien',*MEFRA* 72, 273–335.
Wallace-Hadrill, A.
   1987   'Time for Augustus: Ovid, Augustus and the *Fasti*', in M. Whitby, P.R. Hardie, and M. Whitby (eds.) *Homo Viator*, 221–30, Bristol.
West, D.
   1991   *Virgil, the* Aeneid*: A New Prose Translation*, Harmondsworth.
Wiedemann, T.
   1992   *Emperors and Gladiators*, London.
Wiseman, T.P.
   1995   *Remus: a Roman Myth*, Cambridge.
Woodman, A.J.
   1983   *Velleius Paterculus: the Caesarian and Augustan Narrative (2.41–93)*, Cambridge.
Yavetz, Z.
   1984   'The *Res Gestae* and Augustus' public image', in F. Millar and E. Segal (eds.) *Caesar Augustus: Seven Aspects*, 1–36, Oxford.

10

NON ENARRABILE TEXTUM?
THE SHIELD OF AENEAS AND
THE TRIPLE TRIUMPH OF 29 BC
Aeneid 8.630–728

Alexander G. McKay

temptanda via est (*Georgics* 3.8)

This paper will argue that Vergil's great shield of Aeneas, divinely crafted by the Lord of Fire for the fated champion, follows patterns and conventions favoured by Roman artists and that the shield's panels provide a veritable "filmic" documentary of Italic history and Roman triumphs. My approach will also concentrate on reading the city and its "memorials of bygone men" (*virum monimenta priorum, Aen.* 8.312) in close conjunction with the shield's panels in the belief that therein lies the inspiration as well as the thematic unity of the shield. I shall argue that Vergil's fictional shield features vignettes that are relevant to Roman triumphal parades – to those celebrated multimedia events where captives and booty were the visible testimony of victory, where war art, paintings and sculptures entertained jubilant spectators. I shall suggest that the shield is a camera with its lens focused on turnings, monuments, cityscape elements, not always in precise succession, but within the orbit of the processional march from beginning to end. Scholars have reflected often on topographical and monumental associations in the shield panels but have not convinced themselves that the *cursus triumphalis* might be particularly apposite.

The Fire-Lord's prophetic shield is introduced, with a measure of ambiguity, as "an indescribable fabric" – *non enarrabile textum*. It is portrayed throughout in terms of metal: gold (which predominates), silver, bronze, and iron, a medley of metals and of the Ages. The immobility of the relief pictures is countered and balanced by the masterly fusion and interplay of metals in the design, and by vivid painterly description. So the poet's and the artist's craft, frequently suggestive of a painted frieze, fuse in an uncanny fashion. By using colour terms throughout and by means of demonstrative insertions, *aspiceres* (650), *videres* (676, 691), *cernere erat* (676), *credas* (691), Vergil gives the illusion that he is show-casing an artwork for a spectator's wonder and enjoyment.

The double aspect of metallic relief and painting (sculptural and panel) is no doubt deliberate. Vergil' s pictorial vividness, colour uses and *demonstratio* are something more than an historian's device, for behind these artistic idiosyncrasies stands the imaginary spectator, the eyewitness in the context of an art gallery, a pictorial exhibition or parade of exhibits. Frieze and painting are central to our understanding of the shield's *enarrabile textum*.

Although no complete examples of triumphal painting are extant, we can be certain that they were normally commissioned by the victorious general to be carried in his triumph. After being displayed in the *pompa triumphalis*, the art works could be exhibited in temples or in public buildings. The panel paintings were of a documentary nature, tableaux delineated in registers or in serial form, perhaps in ribbonlike strips, exhibited sequentially during the *pompa*. The repertoire would include views of cities and territories, sometimes even maps, on which were depicted, in small scale, battles between Romans and their enemies, the siege of cities, the flight of enemy leaders, and the destruction of enemy territory.[1] Vergil's serial style, and the sometimes layered presentation of episodes on Aeneas' shield, seem entirely apposite to the Roman tradition of triumphal art. Granted that triumphal war art may inform the shield texture, what about ecphrastic precedents, inspirational paradigms for Aeneas' imaginary shield?[2] Certainly Homer's shield of Achilles and the Hesiodic Shield of Heracles are involved; more realistically perhaps Pheidias' shield of the Athena Parthenos, along with a host or miscellany of other suggestive paradigms in commemorative painted friezes and diminutive masterpieces in cameos and gems, of the sort that Paul Zanker has assembled and assessed with uncommon perception in *The Power of Images in the Age of Augustus*.[3]

Homer's shield of Achilles, greatest of the Achaeans, is a microcosm of the society and a vision of the cosmos within which Achilles fights and dies. Figural conceptions generally highlight the pervasive tension in the design, the Lévi–Straussian bipolarity which sets the city at peace alongside the city at war, and so forth. The outer ring apparently portrays the River of Ocean; a religious dance may be the central device. *Sed grammatici certant*. Richard Thomas argues that the Homeric shield has no centrepiece, that the design reveals no item specified as central.[4]

The Hesiodic shield of Heracles is more elaborate: the central boss depicts Phobos (Fear) and Eris (Strife), allegorical figures encircled by a frieze of lions in combat with wild boars; the next encircling frieze contains two scenes: the battle of Lapiths and Centaurs, hybrid creatures who tried to carry off the bride of the Lapith king from his wedding feast (a precursor of the Rape of the Sabine Women?), and a harbour scene, where dolphins and fish and a fisherman are involved; another frieze incorporates two scenes again: a battle scene, which is adjacent compositionally to a Perseus episode, and an urban scene, with vignettes of peace and plenty, adjacent to the relaxed harbour scene. Finally, the River of Ocean frames the tondo. The polarities are readily apparent: Lapiths vs. centaurs; Perseus vs. the Gorgons; a battle scene and a society at peace.[5] Homer's and Hesiod's shields are imaginary constructions, ecphrases in the true sense of the term. The Shield of Athena Parthenos, masterpiece of the sculptor Pheidias, completed in 438 BC, is something else. Philip Hardie wonders whether "in the broad planning of the themes of his Roman shield, Vergil was influenced by the great sacred monument in which the Athenians had expressed their ideal of rational empire."[6] Because it was celebrated (even notorious) throughout history, Pheidias's shield was probably familiar to Vergil through autopsy or through reproductions available in Italy.[7]

The outer ring of the Pheidian shield featured repoussé figures of Amazons battling with Athenians; a Gigantomachy, rendered in low relief, graced the concave interior. Evelyn Harrison[8] argues that the rocky landscape of the shield's exterior represented the acropolis, with the antique ruler Cecrops at the summit defending the Temple of Athena (Manlius' post on Rome's Capitoline hill is a suggestive parallel); scenes of defeat and death are relegated to the bottom of the Parthenos shield. The gigantomachy of the shield's concave side was probably encircled by the River of Ocean, with the victory of the Gods over the Giants paralleling Athens' victory over the Amazons on the exterior.

The Athenian paradigm seems entirely pertinent to Vulcan's creation for Trojan Aeneas: Vergilian ecphrases elsewhere portray Trojan women offering a *peplos* to the Palladium, and Amata's Italian women are engaged in a comparable exercise. Both vignettes seem to draw on Vergil's acquaintance with the Parthenon's east frieze, and the detail of the serpents finding refuge under Pallas's shield after the Laocoon episode may also owe something to the Pheidian paradigm.[9] Of course, the suggestive analogy between Athens' victory over the

Alexander G. McKay

Persians and Octavian's Actian victory over Cleopatra's barbaric, monstrous horde is and no doubt was an inevitable association; and the gigantomachy (Athenian and Pergamene), as Philip Hardie has demonstrated,[10] is certainly an identifiable ingredient in the depiction of the Battle of Actium on the shield of Aeneas. There is general agreement that Vergil's shield of Aeneas marks the climax of *Aeneid* 5–8, the books that lie at the heart of the tripartite epic's substructure, and that it accents the fulfilment of Jupiter's forecast for Aeneas and his Aeneadae/Julian descendants. Octavian's principate appropriately ennobles the centre of the shield, the culmination of the march of time and destiny. The progressive spiral of time is one of Italian history (*Italas res*) and of Roman triumphs (*Romanorumque triumphos*). The shield provides Aeneas and its viewers with bird's-eye views in sequence, a compendium of wars fought and victories won in chronological order – *pugnata in ordine bella* (629). Battles and recurrent civil wars, and the victories and celebrations that attach to wars and perils overcome, dictate the historical composition (*extum*) of the shield.

Vergil's advice, however direct, generally fails to guide scholars who have chosen to follow *diversae variae viae* of construction and explication. The majority have sensed a merger of regal and republican history, either as balancing scenes, or in a chiastic mode. Specific allocation of events and individuals has always been contentious, but the commonest resort is to locate scenes from regal and republican Rome within the outer circular border, featuring the Capitoline panels at the summit and the punishment of the traitor Mettus Fufetius and the Underworld scene at the bottom of the circuit; the battle scenes at Actium and the triumph, including the marchpast of nations, are commonly assigned as an ensemble to the central ring or emblema at the centre. Page DuBois stands back and detects a tripartite model of Roman history in the shield ecphrasis, arguing that "The ecphrasis of the shield builds, in its three sections, to the timeless, triumphant presence of Augustus."[11]

My preference is for three concentric circles with a quartet of scenes from "regal history" depicted in the outer circle, then another quartet of scenes from "republican history", including the Battle of Actium, in the inner ring (*in medio*, 675), with the emblema highlighting the triumphal parade and Augustus' review of subject *gentes* and subjugated territories.

The swelling sea and the cavorting silver dolphins are best assigned to the Actian battle tableau. In my hypothetical construction the dolphins in their blue enamel setting define and encircle the Actian event and accent a pervasive element that has implications for Agrippa's and Octavian's victory. The common association of dolphins with Apollo (Delphinios) and with Venus Marina (*Aeneadum genetrix*) may also be sensed. Godefroid de Calataÿ and Joël Thomas have sensed zodiacal symbolism in the epic and, because the dolphins are enhanced in the shield's design, they assign Book 8 to *Pisces*.[12] We remember too that the Prima Porta Augustus, with its figured cuirass and cosmic imagery, has a dolphin and supporting Cupid at its base.

Many of us, consciously or unconsciously, have traipsed over some sectors of the *cursus triumphalis* in our pilgrimages to Rome, but few, I venture to say, have made the four kilometer victory march with Vergil's Eighth *Aeneid* in hand, and with the Shield ecphrasis as counterpoint along the route.[13] To what end? How accurately and completely can we reconstruct the parade route of Octavian's triumphs, or of triumphs earlier or later?[14] Dio and company provide details rather than the actual route. However, patterns extending from ancient days, from Romulus to Julius Caesar's most recent "performance", were generally constant, and the parade route by the time of Pompey, Julius Caesar and Octavian was virtually canonical.[15]

The lower Campus Martius was the mustering site; the army assembled there and no doubt camped there overnight in the Circus Flaminius, locale for triumphal monuments, temples and porticoes associated with victories. Before the parade began, congratulatory speeches, awards and distinctions, and, no doubt, a review of the troops, fueled the parade's excitement. Thereafter, the general mounted his gilded chariot to cross the pomerium and so initiated the parade past the recently restored Temple of Apollo Sosianus and the Temple of Bellona, past the Theatre of Marcellus site and the Forum Holitorium, crossing the Vicus Jugarius to the Forum Boarium with its Herculean and Victory associations, and on to the Circus Maximus. After parading around the *spina* of the racetrack, to the delight of the 150,000 spectators, the *pompa triumphalis* left the circus through the *carceres*, skirted the Palatine with its grandiose marble monuments and aristocratic mansions, continued past *Capita Bubula* at the northwest end, where Octavian had been born in 63 BC, to the Fornix Fabianus and the Temple of Jupiter Stator; thence along the Upper (Summa) Sacra Via, the "Highway to Heaven", towards the Regia and the Vestal complex, the Temple of the Deified Julius, along the Lower Sacra Via past the Basilica Aemilia and Fulvia and the Temple of Janus (with its doors firmly shut), under the Arcus Actiacus (accepting Coarelli's 1995 location over Nedergaard's 1995 position), pausing while designated criminals were despatched at the Carcer/Tullianum, and so to the Capitoline Incline (Clivus Capitolinus) and the ultimate goal, the Temple of Jupiter Optimus Maximus for sacrifice and offerings to the god and a gala banquet in the temple precinct. The long day's journey ended when the charismatic general was escorted home to the music of flutes.

The order of the displays was fixed: first, spoils captured from the enemy, arms, gold, silver, and jewellery, with "enactment" floats, documentary paintings and reliefs illustrating important events, and explanatory placards (*praefationes*); then war prisoners, with captured princes and nobles as feature attractions. Augustus gloated that kings and princes were exhibited in his parade, although Cleopatra, *non humilis mulier*, could only be exhibited as a waxen (?) image on a special float, or perhaps carried on a platform (*ferculum*). Crowds must have clustered on temple steps, balconies and the roofs of residences, in Circus Maximus stalls, in bleachers erected along the route, and in the galleries of basilicas and on the roofs of retail shops overlooking the tumultuous Sacra Via below.

How closely does the "circuit" of the shield's images adhere to the *cursus triumphalis* which certainly features in the shield's narrative? Diane Favro provides an important reminder in her reading of the shield's primary locale, the Tiber-side city, that "the path of the procession exhorted all observers to 'look behind' to the future. Each procession was part of an urban continuum, a street connected in time as well as in space with the past and future of the Roman state, the triumph ritual, and the topography of Rome."[16] My intention is to show that the ritualistic route of the *pompa triumphalis* enables us both to comprehend the Vergilian shield panels and to appreciate that the triple triumph, Illyrian, Actian and Alexandrian (13–15 August, 29 BC), was basically a religious and political event.

Where does the symbolism and the action within the ecphrasis begin? Of course, at Rome's origin, with Panel I (630–4), portraying the green cave of Mars, the Cave of the Lupercal at the south west foot of the Palatine, with the recumbent, relaxed she-wolf nursing the newborn foundling twins, fearless (*impavidos*) under her protection. It is a vivid, sympathetic rendering, an appealing embodiment of the collective popular memory. Mars and the *lupa* are entirely relevant for the shield because the wolf was a favoured decoration for military armament and a legionary symbol.[17] As we leave the Palatine Cave behind following the tracks of the *pompa triumphalis*, let us remember that the parade passed along the south-west and southern slopes of the Palatine, and that the scenography of the hill above was impressive.

The Domus Augusti (post 36 BC) extended along most of the Scalae Caci on its east side; to the west at its base was the aforementioned Cave of the Lupercal and at the summit the Hut of Romulus (evoked in Evander's "palace" during Aeneas' tour with Evander). The Temple of Victory, possibly restored in 27 BC, the Temple of the Magna Mater, and the Temple of Jupiter Victor were dominated now by the gleaming carrara marble facade of the new Apollo Temple, with the Sun Chariot at the apex of its pediment.[18]

Octavian's Palatine Temple of Apollo, Diana and Latona was visible to the parade, a splendid complement to earlier constructions on the hill. The completion of the Temple of Victory in the early third century, in Wiseman's view, signalled the evolution and gradual alteration of the Palatine's elite residential quarter: "The effect must have been like that of the entrance to an acropolis, and the choice of Victoria (Nike) for the temple at the gate suggests that the Athenian acropolis may have been in the architects' minds."[19]

Vergil indicates that the next shield panel (II, 635–41) is "nearby" (*nec procul hinc*), not only in the restrictive shield space, but in historical time as well, and, from my standpoint, implicit to the parade circuit: the Circus Maximus crowded with spectators at the uncivilized, unprecedented rape of the Sabine Women during the games by the sons of Romulus; the ensuing war, novel (*novum...bellum*) in its guise as civil war involving Romulus, *senex* Titus Tatius and stern figures from Cures (*Curibusque severis*); and finally, a peace settlement involving both kings.[20]

The vignette of the Rape recalls the sculptured version in the Basilica Aemilia, along the parade route, of the legend of Romulus and Rome's foundation, a marble frieze (*c.* 34 BC) set into the lower entablature of the interior's double colonnade. The portion of the frieze highlighting the Rape of the Sabines supplies the context for the event, the festival of Consus (Consualia) with its featured mule cart race. On the left two Romans carry off two struggling Sabine women, and the scene ends with a seated figure, a goddess or personification. Farther right, in an adjacent scene, two women are about to lead a mule cart which is probably reserved for the seated goddess.[21] A row of shops opening on to a capacious portico ran along the forum side of the lawcourt, providing access, with galleries above, for spectators at gladiatorial combats, or parades at the Forum level.

Servius identified the peace treaty's Altar of Jove (640) with the Temple of Jupiter Stator, vowed by Romulus during the war with the Sabines. But Vergil transfers the Sabine treaty, solemnised by the "striking" of a pig, to the temple of Jupiter Feretrius on the Capitoline where Romulus, after killing Acron, king of the Caeninenses, and celebrating the first triumph, dedicated the *spolia opima* to the newly established cult. Another component of the Basilica Aemilia's frieze depicts the combat of Romulus with Acron and includes the trophy of the *spolia opima* that Romulus carried to Rome.

Thereafter, "not far from here" (*haud procul inde*), a spatial designation within the shield's design, in the lowest segment of the outer circle, Vergil inserts Panel III (642–5), containing the aftermath of the ghastly execution of the treacherous Mettus Fufetius, dictator of Alba Longa, by Rome's third king, Tullus Hostilius: the dragging away of the bloody remains of the perfidious Alban, who had been torn apart by two four-horse chariots driven in opposite directions.[22] West thought, aesthetically, that the atrocity was included "for the perspective interest of the four-horse chariot and the blood dripping from the brambles."[23] Maybe, but the implications of the horrendous execution are also important, perhaps more important than the blood-stained brambles, for the scene appears to be juxtaposed with that of Catiline (in torment) and Cato Uticensis (in bliss) in the Republican panel directly above the atrocity and the peace settlement of Regal times.

Tullus Hostilius, an expansionist military king, was celebrated both for the siege and destruction of Alba Longa and for his victories, and so exemplified archetypal *virtus* and stringent morality. Rome memorialized his power to chastise in the Tullianum, the lower level of the State Prison (Carcer) alongside the Capitoline Hill, the one-time Curia Hostilia and the Comitium.[24] The carcer, foreshadowed by the Tullus/Mettus episode, was dreaded terminus for notorious prisoners in the triumphal parade, persons guilty of supreme offences against Rome; they were conducted there for execution by strangulation before the victory parade ascended the Capitoline Hill.

Finally, in Panel IV (646–51), last in the frame of the "regal history" of birth, preservation and expansion, there appears a transitional event, one involving regal and republican personalities: Vulcan's action-shot pictures Etruscan Porsenna besieging the city of the Aeneadae, intent on restoring Tarquinius Superbus in 508 BC; on either flank are depictions of the heroic exploits of Horatius Cocles at the *pons Sublicius*, Tiber-side, and of the cross-Tiber swimmer, Cloelia, who won freedom for herself and other hostages by her courage. Rome's first bridges, the Pons Sublicius, and the Pons Aemilianus, were access routes for the Forum Boarium and both were prominent landmarks on the victory parade route.[25]

To recapitulate, the shield's repertoire of miraculous deliverances and heroic exploits, of punishment, defeat and triumph in the regal period, seems to derive from and associate with locales and stages of the *pompa triumphalis*: I. Palatine hill; II. Circus Maximus, Temple of Jupiter Feretrius; III. Curia, Carcer, Tullianum; and IV. Pons Sublicius, and the Tiber. All the tableaux contain or imply stations or visible memorials along the processional route.

The inner ring offers a Republican medley, another quartet of events and notable, noteworthy persons. Panel V (652–62), at the top (or summit, since *summo* is an ambiguous usage), is a triptych which highlights Manlius Torquatus defending the Tarpeian citadel (*Tarpeiae Manlius arcis*) and the lofty Temple of Jupiter. One may imagine that Romulus' freshly thatched "palatial" hut lies on one side, while the other side features Juno's 'alarm system', a silver goose flying through a golden porticoed precinct; gaudy Gauls are below, making their night assault through thickets, scaling the Capitoline heights.

There are suggestive associations in Vulcan's panel:[26] in the Temple of Capitoline Jupiter, and in the Tarpeian arx, site of the treachery of the foolish virgin Tarpeia who betrayed the citadel to Titus Tatius, the Sabine commander. A marble depiction of the punishment of her treachery is yet another segment of the repertoire of the Basilica Aemilia's interior frieze. Scholars concur nowadays in placing the Tarpeian Rock on the Arx instead of the Capitolium. Wiseman bolsters his argument by pointing out that the Tullianum, Tullus Hostilius' memorial, lies at the foot of the Arx and the two are interrelated. The Temple of Juno Moneta dominated the Arx in Vergil's time, and was close to the spot where Wiseman and Coarelli have speculated that the Tarpeian Rock must have been.[27] The Hut of Romulus, twin to the Palatine version which was granted equity by reason of Augustus' concern for association with Romulus, by its hilltop location accented the associative role of Jupiter in Rome's beginnings.[28]

Vergil's portrayal of the Gallic attack may be indebted to the figured ivory-panelled doors of the new Palatine Apollo Temple; one of the leaves rendered the supernatural repulse of forces led by the Gallic king Brennus in 279 BC when they attempted to sack Apollo's sanctuary under Parnassus. Hardie has detected Pergamene political iconography and Attalid parallels in the Gallic panel, a Gigantomachy in miniature, where Gallic hubris strives ineffectually to scale Jupiter's heights, a scene which implies "divine assertion of cosmos over chaos".[29] The Gallic attack imperils two revered memorials of Rome's genesis and evolution: the hut/palace of Romulus, freshly thatched, and the Temple of Jupiter Optimus Maximus, durable symbol of the sanctity of Rome's power.

The Gallic withdrawal in 390, and Camillus' unstated earlier capture of Veii in 395 BC, two dangers triumphantly averted, provide a context for religious celebrations that dominate Panel VI (663–9): the Salii, Dancing Priests of Mars, with head-quarters at the Regia, replete with their figure-of-eight ancilia, sacred shields that had fallen from heaven as guarantors of Rome's destiny, strut their stuff; the naked Luperci, based at the Lupercal shrine, sport wool-tufted caps appropriate to their role as *flamines*; and to complete the trio of cult services, Vulcan sculpts *castae...matres* who were privileged to travel through the city in their upholstered carriages because they had been generous donors of their golden ornaments to the Republican cause.[30] The Basilica Aemilia frieze includes a meeting of the matrons of Rome. Their convocation in the Temple of Juno Lucina marked the first festival of the Matronalia, a festival no doubt memorialized by Vergil's vignette. Eden notices that Augustus is involved in comparable action later on in the final shield panel when the *matres* appear once again ...*omnibus in templis matrum chorus* (718).

Hardie's argument that the Gallic panel concludes with an allusion to Rome's victory and its triumphal sequel, and so balances the final scene of Actium and the triple triumph of Octavian, helps to corroborate my thesis. Locale and monument are once again clearly defined and complementary topographical stations on the *cursus triumphalis* in the sequence of panels, though not always serially presented, are discernible: V. The Capitoline Hill, Tarpeian Rock, the Arx and Juno's Temple precinct (with the silver goose),and the Hut of Romulus; VI. Intimations of the Regia (haunt of the Dancing Priests) along the Sacra Via, the Lupercal Shrine (Palatine) and the Temple of Juno Lucina on the Cispian Hill above the Clivus Suburbanus. The aforementioned cults and their locales (Regia, Temple of Juno Lucina, Cave of the Lupercal) are both timely and timeless for the triumphal procession, and they are entirely relevant to Octavian's concern for the religious and moral regeneration of a war-weary, demoralized citizenry.

Thereafter, with Panel VII (666–70), "far removed" (*hinc procul*), a spatial and temporal distancing of three centuries yawns open, with a shift from earthly scenes to infernal realms, to the *annus mirabilis* of 63 BC (Octavian's birth year) recalled in a divided cameo involving Catiline, the celebrated revolutionary, undergoing punishment in Tartarus, a punishment Vergil equates elsewhere with those of the Lapiths and Ixion for violations of justice (*Aen*. 6.602–3), and Cato the

Younger (obit 46 BC) administering justice to righteous souls in Elysium.[31] What possible streetside memorials or monumental buildings can be conjured from an underworld sketch? Catiline inevitably evokes the Temple of Jupiter Stator, where Cicero delivered his indictment, and where M. Porcius Cato (Uticensis), strict moralist and rock-ribbed Republican die-hard, countered Caesar's more lenient attitude to the Catilinarian accomplices with an appeal for execution. The debate was recorded by Sallust in his account of proceedings in the Temple of Jupiter Stator on 5 December 63 BC. Is it unreasonable to conjecture that Vergil's vignette of the die-hard Stoic may owe something to Cato's decisive intervention on that occasion? Cato as "martyr to liberty", with his contempt for Caesar after Thapsus (46 BC), is bleached out in the shield panel in favour of his role as staunch defender of order and of justice. As praetor in 54 BC, Cato had applied his strict morality to judicial matters; so in the afterlife he is portrayed as champion of justice, resident and ministering to the *secretos pios* in Elysium. Notwithstanding, Vergil's contemporaries must have shuddered at the recollection of his disembowelling himself at Utica to escape Caesar's tyranny! The Temple of Jupiter Stator, a common factor for both saint and sinner, was located just outside the Porta Mugonia, another viewing stand for the triumphal parade at the end of the Clivus Palatinus.

Gurval argues that "The scenes depicted on the hero's shield proceed in a swift and uneven movement. Vergil compels his reader to shift back and forth, up and down around the armor's edges before focusing on the dramatic centerpiece. The progression of historic events is chronological but uneven."[32] Certainly Panel VIII (671–713), the battle of Actium, features an action far from the capital. This final Republican ring panel follows the conventions of war art, highlighting battle preparations, the engagement, and the final phase of the action off Actium. The battle is portrayed partly as civil war between Roman commanders, partly as a cosmic struggle between East and West. Bellona and Discordia are there, with Neptune and Minerva as Roman champions, and, crucial to the outcome, Apollo as an armed *deus ex machina*.[33]

Servius hesitated over *in medio classis aeratas* (675): *utrum clipeo an mari*? Richard Thomas aligns himself with Heyne, Wagner, Forbiger and a host of others in preferring *clipeo* to *mari*, and underscores his perception of the Actian battle as an ecphrastic centerpiece by noting a formulaic factor in Vergil's description, and that "these lines occur in the exact center of the *descriptio* of the shield (49 lines preceding them,

51 following)."[34] Although Thomas concedes that Servius's disquietude over the ambiguity may be the proper response to *in medio* as a designation, a less stringent response might suggest that the Actian event is enacted "inside" a marine frame, enlivened by dolphins, attributes of Neptune, Apollo (Delphinios) and Venus Marina. We need to remind ourselves that although the Actian triumphal parade was central in the three-day celebration, the parade celebrating the capture of Alexandria, victory over an inimical foreign power, was evidently the most eye-catching.

Hardie's[35] assessment of the Actian panel as another cosmic icon, infused with gigantomachic elements, certainly responds to the height and scale of the Egyptian armada; their captured *rostra* later bedecked the platform of the Temple of Divus Julius at the center of the Forum Romanum and the great platform at the victory site of Nicopolis. Dio notes that Antony's ships were equipped with towers that were enormous and that Octavian's fleet was diminutive by comparison.[36] Vergil pictures the opposing forces displaying hostile symbols: Cleopatra's Isiac sistrum, ominous twin snakes behind her, and bestial, barking Anubis; Octavian's *sidus Iulium* (set atop the cult statue of Julius Caesar in his newly consecrated temple) and the *corona navalis* of Agrippa, awarded first after the defeat of Sextus Pompey at Naulochus and again after Actium, with Neptune, Venus, and Minerva 'on side'. In the midst of the action (*medio in certamine*) are Mars, Dirae, Discordia, and Bellona. The epiphany of Apollo Actius is decisive: Egyptians, Indians, Arabs and Sabaeans are confounded and flee in terror. The final image of the Nile, grieving for its defeated manpower and queen, a subjugated natural wonder now, recalls paintings of enemy territory exhibited in triumphal parades.[37]

Memorials and landmarks in the shield's Republican ring are manifold, all stations along the *cursus triumphalis*, all places and environs replete with traditions and personalities: the Capitoline Hill, the ultimate goal, and the Temple of Jupiter Optimus Maximus; the Temple of Juno and the Temple of Jupiter Feretrius; the Regia and, by implication, the Vestal precinct; the Basilica Fulvia et Aemilia with shops, steps and gallery and its internal "historical" frieze; the Temple of Jupiter Stator, the Carcer, and the newly inaugurated Julian monuments of the Forum Romanum: the Temple of the Divus Julius, where the cult image was crowned by the Julian star; and the Actian triumphal arch (a *quaestio vexata* still), to the north of the newly dedicated temple, marching towards the Vesta temple and the ramp to the Palatine, and past the new speakers' platform of the Temple of Deified

Julius with the inset bronze *rostra* from the wasted fleets of Antony and Cleopatra.

Finally, Panel IX (714–31), in my view, the central panel, reverts to Rome conceived now as centre of the *oikoumene* with its cosmocrator, in a panegyrical diptych that distinguishes the central boss, the umbilicus, of the shield.[38] Vergil signals the change of locality abruptly with "now Caesar, carried within the walls of Rome in triple triumph" (*at Caesar, triplici invectus Romana triumpho/moenia*). Here is the culmination: Octavian–Augustus no longer shares the limelight with Agrippa, and there are no reminders of murderous civil strife. The sequence of action-shots is upbeat and eulogistic, broadcasting a message of optimistic imperialism. The work of art, within a work of art, in the larger context of past, present and future of Book 8, culminates in Octavian's triumphal entry into Rome, an event marked by his pious reverence for Italian gods in the dedication of three hundred shrines, by the boisterous parade, by performances and tumultuous applause, proceeding past memorials of yore, signalling the end of wars and of the artificer's programme of *res Italas Romanorumque triumphos*. Augustus (after 27 BC) appears in gold relief seated on the *sella curulis* on the steps of his dazzling Temple of Palatine Apollo, on the threshold of Apollo's temple, reviewing a procession of ethnic personifications, of conquered, pacified tribes: Nomads and ungirdled Africans, Lelegae and Carians from Asia Minor, arrow-bearing Geloni from the Scythian frontiers, Morini from northern Europe, Dahae from the East, and three rivers, natural wonders, the Euphrates and Rhine, and Araxes, token of the Parthian kingdom. Vergil's role as *vates*, as patriotic prophet of Roman triumphs to come, no doubt dictated his choice of participants in the imaginary review, but Servius found the paradigm for Vergil's post-Actian parade of peoples carrying tokens of their submission in the Porticus ad Nationes.[39] The spoils fastened to Augustus' proud palace doorposts (*superbis/postibus*), can hardly be seen as ambiguous or ominous in the overall context of thanksgiving.[40] The interior frieze of the restored Temple of Apollo Sosianus provides a "frozen" episode of the 29 BC triumphal parade, telescoped and imaginatively reconstructed in Vulcan's *capo lavoro*: butchers (*popae*) lead three bulls for sacrifice accompanied by trumpeters; and young men, wearing tunics, carry a platform (*ferculum*) exhibiting a trophy and two captives.[41] Vergil's scene of the imperial review is, in all likelihood, imaginary but it is certainly complementary to the historical parades. After the overseas conflict, and the colourful, expansive, "wide-angle screening" of the battle at Actium, we return to the urban scene, to Rome's cityscape once more, to the Temple of the Palatine triad. Hardie's response to its visual implications is spirited: "The combination of allusion to sun-god, sitting in review, with a catalogue of peoples points to the common Roman *topos* of universal empire as comprising all the lands that the sun beholds in his daily passage from east to west."[42] Edgeworth argues that the final tableaux are a conflation of three major elements: (1) Augustus' triple triumph, August 13–15, 29 BC; (2) the dedication of the Temple of Apollo on the Palatine, October 9, 28 BC; and (3) Vergil's symbol-rich imagination.[43] If, as I believe, the princeps appears at the centre of the final umbilical tableau, a Vergilian precedent must come to mind: the metaphorical temple at the centre of the *Georgics* where the triumphator occupies the centre of the poet's projected temple.[44] If the Third *Georgic*, in whole or part, had been composed by 29BC when Vergil read his verses to Octavian over four successive days during that summer, the poet's temple and Aeneas' shield were both inspired by the triple triumph.

Vergil has unquestionably telescoped Octavian's three-day triumph, and it is entirely possible that the poet also conflates the festal sequence of events thereafter, 18 and 28 August, 2 September (the second anniversary of Actium), and 23 September, Augustus' birthday and cult festival of Mars, Neptune and Apollo, into his celebratory pageantry. Maybe it witnesses to the first anniversary of the temple's dedication (9 October). The triumphal procession, and the vision of Augustus as imperial *patronus* receiving the *submissio* of his *clientes*, of the cosmocrator and *soter* in the Apollo precinct, are gala events, original or resurrected spectacles that excite fervent eulogy.[45]

Vergil's locale for the review and marchpast of subject nations has been questioned by Maria Chioffi[46] who argues that because the Palatine Apollo Temple's courtyards could not accommodate the marchpast of tribes and symbolic figures conjured by Vergil, the poet's setting must be the newly refurbished Temple of Apollo Sosianus near the Theatre of Marcellus. Her solution is ingenious, but the alternative space seems unlikely to me. In the imaginary world, and in the real world, thresholds are conceived as transitional spaces, standing between the natural world and the world tamed by men's hands.[47] It seems better therefore to assume that by seating the princeps above the rising steps of the Apollo Temple the poet implies that the saviour figure is in transition, half-way between manhood and deification. This may seem to be too bold a flight of imagination to some, but in this respect Antoinette Novara[48] cautions Vergil's readers to appreciate that the shield's "prophecy" differs from Anchises' forecast in

Hades which the poet has largely to transcribe; the poet's role has changed in Book 8 and the scene on the shield is prophetic by virtue of the memory of the poet, who envisions this future because it is for him already largely realized.

Hardie's verdicts on the ecphrasis are, to my mind, incisive and reasonable, that "as cosmic icon the Shield of Aeneas is the true climax and final encapsulation of the imperialist themes of the *Aeneid*", and that the tableau of Actium is "a blend of cosmic allegory and political ideology".[49] The shield, and its final central vignettes, memorializes a great event, the triumph of Octavian, and the recovery of peace after a century of civil wars. For the man in the Roman street, and for aspiring, ambitious parties, the parade was always the fitting commemorative. "Of all the special events, triumphal processions must have made the deepest impression. They condensed the attractions of a parade, conquest, bloodshed, and hero-worship into a single day... They were the most intense, most spectacular pageant the city had to offer."[50] Signposts of the triumphal route seem to be reflected in every segment of the shield, and every image adds impressively not only to the spectator quality of the great shield but also to the crescendo of jubilation and to the postlude of the Augustan achievement. Gurval's lynx-eyed response to the shield's message and to competing "voices" in its components, differs markedly from my more positive, optimistic assessment. He suggests that "To seek the political or private concerns that motivated the poet in his narrative discourse on the hero's shield is a vain and disconcerting effort."[51] I have suggested a hitherto unnoticed context for the apparent progress of the shield's narrative. There are also, doubtless, reverberations of the Senate's golden shield, presented to Augustus in 27 BC, inscribed with a quartet of Augustus' life-saving virtues: courage, clemency, justice and devotion (*virtus, clementia, iustitia, pietas*).[52] But Vulcan's shield was designed above all to signal the end of civil wars and the achievement of a matchless victory and peace. With the passage of years, and in Vergil's lifespan, "symbolism" replaced objectionable "details" and Horace, Vergil, and Propertius together mark developmental stages of the myth: the Battle of Actium as a political contest and as a battle of individuals and dynasts, shifted perceptibly to the consequences of victory, to Augustus as saviour of the Roman world from self-destructive civil war and enemy aggression, to the venerated guarantor of Roman civilization and prince of peace, to the "man at the center" whom Vergil chooses to highlight at the center of his imaginary shield. The *orbis* of the shield is transformed finally into an emblem of *orbis terrarum*, a massive Atlantean burden which prefigures Rome's future empire, a burden which Aeneas–Augustus carries piously into a beckoning future.

NOTES

The Scenes represented on the Shield of Aeneas

The Regal Period
(1) The She-Wolf and the Twins (630–4)
(2) The Rape of the Sabines; war between Romulus and Titus Tatius; ceremonial peace treaty (635–41)
(3) The punishment of Mettus Fufetius by Tullus Hostilius (642–5)
(4) Porsenna besieging Rome to restore Tarquinius Superbus; the heroic exploits of Horatius Cocles and Cloelia (646–51)

The Republican Period
(5) Manlius defending the Capitol and the Gauls' night attack (652–62)
(6) Religious celebrations: Salii, Luperci, and *castae...matres* (663–6)
(7) Catiline punished in Tartarus; Cato administering justice to the righteous (666–70)
The sea, with billows and dolphins, a transitional passage (671–4) setting the scene for
(8) Naval preparations off Actium; the battle and intervention of Apollo; rout of Antony's forces and flight of Cleopatra (675–713)

Centerpiece
(9) Octavian's triumphal entry into Rome with festival and rejoicing, *omnibus in templis matrum chorus* (714–19); Augustus, seated in front of the Palatine Apollo Temple, reviews conquered nations and people (720–8)

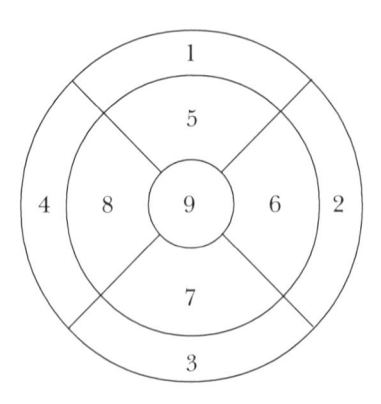

References to the text of Vergil are to the *Aeneid* except where otherwise indicated.

[1] For *imagines, tabulae pictae*, representational artworks, consult: Frova, 372–4; Holliday, 3–8; Brilliant (1967) 137–47; (1984), chapters 2, 3; Gregory (1994) 84: "The images and paintings, together with the ritual procession, trumpeters, captives and booty – and of course reactions from the spectators – expose the triumph as a truly multi-media event."

[2] On ekphrasis, viewer response to the visual arts, see Thomas (1983) 175–84; Fowler, 25–35; Boyd (1995) 71–90.

[3] See Zanker (1988) 167–238.

[4] Thomas (1989) 177. On the great shield of Achilles, see Holloway (1973) 71–3 and fig. 51; Atchity (1978) 158–87; Becker (1995) argues that ecphrasis in the *Iliad* conditions and instructs audience-response to the epic, a notion that may also be extended profitably to Vergil's usages. Hardie reviews allegorical interpretations of the Homeric shield: 25–32; 66–7; 340–75.

[5] On the "Hesiodic" Shield of Herakles: Holloway (1973) 71–3 and fig. 52.

[6] Hardie, 99.

[7] Cohon (1991) 22–30.

[8] Harrison (1981) 281–317. See also N. Leipen, *Athena Parthenos: A Reconstruction* (Toronto, 1971).

[9] Pheidian paradigms: 1, 479–82; 11, 477–9; 2, 225–7 (serpents and Minerva's shield).

[10] Hardie, "Gigantomachy in the *Aeneid*, I, II."

[11] DuBois (1982) 47. Eigler (1994) explores the manifold implications and applications of "indescribable fabric" (*non enarrabile textum*).

[12] De Calataÿ (1993) 318–49; Thomas (1991) 303–8.

[13] For "triumphal" links between Aeneas and Augustus at Pallanteum/Rome: consult Grimal (1951) 51–61; Renaud (1990) 111–16.

[14] For *testimonia*, the triumphal route, paraphernalia, and descriptive commentary see: Chioffi (1990) 275–9; Favro (1994) 151–64; Gurval, 25–34; Kuttner (1995) 143–52; Künzl (1988) passim; Renaud (1990) 147–51.

[15] Julius Caesar's quadruple triumph was a dazzling precedent for Octavian: cf. Suetonius, *Iulius*, 37.1; Dio Cass. 43.19.1; Weinstock (1971) 60–79.

[16] Favro (1994) 155.

[17] For commentary on Panel I, and on all subsequent panels, always consult Eden, Gransden, and Gurval. Access to the Palatine House of Augustus led from the Lupercal (the founder's shrine), up the Clivus Victoriae or Scalae Caci to the summit where Augustus was neighbour to Magna Mater and Apollo Actiacus. For the nurturing wolf, consult Cécile Dulière (1979) passim; Delz (1966) 224–7.

[18] For Palatine landmarks consult: Coarelli (1981), Stambaugh, and Richardson. Wiseman (*L'Urbs*, 1987), 393–413, is richly informative on The Temple of Victory, The Temple of Magna Mater, and the Temple of Jupiter Victor. Aeneas' first impression of the Daedalic Temple(s) of Apollo at Cumae, resplendent with gilded roof tiles and relief-work door panels, prefigures the Palatine scenography encountered during Octavian's triumphal parades. For Octavian's Palatine Apollo Temple, see *infra* (note 38). Propertius, *Elegies*

2.31.1–16 provides an eyewitness description on the occasion of its dedication.

[19] Wiseman (*L'Urbs*, 1987) 400. Cf.Wiseman (*Roman Studies*, 1987) 187–204; (*JACT*, 1987) 3–6.

[20] Cf. Gurval, 219–20.

[21] Cf. Albertson (1991) 801–15.

[22] Cf. Gurval, 220–3: "The violent and gruesome nature of this scene scarcely fits with prevailing interpretations about the hero's shield and its supposedly celebratory and positive tone." 221. Zetzel (1996) 312–13, argues that the Mettus Fufetius episode is inconsistent with the idea of Rome's virtuous rule, and reminds readers that "the horrific dismemberment of Mettus Fufetius may have been interpreted as an example of the importance of *fides*, but it was singled out even by Livy as an example of barbarity that was never to be repeated" (312). Antony, who broke the treaty of Brundisium (40 BC) provides a parallel.

[23] West (1975–6) 3.

[24] See Richardson, s.v. *Carcer*.

[25] Cf. Gurval, 223–5. Vergil's Porsenna episode chronologically follows after the expulsion of the Tarquins and the Republic's foundation, and so is technically detached from the Regal context. However, the heroic acts of Horatius Cocles and of Cloelia also highlight the "bridge" from Regal to Republican norms, and juxtaposition with the Actium panel (VIII) points up the deep-seated reaction to 'alien' tyranny and aggression. Porsenna was finally defeated by Aristodemus, the tyrant of Cumae.

[26] Cf. Gurval, 225–8: "The largest, most elaborate and confusing scene on the hero's shield before the centerpiece of Actium and the Augustan triumph" (225). For Tarpeia and the rock, see Coarelli (1981), and Hinard (1987) 116–19.

[27] On Manlius, Juno's Temple precinct and the honking sentry, see Wiseman (*Roman Studies*, 1987) 225–43; Coarelli (1981); Horsfall (1981) 298–311. Cohon (1991) 28 suggests deliberate artistic similarities between Cecrops and Manlius in their defensive roles.

[28] The Capitoline Hut of Romulus 'competes' with the Palatine version, neighbour to Augustus' residence. For the *casa Romuli* on the Capitoline, see Vitruvius 2.1.5, Seneca, *Contr.* 2.1.5, and *CIL* XVI.23. The Villanovan hut beside the Palatine Temple of Magna Mater, at the summit of the *scalae Caci*, was assigned to various tenants: Faustulus, Remus, and Romulus. See Balland (1984) 57–80.

[29] Hardie (120–5) detects elements of the mythic Gigantomachy in the Gallic assault on Olympian Jupiter's Capitoline domain. Zetzel (1996, 31) accepts the Gauls as "typological precursors of the barbarian east, which is defeated in the central panel of the shield itself, the battle of Actium". My contention is that the central boss, portraying the triumphal parade and aftermath, directly juxtaposed with the Capitoline episode above, aligns the Palatine Triad, token of the new dispensation, with the time-honoured goal of the *cursus triumphalis*, the Temple of Jupiter Optimus Maximus Capitolinus.

[30] Cf. Gurval, 228, contra Hardie, 125. For Mars' dancing priests, cf. Eden (1973) 78–83; for the Lupercal shrine, the Regia, and the Temple of Juno Lucina, consult Richardson and Coarelli (1985). For the *castae...matres* (second

of three examples of female sacrifice, patriotism, and piety on the shield) and the Matronalia, see Albertson (1991) 801–15.

[31] Catiline, prototype of the enemy of the Republic, competes with Cato Uticensis, its defender. See Savage (1940–1) 225–6; Ziolkowski (1989) 225–39.

[32] Cf. Gurval, 229.

[33] Cf. Gurval, 229–40; Zetzel (1996) 309–19.

[34] Thomas (1983) 179.

[35] Hardie, 98–110.

[36] Dio, 50.23; cf. Plutarch, *Antony*, 64, 78, 84. For a concise account of Vergil's reconstructed battle, "the largest assembly of naval forces in antiquity", the battle site, strategy and events, see Wallace–Hadrill (1993) 1–9. "(Octavian's) triremes were technically outclassed by the fourteen-bankers of Antony, vast hulks which men compared to Cycladic islands (Virgil, *Aen.* 8.691)." 3. See also Horsfall (1981) 3–7.

[37] Cairns (1984) 153–4, speculated that Propertius' poetic account of the Battle of Actium (4.6) might describe a painting exhibited in the Palatine Apollo precinct.

[38] Vilatte (1991) 312 consigns the Actian "scenes" to the central boss, "l'*omphalos* élevé, parce qu'elles représentent à la fois le coeur de l'Histoire et le centre géographique de l'*oikumène*, lieu matérialisé par le haut promontoire d'Apollon". But Actium was hardly the world's center. The Temple of Apollo Palatinus (a.k.a. Actius, Actiacus, Navalis, Rhamnusius) to my mind occupies the shield's omphalos, is central to the *orbis* of the shield's design and is, nobody contradicente, the 'hallmark' building of the Augustan *urbs Roma*. Vergil's description seems to provide a pendant to the celebrations at the Ara Maxima which marked Aeneas' arrival at Evander's Pallanteum; perhaps it embodies an anniversary celebration of the dedication of the Apolline Temple. The implications of the locale, the complex of temple, palace, portico, and libraries, and the posture of Augustus (720–3) as *praesens deus* (cf. Horace, *Odes* 3.5.2) are treated by Galinsky (1995) 213–24, Kuttner (1995), and E. Lefèvre (1989).

[39] Servius, ad *Aen.* 8.72. Augustus' Porticus ad Nationes exhibited *simulacra omnium gentium*, all embraced by the Augustan ecumenical orbit. Coponius's sculptured images of fourteen peoples (*simulacra gentium:* Suetonius, *Nero* 46) over whom Pompey triumphed were a feature of his theater complex (Pliny, *HN* 36.41 *Ex* Varro).

[40] Rowland (1968) 832–42, argues otherwise: "The pageant of Rome's future on the shield seems to end on a note of triumph; perhaps…in a very subtle fashion, it is not so triumphal after all." For *spolia* in a palace-temple context, cf. Wiseman (*L'Urbs*, 1987) 394–6.

[41] For details on the temple of Apollo Sosianus (Medicus) and its small interior frieze, consult Coarelli (1981), Stambaugh, and Richardson; La Rocca (1985) 94–5, figs. 22, 24; id. (1988) 121–36; Zanker (1988) 68–9; Gurval, 115–19. The dedication day for Sosius' "revised version" of the antique shrine was 23 September, 28 BC, Augustus' birthday.

[42] Hardie, 357.

[43] Edgeworth (1986) 146. Ovid (*Tristia* 3.1.59–60) describes the temple as

rising *gradibus sublimia celsis...* conforming to the high stepped podia of Italic temples.

[44] Cf. Drew (1924) 195–202.

[45] Gabelmann (1986, 281–300) rejects *submissio* (*proskynesis*) as non-Augustan procedure on rather precarious grounds. Contra: Kuttner (1995) 82–83: "Augustus receiving the homage of a varied group of conquered barbarians, men, women and children".

[46] Chioffi (1990) 275–9.

[47] Cf. Edgeworth (1986) 145–60.

[48] Novara (1986), "Le *Vates* et le Bouclier prophétique", 89–129.

[49] Hardie 339, 342.

[50] Stambaugh 239.

[51] Gurval, 246. Gurval (214–15, and elsewhere) detects negative soundings in the pre-Augustan events, subtle tensions, horror and tragedy, that stray into the imaginatively conceived cameos and ultimately affect the vignettes of Actium and the Augustan triumph. But negative "voices" in a triumphal "parade", in a quintessential Roman institution, always the occasion for positive panegyric, and in Vergil's instance, extending to gigantomachic description, strains credulity. Gurval's portrait of a morally distressed, recalcitrant epic poet often seems out of step with Livy's prose epic; Livy links Octavian's Actian victory with the closing of the Janus Temple doors, signalling the welcome cessation of wars throughout the empire (1.19.3).

[52] Cf.Galinsky (1996) 80–8; Wallace Hadrill, (1993) 7, captures the essence of the victory and the myth-making of Actium: "It was a battle for Roman values, to save the Roman world from a frontal assault on its gods, its ideals, its moral fabric... Appropriately enough, on a shield made by one god (Vulcan) and commissioned by another (Venus), it is seen as a battle of the gods, who embody the values of Roman and alien, of good and evil."

Bibliography

Albertson, F.C.
   1991   "The Basilica Aemilia frieze: religion and politics in late Republican Rome", *Latomus* 49, 801–15.

Atchity, K.J.
   1978   *Homer's Iliad: The Shield of Memory*, Carbondale.

Balland, A.
   1984   "La *casa Romuli* au Palatin et au Capitolin ", *REL* 62, 57–80.

Becker, A.S.
   1995   *The Shield of Achilles and the Poetics of Ekphrasis*, Lanham, Md.

Boyd, B.W.
   1995   "*Non enarrabile textum*: ecphrastic trespass and narrative ambiguity in the *Aeneid*", *Vergilius* 41, 71–90.

Brilliant, R.
   1967   *The Arch of Septimius Severus in the Roman Forum*, ch. 11, "The triumphal register", 137–47, Rome.
   1984   *Visual Narratives, Storytelling in Etruscan and Roman Art*, chs. 2, 3, Ithaca.

Cairns, F.
    1984   "Propertius and the Battle of Actium", in T. Woodman, and D. West (eds.) *Poetry and Politics in the Age of Augustus*, 129-68, Cambridge.
Chioffi, L.
    1990   "triumphus", *EV* 5, 275-90.
Coarelli, F.
    1981   *Guida archaeologica di Roma*, Roma.
    1985   *Il Foro Romano II. Periodo repubblicano e augusteo*, Roma.
Cohon, R.
    1991   "Virgil and Pheidias: The shield of Aeneas and of Athena Parthenos", *Vergilius* 37, 22-30.
De Calataÿ, G.
    1993   "Le zodiaque de l'Énéide", *Latomus* 52, 318-49.
Delz, J.
    1996   "Die Säugende Wölfin auf dem Schild des Aeneas", *MH* 23, 224-7.
Drew, D.L.
    1924   "Virgil's marble temple (*Georgics* III.10-39)", *CQ* 18, 195-202.
Dulière, Cécile.
    1979   *Lupa romana. Recherches d'iconographie et essai d'interprétation*, Brussels and Rome.
Dubois, Page.
    1982   *Rhetorical Description and the Epic*, Cambridge.
Eden, P.T.
    1973   "The Salii on the Shield of Aeneas:*Aeneid* 8.663-6", *RhM* 116, 78-83.
    1975   *A Commentary on Virgil: "Aeneid" VIII*, Leiden.
Edgeworth, R.J.
    1986   "The ivory gate and the threshold of Apollo", *C&M* 37, 145-60.
Eigler, U.
    1994   "*Non enarrabile textum* (Verg. *Aen*. 8.625): Servius und die römische Geschichte bei Vergil", *Aevum* 68, 147-64.
Favro, D.
    1994   "The urban impact of Roman triumphal parades", in D. Favro (ed.) *Streets: Critical Perspectives on Public Space*, 151-64, Berkeley.
Fowler, D.
    1991   "Narrate and describe: the problem of ekphrasis", *JRS* 81, 25-35.
Frova, A.
    1972   *L'Arte di Roma*, Rome.
Gabelmann, H.
    1986   "Zur Schlussszene auf dem Schild des Aeneas (Vergil *Aeneis* VII. 720-8", *RM* 93, 281-300.
Galinsky, K.
    1995   *Augustan Culture: An Interpretive Study*, Princeton.
Gregory, A.P.
    1994   " 'Powerful images': responses to portraits and the political uses of images in Rome", *JRS* 7, 80-99.

Grimal, P.
   1951   "Énée à Rome et le triomphe d'Octave", *REA* 53, 51–61.

Gurval, R.A.
   1995   *Actium and Augustus. The Politics and Emotions of Civil War*, Ann Arbor.

Hardie, P.
   1986   *Virgil's "Aeneid": Cosmos and Imperium*, Oxford.

Harrison, E.
   1981   "Motifs of the city-siege on the shield of the Athena Parthenos", *AJA* 85, 281–317.

Hinard, F.
   1987   "Spectacle des exécutions et espace urbain", in *L'Urbs: espace urbain et histoire*, Collection de L'École Française de Rome 93, 393–413.

Holliday, P.
   1980   " 'Ad triumphum excolendum': the political significance of Roman historical painting", *Oxford Art Journal* 3.2, 3–8.

Holloway, R.R.
   1973   *A View of Greek Art*, Providence.

Horsfall, N.
   1981a   "From history to legend: M. Manlius and the geese", *CJ* 76, 298–311.
   1981b   "The battle of Actium: myth and reality", *Classicum* 18.7, 3–7.

Künzl, E.
   1988   *Der römische Triumph. Siegesfeiern im antiken Rom*, Munich.

Kuttner, A.
   1995   *Dynasty and Empire in the Age of Augustus. The Case of the Boscoreale Cups*, Berkeley.

La Rocca, E.
   1985   *Amazzonomachia: Le Sculture frontali del tempio di Apollo Sosiano*, Rome.
   1988   "Der Apollo-Sosianus-Tempel", in *Kaiser Augustus und die verlorene Republik*, 121–36, Mainz-am-Rhein.

Lefèvre, E.
   1989   *Das Bild-Programm des Apollo-Tempels auf dem Palatin*, Konstanz.

Leipen, N.
   1971   *Athena Parthenos: A Reconstruction*, Toronto.

Nedergaard, E.
   1988   "Zur Problematik der Augustusbögen auf dem Forum Romanum", in *Kaiser Augustus und die verlorene Republik*, 224–39, Mainz-am-Rhein.

Novara, A.
   1986   *Poésie virgilienne de la mémoire: Questions sur l'histoire dans l'Énéide 8*, Clermont-Ferrand.

Ravenna, G.
   1988   "Scudo di Enea", *EV* 4, 739–742, Rome.

Renaud, C.
   1990   *Studies in the Eighth Book of the "Aeneid": The Importance of Place*, Diss., University of Texas, Austin.

Richardson, L., Jr.
   1992   *A New Topographical Dictionary of Ancient Rome*, Baltimore.

Rowland, R.J.
   1968   "Foreshadowing in Vergil *Aeneid* VIII.714–28", *Latomus* 27, 832–42.

Savage, J.J.
   1940-1 "Catiline in Vergil and in Cicero", *CJ* 36, 225–6.

Stambaugh, J.
   1988   *The Ancient Roman City*, Baltimore.

Thomas, J.
   1991   "Le sens symbolique de la bataille d'Actium (Énéide VIII.671–728)", *Euphrosyne* 19, 303–8.

Thomas, R.
   1983   "Virgil's ecphrastic centerpieces", *HSCPh* 87, 175–84.

Vilatte, S.
   1991   "Pensée et esthétique chez Virgile: le bouclier d'Énée", *LEC* 59, 307–22.

Wallace Hadrill, A.
   1993   *Augustan Rome*, London.

Weinstock, S.
   1971   *Divus Julius*, Oxford.

West, D.A.
   1975/6 "*Cernere erat*: The shield of Aeneas", *PVS* 15, 1–6. Reprint, in S.J. Harrison (ed.) *Oxford Readings in Vergil's "Aeneid"*, Oxford, 1990, 295–304.

Wiseman, T.P.
   1987   "*Conspicui postes tectaque digna deo*", in *L'Urbs: espace urbain et histoire*, Collection de L'École Française de Rome 93, 393–413.
   1987   "Reading the city: history, poetry, and the topography of Rome", *JACT Review*, Second Series 1 (Summer), 3–6, including plan.
   1987   "Topography and rhetoric: the trial of Manlius", in T.P. Wiseman, *Roman Studies: Literary and Historical*, 225–43, Liverpool.

Zanker, P.
   1988   *The Power of Images in the Age of Augustus*, transl. A. Shapiro, Ann Arbor.

Zetzel, J.
   1996   "Natural law and poetic justice: a Carneadean debate in Cicero and Virgil", *CPh* 91, 297–319.

Ziolkowski, A.
   1989   "The sacra via and the temple of Jupiter Stator", *Op.Rom.* 17, 225–39.

11

THE SWORD-BELT OF PALLAS: MORAL SYMBOLISM AND POLITICAL IDEOLOGY
Aeneid 10.495–505

Stephen Harrison

And so saying he pressed the corpse with his left foot, stripping off the monstrous weight of Pallas' baldric and the abomination stamped upon it: the foul slaughter of a band of young men under the cover of one wedding-night, and bloodstained marriage-chambers, which Clonus the son of Eurytus had embossed with much gold. In this booty Turnus now triumphed, and rejoiced at his acquisition. How ignorant of destiny and of their future lot are the minds of men, and how unable to observe due measure when uplifted by good fortune! There will be a time for Turnus when he will wish he had bought Pallas' safety at a great price, and when he will hate these spoils and the day he got them.[1]

> et laevo pressit pede talia fatus
> exanimem rapiens immania pondera baltei
> impressumque nefas: una sub nocte iugali
> caesa manus iuvenum foede thalamique cruenti,
> quae Clonus Eurytides multo caelaverat auro:
> quo nunc Turnus ovat spolio gaudetque petitus.
> nescia mens hominum fati sortisque futurae
> et servare modum rebus sublata secundis!
> Turno tempus erit magno cum optaverit emptum
> intactum Pallanta, et cum spolia ista diemque
> oderit.

I. Moral Symbolism: the search for a *nefas*

In this famous passage of the *Aeneid* Turnus, having killed Aeneas' youthful ally Pallas and given a vicious message to be returned with the corpse to the youth's father, despoils his victim's corpse of a baldric or sword-belt with an elaborate design, on which the narrative lingers

Stephen Harrison

in some detail. Despite the absence of proper names or other explicit indications of identity,[2] Vergilian commentators since Servius[3] have agreed that the event depicted on the sword-belt belongs to the myth of the Danaids, the fifty daughters of the Egypto-Greek king Danaus who were married to their fifty cousins the sons of Aegyptus, but ordered to slay their husbands on their wedding night. Forty-nine of them did so, but the fiftieth, Hypermestra, refused to kill her husband Lynceus. The other criminal Danaids were traditionally depicted as being punished in the Underworld, though there were other versions in which they were purified of blood-guilt and even achieved second marriages.[4]

Modern interpreters of the *Aeneid* are generally agreed that the meaning of the Danaid myth here is symbolic, though the precise nature of that symbolism has been much debated. The word *nefas*, emphatically placed immediately before the description proper, suggests that the scene on the sword-belt is a moral abomination, an unspeakable act. This invites the reader to look for another *nefas* in the narrative context of the *Aeneid*. This symbolic approach is encouraged by a passage of Statius which uses the Danaid myth in a clear allusion to *Aeneid* 10.497–9. In the first part of *Thebaid* 4, the Seven against Thebes and their forces are listed in a formal catalogue and their personal arms described. Among them is the Argive Hippomedon, whose vast shield bears a Danaid device (4.131–5):[5]

> The fiery circle covered right over his shoulders and chest, and alive in its gold, perfectly worked, was the night of Danaus: the fifty guilty marriage-chambers burn with the black torch of the Furies, and the father himself, in the bloody doorways, praises the abomination and inspects their swords.

>   umeros ac pectora late
> flammeus orbis habet, perfectaque vivit in auro
> nox Danai: sontes Furiarum lampade nigra
> quinquaginta ardent thalami; pater ipse cruentis
> in foribus laudatque *nefas* atque inspicit enses.

The verbal and thematic echoes confirm the link with Pallas' sword-belt.[6] Statius, like Vergil, concentrates on the violation of the marriage-chambers by murder, but the emphasis is clearly different; the leading role given in the Statian version of the Danaid myth to the father Danaus (*nox Danai*, not *nox Danaidum*), whose motivation for his appalling behaviour is a bitter quarrel with his brother Aegyptus, plainly echoes the narrative context of the *Thebaid* and suggests the function of the shield's symbolism within that work. Hippomedon will use this shield in a similarly vicious dispute between the brothers Eteocles and Polynices which leads to multiple deaths, not least to his own (cf. *Thebaid* 9.222–569), and the *nefas* it displays is the *nefas* of Polynices' ultimately fratricidal attempt to regain Thebes (cf. *Thebaid* 1.86), a *nefas* in which Hippomedon himself, as one of the Seven, is fundamentally and disastrously implicated. Though the Danaids themselves (as in Vergil) are here mentioned only by implication, their crime is symbolic of the criminal intentions of Hippomedon and the cause he espouses, especially as it is depicted on a shield, an artefact which he is to use in the criminal war of the Seven.

Several points emerge from this Statian parallel which illuminate the Vergilian passage. First, the Danaid story is clearly presented as an Argive legend, an evident stress on its local origin, just as Capaneus, another Argive, has devices connected with the Argive hero Hercules on his shield, whose description follows shortly afterwards (*Thebaid* 4.165–72).[7] Second, its symbolic aspect as a token of criminality is plainly relevant to its bearer: like the shield of Turnus in the *Aeneid*, which displays an emblem of the similar divinely-maddened Io (7.789–92), the shield-device reflects the characterisation of its owner.[8] This aspect of wearer-relevance generates a real problem in the Vergilian passage: who is the primary wearer of Pallas' sword-belt, and whose characterisation should it reflect? Is it Pallas himself, for whom it was made, or Turnus, who has just appropriated it, or in some sense both of them? Third, the Statian emphasis on Danaus and the frenzy of family killing suits the context of the fratricidal Thebaid particularly well; we might expect a similar thematic fit for Vergil's version of the Danaid myth within the *Aeneid*. All these issues will be closely relevant in interpreting the sword-belt of Pallas.

The modern history of the symbolic interpretation of the sword-belt, like so much symbolic criticism of the *Aeneid*, begins effectively with Pöschl: 'The crime of the Danaids as pictured on Pallas' sword belt – the *nefas* and the *cruenti thalami* – is related to the "bloody marriage" which Turnus will celebrate. This is mentioned at the very moment when Turnus robs Pallas of his arms. Turnus collects his own death with the belt.'[9] Here the Danaid myth foreshadows Turnus' death – he too will perish before he can become a bridegroom; indeed, as he himself sees it, he is fighting the war for the hand of his bride Lavinia. Less sympathetic to Turnus are the views of Otis, who regards the sword-belt as 'fitting booty for the breaker of a marriage-treaty'[10] (like the Danaids, Turnus seeks to rupture a marriage-pact by killing), and Knauer, who in a brief footnote argues that 'Not only does Turnus steal the *balteus*, but he also "steals" the crime, at least in the way that Vergil formulates it...here there still remains much to elucidate.'[11] Here Knauer rightly draws attention to the clearly symbolic *rapiens... nefas*, with its implication that Turnus takes on the criminal act shown on the belt along with the belt itself: Turnus himself is a latter-day Danaid, somehow inheriting the crime of his mythological analogues, though Knauer wisely suggests that this is not the whole story.

The connection of the *balteus* with Turnus has been further explored by Schlunk, who argues for its psychological symbolism as a token of Turnus' unrestrained and intemperate act in despoiling Pallas.[12] Schlunk points to the allegory of the intemperate souls of Plato's *Gorgias* (493a–d), who are represented as pouring water from leaky sieves into leaky jugs in the Underworld, and that of the similarly ineffective young female water-carriers in the Underworld as allegorised by Lucretius (3.1003–10), usually thought to be the Danaids, whose punishment is similarly symbolic of the insatiability of their desires.[13] These allegorical uses of the Danaids' traditional infernal punishment of carrying water in leaky vessels[14] suggest, Schlunk argues, that the indirect allusion to the Danaids in Vergil, which does not mention their punishment, can nevertheless evoke the allegorical interpretation of their crime as intemperance. Though this has some attractions, especially given the Vergilian comment on Turnus' deed at 10.501–2, which stresses that it shows the intemperate confidence of momentary success, there is some difficulty for the reader, however alert, in making the required series of interpretative jumps. The Danaids must be identified (easy enough), their traditional punishment recalled (in a context where the stress is on the deed and the punishment is not mentioned),[15] and the allegorical interpretations of that punishment brought to bear on the character of Turnus.

Another, radically different, view is taken by Eva Keuls, who relates the *nefas* of the Danaids to the character of Aeneas. She argues that the sword-belt alludes to the characterisation of the Danaids in Aeschylus' *Supplices*, who in her view begin as gentle but are forced to bloodshed by the intolerable provocation of others. This development she sees as analogous to that of Aeneas: 'in the thickening gloom of the final books of the *Aeneid*, the description of Pallas' belt in Book 10 foreshadows the similar hardening of Aeneas into a cold-blooded killer'. This is confirmed for her by the later description of Pallas' sword-belt as *saevi monumenta doloris* (*Aen.* 12.945): 'The "savage sorrow" of the Danaids is also that of gentle Aeneas, dragged by an inexorable chain of events into the brutality of war.'[16] Though this is an ingenious theory, there are several objections to be made. First, it is not clear that the Danaids at the beginning of Aeschylus' *Supplices* are gentle and mild: even there they show some potential for their later acts of violence.[17] Second, the idea of 'gentle Aeneas' surely over-simplifies the complex character of one who from the beginning of the poem is a mighty warrior with a strong Iliadic record in war: while there is no doubt that Aeneas is initially unwilling to fight in Italy and needs several times to be provoked to action, once he is engaged in battle he is far from gentle, especially in his frenzy after the death of Pallas in Book 10.[18] Third, and most important, Aeneas is not present at the killing and despoiling of Pallas, and has no connection with this sword-belt until he sees it at the end of Book 12. It is possible at that point that the sword-belt and its iconography are to be connected with the killing of Turnus, but in Book 10, any immediate reading of the symbolism of the sword-belt is surely more likely to concern the present characters of Pallas and Turnus rather than the absent Aeneas.

The most influential recent interpretation of the sword-belt is justly that of Conte.[19] He argues that the violent *mors immatura* of the young Pallas without the chance to marry is closely parallel to the fate of the sons of Aegyptus, similarly deprived of the hope of maturity and progeny through their murder by the Danaids, and that it is this which makes Turnus' action in killing Pallas a *nefas*. This has the considerable virtue of providing a reading of the sword-belt which is relevant both to its former owner Pallas and to its new owner Turnus, and which reflects in its interpretation the text's evident stress on the victims of the Danaids rather than the Danaids themselves. Two issues seem worth taking up here. First, is it the fact that Turnus kills the young Pallas which is a *nefas*? After all, Turnus is only doing what all warriors are supposed to do in epic and indeed all war situations: killing the enemy, and an important enemy commander at that, who has himself already killed many of Turnus' men earlier in this same book (10.379–425). Admittedly, Turnus' seeking out of Pallas and his taunting him with the prospect of his father Evander's loss of his son is unpleasant and repulsive, but it is Homeric in flavour and similar to the actions of Aeneas when he comes to take revenge for the death of Pallas later in the book (10.510–605): if all killings with taunts are criminal, then many heroic killings will attract that label. But killing the enemy is not wrong in ancient epic or ancient warfare; killing an enemy who is weaker than yourself is not wrong either – it is what inevitably happens, except in special cases like the killing of Achilles, where Paris needed both a long-distance weapon and the help of a god in order to dispatch a hero greater than himself. Though Turnus is certainly excessive in his taunts to Pallas, especially in the idea that Pallas' father Evander should be there to watch the fun (10.443 *cuperem ipse parens spectator adesset*), with *spectator* suggesting going to watch a gladiatorial contest or particularly interesting execution in the arena, killing him is not wrong in itself.

But there is an offence here, as Heinze and others have seen.[20] *Gaudetque potitus* (500) indicates that Turnus keeps the sword-belt of Pallas for himself and puts it on; he is clearly wearing it at the end of the poem. This is wrong in terms of ancient religious thought and practice: the spoils of the dead were in some sense taboo and should be dedicated to the gods. As Hornsby has pointed out in an important article, Aeneas himself always dedicates spoils to the gods, and those who keep or seek to keep the spoils of the dead in the *Aeneid* usually come to grief.[21] Euryalus is killed because of the flash of his stolen helmet, which gives him away in the moonlight (9.365–6), Camilla dies through pursuing Chloreus for the sake of his golden armour, which she wanted for herself (11.781–2), and Turnus himself is of course another example of this pattern: it is the wearing of the plundered sword-belt of Pallas which finally leads to Turnus' death at the hands of Aeneas (12.940–9).

So Turnus' offence is to wear the sword-belt, not to kill Pallas; the death of Pallas is tragic and lamentable, but it is not in itself a crime. How does this relate to the identification of an analogue for the *nefas* of the Danaids in the plot of the *Aeneid*? Here we return to the details of the Danaid story. The killing of the sons of Aegyptus in the Aeschylean version (and I agree with Keuls that this is the version most easily available to the *Aeneid*) was probably presented as a crime against Zeus Xenios, the protector of guests, since in the Aeschylean version the marriages plainly occurred in Argos, where Danaus is host and Aegyptus and his sons are guests.[22] The *nefas* is not just the horror of family killing but also the violation of the bond of *xenia*, guest-friendship, implicit in the Danaids' deed. Vergil's text, though not explicit on this point, seems to indicate this kind of idea in the graphic language of the passage, which refers literally to the bloody pollution of the marriage-chambers (*foede*, *cruenti*), the physical mark of the religious pollution of the host-guest relationship (the *thalami* are in the house of Danaus, if the Aeschylean scenario is being followed). Like Danaus and his daughters, Turnus enacts a killing which is not itself intrinsically criminal; the Danaids are being forced to revenge by their father in pursuance of his quarrel with his brother and under some provocation from Aegyptus and his sons, who are in effect forcing them into marriage, and have a case which was no doubt strongly argued in the third play of Aeschylus' trilogy, in which (like Orestes in *Eumenides*) they seem to have been purified of blood-guilt.[23] The killing is condemned not for itself but for its surrounding circumstances: religious transgression takes place in Turnus' appropriation and wearing of the sword-belt, which he should have dedicated to the gods, an act which symbolises his high-handedness in the manner of Pallas' death, just as religious transgression takes place in the choice of the wedding-night and the context of hospitality for the Danaids' slaying of the sons of Aegyptus.

But the relevance of the sword-belt to Turnus is not limited to describing his act of wearing the spoils as nefarious, though that is important. Knauer's idea that the *nefas* of the Danaid story somehow passes from Pallas to Turnus in the act of appropriating the sword-belt can be turned in a different way using Conte's notion of the Danaid story as primarily concerned with *mors immatura*: the sword-belt itself in a sense passes on the tragic early death depicted, communicating it as if by contagion to Turnus himself.[24] Turnus, like Pallas, will be killed before he reaches maturity and marriage; this is tragic, and doubly tragic because Turnus does not know his future fate, or recognise that it is inscribed on the sword-belt of Pallas. The following narratorial comment *nescia mens hominum* (501) alludes directly to this tragic dramatic irony: the narrator and the reader, through the fact that the narrative lingers over the description of the sword-belt, can see that the Danaid story looks forward to Turnus' own death, but Turnus, caught up in the excitement of victory, cannot see this himself. Indeed, in many ways the Danaid myth fits the story of Turnus more closely than that of Pallas. Both Turnus and the sons of Aegyptus are killed in a dispute connected with marriage.[25] Both share an Argive connection: considerable stress is laid in the *Aeneid* on the connection between Turnus' city of Ardea and its traditional claim to be an Argive colony, and indeed on Turnus' own Argive heredity.[26] As Breen has pointed out, Turnus' city of Ardea was founded according to Vergil by Danae, direct descendant of the one Argive royal bloodline which survived the *nox Danai* (her father Acrisius was the grandson of Hypermestra and Lynceus).[27] The iconography of the sword-belt of Pallas is not the only portentous Argive design associated with the arms worn by Turnus: as already noted above, in the Catalogue of Latins he is shown with Io on his shield, a sign both of his Argive ancestry and of the fact that like Io he has been driven out of his senses by the intervention of Juno, who is herself the traditional patron deity of Argos.[28]

So the sword-belt of Pallas contains in its design the seeds of Turnus' own tragic destruction as well as a reflection of the killing of the youthful Pallas by which he acquired it and the religious violation through which he wears it. In narratological terms, the ekphrasis of the sword-belt is both an analepsis, a flashback to the past, looking back to the killing of Pallas which has just occurred, and a prolepsis, an anticipation of the future, looking forward to the death of Turnus himself at the end of the poem. To make a link with Aeneas' killing of Turnus does not require following Keuls in comparing Aeneas with the Danaids as a 'cold-blooded killer'; Aeneas' natural instinct is for *clementia*, and it is his duty to avenge the dead Pallas which drives him to kill Turnus, one form of *pietas* overcoming another in a tragic conflict rather than the triumph of *nefas* over *fas*.[29] For both Pallas and Turnus, the highlighting of the Danaid design on the deadly artefact they share shows their common fate, that of young men of marriageable age who lose their lives before they can marry and reproduce, the tragedy of all forms of war, which reverses the natural sequences of human existence in ensuring the death of the young.[30] The primary emphasis in the text at *Aeneid* 10.497–9 is on the tragic death of the victims, and the abomination of the death of unfulfilled youth, not on the criminality of the perpetrators. The religious violation in both cases is committed in ignorance or under great pressure: Turnus does not know how great his error is in putting on the sword-belt (10.501 *nescia mens hominum*), while the Danaids are forced to their crime by the competing demands of father and cousin/husbands. It is a tragic and not a triumphant irony that Turnus in the poem's last scene follows Pallas and the sons of Aegyptus, all victims of bloody quarrels whose young lives are violently and prematurely cut short. This lamentable fact is the *nefas* in which all of them share, the tragic death before their time of young men caught up in struggles they cannot control. In linking both Pallas and Turnus with the sons of Aegyptus in this way, the *Aeneid* highlights as often the sufferings of the victims of war.

II. Political ideology: the Danaids in Augustan Rome

So far I have considered the relevance of the Danaid myth within the ideological and narrative scheme of the *Aeneid*. I turn now to its larger context in Augustan Rome. The prominence of the Danaid myth in Augustan poetry has often been noted: apart from Vergil, Horace narrates the story of Hypermestra at length in *Odes* 3.11, Ovid's fourteenth epistle in the *Heroides* is from Hypermestra to Lynceus, and there are a number of incidental mentions.[31] In all Augustan allusions to the Danaids, their deed is condemned, as indeed in Vergil's *nefas*.[32] This negative character of the Danaids is important not only for its coherence with the Vergilian interpretation, but also in understanding the ideological impact of the Danaid myth in the famous Augustan building project which has often and plausibly been connected with the prominence of the story in Augustan poetry.[33] Between the columns of one of the two long porticoes in front of Augustus' temple of Palatine Apollo stood statues of the fifty Danaids, apparently depicted at the moment of murder.[34] Three contemporary poetical descriptions of this sculptural ensemble have been preserved, one in Propertius and two in Ovid. First, Propertius 2.31:

> You ask why I come to you somewhat late? Apollo's golden portico has been opened by mighty Caesar. The whole of it had been marked out for a promenade with Afric columns, between which stood the daughters of old Danaus. Here I thought that Phoebus' statue was fairer than Phoebus himself as he sang with silent lyre and parted lips of marble; and around the altar stood Myron's herd, four steers by the sculptor, statuary which seemed to be alive. Then in the middle rose the temple, of dazzling marble, dearer to Phoebus even than his Ortygian home: upon the pediment of this stood the chariot of the Sun, and doors which were a famed piece of African ivory; one door lamented the Gauls cast down from Parnassus' peak, the other the deaths connected with Niobe. Then between his mother and his sister the god of Pytho himself, wearing a long cloak, plays and sings (tr. Goold, 1990).[35]

> Quaeris, cur veniam tibi tardior? aurea Phoebi
>   porticus a magno Caesare aperta fuit.
> tota erat in spatium Poenis digesta columnis,
>   inter quas Danai femina turba senis.
> hic equidem Phoebus visus mihi pulchrior ipso
>   marmoreus tacita carmen hiare lyra;
> atque aram circum steterant armenta Myronis,
>   quattuor artificis, vivida signa, boves.
> tum medium claro surgebat marmore templum,
>   et patria Phoebo carius Ortygia:
> in quo Solis erat supra fastigia currus,
>   et valvae, Libyci nobile dentis opus;
> altera deiectos Parnasi vertice Gallos,
>   altera maerebat funera Tantalidos.
> deinde inter matrem deus ipse interque sororem
>   Pythius in longa carmina veste sonat.

From this, the most detailed ancient description of the Palatine temple and its surroundings, we learn that apart from four sculptures of steers by Myron next to the altar, presumably a witty evocation of sacrificial animals (Apollo's altar will never be short of victims), the other external decorations were a marble statue of Apollo playing the lyre, and the ivory-panelled doors with their historical and mythological designs – one depicting the repulse of the Gauls from Delphi in 278 BC, the other showing Niobe weeping over the bodies of her children. The meaning of the last two seems clear: in both cases Apollo acts violently to take revenge on those who offend him or violate his places of worship, whether preserving his own oracle from a barbarian invasion or avenging a slight to himself and his family. Niobe of course had boasted that she had many more children than Apollo's mother Leto, and Apollo and Artemis killed them all in revenge; this surely matched Augustus' vengeance for his father Julius Caesar. The link with Actium is clear: there too (as in Propertius 4.6) Apollo took revenge on his enemies and supported his favourite Augustus.[36] There is also a Greek/barbarian element here: the Gauls are northern barbarians repulsed from Delphi, the centre of the Hellenic world, while Niobe is the daughter of Tantalus and by origin a Lydian rather than a Greek. Thus Palatine Apollo becomes the defender of civilization against barbarism, very suitable for a temple celebrating a victory commonly depicted as a defeat of Oriental barbarians such as Cleopatra. This theme of the repulse and defeat of barbarians will be useful in considering the meaning of the Danaid sculptural group within the ensemble.

Of the Danaid part of the scheme we learn relatively little from Propertius: *Danai femina turba senis* simply confirms the presence of the Danaid statues, though *senis* importantly suggests the presence of a likeness of Danaus too. This last detail is confirmed by Ovid's two brief descriptions: *Ars* 1.73–4 'and the female descendants of Belus who dared to prepare death for their miserable cousins, and their father stands there fierce with drawn sword', *quaeque parare necem miseris patruelibus ausae | Belides et stricto stat ferus ense pater*, *Tristia* 3.1.61–2 'where there are the statues alternating with foreign columns, the female descendants of Belus and their father fierce with drawn sword', *signa peregrinis ubi sunt alterna columnis | Belides et stricto barbarus ense pater*.[37] Clearly the sculptural group included a depiction of Danaus himself, with drawn sword, urging his daughters to the deed. A further issue is that of whether the victims were also depicted as well as the murderers: this has obvious importance for any link with the *Aeneid*. The standard modern work on Roman topography claims that the fifty sons of Aegyptus were represented by equestrian statues in the open

The Sword-belt of Pallas: Moral Symbolism and Political Ideology

area opposite the portico of the Danaids, but the only evidence for this is a scholion on Persius 2.56 which claims to report Acro, a dubious and late source which should be treated with scepticism:[38] quite apart from this doubtful provenance, it is surely very unlikely (as several scholars have stressed) that such a large group evidently related to the fifty Danaids would not have been mentioned in the relatively extensive literary sources for the buildings on the Palatine, and especially in Propertius 2.31, which gives an account of the whole complex.[39]

So if the Danaids appeared in the context of Palatine Apollo without their bridegroom victims but with their hortatory father, what symbolic role could they play in the iconography of the Augustan complex? There is little connection of the *Danaid* myth with Apollo in the mythographic or Aeschylean versions,[40] though it is of course true to say that our knowledge of the epic *Danais* is very small,[41] and that Apollo might have played an important part there of which we are ignorant. The question of precisely what the Palatine Danaids represent has been faced by a number of scholars, several of whom have considered it alongside the interpretation of the sword-belt of Pallas in the *Aeneid*:[42] in this treatment, the function of the Danaids on the Palatine will be considered first, and then their function on the belt of Pallas. Paul Zanker has suggested one way in which the Danaids fit into the celebration and monumentalising of Actium on the Palatine, arguing that they were depicted as atoning in Hades for their crimes, in their traditional punishment of fetching water in leaky vessels.[43] Symbolically, this represented general atonement for the blood shed in the years of fratricidal civil war to which Actium put an end. But several arguments against this may be made. First, Ovid's descriptions of Danaus standing with his daughters sword in hand suggests that the moment depicted was that of the killing rather than its aftermath; second, that such a concept would turn Augustus' brilliant marble colonnade into a depiction of the Underworld, surely highly undesirable, and third and most importantly, that the idea of atonement is simply inappropriate to the consistent Augustan presentation of Actium not as a battle to end a civil war but as the triumph of Rome over exotic and oriental barbarians.[44]

An alternative interpretation of the Augustan symbolism of the Danaid sculptures has been advanced by both Simon and Lefèvre.[45] Their line of argument follows the theme of barbarian defeat so evident elsewhere in the Palatine design, and suggests that the Danaids (with their Greek name) stand for the triumph of Greece and therefore civilisation over Oriental barbarism. The sons of Aegyptus, the

Danaids' victims, represent the defeat of their eponymous Egypt, from which both the Danaids and their unfortunate husbands originally came. This interpretation has the great virtue of bringing in the notion of barbarians and Egypt, which is surely likely to be relevant given the context of Actium and its usual presentation as a victory against barbarians, a presentation which (as we have already seen) clearly lies behind the decorations of the Palatine temple. But it is not clear that the Danaids are more Greek than the sons of Aegyptus: though their patronymic suggests an Argive connection, their previous presentation in myth and literature was as strongly Egyptian. In Aeschylus' *Supplices* they are refugees from Egypt who have just arrived in Argos, and their characterization suggests exotic females who do not correspond to traditional Greek notions of women and their role.[46] In the epic *Danais*, the single substantial fragment seems to place the slaying of the sons of Aegyptus in Egypt, rather than in Argos as in Aeschylus and texts dependent on him.[47] The likely absence of any depiction of the sons of Aegyptus is also a problem for this interpretation: if the event celebrated in the Danaid sculptures is the destruction by Europeans of Egypt, then the absence of any symbolic analogue for Egypt is surely a difficulty.

A third line of argument, represented by Kellum, has been to retain the Egyptian connection of the Danaid story, but to argue that it is the Danaids and not the sons of Aegyptus who represent the forces of orientalism and barbarism defeated at Actium, with their Egyptian origin and their monstrous crime.[48] This interpretation has a number of virtues, not least amongst them the fact that the ideological meaning is now vested in the Danaids, who were certainly depicted, rather than in the sons of Aegyptus, who were very probably not. It is precisely the kind of barbarism demonstrated by the spouse-murdering Danaids that Augustus, in Augustan triumphalist discourse, is represented as defeating with Apollo's aid at Actium, the victory celebrated in the Palatine temple; and the depiction of the Danaids in their portico then coheres with the depictions of the Gauls and the Niobids on the doors of the temple in displaying human transgression which Apollo has helped to punish. As Kellum herself argued, the Danaids are surely an appropriate mythological representation of Cleopatra, the official enemy at Actium, defeated through Apollo's help in the Augustan accounts of the battle; it is an interesting fact that one of the Danaids is reported to have been named Cleopatra.[49] Kellum's argument may be supplemented by further consideration of the facts of Cleopatra's career. Cleopatra VII is easily seen as a contemporary Danaid, a

The Sword-belt of Pallas: Moral Symbolism and Political Ideology

woman who was (like the Danaids) both Egyptian and Greek, whose royal family history was almost as colourful and quarrelsome as that of Danaus and the legendary ruling house of Argos. In 51 she married her younger brother Ptolemy XIII, but later sided with Caesar against him in the civil war, in which he was drowned in the Nile in 47 BC. Thereupon Caesar married her to another even younger brother, who became Ptolemy XIV; he was said to have been murdered by her orders when he died in 44.[50] Thus fatal quarrels with male relatives in the context of marriage are a feature of the Cleopatra story, at least as told by her enemies; the parallel with the Danaids is hard to deny. Just as the crime of the Danaids depicted on Pallas' sword-belt is a monstrous *nefas*, so too Cleopatra herself, attempting to do the unspeakable in overcoming Augustus and becoming mistress of Rome as Antony's wife, is a *nefas* in Vergil's description of Actium on the Shield of Aeneas (*sequitur (nefas) Aegyptia coniunx*, 8.688, 'there follows (abomination!) his Egyptian wife'), and a *fatale monstrum*, 'deadly monster', in Horace's Cleopatra ode (1.37.21). The leadership of an Eastern woman in the war against Augustus (and the fact that she is married to the Roman Antony) is presented as an ideological outrage, a perversion of an expected gender-role,[51] just like the 'unfeminine' actions of the Danaids, brides who show very different qualities from those expected of young girls in their position in the Roman world.

If the Danaids are in some sense parallel with Cleopatra, the criminal Egyptian woman, this raises the question of the prominence of Danaus, which has already been noted as a prime feature of the Palatine scheme. Lefèvre, following his view that it is the Aegyptids and not the Danaids which represent the forces of evil, has argued that Danaus is closely connected with Apollo, who in Pausanias' version of the Danaus-story helps Danaus gain the kingship of Argos and is honoured in recompense with a temple. Danaus, like Augustus, is thus a virtuous protegé of Apollo, depicted in a virtuous act: 'Danaus' raised sword was not the sign of an aggressor who committed an injustice, but the symbol of a defender, who had warded off a threat of injustice.'[52] But the fact that Ovid (above) describes the figure of Danaus with drawn sword as *ferus* and *barbarus* suggests that this was not the immediate interpretation of the contemporary viewer; and both this and the representation of the Gauls and Niobids on the temple doors as multiple enemies overthrown by Apolline might suggests the opposite interpretation, that Danaus is associated with his daughters as a perpetrator of barbaric *nefas*, as in his depiction in Statius' *Thebaid* (see above). Lefèvre himself has followed Zanker's

235

suggestion that Danaus and his non-depicted brother Aegyptus represent the 'fratricidal' war of Augustus and Antony; but it might be better to reverse the comparison and (with Meyer) to see Danaus, prime mover in internecine strife and encourager of nefarious females, as representing Antony. Though Augustus had in 32 carefully declared war against the foreign queen Cleopatra rather than his Roman former brother-in-law,[53] Antony could still be represented in the triumphal Augustan discourse of Actium as her coadjutor in crime: like Danaus, Antony urges a closely-linked female to barbarous deeds.[54] It is interesting to note that, just as Turnus is descended from Danaus, so is Antony: he claimed to be the descendant of Hercules, the putative great-grandson of Perseus, who was grandson of Acrisius, who was great-grandson of Danaus.[55] Antony's legendary genealogy is clearly relevant to the iconography of the Palatine complex in other ways: Kellum has plausibly argued that the terracotta plaques discovered on the Palatine in 1968, which display the struggle between Apollo and Hercules for the Delphic tripod, also allude to Antony's Herculean descent, and that Hercules' defeat in that struggle mirrors his descendant's defeat at Actium at the hands of Augustus and Apollo.[56]

Placed in the portico of Augustus' temple of Palatine Apollo, the depictions of the Danaids, barbarians prepared to commit the most appalling crimes, are trophies representing the kind of monstrous opposition overcome at Actium through the support of Apollo, who matches Augustus in his role as civilised victor over barbarians. The Egyptian connection of the Danaids, the link of Danaus and Antony and of the Danaids and Cleopatra make them a plausibly specific symbolic representation of contemporary enemies. No doubt, like many other sculptures in Augustan monuments, the Danaids were taken from the cities and sanctuaries of the conquered, like the statue of Apollo as citharode by Scopas which was one of the main ornaments of the Palatine complex (Pliny, *NH* 35.27, 93); they may even have come from Alexandria itself, the capital of Antony and Cleopatra, like Apelles' picture of Alexander triumphing over War (ibid. 36.25) which evidently formed a model for the Vergilian description of Furor at *Aeneid* 1.294–6.[57] The appropriation of these sculptures is a further mark of their function as trophies over the defeated at Actium: they display Rome's power over the Greek East both at the obvious level of *spolia*, and at the metaphorical level of mythological statements about contemporary politics.

It remains to consider how this interpretation of the Danaid statues fits in to the interpretation of *Aeneid* 10.495–505 suggested in the first

The Sword-belt of Pallas: Moral Symbolism and Political Ideology

part of this paper. Vergil's use of the Danaid myth on the sword-belt of Pallas appropriated by Turnus is as we have seen primarily concerned with the moral *nefas* of young males dying before their time, not (as in the Palatine sculptures) with the emphatic display of female and barbarian crime in a context of political propaganda. This marks the different attitude of the *Aeneid* to the suffering of war, more tragic than triumphalist, though Vergil can of course turn on Augustan triumphalism when required (as on the Shield of Aeneas in *Aeneid* 8). That the sword-belt of Pallas alludes in some sense to the Augustan monument seems very likely: if the Danaid statues were appropriated from a Greek city conquered in the war against Antony and Cleopatra, they share with the sword-belt not only a common mythological story, but also a common role as spoils taken from the enemy and turned into a display of that enemy's defeat. The triumphalist discourse of post-Actian celebration, represented in the iconography of the Palatine complex, is reappropriated by Vergil to serve a more meditative and tragic view of war. The Danaid story can be seen not only through the nefariousness of the perpetrators, but also through the pitiable suffering of the victims and the tragic irony of their ignorance. But this is not to argue that the *Aeneid* undermines or deconstructs the symbolic triumphalism of the Palatine Danaids: in the sword-belt of Pallas and its ornamentation the *Aeneid* offers not a specific condemnation of the victor (whether Turnus, Aeneas, or Augustus), but rather exposes with all its tragic force the lamentable and irreversible catastrophe of premature death. The different approaches to the Danaids in the Augustan monument and the *Aeneid* reflect the difference between the demands of public politics at a time of propagandistic triumph, and a more thoughtful and measured view of war and its consequences in a slightly later literary context.

Notes

[1] Translation from Harrison (1991) 99. This paper enlarges and modifies the rather compressed and dogmatic discussion of the sword-belt of Pallas in Harrison (1991) 198: the views of other scholars are here given fuller and (I hope) juster treatment.

[2] A technique usefully termed 'implicit myth' by Lyne (1987) 139–44.

[3] Servius on *Aeneid* 10.497: *insculptum Danaidum nefas*. D. Servius then adds an extensive version of the Danaus story. For other versions cf. Hyginus, *Fab.* 168. Apollodorus, *Bibl.* 2.1.4–5.

[4] According to Apollodorus, *Bibl.* 2.1.5, they were purified by Athene and Hermes and married off to the victors in an athletic contest (cf. also for the latter detail Pindar, *Pythian* 9.112–16, Pausanias 3.12.2). For their punishment in

the Underworld cf. n. 15 below.

⁵ On this shield cf. also Klinnert (1970) 82–4.

⁶ Cf. 134 *thalami...cruentis* (~ *Aeneid* 10.498 *thalamique cruenti*) and 135 *nefas* (~ *Aen*. 10.497 *nefas*).

⁷ Cf. Harrison (1992). In fact, Hippomedon is related to Danaus, as Turnus is (see n. 27 below); cf. Klinnert (1970) 83.

⁸ Cf. Small (1959).

⁹ Pöschl (1962) 149.

¹⁰ Otis (1964) 356.

¹¹ Knauer (1963) 303, n. 1 (my translation).

¹² Schlunk (1984).

¹³ Cf. Heinze (1897) 189–90.

¹⁴ See especially Keuls (1974).

¹⁵ Though it should here be admitted that the infernal punishment of the Danaids is obviously familiar in the Augustan period – cf. Tibullus 1.3.79–80; Horace, *Odes* 2.14.18–19; Propertius 4.11.27–8; Ovid, *Met*. 4.462–3, 10.43–4. The step to a knowledge of Plato is the hardest.

¹⁶ Keuls (1974) 116.

¹⁷ Winnington-Ingram (1983) 57: Hall (1989) 125 n. 76. The characterisation of the Danaids in Aeschylus is a complex issue; however, cf. Garvie (1969) 211–24.

¹⁸ Cf., e.g., Harrison (1991) 201–2 (with further references).

¹⁹ Conte (1970), largely reprinted in English translation in Conte (1986).

²⁰ Heinze (1915) 209–10.

²¹ Hornsby (1966).

²² Winnington-Ingram (1983) 63–4.

²³ The purification of the Danaids mentioned in Apollodorus, *Bibl*. 2.1.5 is almost certain to have taken place in some form in *Danaides*. the lost third play of the Aeschylean trilogy; cf. Garvie (1969) 211–13; Winnington-Ingram (1983) 70.

²⁴ Cf. Hardie (1993) 33: 'Turnus loses his life because he is wearing another man's armour, the swordbelt of Pallas: and by doing so he transfers to himself the symbolism of the ephebe cut down on his wedding night contained in the swordbelt's scene of the Danaids.'

²⁵ Turnus is also like the Aegyptids in trying to marry his cousin: Amata, Lavinia's mother, is his aunt according to Dion.Hal. 1.64.2 and Servius on *Aeneid* 6.90 and 12.29, though in the *Aeneid* itself this blood-relationship is expressed more vaguely (7.366, 12.29).

²⁶ Cf. *Aeneid* 7.371–2, 409–10 and (implicitly) 789–92; the last two passages, in the poet's own narrative, show that claims about Turnus' Argive ancestry are not just attempts by Amata to make him fit Faunus' oracle as an *externus gener* (7.81–106, 7.367–72).

²⁷ Breen (1986), though her claim (65 n. 2) that Danae was Turnus' grandmother seems unlikely; even if she married Pilumnus (there is no evidence for this – cf. Servius on *Aen*. 7.372), Pilumnus is probably not Turnus' grandfather. (*Aen*. 10.619 gives the true more distant relationship, while *Aen*. 10.76 could be vague and is probably a rhetorical exaggeration – cf. Harrison (1991) 78.)

[28] Cf. Small (1959).

[29] Keuls (1974) 116. The view taken here is essentially that of the ancient commentary of Servius, closer than we to Roman ideological values. On *Aen.* 12.940 it states 'every intention contributes to the glory of Aeneas: for he is both shown to be *pius* from the fact that he thinks of sparing his enemy, and carries the prize for *pietas* from the fact that he kills him; for it is in consideration for Evander that he avenges the death of Pallas'.

[30] Cf. Herodotus 1.87.4: 'No-one is so senseless as to prefer war to peace: for in the latter the sons bury the fathers, in the former the fathers the sons' (my translation).

[31] Collected at Nisbet and Hubbard (1978) 233 (not including *Aen.* 10.497–9); most allude either to the Palatine sculptures (below) or to the Danaids' infernal punishments (see n. 15 above).

[32] Most explicitly at Tibullus 1.3.79–80 *et Danai proles, Veneris quod numina laesit | in cava Lethaeas dolia portat aquas*; Ovid *Met.* 4.462–3 *molirique suis letum patruelibus ausae | adsiduae repetunt, quas perdant, Belides undas.*

[33] First explicitly at Nisbet and Hubbard (1978) 233.

[34] For the most useful modern treatments see Zanker (1983), Kellum (1985), Lefèvre (1989) and Gurval (1995) 123–36.

[35] I give the text and translation of Goold (1990), except that Goold merges this poem with the following one (2.32), perhaps rightly. I disagree with Goold's interpretation of line 14, where he regards *funera Tantalidos* as including the death of Niobe herself: surely the point is that she remains alive to lament her children. I have taken the liberty of altering his version at that point.

[36] It should be evident that my whole interpretation of the Palatine complex is opposed to that of Gurval (1995) 87–136, who attempts to play down the Actium connection.

[37] Belus was father of Danaus (Apollodorus *Bibl.* 2.1.4). The name is ultimately derived from Ba'al, the Baal of the Old Testament; at *Aen.* 1.621 and 1.729 the Phoenician Dido has both a father and a distant ancestor of this name, and the Orientalising colour of the patronymic *Belides* suggests that Ovid viewed the Danaids as 'Orientals', possible corroboration for the view taken of them in this article.

[38] For the 'equestrian' statues cf. Richardson (1992) 14; no doubt this is inherited from Platner and Ashby (1929) 17, but there are other modern believers – cf. Meyer (1983) 93–4, Galinsky (1996) 220. The Persius scholion reads *Acron tradit, quod in porticu quondam Apollinis Palatini fuerunt L Danaidum effigies, et contra eas sub divo totidem equestres filiorum Aegypti*. Villeneuve (1918) xxxvii–xxxviii has a good discussion, suggesting that the reference to Acro may allude not to a Persius commentary by him (for which this report is in effect the only evidence) but to the lost commentary on Horace of which the extant and much later 'Pseudo-Acro' commentary preserves some traces, suggesting that it may garble an original note of Acro on *Odes* 1.31 or 3.11 which did not vouch for the equestrian statues. Caution on the significance of the report for the Palatine complex is also wisely exercised by Kellum (1985), 173, Lefèvre (1989) 13–15 and Spence (1991) 15, and its evidence seems to be discounted by Gurval (1995) 123–31.

[39] Cf. Lefèvre (1989) 14, Spence (1991) 15. It is possible that Propertius omitted the Aegyptids in the interests of poetic economy, but their complete absence outside the Persius scholion is very striking.

[40] However, as Kellum (1985, 173) points out, Apollo was considered as a possible source of help by the Danaids at Aeschylus *Suppl.* 214–5, and it is just possible that it was he who purified them in that trilogy, though Apollodorus suggests that it was Athene and Hermes (see n. 4 above).

[41] Three fragments (only one of more than a line – for which see n. 47 below) and one *testimonium* – cf. Davies (1988) 141.

[42] The first to mention the Palatine link with the Vergilian text was Conte (1970); the first to explore it from an ideological standpoint was Kellum (1985), which should have been discussed by Harrison (1991) 198. See now also Spence (1991), Putnam (1994), Gurval (1995) 124, n. 91 and Galinsky (1996) 221–2.

[43] Zanker (1983), reprised briefly in Zanker (1988), 85–6. For the punishment cf. n. 14 and n. 15 above.

[44] Cf. Syme (1939) 296–9; the recent reassessment by Gurval (1995), though full of interest, does not in my view alter the case.

[45] Simon (1986) 21–4; Lefèvre (1989).

[46] Cf. Hall (1989) 125 n. 76.

[47] fr. 1 Davies 'and then the daughters of Danaus swiftly armed themselves before the river of swift-flowing lord Nile.' καὶ τότ' ἄρ' ὡπλίζοντο θοῶς Δαναοῖο θύγατρες | πρόσθεν ἐυρρεῖος ποταμοῦ Νείλοιο ἄνακτος. The arming of the Danaids is surely for the killing of the Aegyptids and the mention of the Nile locates it firmly in Egypt.

[48] Kellum (1985) 172–5.

[49] Apollodorus *Bibl.* 2.1.5, pointed out by Kellum (1985) 174.

[50] Josephus, *AJ* 15.89, *Ap.* 2.58; the latter passage also accuses Cleopatra of having her sister Arsinoè murdered.

[51] See Wyke (1992) on the gender-role of Cleopatra.

[52] Lefèvre (1989) 19.

[53] Cassius Dio 50.4.4–5; Reinhold (1981–2).

[54] The poetic celebrations of Actium largely omit this idea, being concerned with the demonisation of Cleopatra and the suppression of Antony, but the presentation at *Aen.* 8.685 ff. of Antony as prime mover, bringing Cleopatra with him, reflects a more realistic view in a text which is nevertheless encomiastic of Augustus. (For an interesting and more complex view see Gurval (1995) 234.)

[55] On Antony's claimed Herculean descent cf. Plutarch *Ant.* 1: Pelling (1988) 124; Gurval (1995) 92–3; for the descent of Hercules from Danaus see the genealogies of Apollodorus, *Bibl.* 2.2.1–2.4.8.

[56] Kellum (1985) 169–71.

[57] See D. Servius' note ad loc.

Bibliography

Breen C.C.
   1986   'The shield of Turnus, the swordbelt of Pallas, and the wolf: *Aeneid* 7.789–92, 9.59–66, 10.497–99', *Vergilius* 32, 63–71.

Conte. G-B.
   1970   'Il balteo di Pallante', *RFIC* 98, 292–300.
   1986   *The Rhetoric of Imitation*, Ithaca, N.Y.

Davies, M.
   1988   *Epicorum Graecorum Fragmenta*, Göttingen.

Galinsky, G.K.
   1996   *Augustan Culture*, Princeton.

Garvie, A.F.
   1969   *Aeschylus' Supplices: Play and Trilogy*, Cambridge.

Goold, G.P.
   1990   *Propertius: Elegies*, Loeb Classical Library, Cambridge, Mass. and London.

Gurval, R.A.
   1995   *Actium and Augustus*, Ann Arbor.

Hall, E.
   1989   *Inventing the Barbarian*, Oxford.

Hardie, P.R.
   1993   *The Epic Successors of Virgil*, Cambridge.

Harrison, S.J.
   1991   *Vergil:* Aeneid *10*, Oxford.
   1992   'The arms of Capaneus: Statius*Thebaid* 4,165–77', *CQ* NS 42, 247–52.

Heinze, R.
   1897   *T. Carus Lucretius De Rerum Natura: Buch III*, Leipzig.
   1915   *Vergils Epische Technik*, 3rd edn, Leipzig.

Hornsby, R.A.
   1966   'The armor of the slain', *Philological Quarterly* 45, 347–59.

Kellum, B.
   1985   'Sculptural programs and propaganda in Augustan Rome: the temple of Apollo on the Palatine', in R. Winkes (ed.) *The Age of Augustus*, 169–76, Louvain.

Keuls, E.
   1974   *The Water Carriers in Hades*, Amsterdam.

Klinnert, Th.C.
   1970   *Capaneus – Hippomedon*, Diss., Berlin.

Knauer, G.N.
   1964   *Die Aeneis und Homer*, Hypomnemata 7, Göttingen.

Lefèvre, E.
   1989   *Das Bild-Programm des Apollo-Tempels auf dem Palatin*, Xenia 24, Konstanz.

Lyne, R.O.A.M.
   1987   *Further Voices in Vergil's Aeneid*, Oxford.

Meyer, H.
   1983   *Kunst und Geschichte*, Munich.

Nisbet, R.G.M. and Hubbard, M.
  1978   *A Commentary on Horace* Odes *Book II*, Oxford.
Otis, B.
  1964   *Virgil: A Study in Civilized Poetry*, Oxford.
Pelling, C.B.R.
  1988   *Plutarch: Life of Antony*, Cambridge.
Platner, S.B. and Ashby, T.
  1929   *A Topographical Dictionary of Ancient Rome*, London.
Pöschl, V.
  1962   *The Art of Vergil*, tr. G. Seligson, Ann Arbor.
Putnam, M.C.J.
  1994   'Virgil's Danaid ekphrasis', *ICS* 19, 171–89.
Reinhold, M.
  1981–2 'The declaration of war against Cleopatra', *CJ* 77, 97–103.
Richardson, L. Jr.
  1992   *A New Topographical Dictionary of Ancient Rome*, Baltimore.
Schlunk, R.R.
  1984   'The wrath of Aeneas: two myths in *Aeneid* X', in D.F. Bright and E.S. Ramage (eds.) *Classical Texts and Their Traditions: Studies in honour of C.R. Trahman*, 223–9, Chico, Cal.
Simon, E.
  1986   *Augustus*, Munich.
Small, S.P.G.
  1959   'The arms of Turnus: *Aeneid* 7.783–92', *TAPA* 90, 243–52.
Spence, S.
  1991   'Clinching the text: the Danaids and the end of the *Aeneid*', *Vergilius* 37, 11–19.
Syme, R.
  1989   *The Roman Revolution*, Oxford.
Villeneuve, F.
  1918   *Les satires de Perse*, Paris.
Winnington-Ingram, R.P.
  1983   *Studies in Aeschylus*, Cambridge.
Wyke, M.
  1992   'Augustan Cleopatras: female power and poetic authority', in A. Powell (ed.) *Roman Poetry and Propaganda in the Age of Augustus*, 98–140, Bristol.
Zanker, P.
  1983   'Der Apollotempel auf dem Palatin. Ausstattung und politische Sinnbezüge nach der Schlacht von Actium', in *Città e architettura nella Roma imperiale*. Analecta Romana Instituti Danici, Supplementum 10, 21–40, Copenhagen.
  1988   *The Power of Images in the Age of Augustus*, tr. A. Shapiro, Ann Arbor.

12

FAME AND DEFAMATION IN THE *AENEID*: THE COUNCIL OF LATINS
Aeneid 11.225–467[1]

Philip Hardie

Vergil's rhetorical skills were already well recognised in antiquity; whether he was more an orator or a poet was a grammarian's question. Modern critics are no less alive to Vergil's ability to turn a rhetorically effective speech in the mouth of a Sinon, a Dido, a Drances. Yet among those who hold that rhetoric is the insidious rot in imperial literature, there is a consensus that in Vergil rhetoric knows its place, and that it is not until the next generation of poets that rhetoric spreads its tentacles into every corner of the poet's art. The aesthetic prejudice that Vergil, as opposed to an Ovid or Lucan, obeys a classical restraint in these matters finds support in the belief that the *Aeneid* tells of a heroism that transcends the political feuding of the late Republic, and so is immune to the conditions that nourish the orator's art, an art that could best be left to its Greek inventors by a Roman people newly recalled to their *Romanitas* (*Aen.* 6.849). This paper is an attempt to resituate the place of rhetoric within the *Aeneid*, with especial reference to the most elaborate and most formal rhetorical exchange between human actors in the poem. The focus of my discussion is not so much on the formal markers of a rhetorical manner, as on the relationship between the truth-functions of rhetoric and of a supposedly authoritative epic voice.

The Council of Latins in *Aeneid* 11 is the single example in the poem of an extended scene of human political debate. A council called by king Latinus to consider future action in the light of Diomedes' negative response to a request for military aid turns into a slanging match between Turnus and an envious Latin, Drances, a character who appears only in this book of the poem. In terms of plot, the function of the exchange between Drances and Turnus is so to exacerbate the

Philip Hardie

furious *uiolentia* of Turnus that, in a moment of bravado, and oblivious to Latinus' earlier proposals of a peaceful accommodation between Italian and Trojan, he declares himself ready to fight a duel with Aeneas. This is the duel which Aeneas earlier in Book 11, in a rhetorical and hypothetical four lines (11.115–18) tacked on to his agreement to allow a truce for the burial of the dead, had suggested would have been a better way of resolving the quarrel than the mass slaughter that has actually taken place in the previous two books.[2] A little later (218–21) we are told that the Latin womenfolk and orphans, egged on by Drances, also call for Turnus to fight it out single-handed. But in the formal council the suggestion seems to exist for Turnus, as earlier for Aeneas, in the realm of rhetoric and hypothesis, for his reaction to the news of the approach of the Trojan army is the same as his reaction to the news at the beginning of *Aeneid* 9 of the temporary absence of Aeneas, namely to effect a full-scale mobilization of his army.[3] Not until the beginning of the next and final book will Turnus once more declare himself ready to fight the duel, only once more for the final resolution of the plot to be deferred by many more hundreds of lines of all-out warfare.

Indirectly, then, this scene of deliberative rhetoric does issue in a positive proposal that will, eventually, yield closure for the whole poem. But within the context of Book 11 Vergil goes out of his way to make it appear that the whole Council is so much hot air:

So they disputed among themselves in deep uncertainty.

> illi haec inter se dubiis de rebus agebant
> certantes... (11.445–6)

– just so much wasted rhetoric. The actors are snatched from these wandering mazes of charge and countercharge by the sudden irruption of other words, those of the messenger announcing the Trojan advance, whereupon the ritualized verbal combat of the council collapses into a Babel of discord ('on every side there was a great clamour of dissenting voices', *hic undique clamor | dissensu uario magnus*, 454–5), as the male citizenry is divided between the young men screaming for war and the elders muttering their disapproval.[4] Turnus cuts through the knot by turning words to action, with a sarcastic repetition of Latinus' opening complaint that debate comes too late, now that the enemy are at the gate;[5] 'without further words', *nec plura locutus*, Turnus rushes out, turning from rhetoric to the clipped commands of the general (463–7).

Modern critics have used two types of approach in order to make sense of this great verbal interlude in the action scenes of the last four books. The first approach has been to ask what the Council tells us about Turnus' character, highlighting certain features of his personality and motivation through the deployment of the *Kontrastfigur* Drances. Thus Peter Schenk analyses the debate for what it can tell him in answer to his question of whether Turnus is a tragic hero or a *Staatsfeind*, a stubborn representative of an older world of heroes, responsible for his own downfall.[6] A rhetorical debate within the text is made to serve an ongoing critical debate about the overall meaning of the text. Schenk himself is unambiguous in his conclusion that Turnus does not deserve the reader's sympathy, but that has not deterred other critics from further disagreement on the matter – *illi haec inter se dubiis de rebus agebant*. P.F. Burke, for one, took the opposite view, arguing that the debate serves to bring out the 'tragedy of Turnus' position', a tragedy located in the irreconcilable 'incompatibility of his political actions with his heroic inner nature'.[7] Burke subtly derives this complexity of character from Vergil's use of a variety of Iliadic intertexts, which Burke suggests are 'designed to create in the mind of the audience a number of simultaneous and quite different possible interpretations of the Drances–Turnus quarrel'. Drances is both a detestable Thersites and a prudent Antenor or Poulydamas; Turnus is both a selfish Paris, and a brave Hector or the good counsellor Odysseus. It is certainly tempting to see some kind of mirror of the contradictions within Turnus in the contradictory Drances, who, to put it crudely, says the right things for the wrong reasons. Burke, in sum, puts his finger on ambivalences that have their origin in textual (or intertextual) phenomena, but makes of them merely the vehicle for contradiction in the 'real' characters of the actors represented in the text.

The second approach to the Council looks beyond the legendary action of the *Aeneid* to the contemporary and recent historical context of Vergil's own day. This is Drances as Cicero,[8] or, in the more nuanced and persuasive formulation of Antonio La Penna,[9] Drances as the type of the demagogic *popularis*, more a Catiline than a Cicero, the kind of politician whose specious championship of popular grievances caused so much trouble in the later Republic. The debate then makes an ideological point about the undesirability of political ambition; this is the kind of thing that ruined the Republic, demonstrating the necessity of an Augustus to keep in check the re-emergence of the *seditio* that is calmed by the statesman in the first simile of the poem (1.148–53). La Penna offers us a contrast between the disparagement of ambition pursued through rhetorical skill in this passage, and the encouragement of ambition pursued through military excellence in the episode of Nisus and Euryalus in Book 9, whom La Penna compares to the type of the as yet unsung young warrior who seeks to distinguish himself in the eyes of his superiors, like a Caesarian centurion in the eyes of Caesar.

The effect of both approaches is to bracket the rhetoric of the episode: in the Schenk/Burke approach by making of rhetoric's twisty nature a way of bringing out something essential in human character, or in La Penna's approach by establishing an opposition between rhetoric and plain dealing, between hypocrisy and political honesty. My aim is to question the validity of this bracketing of rhetoric and of its effects within the text. Is it, in fact, so easy to separate out the versions of reality presented by a Drances or a Turnus in the heat of debate from the true story to which the epic narrator gives us access? Is the fame that the epic poet offers his characters to be located in a verbal world completely separate from the defamation dealt out in political invective? To put it another way, what are the limits of rhetoric within the *Aeneid*?

One answer to that question was given by Denis Feeney in his article 'The taciturnity of Aeneas', in many ways the best treatment of the topic of rhetoric in the *Aeneid*.[10] He argues that the relative taciturnity of Aeneas, seen for example in his unwillingness to engage in debate with Dido, is the narrative expression of Vergil's conviction that (in Highet's formulation, endorsed by Feeney, 185) 'powerful oratory was incompatible with pure truth'; or, in his own words (186), 'powerful language distorts reality, or the truth, in its single-minded pursuit of its particular aim; and it exploits ungovernably the emotions of speaker and audience'. Vergil is enlisted in the line of criticism of rhetoric that goes back to Plato. So convinced is Feeney, in 1983, of this reading that he fails to notice the irony when he suggests (188–9) that the closest analogue for the repressed Aeneas is not Augustus, but Tiberius – the arch-dissimulator.[11] This model of a simple contrast between an honest, to-the-point, use of language and a devious long-winded use also underlies the interesting article by J.P. Lynch on the speeches of Laocoon and Sinon in *Aeneid* 2, read respectively as models of Catonian straight speaking ('hold fast to the subject-matter, the words will follow', *rem tene, uerba sequentur*) and a sophisticated and sophistic rhetoric that follows the rules of the Greek handbooks.[12]

Feeney in 1991 might have thought somewhat differently, to judge from his discussion in *The gods in epic* of the role of Jupiter and his words, where he concludes that *Fatum*, the word of Jupiter, cannot be

Fame and Defamation in the Aeneid: the Council of Latins

taken as an objective criterion of truth external to the text.[13] Jupiter's most impressive definition of *Fatum* occurs in the speech which concludes the Council of Gods at the beginning of Book 10, a scene of *seditio* on Olympus that demands to be read in close conjunction with the Council of Latins in Book 11. On the surface the words of Jupiter oppose the fixities of Fate to the windy distortions of the rhetoric of Venus and Juno; but whether Jupiter himself speaks crooked words, whether his own appeal to the immutable sanctions of Fate conceals anything but a wordy vacuum, has been the subject of intense discussion in recent years.

In his 1983 article Feeney identifies a coincidence between the hero's version of events and narratorial actuality in Aeneas' statement at the beginning of his reply to Dido at 4.337, 'let me speak a few words to meet the case', *pro re pauca loquar*.[14] But Aeneas' opening gambit, implying a simple distinction between facts and words, is of course itself a rhetorical ploy; as Pease notes 'Most orators...begin by announcing their intended brevity.' No commentator doubts the rhetorical weight of Drances' opening words at 11.343-4:

> You consult us on a matter clear to all and in no need of my words.

> > rem nulli obscuram nostrae nec uocis egentem
> > consulis.

The *res/uerba* opposition comes into play at various key points in the Council of Latins. The topos of proper times for action and for speaking, which goes back to the Homeric models for the debate,[15] introduces Latinus' speech at 302-4:

> For my part, O men of Latium, I would have wished, and it would have been better so, to have decided this great issue long since, and not be summoning a council at a time like this with the enemy sitting by our walls.

> > ante equidem summa de re statuisse, Latini,
> > et uellem et fuerat melius, non tempore tali
> > cogere concilium, cum muros adsidet hostis.

summa de re may mean either 'in matters of state' (the *res publica*), or 'about the critical situation';[16] in either case there is an implied opposition between words and action: the *summa res* requires immediate action in accordance with verbal decisions previously taken.

Turnus' reply to Drances begins with a scornful contrast between Drances' 'copious supplies of words', *larga...copia fandi*,[17] and the physical action, *manus*, required by war. The taunt echoes two remarks in *Iliad* 2, a book which more than any other explores the proper limits

Philip Hardie

of public words: firstly Odysseus' castigation of Thersites as 'irresponsible with words, for all that you are a ready talker' (*Il.* 2.246, followed by eighteen more lines of Odysseus' ready speech), and secondly the disguised Iris' gentler rebuke to Priam, 'you are always ready with endless words, as formerly in peace; but now unavoidable war has broken out' (2.796–7). One of the ironies of Turnus' reply is of course that he himself displays a great *copia fandi;* his reply is twice as long as Drances' speech (67 to 33 lines), and is a powerfully composed piece of rhetoric, of which Heyne commented, 'I think that nothing could be found in Greek authors, let alone Homer, that comes closer to the art of declamation.' Heinze remarks, 'it is only in Turnus' speech that one finds anything like a rhetorical emphasis on its arrangement: this is intended to make a clear-cut division between the well-considered *oratio deliberativa* [11.410 ff.] and the heated *invectiva* of the first part of the speech'.[18] Very different is the reply given by Ascanius to another of the *Aeneid*'s rhetoricians, Numanus, a character who in certain respects is a double of Drances.[19] Ascanius' first response is verbal, but instead of countering his human opponent's distortions he addresses a five-line prayer to Jupiter, before he kills Numanus with a single arrow-shot, accompanied by the five-word taunt 'go and mock bravery with proud words', *i, uerbis uirtutem inlude superbis*, 9.634.[20] Turnus by contrast strings out the opposition between *uerba* and *uirtus* over the first fourteen lines of his speech (*uerbis*, 11.380; *uirtus,* 386). He responds in imagined, rather than actual, deeds ('let's go into battle together, and then see who is the braver', 389–91); and uses his battle-tested right hand in the service of his rhetorical *actio*:

> You will never lose your life by this right hand (don't flinch!)
>> numquam animam talem dextra hac (absiste moueri)
>> amittes   (408–9)

– playing Drances' own game (see 348). Not until a critical moment near the end of the poem does Turnus finally translate the rhetorical antithesis between words and deeds into an immediate determination to act:

> Shall I allow the houses to be destroyed (that was all I needed), and shall I not refute Drances' words with my right hand?
>> exscindine domos (id rebus defuit unum)
>> perpetiar, dextra nec Drancis dicta refellam?'[21]
>>   (12.643–4)

The participants in the debate use traditional Homeric contrasts between words and deeds, in respect both of the proper occasion for saying and doing, and of the difference between the good speaker and the good fighter.

One of the most serious criticisms of rhetoric, however, is that it confuses the boundary between words and deeds, appearance and reality. Feeney spotlights this issue in discussing Aeneas' injunction to Dido at 4.338, 'don't pretend', *ne finge*, a verb found also in the debate in 11, once in the mouth of Drances ('you pretend that I am your enemy, and if I am I don't care', *inuisum quem tu tibi fingis (et esse nil moror)*, 364–5), and once in the mouth of Turnus ('or when he pretends to be terrified when I speak, a rogue's trick', *uel cum se pauidum contra mea iurgia fingit, | artificis scelus*, 406–7). Feeney states that the word 'pinpoints with some precision the moulding and misrepresentation which is part of the orator's stock-in-trade';[22] he cites two other passages in which *fingo* is used in relation to speech. The first occurs in the sleeping Turnus' rebuke of the disguised Allecto, 'do not invent such fears for me', *ne tantos mihi finge metus*, 7.438. This is a dangerous thing to say to a Fury who has the supernatural power to work real changes on the human *psyche*: her response to Turnus' charge of being a silly old woman of whom 'old age is making a fool with false fears, amidst the wars of kings' (7.452–3, repeating, mostly verbatim, 440–2) is to plunge a hallucinatory torch into Turnus' breast;[23] as a result 'a great terror burst in upon his sleep', *olli somnum ingens rumpit pauor*, 458. By poetic justice fear is the first of the emotions to afflict the scornful Turnus. The Council in Book 11 shares with the Allecto scene in Book 7 both the motif of the fabrication of fear (11.406), and the motif of the incendiary effect of taunting words: Turnus' reaction to Drances' speech at 11.376:

> Turnus' violent anger blazed out at these words.
>
> talibus exarsit dictis uiolentia Turni.

reproduces Allecto's reaction to Turnus' dismissal of her first speech at 7.445:

> Allecto blazed out in anger at these words.
>
> talibus Allecto dictis exarsit in iras.

Feeney's last example of *fingo* with relation to speech is the description of *Fama* at 4.188 as:

As tenacious of her lies and distortions as she is a messenger of the truth.

> tam ficti prauique tenax quam nuntia ueri.

Here we move clearly from the sphere of rhetoric into a making of

Philip Hardie

fictions that is hardly to be distinguished from the work of the poet. This line ascribes to a personification with a Hesiodic ancestress in the *Works and Days* that power to deal equally in falsehood and truth which the Muses claim for themselves at the beginning of the*Theogony* (27–8).

The Vergilian connections between Allecto, *Fama*, panic and the power to create convincing fictions are reworked in Flavian epic. At *Thebaid* 7.108–44 Statius describes the person and powers of *Pauor* in a way that clearly brings out the similarity between the effects of panic-driven rumour and the work of the poet: he is 'an authority good at making himself believed in everything', *bonus omnia credi auctor*, 112–13. In a manner analogous to the working of poetic*enargeia* 'his pitiful victims think that they have actually seen [his illusions]', *miseri uidisse putant*, 116. Like the Latin epic poet 'he imitates the sounds of men's armour and of horses' hoofbeats', *arma uirum pulsusque imitatur equorum*, 120. Panic works a suspension of disbelief, and mimics the working of inspiration: 'in their terror they take everything as true. But when undisguised he fell upon the crazed men...', *nil falsum trepidis. ut uero amentibus ipse | incidit...* (131–2; the verb is that applied to the poet's own inspiration at 1.3, 'the Muses' heat has fallen on my mind', *Pierius menti calor incidit*). In the Lemnian episode at *Argonautica* 2.115–34 Valerius Flaccus has Venus enlist the services of *Fama* to perform the work of the Vergilian Allecto, in a way that also replicates the fictions of the poet of epic warfare:

> Overturn all their households, appearing as when you run before war, when you invent a thousand trumpets and warriors marching on the plain and the snorting of unnumbered horses.
>
> et cunctas mihi uerte domos, praecurrere qualis
> bella soles, cum mille tubas armataque campis
> agmina et innumerum flatus cum *fingis* equorum.
> (2.128–30)

The verbal creation of the *pathos* of fear is also a goal that the epic poet shares with the tragedian, and a point at which Heinze identifies an equivalence between the emotional effects striven for by the tragedian and by the rhetorician.[24] Horace describes the psychological effects of drama at *Ep.* 2.1.210–13:

> I would believe that the poet could walk on a tightrope, who on the basis of nothing pains, angers, and soothes my heart, and fills me with false fears, like a magician, and transports me now to Thebes, now to Athens.
>
> ille per extentum funem mihi posse uidetur
> ire poeta, meum qui pectus inaniter angit,

Fame and Defamation in the Aeneid: the Council of Latins

> irritat, mulcet, *falsis terroribus implet*,
> ut magus, et modo me Thebis, modo ponit Athenis.[25]

Drances' rhetoric is introduced with the line:

> He rose and with these words loaded and heaped up their anger.
>
> surgit et his onerat dictis atque aggerat iras.
> (11.342)

The last four words reproduce the second half of the line that describes the effects of *Fama* on Iarbas at 4.197:

> With her words she fired his spirit and heaped up his anger.
>
> incenditque animum dictis atque aggerat iras.

The image of fire in the first half of that line is paralleled in the description of the effects of Drances' speech on Turnus at 11.376, *talibus exarsit dictis uiolentia Turni*. Feeney points to Aeneas' use of the verb *incendere* in his plea to Dido at 4.360:

> Stop inflaming me and yourself with your complaints.
>
> desine meque tuis incendere teque querelis.

– and produces examples of the semi-technical application of *incendo* and related words to the emotional effect aimed at by the orator.[26] But again this is only part of the story. *incendo* is indeed used in the *Aeneid* of the disruptively inflammatory effects of speech, above all female speech, as here, and at 9.500 (the mother of Euryalus) 'as she inflamed their grief' *illam incendentem luctus*, and at 11.147 (the mothers in Evander's city) 'they inflame the grief-stricken city with their cries', *maestam incendunt clamoribus urbem*, and at 12.238 (Juturna in disguise) 'with such words the young men's minds were inflamed', *talibus incensa est iuuenum sententia dictis*.[27] But the verb is also used of the positive excitement of male courage and virtue, as at 9.788 'inflamed by these words (Mnestheus' rebuke)', *talibus accensi*, or 10.368 (Pallas) 'now with prayers, now with harsh words he inflamed their courage', *nunc prece, nunc dictis uirtutem accendit amaris*, and most importantly at 6.889, the line that rounds off the Parade of Heroes:

> He inflamed his spirit with a love for the fame that was to come.
>
> incenditque animum famae uenientis amore.[28]

incenditque animum is the first half of that same line describing the deleterious effects of *Fama* at 4.197, whose second half is repeated in the line introducing Drances' speech (11.342). The Speech of Anchises both in overall outline and in allusive detail is an encapsulation of Ennius' *Annales*, and Anchises' historical protreptic has the effect on Aeneas which Ennius meant his epic to have on the Roman reader. *incendo* is also the carefully chosen verb that Fronto uses to describe the effect of reading Ennius:

> Then, when the desire to read had come over you, you would either polish yourself with Plautus, or glut yourself with Accius, or soothe yourself with Lucretius, or inflame yourself with Ennius.
>
> mox, ut te studium legendi incessisset, aut te Plauto expolires aut Accio expleres aut Lucretio delenires aut Ennio incenderes.
>
> (p. 212, van den Hout)

In the extended description of Drances that introduces his speech in the Council, his driving motive is identified as envy, *inuidia*, aroused by the *gloria* of Turnus (11.336–7). Drances comes close to being a personification of *Inuidia*, a sibling of the personification of *Fama*, as Ovid intimates when he models his *Inuidia* on the Vergilian *Fama*.[29] Envy is aroused by Fame, and is in competition with Fame; envy is an inevitable product of the *certamen gloriae* that fuels Republican politics.[30] *Inuidia* and *Fama* (or *Gloria*) go together as the negative and positive aspects of the power of the word to establish a reputation. At his earlier appearance in *Aeneid* 11 (122–32) Drances had already been introduced as motivated by hatred of Turnus,[31] but his first words were ones of praise rather than blame. His very first words, indeed, are 'O in fame...', *o fama*. The first two lines of his address to Aeneas are an encapsulation of the subject of the *Aeneid* viewed as praise poetry:

> Great in fame, greater in warfare, hero of Troy, with what praises shall I bring you level with the sky?
>
> o fama ingens, ingentior armis,
> uir Troiane, quibus caelo te laudibus aequem?[32]
>
> (11.124–5)

The use of the degrees of the adjective *ingens* suggests epic's hyperbolical urge to magnify, to identify a greatest hero: the comparative *ingentior* is found only here in the classical period; the superlative *ingentissimus* is never found until late,[33] but is implied if it is true that no greatness can exceed equivalence with the heavens. Furthermore the first two words of the poem are repeated, in different cases, over the line-ending of 124–5 *armis,* | *uir*.[34] The two lines also engage with the opposition of *res* and *uerba*: the first five words chiastically highlight the superiority of deeds, *arma*, over words, *fama*.[35] But in the

Fame and Defamation in the Aeneid: the Council of Latins

third part of this *auxesis* Drances undoes the words/deeds opposition by his implication that the superlative of *ingens* will be conferred by his, Drances', own verbal skills. Gransden notes ad loc., 'Aeneas was, of course, subsequently deified', so that even in the use of the phrase *caelo te...aequem* there is an equivocation between a purely verbal magnification and a literal elevation to the skies, an equivocation that may be paralleled in other instances of the poem's central image of the journey to heaven.[36] If we are tempted to feel that Drances' dishonourable motives push him over the top in his praise of Aeneas, we should remember that these are the terms that Aeneas had used at 1.378-9 in defining to Venus his own heroic status within the Homeric tradition: 'I am pious Aeneas...known through fame above the skies', *sum pius Aeneas...fama super aethera notus* (an elevation echoed in the final divine authorization of Roman greatness at 12.838-9, 'thence you will see the race that will arise with the mixture of Italian blood soar over men and gods in piety', *hinc genus Ausonio mixtum quod sanguine surget, | supra homines, supra ire deos pietate uidebis*). In the rhetorical *dubitatio* in the next line:

> Shall I first admire your justice or your labours in war?
>
> iustitiaene prius mirer, belline laborum?
> (11.126)

Drances again mouths panegyric formulae already familiar from Ilioneus' praise of Aeneas at 1.544-5:

> Our king was Aeneas, who had no equal in justice and piety, and no equal in the field of battle.
>
> rex erat Aeneas nobis, quo iustior alter
> nec pietate fuit, nec bello maior et armis.

There are other similarities between the scene where Ilioneus speaks at the court of Carthage and this scene: Ilioneus is described as *maximus* (1.521), Drances as *senior* (11.122), and the reaction to both of their speeches is described in the same way ('So spoke Ilioneus, and all the Trojans to a man murmured in agreement', *talibus Ilioneus; cuncti simul ore fremebant | Dardanidae*, 1.559-60; 'These were his words, and they all murmured the same things with one voice', *dixerat haec unoque omnes eadem ore fremebant*, 11.132). Ilioneus, the Trojan spokesman at Dido's court, finds himself in a situation where it is essential to persuade the audience of the character of the petitioners; but the rhetoric in his use of the conventional panegyrical division of the king's virtues into those of peace and war was sufficiently veiled for Francis Cairns to

Philip Hardie

take it as the epic's normative image of Aeneas as the 'good king'.[37] Gransden, by contrast, feels uneasy with the distasteful mouthpiece of praise in Book 11 (on 124–6): 'It is a *donnée* of Aeneas' character as a good king that he excelled both in moral virtue (*pietas*) and in military prowess: cf. 291–2, and 1.544... Here the intention is to flatter: Drances is thinking of himself, not of Aeneas, and the emphasis of his words falls on the two first-person singular verbs, *aequem, mirer*, "how am *I* to match your praises, where shall *I* start?", etc.' This is a desperate shift; Drances may have his reasons, but he is too good an orator to betray self-centredness in this way.[38]

Drances' praise of Aeneas is soon echoed in the reported words of Diomedes at 11.291–2 (referring to Hector and Aeneas):

Both noble in their courage, noble in their skill in arms, but Aeneas the greater in piety.

> ambo animis, ambo insignes praestantibus armis,
> hic pietate prior.

This reproduces the dichotomy between virtues of war and peace, but is closer in verbal formulation to Ilioneus' words at 1.544–5.[39] In Diomedes have we at last found an impartial witness? He too is making a case, under pressure of the need to justify to Latinus his refusal to send military aid. The division of virtues between military ability and *pietas* serves an immediate function in its context: Aeneas' military ability is a reason for not fighting him ('make sure that your weapons do not clash with his', *ast armis concurrant arma cauete*, 293), while his outstanding *pietas* is a reason for extending right hands in a religiously sanctioned treaty ('let your right hands come together in a treaty', *coeant in foedera dextrae*, 292).[40] There are other features of Diomedes' speech that suggest that he is slanting his account. He claims that the reason for the ten years' delay in taking Troy was the combined strength of Hector and Aeneas. Now while there are passages in the *Iliad* where Hector and Aeneas are jointly said to be the best Trojan warriors,[41] traditionally Hector alone is the *belli mora* ('the Greeks... whom Hector put off until the tenth year', *Danais...decimum quos distulit Hector in annum*, 9.154–5).[42] Diomedes' recollection of Aeneas' awesome presence in battle (282–4) hardly matches *our* recollection of the encounter between the two men in the *Iliad* (5.297–317).[43] Nor are the Trojans the only object of Diomedes' tinted gaze; he opens his speech with a characterization of the Latins that bears at best a partial correspondence to the reality:

O blessed peoples, Saturn's kingdom, the ancient Ausonians, what

Fame and Defamation in the Aeneid: *the Council of Latins*

Fortune disturbs your peace, and persuades you to stir up unknown wars?

> o fortunatae gentes, Saturnia regna,
> antiqui Ausonii, quae uos fortuna quietos
> sollicitat suadetque ignota lacessere bella?
> (11.252-4)

Conington comments 'Virgil wavers, as we have seen, between two views of the past of Italy, a legendary and a semi-historical one: here he adopts the former, as if the Italian nations still lived in the halo of the golden age and knew nothing of war.' This is Italy as we see it at the end of the second Georgic. Of course it is not the narrator Vergil who here adopts this view of Italy, but a character Diomedes, in whose mouth it is a powerful opening rebuke to the Latins' desire for war, and also prepares the ground for an analogy between the Greeks' violation of a sacred people protected by the gods (*uiolauimus*, 255; *uiolaui*, 277) and the Latins' mad rush to violate the peace of their own Golden Age existence.[44]

Yet Diomedes is the man in whom we are asked to put our trust – *experto credite* (283). This tag forms part of a network of appeals to evidential certainty, as well as verbal exactness, that stretches over the whole of the Council scene, and which provides an ironic foil to the rhetoric of the several speakers. Latinus is careful to provide the optimal conditions for a faithful account by the envoys of Diomedes' reply:

> He asked the envoys who had returned from the city of Aetolians to tell what reply they brought, demanding to hear every detail in due order. The assembly was called to silence. Venulus obeyed the command and began to speak.
>
> > atque hic legatos Aetola ex urbe remissos
> > quae *referant fari* iubet, et *responsa* reposcit
> > *ordine cuncta suo.* tum facta silentia linguis,
> > et Venulus *dicto parens* ita *farier* infit.[45]
> > (11.239-42)

Venulus' first word is *uidimus*, 'we've seen Diomedes and Argyripa', followed two lines later, at the beginning of the verse, by *contigimus* 'we've touched the hand by which Troy fell' (although already in that last description interpretation begins to creep in: they may have touched the hand, but was *that* really the hand by which Troy fell?). Sight and touch offer the straightest highway to belief according to Lucretius;[46] they are also the two senses on which Latinus will ask the

255

Philip Hardie

Council to base its decisions at 310–11:

> All other resource is shattered and lies in ruins. You can see this with your own eyes. The whole truth is there at your fingertips.

> cetera qua rerum iaceant perculsa ruina,
> *ante oculos interque manus* sunt omnia uestras.

Ocular and physical contact are also, as we have seen, the evidence on which Diomedes claims to base his assessment of the folly of fighting with Aeneas (with *contigimusque manum*, 245, compare the shape of *contulimusque manus*, 283).[47] Drances and Turnus will also appeal to the evidence of direct sensory experience: (Drances) 'we see the whole city slumped in grief', *totamque uidemus | consedisse urbem luctu*, 349–50; 'we've been routed often enough and seen enough funerals', *sat funera fusi | uidimus*, 366–7; (Turnus):

> Who can say I am defeated when he sees the Tiber rising, swollen with Trojan blood, the house of Evander destroyed root and branch and the Arcadians stripped of their arms?

> aut quisquam merito, foedissime, pulsum,
> arguet, Iliaco tumidum qui crescere Thybrim
> sanguine et Euandri totam cum stirpe *uidebit*
> procubuisse domum atque exutos Arcadas armis?[48]
> (392–5)

and:

> That wasn't Bitias' and giant Pandarus' experience of me.

> haud ita me *experti* Bitias et Pandarus ingens.[49]
> (396)

Note also Turnus' 'thought-experiment' at 386–8:

> Now is our chance to test our vigour and valour; the enemies aren't far to seek.

> possit quid uiuida uirtus
> *experiare* licet, nec longe scilicet hostes
> quaerendi nobis.

As the basis for their *propositiones* Drances and Turnus offer two versions of the reality of what has happened on the battlefield. Latinus has given a third, which is the basis for his own *propositio* (314–34); in his case it is clear that a depressive fit consequent on the failure of the mission to Diomedes leads him to an unduly pessimistic assessment of the situation after the battle in the previous book.[50] And in justification of his decision Diomedes, too, has given the envoys a version of the

Fame and Defamation in the Aeneid: the Council of Latins

Trojan War and its aftermath that bears clear marks of being a partial view. Highet adduces the speech of Diomedes in support of his claim that in Vergil the dichotomy between poetry and oratory is false (56–7): 'Diomedes' account of the fates of his comrades is oratorical in purpose and even in structure: the rapid summary of many different episodes is a *percursio*, and the passage contains two *praeteritiones*… Yet, since it summarizes an entire epic poem, the *Nostoi*, it is also a feat of poetic skill…'[51] Highet is concerned chiefly with stylistic and formal features, and stops short of asking how this rhetoricization of poetic traditions may affect the authority of the epic voice. As a summary of a part of the epic cycle, Diomedes' speech has a precedent in the scenes in the temple of Juno in Book 1, whose visual 'rhetoric' has been the subject of much discussion recently: do the scenes function as the pictorial equivalent of epic *praemia laudi* (1.461) that Aeneas reads into them, or do they celebrate Juno's extermination of her foes? Alessandro Barchiesi has recently pointed to a pun in 1.457 'wars already broadcast in fame through the whole world', *bellaque iam fama totum uulgata per orbem*: these are wars that have become tediously familiar through their rehearsal in the epic *Kuklos*, within whose circuit Vergil must define an area for his own, new, epic.[52] The same pun may operate in Diomedes' description of the subject of his *Nostoi* catalogue (after the *praeteritio* of the matter of the *Iliad* in 11.256–7) as 'unspeakable punishments and penalties for our crimes throughout the world', *infanda*[53] *per orbem | supplicia et scelerum poenas* (257–8).

The rhetorical distortion in the speeches of Diomedes, Drances and Turnus, this second and even third narrating of events already told, is not an isolated feature within the poem. Internal narrators are of course a defining feature of the genre of epic, and their narratives are rarely disinterested. Phoenix' use of the example of Meleager in his speech to Achilles in *Iliad* 9 already shows the use of a slanted version of a story to what in a later age would be called rhetorical effect. In the *Odyssey* Odysseus is the masterful and effective narrator of a number of narratives both straight and crooked; the fictional autobiographies that he spins in the second half of the *Odyssey* may be described as retellings of a tale already told, to the extent that they offer other versions of what has happened within the time-span of the poem. On a smaller scale, Richard Martin comments on the speech of Achilles to Thetis at *Iliad* 1.365–412 that 'it recaps in a miniature narrative the first episode in the poem with Achilles' slight reshaping'.[54] But it appears that the *Aeneid*, to an unprecedented extent, invests in internal retellings or redescriptions of epic narratives, whether through

Philip Hardie

flashback or prophecy. In Book 1 Jupiter outlines for Venus' benefit the whole of the 'epic cycle' of future Roman history (and O'Hara has shown how the apparently objective unrolling of Fate in this and other prophecies conceals a degree of what might be called rhetorical selection and slanting);[55] later in Book 1 Aeneas gives his reading of the ecphrasis of parts of the epic cycle as represented in the temple of Juno. Within Books 2 and 3, Aeneas' own, Odysseus-style, narrative of events first told in the *Ilias Parva* and *Iliupersis*, we have the story told by Sinon, whose tissue of truths, half-truths, and lies superimposes on the Odyssean models of tale-telling the influences both of tragedy and of rhetoric. Turnus will describe Drances in words that echo Sinon's ironic invective against Ulysses, whose double in truth he, Sinon, is: with 11.406–7:

> Or when he pretends to be terrified when I speak – a rogue's trick! The fear is a pretence to add sting to his charges against me.
>
> > uel cum se pauidum contra mea iurgia fingit,
> > artificis scelus, et formidine crimen acerbat.

compare 2.124–5:

> Now many began to predict that the rogue's cruel trick would fall on my head.
>
> > et mihi iam multi crudele canebant
> > artificis scelus.[56]

In Book 4 the emergence of competing versions of events is allegorized in the personification of *Fama*. The major ecphrastic prophecies at the ends of Books 6 and 8, the Parade of Heroes and the Shield of Aeneas, are both summary rewritings of Ennius' Roman epic cycle; we have already seen how Anchises turns his preview of Roman history into a rhetorical protreptic for his son. In each case Vergil diverges from his primary Homeric model, the catalogue of heroines in the Nekyia and the Shield of Achilles, by taking as his subject a chunk of central epic narrative that is retold in ecphrastic form. In the last four books, the speeches of Venus and Juno in the Council of Gods present sharply divergent versions of events on earth; another great rhetorical manipulator of reality in these last books is Numanus Remulus, who gives us his version not of events but of the national characters of the two peoples at war. Within the text Ascanius' answer is swift and final; the issues that Numanus raises, however, continue to exercise modern critics. Numanus, as we have seen, has several points in common with Drances; furthermore Numanus is a close relative of *Fama*: 'things worthy and unworthy to relate', *digna atque indigna relatu* (9.595) in shape recalls 4.190 'she sung of facts and fictions', *facta atque infecta canebat*. 'He made himself great with his shouting', *ingentem sese clamore ferebat* (9.597) could equally be said of the self-inflating power of *Fama*; and Numanus' charges of Trojan luxurious decadence overlap with the accusations of decadence made by *Fama* and her human mouthpiece Iarbas. David West in this volume analyses the Sinon-like economies practised on the truth by Juno in her final speech in Book 12.

This obsessive and tendentious re-presenting of parts of the narrative within the narrative might still leave intact the authority of the primary narrator, as occupying a position outside and apart from the biased perspectives of his characters. I have already hinted that it is not possible to disassociate cleanly the overheated deployment of praise and blame by Drances from the poet's own use of words. This raises the general issue of the extent to which the performance of the epic narrator is mirrored in the verbal performances of characters within the narrative. The connection is obvious enough when the character is a bard or poet performing an epic-type song, a Demodocus or an Iopas. Closely related is the phenomenon of the epic hero, Odysseus or Aeneas, who narrates a part of the main narrative through first-person flashback. But how many other kinds of verbal – and indeed non-verbal – performances *within* the narrative mimic the work of the primary narrator? Within the *Aeneid* two extended passages of praise speech or praise ecphrasis that clearly shadow the epic poet's work are the Speech of Anchises and the Shield of Aeneas. I have pointed to the Ennian nature of these passages, but one can go further and say that the characters Anchises and Vulcan, 'not unaware of what the prophets/poets had said', *haud uatum ignarus* (8.627) are surrogates for Vergil and the tradition of Greco-Roman epic that he continues and subsumes in his own poem. The inflammatory effect of Anchises' speech on his son, the effect that is inseparable from the effect of 'bad' rhetoric, is therefore also the effect that the poem we are reading intends to have on us. The personification of *Fama* in Book 4 is, as I will argue at greater length elsewhere, a demonic double of the epic voice and of the epic tradition itself. It is impossible to separate surgically the slander of *Fama* from the praise poetry that is epic; we have seen how the one person Drances is a mouthpiece both for epic *fama* and for *invidia*.

This reflection of the poet's work within his text might be thought to be the product of the late stages of a tradition that has become overly self-conscious, a development that will reach its logical conclusion in

Philip Hardie

the plethora of figures of the poet that inhabit the pages of Ovid's *Metamorphoses*. Yet it may be that we are dealing with a fundamental feature of the genre itself. Richard Martin has argued that the conditions of oral performance of early Greek epic tend to foster an identification between the performance of the narrator and that of his characters, whose speech acts, as narrator, he acts out himself.[57] Martin shows that the main categories of *muthos*, defined as the 'expressive use of language in dispute settings' (the categories of commands, boast and insult contests, and the recitation of remembered events), operate in an agonistic context that is analogous to the agonistic culture in which the poet himself must strive for success. An early example in the *Iliad* of verbal contest for authority is the ἀγορή at which Thersites attempts to blacken the character of Agamemnon. As has often been noted, Thersites' arguments are a parodic repetition of those of Achilles in *Iliad* 1.[58] There is, then, a danger that Thersites' excellence in the art of invective may assume too successful a role in the epic of praise. Nagy suggests that the ignominious worsting of Thersites at the hands of Odysseus is intended to draw the lines around epic poetry, institutionalizing it as a kind of praise poetry in opposition to blame poetry.[59] In the *Aeneid* this silencing of a voice of invective is paralleled in Iulus' swift killing of Numanus. However it is Drances who has the role closest to that of the Homeric Thersites, and Vergil signally fails to write him out of the continuing verbal texture of his epic. As we have seen, in this Council there is no resolution to this endless dispute *dubiis de rebus*, in strong contrast to Odysseus' swift and masterful resolution of the verbal disorder in the Achaean ἀγορή. Drances is not summarily expelled from Vergil's epic. Invective and its effects on an audience are not to be radically dissociated from the narrator's own use of language and from the effects of that language on his audience.

We might rest content with an explanation of the convergence between the performances of narrator and his characters in terms of the generic conditioning of the Homeric tradition. But we might also inquire into the historical determinants that in Vergil's own day reinforced the genre's tendency to identify the poet's verbal performance with that of his hero(es) – and even villain(s). In other words, what kinds of performance in the culture of late first century BC Rome does the *Aeneid* represent, and how might these be mirrored in the poet's own performance? It would be easy to see parallels between Vergil's epic and the commemorative and panegyrical displays of the visual arts and of pageantry and ceremony: Anchises and Vulcan are figures both for the epic poet and for the artists of the great public monuments of Augustan Rome, as well as for the impresarios of triumphs and patrician funerals. The analogy between an epic and a visual iconographic cycle is anticipated by Vergil himself in the Temple of Poetry at the beginning of *Georgics* 3. In *Aeneid* 8 Evander enters as the aetiological expert guiding Aeneas and the reader through the prehistory of Rome, and Evander is also the narrator of an archetypal myth of the victory over a demonized enemy of a hero with Olympian pretensions.[60] The poet of the *Aeneid* too is an expert in Callimachean aetiology and Varronian antiquarianism, as also in the aretalogy of saviour-heroes. In these ways the *Aeneid* represents in localized characters and episodes its own functions as the kind of epic poem that it is.

How then will this totalizing poem negotiate its relationship with the discourse that had become the prime vehicle of verbal power in the late Republic, namely oratory? The poem is hospitable enough to epideictic rhetoric: Ilioneus' outline of a *basilikos logos* to Dido at 1.544–9 fits easily into the poem's own project,[61] as in another way does Anchises' apparent prescripting of Augustus' own *epitaphios logos* for his nephew Marcellus at 6.868–86.[62] Here, through the figure of Anchises, the poet ventriloquizes for his 'hero', Augustus. And what of deliberative rhetoric? My whole argument has tended to the conclusion that in the debates in the divine and human councils of Books 10 and 11 Vergil lets us see how the verbal power-struggles of late Republican rhetoric cannot definitively be separated from the 'rhetorical' effects at which his own poem aims. One major difference between the Homeric poems and the *Aeneid* is obviously the fact that the *Aeneid* is immediately concerned with contemporary politics as the *Iliad* and *Odyssey* are not. Politics is a dirty business; in *this* poem invective cannot be expunged with the nonchalance with which Odysseus pitchforks Thersites out of the *Iliad*. Political demonization is too useful a tool for the new regime. Like Drances, the poet of the *Aeneid* is equally adept at sketching saints and monsters.

Drances is not a nice person; Vergil goes out of his way to reveal the baseness of his motives, so that he and we may feel a healthy superiority in our own humanity and fair-mindedness. Yet it is disconcerting that Drances' policy is the one that the Latins should be following, and that his far-from-disinterested insistence that Turnus actually fight the duel that Aeneas had mentioned in unreal past tenses (11.115–18) does indeed eventually provide the resolution to the plot of the poem.[63] This monster of defamation turns out to collude with the designs of Fate (and the same is true, even more paradoxically, of the Earthborn monstrosity *Fama* in Book 4). But beyond this, the rhetoric deployed by Drances, and by Turnus in response, cannot tidily be ring-fenced from the uses of words elsewhere in the poem. Drances is no simple allegory of Cicero or Catiline, but we will probably not err in hearing in the debate in the Council of Latins echoes of the contests of oratory of the late Republic, which issued in no solution to the political problems of the time. This endless squabbling *dubiis de rebus* could be resolved only by the intervention of the man who claimed to be the descendant of Aeneas. And yet, once a military solution had been achieved, this man too depended on words to consolidate and make palatable the results of his actions. One example of such words is the epic poem the *Aeneid*; the constant bubbling to the surface, in this narrative of unchangeable Fate, of different versions of epic Fame, and the attempt of a series of characters to impose their own rhetorical interpretation of events, serve to remind the reader that although conditions *had* changed, the *princeps* could not escape the necessity of conducting the old Republican*certamen gloriae* by other means.[64]

Turnus presents himself as the man of action in opposition to Drances, the man of words. The most famous debate of this kind in the epic cycle was the debate between Ajax and Odysseus over the arms of Achilles, and it is possible that one or more versions of this debate are among the models used by Vergil in the Council scene.[65] Puccioni[66] sees in the sarcasm, μυκτηρισμός, of Drances at 11.383–91 a reflection of the proverbial Αἰάντειος γέλως, as exemplified in Accius' treatment of the *Armorum iudicium*:

> So it was you, Ulysses, that I saw fell Hector with a stone; it was you I saw shelter the Dorian fleet behind your shield? Then I all trembling called for shameful flight?
>
> > uidi te, Ulixes, saxo sternentem Hectora,
> > uidi tegentem clipeo classem Doricam;
> > ego tunc pudendam trepidus hortabar fugam.
> >   (115–17, Warmington)

Accius is certainly one of the models used by Ovid in his *Armorum iudicium* at the beginning of *Metamorphoses* 13; Turnus' sneering suggestion to Drances that they both go into battle, and then see who's a real man (11.389), may also lie behind Ajax' challenge to Ulysses to recreate an earlier scene on the battlefield (*Met.* 13.77–9).

Ovid introduces the Iliadic section of the *Metamorphoses* with his own rewriting of the Vergilian personification of *Fama* at the beginning of *Met.* 12, signalling in no uncertain way the thoroughgoing relativization of epic authority in what is to follow.[67] Ovid's strategy in his 'Iliad' is to narrate obliquely and through intermediaries: in Book 12 the place of a central Iliadic war narrative is taken by the internal narrator Nestor's lengthy account of the earlier battle of the Lapiths and Centaurs. Because of his age and wisdom Nestor might be thought to embody as close an approximation as possible to an objective epic narrator, so it is disconcerting when at the end, in answer to Tlepolemus' amazement that Nestor has said nothing about Hercules' part in the battle, Nestor replies that he has deliberately avoided praising Hercules' deeds because of his grief for his brother Periclymenus, killed by Hercules;[68] 'For who would praise an enemy?' Zumwalt comments 'What constitutes material for praise...and what is included in or excluded from the epic tradition depends, in part, on personal bias.'[69] When in Book 13 Ovid turns to the subject-matter proper of the *Iliad* he chooses not to narrate, but to orate, through the mouths of Ajax and Ulixes. The truth about the Trojan War, whatever that might be, disappears into the rival versions of the two speakers motivated by self-interest and contempt or hatred for the rival. Words completely occlude deeds, and at the end words win out over deeds:

> The company of chiefs was moved, and the event showed the power of eloquence, and the clever speaker bore off the arms of a brave man.
>
> > mota manus procerum est, et, quid facundia posset,
> > re patuit, fortisque uiri tulit arma disertus.
> > > (13.382–3)

The narrator's summing-up provides a comment on Ajax' opening attempt to establish the proper boundaries between words and deeds:

> So it is safer to contend with feigned words than to fight in battle. But I have no gift for speaking, nor he for action; my strength lies in fierce warfare and the front line, his strength in words.
>
> > tutius est igitur fictis contendere uerbis,
> > quam pugnare manu. sed nec mihi dicere promptum
> > nec facere est isti, quantumque ego Marte feroci
> > inque acie ualeo, tantum ualet iste loquendo.
> > > (13.9–12)

Ulixes' successful use of rhetoric to reshape the Trojan narrative may also be understood as a reflection on tendencies that Ovid will have observed in the *Aeneid*.

Philip Hardie

Notes

[1] I am very grateful to Denis Feeney for his generous comments on a draft of this essay. He tells me that he would now accept that 'anxieties about speech-use go *all the way down*' in the *Aeneid*, but he would not necessarily agree with all the emphases in my argument.

[2] Contrast the relatively straightforward way in which Homeric duels are set up: at *Il.* 3.58 ff., Paris' offer to fight a duel with Menelaus, prompted by Hector's abuse, is immediately taken up by Hector; at 7.33 ff. on the prompting of Apollo and Athene, Helenos persuades Hector to issue a challenge. The absence of a direct challenge by Aeneas is the enabling condition for Drances' accusation that Turnus is a coward (since we cannot imagine that Turnus would really have turned down a direct challenge).

[3] The parallelism between the two Vergilian passages is reinforced by their shared use of a single Iliadic model: one of the models for the descent of Iris at 9.1 ff. is the descent of Iris at *Il.* 2.786–806 (immediately after the Catalogue of Ships) to urge Priam to break off the ἀγορή and instead to marshal his troops to meet the Achaean advance. This is the main model for the arrival of the human messenger at *Aen.* 11.447 ff. which breaks off the Latin *concilium*. In both cases Turnus is quick to 'seize the moment' (see Hardie on 9.12).

[4] The division of opinions mirrors that at 11.215–24; cf. the scene of *discordia* at 12.583–92 when Aeneas attacks the city. *arma manu trepidi poscunt, fremit arma iuuentus*, 11.453, echoes *arma amens fremit, arma toro tectisque requirit*, 7.460; the Latin *iuuentus* is solid with the *iuuenis* (e.g., 7.446) Turnus.

[5] *arrepto tempore Turnus, | 'cogite concilium et pacem laudate sedentes; | illi armis in regna ruunt'* (11.459–61); cf. (Latinus) *'ante equidem summa de re statuisse, Latini, | et uellem et fuerat melius, non tempore tali | cogere concilium, cum muros adsidet hostis'* (302–4).

[6] Schenk (1984).

[7] Burke (1978).

[8] McDermott (1980); Alessio (1993) 83–5.

[9] La Penna (1979).

[10] Feeney (1990, originally published in 1983). Feeney tries to minimize the importance of the debate in *Aen.* 11 (184): 'The set-piece debate in the Latin Senate in Book 11 is a mere shouting match; Latinus' proposals for peace are buried in the exchange of words between Drances and Turnus (225–461). The bedlam is shown for what it is by an interruption: *"illi haec inter se dubiis de rebus agebant | certantes: castra Aeneas aciemque mouebat"* (445 f.). As they tussle away Aeneas acts.'

[11] *Per litteras* Denis Feeney tells me that at the time of writing the article he was 'particularly exercised' by *Aen.* 4.283–4 *heu quid agat? quo nunc reginam ambire furentem | audeat adfatu? quae prima exordia sumat?* Austin's notes ad loc., taking issue with Page, reveal the awkwardness of a critic desperate to absolve the hero from the imputation of the possibility of a calculated rhetoric in *ambire* and *exordia*.

[12] Lynch (1990).

[13] Feeney (1991) 144–5 on the council of the gods; 151–5 on the absence of an Archimedean point of objective 'Fate'.

[14] Feeney (1990) 170. There is a model in Jason's opening gambit to Medea at Ap. Rhod. *Argon.* 3.976-7 οὔ τοι ἐγὼν οἷοί τε δυσαυχέες ἄλλοι ἔασιν ἀνέρες, followed by a less-than-straightforward speech. The precise meaning of δυσαυχέες is disputed (see Hunter ad loc.), but one may compare *Il.* 8.230 κενεαυχής, used of those whose deeds do not match their words.

[15] *Iliad* 2.342-3 (Nestor): 'In vain do we strive in words, and can find no device, although we have been here for a long time'; 16.630-1 (Patroclus): 'The *telos* of war lies in hands, of words in council. Therefore we should not multiply words, but fight' (for the antithesis between valour and wisdom, good at fighting/good in council see Janko on *Il.* 13.726-9). On the relationship of words and deeds in Homer see Parry (1981) 21-7; Barck (1976).

[16] See Austin on the interpretative crux at 2.322 *quo res summa loco...?*

[17] *larga quidem semper, Drance, tibi copia fandi* (11.378) echoes the opening description of Drances as *largus opum et lingua melior* (338): oratory and *largitiones* are two of the major instruments for the distortion of the political process in the Republic.

[18] Heinze (1993) 327.

[19] Like Drances he is puffed up by a high-class relationship, his recent marriage to Turnus' younger sister, which elevates him to *regnum* (of his own antecedents we are told nothing); with *talia iactantem dictis ac dira canentem* (9.621) cf. *cane talia, demens* (11.399). But Numanus is *fortis* (592); he presents himself as a warrior, which Drances has no pretensions to be.

[20] See Hardie ad loc.

[21] Turnus' self-reproach at 12.645 *Turnum fugientem haec terra uidebit?* admits Drances' charge at 11.351 *fugae fidens*. Turnus' monologue in 12 is immediately followed by the arrival of Saces, whose desperate plea to Turnus unwittingly reproduces fragments of the debate in 11; note esp. *miserere tuorum* (12.653 = 11.365). *Drancis dicta refellam* (12.644) picks up Turnus' earlier (thwarted) statement at 12.16 *et solus ferro crimen commune refellam*.

[22] Feeney (1990) 173.

[23] Allecto's 'imaginary' *fax* (of course it is 'just a dream') is followed by the cauldron simile at 462-86, an instance of the epic poet's power to conjure up *simulacra*. There is an analogy between poetic fictionalizing and the supernatural manipulation of (dreaming) reality by a Fury. Note also that the sequence closely anticipates the Ascanius and Numanus scene: like Numanus Turnus ends his rant with advice to the old priestess to leave war to the men (*Aen.* 7.444; 9.620); both men are quickly penetrated by a violent blow. Ascanius' shooting of Numanus lies behind Cupid's peremptory response to the amatory rhetoric of the poet Ovid at *Am.* 1.1.21-4 and to Apollo's put-down of Cupid in the parallel passage at *Met.* 1.463-73, passages given as examples of Ovid's ironic treatment of the power of rhetoric by Tarrant (1995).

[24] Heinze (1993) 371.

[25] See Brink ad loc., in particular on the Gorgianic precedents. It is also one of the powers of *Fama* to effect translocation within the narrative, as for example with her transporting of the reader from Carthage to the kingdom of Iarbas in *Aeneid* 4, or from Aulis to Troy at the beginning of *Metamorphoses* 12.

[26] Feeney (1990) 175-6.

Philip Hardie

²⁷ 12.238 concludes the account of the nurturing of *rumores*, among the Latin spectators of the duel, by Juturna in the disguise of Camers at 12.222–39, and is part of a larger sequence (216–65) which examines the interrelationship of several aspects of verbal report and fame: Camers derives his power over the crowd from his own nobility and *clarum...nomen...uirtutis;* (s)he shames the Latins with the prospect that, while they will lose home and liberty (this is the rhetoric of Drances), Turnus will enjoy an eternal (epic) fame, *ille quidem ad superos, quorum se deuouet aris, | succedet fama uiuusque per ora feretur* (234–5). Camers' production of rumour, cued by the visual trigger of Turnus' pitiable appearance (219–21), has tangible consequences (*ipsi Laurentes mutati ipsique Latini*, 240); this is immediately followed by another visual sign, the omen of the eagle and swan, whose verbal (mis)intepretation by the augur Tolumnius issues in military action at 266.

²⁸ Imitated at Luc. 9.406–7 *sic ille* [Cato] *pauentis | incendit uirtute animos et amore laborum. accendo* is also found in the *Aeneid* in both positive and negative contexts with relation to speech and reputation. Negative: *isque amens animi et rumore accensus amaro* (4.203); *finitimas in bella feram rumoribus urbes, | accendamque animos insani Martis amore* (7.549–50). Positive: *si nulla accendit tantarum gloria rerum* (4.232); *aere ciere uiros Martemque accendere cantu* (6.165: a figure for the poet?); '*arma citi properate uiro! quid statis?*' *Iapyx | conclamat primusque animos accendit in hostem* (12.425–6). How are we to judge *eximiae laudis successus amore* (7.496)? Note also *his dictis incensum* [var. lect.] *animum inflammauit amore* (4.54).

²⁹ See Keith (1992) 130–1. Drances' *frigida bello dextera* (*Aen.* 11.338–9) may be compared with the *ignauum frigus* of the house of Ovidian *Inuidia* (*Met.* 2.763): see Dickie (1975).

³⁰ *gloria Turni* introduces the exchange between Drances and Turnus (11.336), which concludes with Turnus' claim for himself of *gloria* (444); Drances taunts Turnus with his desire for *fama* at 368; Turnus raises the issue of *gloria* at 421 and 431. The inextricable link between envy and glory (or praise) is clear in Roman historians and orators; cf. Verg. *Ecl.* 7.25–8: *pastores, hedera crescentem ornate poetam, | Arcades, inuidia rumpantur ut ilia Codro; | aut, si ultra placitum laudarit, baccare frontem | cingite, ne uati noceat mala lingua futuro.* On envy and praise in Greece see Walcot (1978).

³¹ And also as *senior*, perhaps lending him a certain authority. *senior* is otherwise used of Anchises, Acestes, (the risible) Menoetes, Nautes, Latinus, Galaesus, Tiberinus, Evander, Thymbris, the father of Halaesus, Acoetes, Iapyx: for the most part august company. On *seniores* and the proper order see Ov., *F.* 5.1 ff.

³² Cf. also *o decus Italiae uirgo, quas dicere grates | quasue referre parem?* (11.508–9). Drances' doubt about his ability adequately to praise his subject may be compared with Lucretius' exaltation of Epicurus over the greatest epic hero, Hercules, at *De rer. nat.* 5.1–8: *quis <u>potis est</u> dignum pollenti pectore carmen | condere <u>pro rerum maiestate</u> hisque repertis? | quisue <u>ualet uerbis</u> tantum qui <u>fingere laudes</u> | <u>pro meritis</u> eius possit...nemo, ut opinor, erit mortali corpore cretus. | nam si, ut ipsa petit <u>maiestas</u> cognita rerum, | dicendum est, deus ille fuit, deus, inclute Memmi...* Macrobius (*Sat.* 6.2.33) provides a parallel in Cicero's praise of the

elder Cato, in a lost treatise: *contingebat in eo, quod plerisque contra solet, ut maiora omnia re quam fama uiderentur; id quod non saepe euenit, ut expectatio cognitione, aures ab oculis uincerentur* [= *fr. philos.* 6.14 Müll.], commenting *nec Tullio compilando, dummodo undique ornamenta sibi conferret, abstinuit*: ammunition, perhaps, for those who would see in Drances a figure of Cicero.

[33] *Thes. Ling. Lat.* s.v. Cf. the play with the three degrees of *magnus* (*maior, maximus*) at Ov. *Fasti* 1.603–6 (all outdone by *Augustus*); with two degrees at *Geo.* 2.169–70 *extulit, haec Decios Marios magnosque Camillos,* | *Scipiadas duros bello et te, maxime Caesar*; Ov. *Met.*14.108–9 (the Sibyl to Aeneas) '*magna petis*' dixit, '*uir factis maxime, cuius* | *dextera per ferrum, pietas spectata per ignes*.'

[34] Hardie on 9.57.

[35] For the pairing cf. *Ufens, insignem fama et felicibus armis* (7.745), perhaps to be taken as a hendiadyoin, 'renowned for the fame of his successful arms'.

[36] See Hardie (1986), index s.vv. 'heavens, ascent to'. The 'purely verbal' kind of ascent to the skies is given the authority of the mouthpiece of *Fatum* in Jupiter's climactic words at 1.287–8 *famam qui terminet astris* | *Iulius*.

[37] Cairns (1989) 29–30.

[38] Presumably Gransden would not say the same of Horace, *Odes* 1.12.13–14 *quid prius dicam solitis parentis* | *laudibus…?* See Gow on Theocr. 17.11.

[39] Cf. also the praise of Marcellus at 6.878–80 *heu pietas, heu prisca fides inuictaque bello* | *dextera! non illi se quisquam impune tulisset| obuius armato…*

[40] *pius* is used of Aeneas both at the beginning of the *foedus* scene in *Aen.* 12 and at the point of its disruption: *tum pius Aeneas stricto sic ense precatur* (12.175), and *at pius Aeneas dextram tendebat inermem* (12.311).

[41] 6.77–9; 17.513.

[42] See Tarrant on Sen., *Ag.* 211: the phrase *belli mora* seems to originate with Albucius Silo. Turnus of course has his own reasons for choosing the traditional version.

[43] Stahl (1981) 173–4, comments on *Aen.* 11.283–4 that 'Diomedes… modifies Homer's picture of Augustus' ancestor very favorably', and identifies Diomedes' reassessment as part of the poet's own project. This may be so; my aim is to show that the text reveals the 'rhetorical' nature of what Vergil is about.

[44] For the Golden Age implication of 254 *ignota lacessere bella* cf. 8.112–13: *quae causa subegit* | *ignotas temptare uias?* (hinting at the *topos* of the first ship).

[45] Reinforced by Venulus' closing remarks at 294–5 *et responsa simul quae sint, rex optime, regis* | *audisti et quae sit magno sententia bello*.

[46] 5.101–3: *nec tamen hanc possis oculorum subdere uisu* | *nec iacere indu manus, uia qua munita fidei* | *proxima fert humanum in pectus templaque mentis*, closely following Emped., DK B133.

[47] A PHI search reveals that the sequence -*musque manu*- occurs only in these two places in Vergil.

[48] See the commentators ad loc. on the exaggerations contained in these claims of what can be 'seen'; the Tiber swelling with blood is the kind of vision that a Sibyl has (6.87).

[49] Cf. 11.283 *experto credite*.

[50] 11.231–3: *deficit ingenti luctu rex ipse Latinus:* | *fatalem Aenean manifesto*

Philip Hardie

numine ferri | admonet ira deum tumulique ante ora recentes, where it is uncertain whether the object of *admonet* is focalized through Latinus or the narrator.

[51] Highet (1972) 56–7, referring to Kroll (1924), 240 n. 28 for similar 'Katalog-, Epitomegedichte' in Cat. 64.338 f., *Culex* 304 f., Ov. *Met.* 14.441 f., 566 f.

[52] Barchiesi (1994) 118.

[53] With *infanda* cf. Aeneas' introduction of his narrative of the *Iliupersis*, *infandum, regina, iubes renouare dolorem* (2.3), another internal narrative of a part of the cycle.

[54] Martin (1989) 141. A programmatic internal *r*eperformance near the beginning of the poem? See also Martin 142–3 arguing that Achilles' notorious silence on the subject of the embassy episode at 16.72–3 is a deliberate manipulation of the 'rhetoric' of recollection.

[55] O'Hara (1990) 132–63 on Jupiter's *consolatio*.

[56] Sinon as double of Ulysses: with *fandi fictor Ulixes* (9.602) cf. (Sinon) *prosequitur pauitans et ficto pectore fatur* (2.107). Sinon feigns *pauor* like Drances, according to Turnus, *se pauidum...fingi* (11.406).

[57] Martin (1989).

[58] Note in particular Whitman (1958) 161: 'Few things are more subtle in the *Iliad* than the way in which this "good-for-nothing", the social and physical antitype of Achilles, reiterates the resentment of the hero: the theme of the entire second book is Delusion, and truth can appear only in the mouth of a Thersites.'

[59] Nagy (1979) 253–64, at 260.

[60] See Drew (1927) 31–41: 'Evander and Virgil'.

[61] Tiberius Donatus ascribed the whole poem to the *genus laudatiuum* of rhetoric.

[62] See Norden on 6.868 ff.

[63] The words used by Drances at 11.220–1 in his vicious aggravation of popular hostility against Turnus, *solumque uocari | testatur, solum posci in certamina Turnum*, turn out to be prophetic of the actions of Aeneas at 12.466–7: *solum densa in caligine Turnum | uestigat lustrans, solum in certamina poscit* (both also echo 10.442–3: *solus ego in Pallanta feror, soli mihi Pallas | debetur*). The passage in Book 11 traps Turnus' past and future actions in a contest of blame and fame: the accusations of the grieving womenfolk and children are counterbalanced by the sheltering *magnum reginae nomen* (223) and the support of Turnus' own military *fama* (224).

[64] For examples of the *certamen gloriae* (*honoris, dignitatis, famae, laudis*) see *Thes. Ling. Lat.* iii.879.52–70. In this contest the poet is yoked with the *princeps*: the pairing of statesman and poet is expressed most economically in Vergil's image of *Inuidia infelix* at *G.* 3.37 (hinting at a Pindaric genealogy for the contest between κλέος and φθόνος), notoriously ambiguous between the threat to the poet and the threat to the *princeps*.

[65] For the suggestion that the debate between Drances and Turnus is modelled on that between Odysseus and Ajax see Anderson (1969) Ch. 7, n. 3.

[66] Puccioni (1985) 147, referring to Zenob., *paroem.* 1.43, and to the story of Pleisthenes reciting Carcinus' *Aias*. But Zenobius refers to Aias' mad laughter as he kills the cattle (cf. Soph., *Ai.* 303); the proper reference should be to

Nauck, *TGF* ² 797: Carcinus, *Aias*, Prov. Milleri *Mél. de litt. gr.* p. 355: Αἰάντειος γέλως – λέγουσι δὲ ὅτι Πλεισθένης ὁ ὑποκριτὴς τὸν Καρκίνου Αἴαντα ὑποκρινόμενος εὐκαίρως ἐγέλασε· τοῦ γὰρ Ὀδυσσέως εἰπόντος ὅτι τὰ δίκαια χρὴ ποιεῖν, μετὰ εἰρωνείας ὁ Αἴας τῷ γέλωτι ἐχρήσατο.

[67] See Zumwalt (1977).

[68] '*quid me meminisse malorum | cogis et obductos annis restringere luctus?*' (*Met.* 12.542-3) is reminiscent of the opening of *Aen.* 2; Aeneas, by contrast, does steel himself to speak of *infanda*, but we are reminded that strong emotion may colour the content of his narrative.

[69] Zumwalt (1977) 216-17.

Bibliography

Alessio, M.
    1993   *Studies in Vergil. Aeneid 11: An Allegorical Approach*, Quebec.
Anderson, W.
    1969   *The Art of the* Aeneid, Englewood Cliffs, N.J.
Barchiesi, A.
    1994   'Rappresentazioni del dolore ed interpretazione nell' Eneide', *A&A* 40, 109-24.
Barck, C.
    1976   *Wort und Tat bei Homer*, Hildesheim and New York.
Burke, P.F.
    1978   '*Drances infensus:* A study in Vergilian character portrayal.' *TAPhA* 108, 15-20.
Cairns, F.
    1989   *Vergil's Augustan Epic*, Cambridge.
Dickie, M.W.
    1975   'Ovid, *Metamorphoses* 2.760-64', *AJPh* 96, 378-90.
Drew, D.L.
    1927   *The Allegory of the* Aeneid, Oxford.
Feeney, D.C.
    1990   'The taciturnity of Aeneas', in S.J. Harrison (ed.) *Oxford Readings in Vergil's* Aeneid, 167-90, Oxford. [= *CQ* 33 (1983), 204-19.]
    1991   *The Gods in Epic*, Oxford.
Hardie, P.R.
    1986   *Virgil's Aeneid. Cosmos and Imperium*, Oxford.
Heinze, R.
    1993   *Virgil's Epic Technique*, transl. H. and D. Harvey and F. Robertson, Bristol.
Highet, G.
    1972   *The Speeches in Vergil's* Aeneid, Princeton.
Keith, A.
    1992   *The Play of Fictions. Studies in Ovid's* Metamorphoses *Book 2*, Ann Arbor.
Kroll, W.
    1924   *Studien zum Verständnis der römischen Literatur*, Stuttgart.

La Penna, A.
  1979 'Spunti sociologici per l' interpretazione dell' Eneide', in *Fra teatro, poesia e politica romana*, 153–65, Turin. [= H. Bardon and R. Verdière (eds.) *Vergiliana. Recherches sur Virgile*, 283–93, Leiden.]

Lynch, J.P.
  1990 'Laocoön and Sinon. Virgil *Aeneid* 2.40–198', in I. McAuslan and P. Walcot (eds.) *Virgil:* 112–20, Oxford. [= *G&R* 27 (1980): 170–9.]

Martin, R.P.
  1989 *The Language of Heroes. Speech and Performance in the* Iliad, Ithaca and London.

McDermott, W.C.
  1980 'Drances–Cicero', *Vergilius* 26, 34–8.

Nagy, G.
  1979 *The Best of the Achaeans*, Baltimore.

O'Hara, J.J.
  1990 *Death and the Optimistic Prophecy in Vergil's* Aeneid, Princeton.

Parry, A.M.
  1981 *Logos and Ergon in Thucydides*, New York.

Puccioni, G.
  1985 'Lettura dell' undecimo libro dell' Eneide', in *Saggi virgiliani:* 137–53, Bologna.

Rigney, A.
  1994 'Fame and defamation: toward a socio-pragmatics', *Semiotica* 99, 53–65.

Schenk, P.
  1984 *Die Gestalt des Turnus in Vergils Aeneis*, Königstein.

Stahl, H.-P.
  1981 'Aeneas – an unheroic hero?', *Arethusa* 14, 157–86.

Tarrant, R.
  1995 'Ovid and the failure of rhetoric', in D. Innes et al. (eds.) *Ethics and Rhetoric. Classical Essays for Donald Russell on his Seventy-fifth Birthday*, 63–74, Oxford.

Walcot, P.
  1978 *Envy and the Greeks. A Study of Human Behaviour*, Warminster.

Whitman, C.H.
  1958 *Homer and the Heroic Tradition*, Cambridge, Mass. and London.

Zumwalt, N.
  1977 '*Fama subversa:* theme and structure in Ovid *Metamorphoses* 12', *CSCA* 10, 210–22.

13

THE ISOLATION OF TURNUS
Aeneid Book 12

R.F. Thomas

> We just saw it from a different point of view.
> Bob Dylan, "Tangled up in Blue".

After deciding on the title of this paper, I became more familiar with the article of H.-P. Stahl (1990), which remarks of Turnus (183–4) "he is found to be in considerable isolation". The very word isolation, and the aesthetic response which it evokes, will depend on our perspective on many aspects of this poem. That is a situation with which Vergil presents us. How we proceed will depend on our own experience, on our own judgements of the achievement and ethical situation of Aeneas, of Turnus, even of Augustus. Stahl's procedure is to carry out a sustained attack on the character of Turnus, whom he sees as utterly dark and beyond redemption, a figure to be swept aside by Aeneas, just as Augustus is to sweep aside all the dark forces threatening his own mission. The article is the sole Vergilian offering in a large volume on interpretations of Augustus, which may well reach wide general readership; it will therefore be useful to set forth an alternative reading as a sort of "companion" piece.[1]

Stahl's conclusions are presented at the outset, and may serve as a useful departure point for us:

> In Vergil's version, Aeneas, ancestor of the Julian family, appears in Italy as a peaceful and peace-seeking newcomer. (Perhaps one should call him a homecomer since his distant forefather Dardanus had supposedly emigrated from here, *Aen.* 7.206 f., 240; cf. 3.167.) His journey has been supervised by Fate and by Jupiter (1.261 ff.; 8.381). He is sent under orders of Apollo, god of prophecy, specifically to occupy the land between Tiber and Numicus (7.241 ff.), i.e., territory held by King Latinus' people and by the Rutulians of King Turnus. The ultimate purpose of his arrival, according to divine revelation (7.98–101; cf. 1.286 ff.), is the worldwide rule his descendant Augustus will one day peacefully exercise around here.
>
> Aeneas is not spared the saddening experience of resistance, raised by

an increasing faction of the native population. There is, above all, oracle-defying, sacrilegious Turnus (cf. 7.595) who associates with such tell-tale characters as King Mezentius, most cruel torturer of his own subjects (8.485 ff.) and "despiser of the gods" (*contemptor divum*, 8.7); another close companion of his is Messapus who, on the occasion of a peace treaty, delights in killing a king at the altar in full regalia as, in his words, "a better victim for the great gods (12.289–96)". The Julian ancestor is forced to wage a holy war against the godless opposition.

His greater descendant had to face comparable problems...

Octavian, as his *Achievements* inform posterity (*R.G.* 2), had to defeat the men "who butchered my father" (*qui parentem meum trucidaverunt* – the customary label for a dictator's assassins, we remind ourselves, would be "tyrannicides"), "when they raised arms against the republic", *bellum inferentis rei publicae*. True to his perception of his mission as serving the common weal, he calls his opponents a "faction" (*R.G.* 1), not dignifying them by mentioning a name.

To sum up, then: a just cause; executor of a divine mission; administrator of the nation's interests; facing irresponsible, godless, and criminal factionalism – these are the features shared by the founder of the Julian race (as depicted by Vergil) and by his descendant (as his case is presented by Augustus himself).

That is essentially the substance of the article, although there are thirty-five pages of detail persuading us to feel the justice of this position. Lest it be felt that Stahl is simply being used as a straw man, I would just note that the other recent full treatments of Turnus (by Cairns, [earlier] Hardie, Enger, Schenk and Galinsky) take a similar approach. I will be aligned, on the other hand, with a number of critics, mostly of a preceding critical generation (e.g. Nethercut, Putnam),[2] to whose voices the Augustan critics oppose themselves. Among current critics, I am also most sympathetic with the work of O'Hara.[3] For those who consider sympathy or even support for Turnus a mark of American post-Vietnam aesthetic angst, it is worth quoting a German scholar writing before Vietnam but, more importantly, after he had perhaps had time to reflect on the consequences of his own society's simplistically identifying, *sine humanitate*, enemies of the state:

> In der herabziehenden Deutung der Turnusgestalt liegt etwas von der kleinen und engen Gesinnung der Wissenschaft des neunzehnten Jahrhunderts und auch der politischen Verblendung des zwanzigsten, die immer nach irgendwelchen Parteinahmen fahndet, ohne zu ahnen, wie unendlich erhaben die grossen Genien der Menschheit solchen Ueberlegungen gegenüberstehen.[4]

There is something of the small and narrow outlook of the nineteenth century at the bottom of this downgrading of Turnus. There is also something of the political delusion of the twentieth century which is always choosing ideological sides without the slightest realization of the immense disdain which the great geniuses of mankind have for such considerations.[5]

How to proceed? One could argue with Stahl's details,[6] and one could certainly take issue with his militant tone and comfortable conclusion, which will seem to many, I think, a poor representation of the complexity of the *Aeneid*, and of the contrasting ideologies in which it always deals. So having spent ten pages (199–208) insisting that we must share Aeneas' anger at the utter monstrosity of Turnus' act against Pallas in *Aen*. 10, he deals in half a page with the brutality of Aeneas that immediately follows Turnus' act, asserting that Aeneas is a (good) "Super-Achilles' compared to Turnus as (bad) "New Achilles". On this second half of the book he is chiefly content to be epigrammatic (208):

> Because of space limitations, we have had to exclude a detailed investigation into the terms under which Vergil wishes his reader to view Aeneas' fierce fighting after Pallas' death. Suffice it to say that, against many recent interpretations (mostly of the Two Voices School), a close reading of context and author's interventions results in a positive picture.

No indication that this "fierce fighting" of Aeneas involves human sacrifice, decapitation followed by kicking of the headless trunk, sarcastic rejection of suppliancy, killing of brother before brother and son before father – and Lausus barely gets a mention. Nor is there any treatment of the full-blown *aristeia* of Pallas (10.362–425) that precedes and motivates the young warrior's confrontation of Turnus; for Stahl, who isolates the central encounter of Pallas and Turnus, that encounter is viewed as a "murder" (201–3), as "the reader" is "impregnated with antipathy against cruel Turnus" (205).

But rather than pursue such matters, I would shift the point of view. While allowing that from an Augustan point of view, from the point of view of Augustus himself, and of Aeneas himself, with a few minor adjustments Stahl's reading is a possible one, supported much of the time by the text (from which he frequently departs however), I will focus as strongly as he does on a point of view that allows a competing meaning; that is, my focus will be Turnus. I presuppose and do not deny the Augustan Turnus, but he does have company. Stahl at one point notes "repelled by Turnus' unethical, abominable conduct as depicted in Book 10, the attentive reader will join Aeneas in the end in opting for revenge rather than mercy." Of course it depends on what the reader attends to and what he is discouraged from attending to.

Pöschl presents a more balanced view of Turnus, but for the present purposes I am looking not for balance but for identification of the full voice of Turnus, with all that implies. Stahl claims his own paper "concentrates on, and if possible, limits itself to perspectives that can be demonstrated to flow from the epic's text itself". The word "epic" is frequently evoked in Augustan readings, as a device for validating the Augustan reading, but, be that as it may, my own conclusions emerge also from the Vergilian text, though, not surprisingly, almost never from the same texts Stahl or other Augustan readers treat; and the texts to which I go are almost without exception ignored by Stahl or other Augustan readers. G.B. Conte's formulation reminds us that we must always attend to individual focalizations in this poem; there is no overarching 'epic' or other point of view: "The coexistence of the worlds of Aeneas, Dido, Turnus, Mezentius, and Juturna springs from the fact that Vergil allows each of them an autonomous, personal raison d' être which the historico-epic norm had always denied."[7] Although, then, I do not deny a Turnus focalized from the Augustan perspective, I will look here at the Turnus who keeps him company, and whose full voice still merits critical attention, partly because critics have striven for critical balance – again, not the aim in this study.

The theme of Stahl's article is "the political rival", and he frequently uses the *Res Gestae*, to which the phenomenon of voice might also be usefully applied. Just as behind the voice of Augustus in his claim to have punished those "who butchered my father" there is another perspective, having to do with tyrants and tyrannicides, a perspective which is utterly suppressed in the *Res Gestae*, so behind Aeneas' final words to Turnus, with their invocation of the shade of Pallas, there is another perspective. There was after all another butcher, other than the killers of Caesar, in circulation in the mid- to late 40s. One of the many remarkable differences between the *Aeneid* and the *Res Gestae*, and between their respective authors, is that so far from suppressing that other perspective, the perspective of the public enemy, Vergil's poem nourishes and lingers over it. Where the *Res Gestae* is studiously unaware of Octavian's shortcomings in the court of *humanitas* and *clementia* ("as victor I spared the lives of all citizens who sought pardon", *victorque omnibus veniam petentibus civibus peperci*, 3.1), Vergil remains unblinking in sustaining his focus on the exceptions, on those who lose and die, whether or not they ask for pardon – which incidentally Turnus did, thereby meriting the outcome that the author of the *Res Gestae* claims was the norm.[8] It is also noteworthy that the *Res Gestae*'s anxiety about *clementia* shows that the quality of mercy, and the ethical issues that arise from its being granted or denied, exist in Augustan Rome, and are not conditioned simply by the expectations of Christianity or uneasiness about America's role in Vietnam. The Augustan critics depend on their ability to dismiss as "modern" or "Christian" any tendency to see excess in the actions of Aeneas.[9] The reality however may more likely be that assumptions about optimistic closure and wise and just deities may precisely be conditioned by Judeo-Christian theologies and theodicies.

On one initial point we should be emphatic: Vergil chose to develop the Turnus tradition least favorable to the Trojan element in the Roman mythical history. Whereas the Augustan authors Livy (1.2) and Dionysius of Halicarnassus (1.59–60, 64) promoted the version in which Turnus attacks the Trojans and Latins after they have joined in an alliance and after Aeneas and Lavinia are united, Vergil develops an account, known from Cato, and obviously in the process of being erased by an increasingly sophisticated and national consciousness, in which there is a pan-Italian resistance to the Trojans (Servius ad *Aen*. 1.267, 4.260). To put it another way, in the very tradition from which Vergil draws we find a version, passed over by the poet, in which Turnus is unambiguously a public enemy.[10]

Turnus and Aeneas

Readers of the *Aeneid* have been struck by the fact that Vergil reserves for Turnus, at the moment of his death, a conflated Homeric formula,[11] used once before, for Aeneas, in that strange moment at which we encounter him, a human 'hero', fearing death at sea and wishing he had died at Troy:

> his limbs go slack with chill, *illi solvuntur frigore membra* (12.951)

> Aeneas' limbs go slack with chill, *Aeneae solvuntur frigore membra* (1.92)

M.C.J. Putnam ends his book on the *Aeneid* with a well-known reference to this nexus, still worth quoting. "Now as the poem reaches its climax, it is one of Vergil's most bitter and cogent ironies that he uses this very phrase at the exact moment Aeneas becomes the personification of avenging wrath and brings death to Turnus."[12] In a poem that constantly and powerfully confuses victim and victor, Vergil here gives the most powerful such reversal: Turnus becomes what Aeneas had been when first we saw him, isolated and facing death. Aeneas was buffeted by adverse gods, recently deprived of wife and father, his city fallen and the future dark, unsure whether that future would ever brighten. Turnus on the other hand will move in a direction opposite and reciprocal to Aeneas, from light and tranquillity to darkness, as he confronts death, hostile gods, and loss of betrothed to his enemy.

But to turn more squarely to Turnus, in our very first encounter with him we see a potential Aeneas. We meet him before the arrival of the Trojans, at 7.55–6: "most handsome before all others Turnus sought her hand", *petit ante alios pulcherrimus omnis | Turnus*. As in the final mention of Turnus, so here in the first Vergil seems clearly to bind Turnus to Aeneas, to Aeneas when he too was a "suitor", at 4.141: "most handsome before all others", *ante alios pulcherrimus omnis*. Once again two phrases, not otherwise used by Vergil. Fordyce notes the parallel, but does no more ("again in 4.141 of Aeneas'"), Austin and Williams were unaware of it or chose not to mention it – if the latter, it might be said that implicit denial of intertextual or intratextual patterns is as much a critical strategy as embracing such patterns, and should be recognized as such.

These, then, are simply two of the many ways in which Aeneas and Turnus are tied together, a procedure quite familiar to readers of Vergil, as for instance when Camilla and Turnus die with the same line (11.831 = 12.952). Nethercut points to 2.314 of Aeneas ("crazed, I seize arms", *arma amens capio*) and 7.460 of Turnus ("crazed, he cries for arms", *arma amens fremit*).[13] I choose just one from Book 10, where Vergil brings out the reciprocal relationship between Turnus and Aeneas, vis-à-vis their victims Pallas and Lausus, with a strong intertextual bond, a rare repetition of a name within a line:

[Turnus:] I alone attack Pallas, to me alone is Pallas owed, *solus ego in Pallanta feror, soli mihi Pallas debetur*. (10.42–3)

[Aeneas:] Aeneas chides Lausus and threatens Lausus, *Aeneas…Lausum increpitat Lausoque minatur*. (10.809–10)

Harrison gives the cross-reference without interpretive comment, while Stahl notes of the first instance that Pallas' name is "emphasized twice in the same line", but has nothing on the second.[14] Now we can of course talk about the differences between the two passages and the two characters, but similitude and parallelism are essential to any such discussion.

Vergil also brings Aeneas and Turnus together through simile. As much as any poet Vergil realized the potential of the simile to suggest connections and communicate meaning. While it is true that much of the power of simile may be to suggest difference ("the slippage between tenor and vehicle" if we will),[15] it is also true in the case of the Vergilian simile, within the emphatic distinction between the worlds of tenor and vehicle, that some crucial similitude is always the rule. Scholars, such as O'Hara, have talked about the notion of "trespass", the eliding of what should be an impenetrable boundary between narrative and simile, and this is one of the ways Vergil brings two worlds into close alignment. Almost all of Vergil's similes are adapted from previous literature;[16] in such circumstances the alterations of detail will be particularly significant. In other words, the identification of the model is simply the beginning, and potentially the foundation, of interpretation. Simile may serve as a potent tool for subversion of the surface level, a possibility which we shall see realized.

At 12.500–47 Vergil gives a rare double *aristeia* of Aeneas and Turnus, a passage analyzed by M.M. Willcock.[17] The effect of this doubling up, unique in the tradition of the *aristeia*, is to approximate the two warriors to each other. Vergil begins with the standard language but even here, as throughout the passage, the focus is on balance and duality, and although the Iliadic background (viz. the last part of *Il.* 20) is present throughout, this new focus is Vergilian:

> What god could now set forth for me so much woe, what god sing the varied slaughters and death of leaders, whom now Turnus, now the Trojan hero drives across the whole plain?
>
> quis mihi nunc tot acerba deus, quis carmine caedes
> diversas obitumque ducum, quos aequore toto
> inque vicem nunc Turnus agit, nunc Troius heros
> expediat?   (12.500–3)

This passage is composed with great artistry: the narrative of the exploits of the two (505–20) alternates its focus – 4 lines for Aeneas, 4 for Turnus, 3 for *ille* (Aeneas), 5 for *hic* (Turnus); in all, each kills 5 warriors.[18] And we are now ready for the simile that brings them even closer together, as they are *both* compared to the same phenomena, to twin forest fires, and to raging rivers (12.521–5). The adaptation is from *Iliad* 14.394–9 (Greeks and Trojans as surf and forest fire), and 20.490–2 (Achilles as forest fire), but the doubling and the conflation effected by that doubling is Vergilian, the result the close binding of Aeneas and Turnus (*non segnius ambo | Aeneas Turnusque...*, 12.525–6). In the battle-narrative following the double simile we again see killing of individuals (529–47): *hic* (Aeneas) kills Murranus; *ille* (Turnus) kills Hyllus; Turnus kills Cretheus; Aeneas kills Cupencus; in all each kills two, and the balance is perfect. Through narrative and simile, in fewer than fifty lines, Vergil has blended Aeneas and Turnus so that they have become doublets of each other, a process unprecedented even in the Achilles/Hector duality.[19]

R.F. Thomas

The death of Aineias and beyond

But the killing is *not* finished; there remains one victim, Aeolus, whose death at the hands of Turnus receives an extended apostrophe:

> You too, Aeolus, the Laurentian fields saw perish and go sprawling on the earth. You fall dead, you whom the Greek squadrons could not bring down, nor Achilles, sacker of the realm of Priam; here was the boundary of your death; your high home was under Ida, your high home was at Lyrnessus, but your sepulchre on Laurentian soil.

> te quoque Laurentes viderunt, Aeole, campi
> oppetere et late terram consternere tergo.
> occidis, Argivae quem non potuere phalanges
> sternere nec Priami regnorum eversor Achilles;
> hic tibi mortis erant metae, domus alta sub Ida,
> Lyrnesi domus alta, solo Laurente sepulcrum.
>   (12.542–7)

Williams (1973) ad loc. points to the parallel with Aeneas' words at 2.195–8, capturing the disastrous results of Sinon's lies:

> they whom Diomedes could not break, nor Achilles of Larissa, nor ten long years and a thousand ships.

> quos neque Tydides nec Larisaeus Achilles,
> non anni domuere decem, non mille carinae.

But the connection to Aeneas is even closer, establishing itself through the intricacies of Vergilian intertextuality. This Aeolus of Book 12, otherwise unknown to fame, is said to have escaped death at the hands of the Greeks, and specifically at the hands of Achilles, sacker of the realm of Priam. We think of Troy, but we also think of Lyrnessus, that being where Vergil situates the home of Aeolus. It is time to look to *Iliad* 20, whose contents, as a prelude to the final encounter of *Iliad* 22, are crucial to the movement of *Aeneid* 12.

Iliad 20 contains the *aristeia* of Achilles, and treats his attempt against Aineias, whom Poseidon will remove from danger, leaving Achilles to focus his attention on Hector. I am concerned with the relationship of Achilles and Aineias in the *Iliad*, as it reflects on that of Turnus and Aeolus – and Aeneas – in the *Aeneid*. In the lines quoted above, Aeolus receives an epigram:

> hic tibi mortis erant metae, domus alta sub Ida,
> Lyrnesi domus alta, solo Laurente sepulcrum.
>   (546–7)

The sentiment, and the wording, as the commentators note, is based closely on that of *Il.* 20.390–2, Achilles' vaunt to Iphition, the *first* person he kills in his rampage after his frustrated attack on Aineias:

> Here is your death, but your birth-place is at Lake Gyge, where your ancestral domain lies, by the fish-filled Hyllus and swirling Hermus.

> ἐνθάδε τοι θάνατος, γενεὴ δέ τοί ἐστ᾽ ἐπὶ λίμνῃ
> Γυγαίῃ, ὅθι τοι τέμενος πατρώϊόν ἐστιν,
> Ὕλλῳ ἐπ᾽ ἰχθυόεντι καὶ Ἕρμῳ δινήεντι.

In both cases the limits of life and death are tied to birthplace or domicile, and death away from that place: Iphition, born around Lake Gyge in southern Mysia, dies at Troy; Aeolus, whose home is Lyrnessus, dies in Latium. A few lines earlier Hector had ended his self-exhortation to fight Achilles with an artful epanalepsis of a hemistich, of which there are only three examples in the *Iliad*:[20]

> I go to face him, though he has hands like fire, though he has hands like fire, and strength like blazing iron.

> τοῦ δ᾽ ἐγὼ ἀντίος εἶμι, καὶ εἰ πυρὶ χεῖρας ἔοικεν,
> εἰ πυρὶ χεῖρας ἔοικε, μένος δ᾽ αἴθωνι σιδήρῳ
> (20.371–2)

Vergil's crafting of a similar epanalepsis precisely in the epigram of Aeolus (*domus alta sub Ida | Lyrnesi domus alta*), as the Hector figure is killed by Turnus the Latin Achilles, serves to create a profound intertextual and contextual bond with the Homeric situation.[21]

But now to Achilles and Aineias. Poseidon's rescue of Aineias from Achilles in *Il*. 20 was not the first time the hero was so saved: Zeus had rescued him from Achilles once before – at Lyrnessus, the home of our Aeolus in the *Aeneid*. Three times the Homeric text draws attention to this story (19.291–4, 20.89–96, 20.189–94), perhaps part of a lost Greek *Aeneid* tradition: at 19.291–4 Briseis, without mentioning Aineias, tells of her capture and of the sack of her city, along with Achilles' slaughter of her husband and brothers. At 20.89–96 Aineias himself, explaining that this is not the first time he stood up to Achilles, who had come after his cattle on Mt. Ida when he sacked Lyrnessus and Pedasus. And at 20.188–94 Achilles reminds Aineias of this fact, with slightly different detail, and now showing awareness of Briseis' version:

> "Or do you not remember when, away from your cattle and alone, I hotly chased you on swift feet down Mt. Ida? Then you ran away and did not turn back. And from there you fled into Lyrnessus; but I pressed my attack and destroyed it with the help of Athena and father Zeus. And I took the day of liberty from their women and led them off as booty; but Zeus and the other gods saved you."

> "ἦ οὐ μέμνῃ ὅτε πέρ σε βοῶν ἄπο μοῦνον ἐόντα
> σεῦα κατ' Ἰδαίων ὀρέων ταχέεσσι πόδεσσι
> καρπαλίμως; τότε δ' οὔ τι μετατροπαλίζεο φεύγων.
> ἔνθεν δ' ἐς Λυρνησσὸν ὑπέκφυγες· αὐτὰρ ἐγὼ τὴν
> πέρσα μεθορμηθεὶς σὺν Ἀθήνῃ καὶ Διὶ πατρί,
> ληϊάδας δὲ γυναῖκας ἐλεύθερον ἦμαρ ἀπούρας
> ἦγον· ἀτὰρ σὲ Ζεὺς ἐρρύσατο καὶ θεοὶ ἄλλοι."

This is the only role of Lyrnessus in ancient literature;[22] it is the city sacked by Achilles, the city from which Aineias was rescued by Zeus. When Vergil presents us with an Aeolus who suffers death at the hands of Turnus, the Latin Achilles, after having evaded the Greeks, and specifically the real Achilles, sacker of Priam's realm, an Aeolus who also comes from Lyrnessus and Mt. Ida, and whose epitaph recalls the language of Hector, as well as that of Achilles after the rescue of Aineias, we are perhaps permitted to ask whom this person represents, in the Vergilian setting, and to wonder why all these resonances occur.

I would suggest that in fact Vergil's Aeolus symbolizes the figure he mirrors so markedly, the Homeric Aineias, actually done away with by Turnus, the Latin Achilles, who now finally succeeds, where his Homeric predecessor could not at Lyrnessus and Troy. But it is only the *Homeric* Aineias who is removed in the form of Aeolus. The imbalance created by Turnus' killing an extra warrior, a substitute Aeneias, at the end of the double *aristeia*, disrupts the closure of this otherwise perfectly balanced passage, and creates a suspense that will be resolved at the end of the poem when the new Roman Achilles kills Turnus, who at that point becomes the Latin Hector. What started out as balance becomes very different, as the scales are seen to tip in Aeneas' favor.[23]

Now the Sibyl had of course told Aeneas of the new Achilles:

> another Achilles is now sprung forth in Latium, himself the son of a god.

> alius Latio iam partus Achilles,
> natus et ipse dea.   (6.89–90)

The commentators, since Servius, note that this must be Turnus. Some also point to *Ecl.* 4.34–6:

> there will then be a second Tiphys and a second Argo to carry chosen heroes, there will be another set of wars, and once again will a mighty Achilles be sent to Troy.

> alter erit tum Tiphys et altera quae vehat Argo
> delectos heroas; erunt etiam altera bella
> atque iterum ad Troiam magnus mittetur Achilles.

A second time: *alter...altera...altera...iterum*. Why did the Sibyl not say

The Isolation of Turnus

alter...Achilles, another Achilles for the Trojans to face? Servius adverts to the obliqueness of these words, quoting Vergil's assessment of her speech (100): *obscuris vera involvens*. The Sibyl's words foretell of another Achilles, Turnus, but her words, wrapping truth in obscurity, allow intimation of another (*alius*, potentially a third, rather than a second, *alter*), Aeneas himself: as the Cumaean song of *Ecl.* 4 predicted another Achilles to go to Troy, the Sibyl at Cumae talks of yet another Achilles who comes into being in Latium.[24]

Now to resume the theme of parallelism, it is frequently noted that animal similes are applied to Turnus rather than Aeneas, but that is not always the case.[25] M.C.J. Putnam has studied the connection of the bull similes of *Aeneid* 12 to lines from the *Georgics*, from which the *Aeneid* similes closely draw.[26] Together they conspire to suggest the erotic motivation of Turnus, but not Turnus alone. The first hint comes at 12.101-8, where Turnus is compared to an exiled bull, preparing for its return (cf. *Geo.* 3.232-4); I include the surrounding narrative:

> Turnus is driven by this fury, shooting sparks from his blazing face, fire flashing from his fierce eyes, just as when a bull at the battle's start calls up fearful bellowing or tries putting his anger into his horns by charging a tree trunk, and gores the air with butting or paws the sand, and scatters it in prelude to the fight. Meanwhile, no less savage in his mother's arms, Aeneas sharpens his battle spirit and stirs himself up with anger.

> his agitur furiis [Turnus], totoque ardentis ab ore
> scintillae absistunt, oculis micat acribus ignis,
> mugitus veluti cum prima in proelia taurus
> terrificos ciet aut irasci in cornua temptat
> arboris obnixus trunco, ventosque lacessit   105
> ictibus aut sparsa ad pugnam proludit harena.
> nec minus interea maternis saevus in armis
> Aeneas acuit Martem et se suscitat ira.

Turnus as enraged bull, then. But the continuation of the narrative creates a particular effect: *nec minus interea...acuit* (107-8) looks across the simile to the rage and battle preparation of Turnus before the simile (cf. *acribus*, 102; *acuit*, 108). But in the absence of any mention of Turnus at the close of the simile, and with the postponement of *Aeneas acuit* to 108, the reader is in momentary confusion about the relationships between simile and narrative, for the line *nec minus interea maternis saevus in armis* which in fact will connect Aeneas to Turnus, may seem to be connecting somebody (Aeneas) to the bull. The phrase *nec minus* qualifies *acuit*, but its potential, in the apparent syntactical completeness of 107, to be taken with *saevus* binds to the bull as well as to Turnus. In short, in this passage Turnus is driven by rage, Aeneas is savage and filled with anger; in between is the bull, to whom both men are linked, in a radical shift where the focus of the narrative imperceptibly moves, because of the ambiguity of the frame, from one warrior to the other. Where a simile normally connects the narrative frame in an A–B–A progression, this simile proceeds A–B–C, the effect being to link A (Turnus) and C (Aeneas). This connection prefigures the other exception to the tendency for the similes to distinguish the two warriors: at 12.715 Aeneas and Turnus are equated through the powerful and elaborate simile of bulls fighting for the herd (*Aen.* 12.715–22; cf. 716 *duo...tauri*).[27] For now I would simply note that one of the functions of the simile is to bring the two adversaries into a close connection and confrontation, as the narrative immediately reflects:

> Just so Trojan Aeneas and the Daunian hero clash with their shields, a huge crash fills the sky.

> > non aliter Tros Aeneas et Daunius heros
> > concurrunt clipeis, ingens fragor aethera complet.
> > (723–4)[28]

Nowhere else in the poem does such balance occur between two warriors, and Vergil immediately produces his adaptation of the Homeric scales of Zeus, as the binding and then separation (*aequato... diversa*) of the two occurs on a cosmic level:

> Jupiter himself holds up two scales with equal balance, and puts in the different destinies of the two, whom the struggle dooms and with whose weight death sinks down.

> > Iuppiter ipse duas aequato examine lances
> > sustinet et fata imponit diversa duorum,
> > quem damnet labor et quo vergat pondere letum.
> > (12.725–7)

The final duality (*fata...diversa duorum*) is only apparent, as both relative clauses in reality defer the superficial appearance of duality (*quem...et quo*), referring not to the fates of the two, but to the doom, doubly stated, of Turnus.

If the simply Augustan view of Turnus is all that the genius of Vergil could comprehend, all that the attentive reader is to take away, why muddy that view by equating the two adversaries so, all the while departing from the Homeric precedent and reshaping it precisely to effect connection rather than distinction? I would mention here, but will not pursue, the issue of Turnus' similarity to Dido, a theme that

The Isolation of Turnus

Putnam has covered well. I do agree, though, with Stahl (1990, 180) that Putnam (1965, 193) cannot stand: "It is Aeneas who loses at the end of Book XII, leaving Turnus victorious in his tragedy." That is very definitely a Christian view. Nobody wins at the end of this poem, certainly not Turnus.

Turnus and the Scipios
We have mentioned the initial description of Turnus, and its connecting him to Aeneas (*petit ante alios pulcherrimus omnis* | *Turnus, avis atavisque potens*, *Aen.* 7.54–5). But these words also evoke the death of Turnus. His end is hinted at in his very first mention. He is named, along with reference to his appearance and his lineage. The style and content give the effect of an embedded sepulchral epigram, as is even more strongly the case later in Book 7, after Allecto has had her effect, and as the Rutulians follow their leader into battle:

> This man was moved by the shining glory of his looks and his youth, this by his royal lineage, this by the famous deeds of his right hand.
>
> hunc decus egregium formae movet atque iuventae,
> hunc atavi reges, hunc claris dextera factis.
> (473–4)

Williams (1973) and Fordyce (1977) ad locc. have nothing to say about these lines, which do ennoble Turnus, but they do more than that. Even more than the details at 7.54–5, the subject matter, and the careful rhetorical ordering (*tricolon decrescens* with anaphora of *hunc*, with each colon recording a virtue of Turnus: youthful good looks, ancestry, deeds), all these features conspire to give the impression of sepulchral epigram. We are quite close to the republican political and aesthetic ideal, as reflected in the epitaph of, for instance, L. Cornelius Scipio Barbatus, consul in 298, written in Saturnians some time after his death:

> Cornelius Lucius Scipio Barbatus, son of Gnaeus, wise and brave man, whose looks were the equal of his valor, who was your consul, censor, aedile, captured Taurasia, Cisauna in Samnium, subjugated all Lucania and took hostages.
>
> Cornelius Lucius Scipio Barbatus
> Gnaivod patre | prognatus, fortis vir sapiensque,
> quoius forma virtutei parisuma | fuit,
> consol censor aidilis quei fuit apud vos,
> Taurasia Cisauna Samnio cepit
> subigit omne Loucanam opsidesque abdoucit.
> (*CIL* I² 6, 7 Buecheler, *CLE* 7, Ernout, *Recueil* 13)

R.F. Thomas

In form too, there is an approximation to epigram in Vergil's couplet: the two lines are in a sense a mimesis of an elegiac couplet, with the second line reproducing (as best it can) the pentameter of the elegiac couplet, the meter of epitaph. The strong break at the third foot strong caesura in the second line (i.e., the central break point of the pentameter), along with the fact that by this point a tricolon is clearly under way, produce assimilation to a type of couplet quite common in the real sepulchral tradition, for instance the opening couplet of *CLE* 958, the epitaph of another Scipio, M. Cornelius Scipio Hispanus, praetor peregrinus in 139 BC:

> virtutes generis mieis moribus accumulavi,
> progeniem genui, facta patris petiei.

And again we find lineage and deeds, as with the couplet on Turnus. The style is evident in a number of sepulchral and dedicatory epigrams which consist simply of elegiac couplets showing the same structures; one will serve as an example:[29]

> Patricium domus haec aeterna laude tuetur:
> astra tenent animam, caetera tellus habet.

The same style abounds in the Greek sepulchral tradition,[30] and we even find, in the later Latin tradition, stichic dactylic hexameters producing this mimesis of the elegiac couplet that I am claiming for Vergil:

> hic iacet Helpidius fatis extinctus iniquis
> egregius iuvenis, causarum orator honestus.   (*CLE* 425)

> hic iacet Heraclius nimium dilectus amicus,
> eloquio primus, nulli probitate secundus.   (*CLE* 753)

Buecheler notes of this last example "Vergilii Turnus *haud ulli virtute secundus*", which is highly relevant to the current discussion: the composer of this (Christian) epitaph has adapted Turnus' *devotio*, his consecration of his life to the infernal gods on behalf of his country – again we are in the world of Roman republican military heroism:

  To you and to my father-in-law Latinus, I, Turnus, second in valor to
  none of the men of old, have devoted this life of mine.

> vobis animam hanc soceroque Latino
> Turnus ego, haud ulli veterum virtute secundus,
> devovi.   (11.440–2)

It is difficult not to see, and others have so seen (see Gransden, ad loc.),[31] a reference to the Decii, and their semi-mythical *devotio* of themselves, a paradigm of selfless republican patriotism. C. Bennett Pascal tries to dissuade us from seeing a real *devotio* in the words of Turnus, but as Matthew Leigh argues, Turnus qualifies eminently;[32] nor, as he says, should we "dismiss this as just his self-serving rhetoric".[33] The *ThLL* also weighed in against the natural meaning, feebly making our example a solitary exception to the collection of military devotions: "*aliter* [unspecified as to how] Verg., *Aen*. 11.442".[34] At the moment of the *devotio*, regardless of whether it will be played out to its end, the Roman reader will have sensed republican military heroism. Indeed, with Turnus' words *haud ulli veterum virtute secundus*, focalized from the time of Vergil, with "deviant focalization", if we will, the *veteres* to whom Turnus claims to be equal, will in a sense be republicans, even the Decii, *veteres* from the perspective of Vergilian time.[35] Vergil, then, from the very beginning, gives us intimations of the doom of Turnus, and he does so in terms strongly reminiscent of heroic, Roman, republican death.

Turnus and Allecto
Some, like Stahl, more or less ignore the early appearance of Turnus, preferring to analyze his character only from the perspective of its state after the visitation of Allecto.[36] There is unlikely to be resolution of the issue of what Allecto represents, a metaphor for Turnus' inherent and innate rage, disorder and godlessness, or the imposition, comprehensible in a system in which the gods function as characters who cause certain effects and produce certain results among mortals, of a destructive force that suits the design of Juno. I will not engage this question at any great length, but would state that when the narrative has a deity, specifically Juno, send a Fury against a character in a poem, and when that Fury is described as physically coming to that character and inflaming him with rage, criticism which ignores the external aspects of that carefully elaborated act in its interpretation of the nature of the character in question will not be sufficient.

Rhipsaspia
Again, I am not contesting the fact that Turnus acts against the will of Jupiter. We will examine later whether Turnus in fact realizes that the cosmos and its ruler are against him, and what I am now suggesting is that focusing solely, or even predominantly, on the rage and anger of Turnus is a huge simplification of the complexity of Vergil. That simplification is most apparent in the reaction of Augustan readers to the arms of Turnus, another area in which he is clearly parallel in

some fashion to Aeneas:

> Turnus himself, outstanding in physique, moves armed among the chiefs, a whole head higher than the rest. His tall helmet, crested with triple plume, supports a Chimaera breathing Aetna's fire from her jaws; the more the fight grows with blood poured forth the more she rages savage with her gloomy fires. But on his smooth shield is imprinted Io with horns upraised, already grown over with bristles, already a heifer, a momentous portrayal, and Argus, guardian of the girl, and her father Inachus pouring out his river from engraved urn.

> ipse inter primos praestanti corpore Turnus
> vertitur arma tenens et toto uertice supra est.
> cui triplici crinita iuba galea alta Chimaeram
> sustinet Aetnaeos efflantem faucibus ignis;
> tam magis illa fremens et tristibus effera flammis
> quam magis effuso crudescunt sanguine pugnae.
> at levem clipeum sublatis cornibus Io
> auro insignibat, iam saetis obsita, iam bos,
> argumentum ingens, et custos virginis Argus,
> caelataque amnem fundens pater Inachus urna.
> (7.783–92)

Two lines introduce Turnus, with four lines for the helmet, with its depiction of the Chimaera, and four for the shield, on which is figured the metamorphosed Io.

The treatment of Philip Hardie is instructive.[37] Building on earlier Augustan readings of the description,[38] he first notes as others have the parallel between the shield of Aeneas (with its "depiction of the political values for which Aeneas stands") with the depiction of Turnus' "figured helmet and shield", concluding, rightly, that "the positioning of the two arming scenes, at the ends of the seventh and eighth books respectively, invites comparison between the two". As a precursor to his next chapter, which studies the last four books of the *Aeneid* as the "working out of the Gigantomachic image on a strictly human level", he finds, reasonably, that:

> In the Vergilian version of this war of images the chthonic and Gigantomachic threat posed by Turnus is countered by the Olympian defeat of Gigantic forces on the Shield of Aeneas.

But in quietly moving as he does from stating a parallel between Aeneas' shield and Turnus' helmet and shield, to Turnus's helmet, he avoids having to mention Turnus' actual shield (he only cites 783–8, on the helmet), which one would think might also bear *some* comparison with the shield of Aeneas. But you cannot tell from Hardie's

400 pages that Turnus carries anything into battle other than a helmet depicting the Chimaera, and a shield of some sort. Io is nowhere to be found, in the text, or in the index (where "Chimaera" receives two entries).[39] All that *Cosmos and Imperium* tells us of the armor of Turnus is that it depicted the Chimaera.

That is one way to deal with Io, the ancestress of Turnus, she who was raped by Aeneas' ancestor, Jupiter (we will look to Juturna later) and then infuriated by the gadfly, inflicted by Juno, dispatcher of Allecto against Turnus.[40] S.G.P. Small found another procedure. With good bibliography and careful research she shows that Vergil, by placing the Chimaera on Turnus' helmet, connotes for the wearer a chthonic, irrational, violent nature: "Under the influence of Juno and the Fury [that, at least, is conceded], Turnus' personality has undergone a terrible transformation; it has become a force for evil, as disorganized, divided and (in terms of Vergil's theology) unnatural as the image of the monstrous Chimaera upon his helmet."[41]

So far, much like Hardie, who cites Small. But what about Io? Small gets rid of her in a different way: it is not Vergil who has chosen the icon (as he apparently *did* with the Chimaera), but rather Turnus, a distinction that finds no justification from the text. Here is Small: "We can readily understand why Turnus has chosen this emblem...Turnus has therefore adopted this blazon...Turnus thinks of himself as a kind of second Achilles (9.742)."[42] Although Small allows some of the connections between Io and Turnus ("it must be admitted that the Io emblem gives the reader a much more favorable impression of Turnus' character than does the fire-breathing Chimaera"), she proceeds to make some distinctions: Io was simply sinned against – "She does no one any harm" she says, and, "Through Epaphus, Io becomes the ancestress of a glorious line of kings and heroes." Turnus, on the other hand, "though equally a victim...is far from harmless. He is transformed into an instrument of destruction." Small concludes that "the discrepancies between the fate of Turnus and that of his great ancestress are so striking that they make a mockery of the claims implied by his wearing the image of Io on his shield". This interpretation is utterly fanciful. Io is on the shield; she is closely associated with Turnus, and later in the narrative she will in a sense "return," in the form of Turnus' sister, Juturna. We will also see Jupiter, who has to do with all three mortals, Jupiter who for Small has been transformed in the *Aeneid* from the rapist to something lofty and almost Christian – "The evolved Jupiter whose will [Turnus] opposes is no tyrant but a wise and just god." Go ask Juturna, whose rape by Jupiter is twice mentioned in *Aen.* 12 (140–1, 878), the second time subsequent to the final appearance of Jupiter. For Io and the shield, then, we have either Hardie's silence or Small's paradigm shift and attempt to argue away the relevance of Io to Turnus. Hardie does not mention Small's article except in relation to the Chimaera, which I take as confirmation of the weakness of her attempt to distinguish Io from Turnus.

The duality must be allowed to stand, and to remain in the poem, until its last line. The duality and contrast is there, as the word *at* (789) shows. Io is on the shield, placed there by the narrator and the poet, and appropriate to the warrior who will, like his ancestress, suffer at the hands of Jupiter, and of Juno.

Simile and the Augustan reading

We have already seen two similes and their surrounding narrative that have the effect of equating Turnus and Aeneas. Other similes of Book 12 seem to me, at least in many of their details, to work against a simply Augustan reading of Turnus and Aeneas, to take us out of the easy conclusions that such a reading is always trying to make. They do so in two further ways: by embedding disconsonant elements that work against the simply Augustan reading; by the invocation of frailty and pathos precisely where the Augustan, and the traditionally heroic, narrative calls for weighting the scale in favor of Aeneas. Simile, I will suggest, becomes a vehicle for subverting the epic's authoritative voice.

As for the embedding in a simile of material that deflects the Augustan reading, the very first simile of Book 12 provides a well-known example:

> As in the Punic fields a lion, his breast deeply wounded by hunters, only then is stirred to war and rejoices to shake his flowing mane from its neck, and fearlessly breaks off the weapon the brigand has stuck in him, and roars with bloody mouth: just so does violence take fire and grow in Turnus.

> > Poenorum qualis in arvis
> > saucius ille gravi venantum vulnere pectus
> > tum demum movet arma leo, gaudetque comantis
> > excutiens cervice toros fixumque latronis
> > impavidus frangit telum et fremit ore cruento:
> > haud secus accenso gliscit violentia Turno.
> > > (12.4–9)

Brooks Otis drew attention to the fact that the simile presents Turnus as a *wounded* lion – the simile is Homeric (*Il.* 20.164 ff., though Achilles, the lion figure there, is not wounded); in this respect Turnus is very much like the Dido of Book 4 who is compared, of course, to a wounded doe (4.68–73), and, in the simile of *Aen.* 12, there may be significance in the lion's location *Poenorum...in arvis* (Dido's territory). The designation perhaps takes us back also to *Georgics* 3.249, where Vergil talks of the danger of wild animals afflicted by the fire and madness of passion: "ah, a bad time that to wander in Libyan fields!", *heu male tum Libyae solis erratur in agris.*[43] Otis does not here go along with Pöschl's claim, which obviously seems right to me, for Turnus' original innocence. Another detail of the simile that disrupts any straightforwardly Augustan status for the simile, is the designation of the lion's antagonist as a *latro* (12.7), a "robber", "brigand", with its probable etymological root of "mercenary" frequently felt. It is difficult not to identify Aeneas with this *latro*, at least on some level.[44] Williams' comment, ad loc., is a fairly typical way of proceeding when the language of this poet becomes difficult:

> 7. *latronis*: 'the huntsman', an unusual sense of the word, which normally means 'brigand'.

As with Turnus' *devotio*, unsubstantiated philological assertion resolves the issue. The support in this case comes from Servius (LATRONIS *insidiatoris, a latendo; sed* modo venatoris) quoted with other material by the *ThLL*, which on this basis produces a separate class of meaning for the word, occurring only at 12.7:[45] "*audacius de venatore*: Verg. aen. 12,7." This category is produced by a philological collective simply so we may avoid associating "Aeneas" and "*latro*", but that is what we must do, for it is what Vergil has done.

But it is in the second typology, that of the disturbing detail, that Vergil takes the reader to a point where the simply Augustan reading is hard to sustain. I have in mind the simile and narrative of 12.473–8. As Aeneas closes in on Turnus, tracking him through the gloom (466–7), Juturna, terrified for her brother, replaces and takes on the form of his charioteer, Metiscus, and proceeds to pick her way through the battlefield so as to keep Turnus from battle. In an apparently original simile, a rarity for Vergil, Juturna is compared to a swallow (12.473–8). As commentators note, the simile is markedly Roman, with the rich man's house (*divitis aedes*), with its atria, porticoes and pools. What is noteworthy for our purposes is that the simile is a complete focalizing of the emotions of Juturna: (*pabula parva legens nidisque loquacibus escas*) – the swallow's actions are tied to the needs of her family, and the simile converts that family from warrior brother to hungry nestlings, elsewhere in Vergil the victims of aggression, usually by agricultural man, man in the age of Jupiter (*Geo.* 2.207–11). This aspect of the simile may seem inappropriate until we realize the state Turnus is entering – "As flies to wanton boys…'

Details of the swallow simile are particularly marked in that there is no model for it; the last major simile of the Book gains power particularly from its distinction from its model, it is one of the most powerful moments in all of Vergil, and it takes us far from the Augustan reading. Turnus has just failed in his attempt to throw the rock:

> And as in our dreams, when drooping rest has pressed our eyes with night, we seem vainly to want to push forward our eager course, and in mid effort worn out we sink down; our tongue is powerless, gone from our body is the familiar strength, nor do voice or words come forth: so for Turnus…

> > ac velut in somnis, oculos ubi languida pressit
> > nocte quies, nequiquam avidos extendere cursus
> > velle videmur et in mediis conatibus aegri
> > succidimus; non lingua valet, non corpore notae
> > sufficiunt vires nec vox aut verba sequuntur:
> > sic Turno…   (12.908–13)

Critics point to the model, the simile occurring as Hector is pursued by Achilles:

> As in a dream a man cannot pursue one who runs away, nor can the one escape nor the other pursue him, so that he cannot run and catch him, nor the other get away.

> > ὡς δ' ἐν ὀνείρῳ οὐ δύναται φεύγοντα διώκειν·
> > οὔτ' ἄρ' ὁ τὸν δύναται ὑποφεύγειν οὔθ' ὁ διώκειν·
> > ὣς ὁ τὸν οὐ δύνατο μάρψαι ποσίν, οὐδ' ὃς ἀλύξαι.
> >   (*Il.* 22.199–201)

Some critics also point to the differences, though none that I have found is sufficiently emphatic about those differences. We are again dealing with focalization, or point of view: Vergil has removed the Achilles figure and the reciprocity of the dream (pursuer cannot catch pursued, nor can pursued evade pursuer).[46] The focus is simply and squarely on Turnus, whose efforts, and whose efforts alone, fail. In that distinction there is a world of difference. Williams notes the application just to Turnus, and also observes that Vergil "has retained the eerie impression of an unreal world and strengthened it by applying it personally with the use of the first person verbs *videmur*, *succidimus*."[47] But surely this change does more than that. This simile is unique in Vergil, and the uniqueness resides in the introduction of first persons. The effect of these is to involve Vergil, and us as readers, precisely in the failure of Turnus: he has become one of us, a very human creature, who has just realized that the cosmic order is against him. The simile, and in particular its distinctions from the Homeric model, align Vergil, Turnus and the reader in a shared focalization, the point of view of the victim.[48]

Turnus and prognostication

Turnus' realization of his desperate status comes just 12 lines before the simile, with his response to Aeneas at 12.894–5:

> Your angry words do not terrify me, fierce one; it is the gods that terrify me, and having Jupiter as my foe.

> > non me tua fervida terrent
> > dicta, ferox; di me terrent et Iuppiter hostis.

For the first time, his analysis of the situation is correct. Now this revelation comes soon after his sister Juturna has withdrawn, driven off by the Jove-sent Fury, as he echoes her lament, and shares her recognition of the reality that is about to oppress him:

> Do not terrify my fearful soul, ill-omened birds: I recognize the deadly sound of their beating wings, nor do the haughty commands of high-minded Jove escape me.

> > ne me *terrete* timentem,
> > obscenae volucres: alarum verbera nosco
> > letalemque sonum, nec fallunt iussa superba
> > magnanimi Iovis.

Relevant here is the contrast between Turnus' final recognition and his delusion elsewhere in the poem, for instance at 9.128–9, where he supposes, I would think quite reasonably from *his* perspective, that in doing away with the Trojan ships (they turn into Nymphs), the gods are supportive of the Italians:

> These signs attack the Trojans, from whom Jupiter himself has taken away his usual help.

> > Troianos haec monstra petunt, his Iuppiter ipse
> > auxilium solitum eripuit.

Hardie, who well connected the two passages, called this a "boastful reaction" to the metamorphosis; but it seems to me more in the nature of an interpretation, and one which is reasonable – the Trojans have been deprived of their ships from his point of view – if wrong.[49] And we as readers know that it is wrong, having been aware for several books that the miraculous ships are firmly on the side of Aeneas; the result is a strong instance of the "isolating" of Turnus, whose ignorance is in contrast to the knowledge of the reader as of the other characters of the poem. Likewise at 9.133-4, in diction which ominously prefigures his final recognition of Jupiter's hostility, Turnus states that he does not fear whatever fates the Phrygians boast of (*nil me fatalia terrent | si qua Phryges prae se iactant*), but will drive the guilty race from his land. Hardie (ad 9.133-4) connects this "rash dismissal of the gods' fate-revealing oracle" with Turnus' "panic-striken recognition of the truth at the end of the epic". The extreme Augustan interpretation fails however to allow a focalization of the situation from Turnus' viewpoint, a failing not shared by Vergil. Turnus is not dismissing any "gods' fate-revealing oracles". Rather he is claiming they are false, Trojan propaganda (*si qua Phryges prae se iactant*). He distinguishes his rival's mother from the rest of the gods, and he claims the validity of his own fates and his role as expeller of the invaders and avenger of his thwarted nuptials.

Turnus is wrong, but that is a very different matter, and it is worth enquiring what aid he has had to guide him to the truth and inevitability of his diminished state? On the divine level, he is quite simply alone from the beginning, and in this he is markedly distinct from Aeneas. Hardie (1994) at one point refers to Turnus' ignorance as to divine activity: "he presumably does not know that it took the same god to destroy [the walls of Troy], a fact known only too well to Aeneas after the vision granted him by Venus" (ad 9.145). One could repeat that statement at a number of points through the poem. Juno uses Turnus, sends him apparitions and Furies so he will further her plan, while Aeneas receives help at every turn (from Venus, the Penates, the Sibyl, Anchises, Tiber), and he does so because his destiny is Rome's. But what sort of world is it that in the context of that necessity presents a figure who fails to see true signs and who misinterprets because of insufficient help? We should keep in mind that the original prophecy of 7.68-70 is presented to Latinus, not to Turnus, who has no personal autopsy. Nor does Vergil anywhere tell us that Latinus informed him of it; Rumor circulated it (7.102-6). The question is not whether the prophecy occurred, but whether Turnus is ever helped by divine signs.

On the contrary, Turnus receives Allecto, disguised as the aged (and real) Chalybe, and Turnus (reasonably) misinterprets the ship metamorphosis. In contrast to the help Aeneas received from Tiber and from Venus in the opening and closing frames of Book 8, at 9.1-24 Iris, sent to Turnus by Juno as she was to the dying Dido in the poem's mirrored position at the very end of *Aen.* 4, encourages him that

The Isolation of Turnus

military activity is timely; her closing words are particularly urgent:

> Now is the time to call for horses, now for chariots. End all delays and seize the camp in its turmoil.

> nunc tempus equos, nunc poscere currus.
> rumpe moras omnis et turbata arripe castra.

Turnus recognizes Iris (9.16 *agnovit*), ponders the omen, and responds appropriately by accepting it after due deliberation ("I follow these great omens, whoever you are that calls me into arms", *sequor omina tanta, quisquis in arma vocas*, 9.21–2).[50] Unlike Aeneas, he is unaware of who sent Iris, but the omen and words of Iris encourage him to proceed, and his decision, if wrong, is again not unreasonable. Similarly at 12.620–30 he receives encouragement to proceed into battle from Juturna (disguised as his charioteer Metiscus), like Iris sent by Juno (628–35). Although Turnus has long recognized his advisor (*et dudum agnovi*), and although the deception of Juturna does not work (*et nunc nequiquam fallis dea*), he is less sure of the reasons for her presence, as he wonders which of the Olympians has sent her to share in his troubles (634–5 *sed quis Olympo | demissam tantos voluit te ferre labores?*). But by the end of this speech, even before he hears of the capture of Latinus' city and the death of Amata, Turnus realizes his isolation, as he prays to the only gods he is sure of, the shades of his ancestors:

> O you shades below, be kind to me, since the gods above have turned away their favor.

> vos o mihi, Manes,
> este boni, quoniam superis aversa voluntas.[51]
> (12.646–7)

He is not far from the self-knowledge of his final recognition: *di me terrent et Iuppiter hostis* (895).

Tolumnius, who urged the Latins to break the treaty – in the absence of Turnus it should be stressed – likewise failed as an interpreter.[52] Here too Juno-sent Juturna was the instrument, sending the portent of the swans' eviction of the eagle. Tolumnius recognises and accepts the omen (*accipio agnoscoque deos*, 12.260), taking it, reasonably but wrongly, to indicate that Aeneas can be driven out.

I would like to look at a final instance of failed interpretation, again where Turnus reacts reasonably from the perspective of *signa*, but perhaps wrongly. I speak of Lavinia's blush, virtually the only thing for which she is known in the poem, to which, paradoxically, she is so central. Critics are concerned mostly with the meaning, absolutely stated, of her blush; mine is with the reception of the blush, specifically the reception by Turnus. The lines in question are *Aen.* 12.54–71: Amata begs Turnus, only respite of her old age, and last defense of the house of Latinus, to quit battle with the Trojans; she will die with him rather than see Aeneas as a son-in-law (*nec generum Aenean captiua uidebo*, 63). The focus then shifts immediately to Lavinia, who reacts famously:

> Lavinia heard her mother's speech, her burning cheeks wet with tears, as a deep blush kindled its fire and spread across her heated face.
>
> > accepit vocem lacrimis Lauinia matris
> > flagrantis perfusa genas, cui plurimus ignem   65
> > subiecit rubor et calefacta per ora cucurrit.

Then the simile (67–9) and another abrupt change of focus to the famous reaction of Turnus:

> He, thrown into a turmoil of love, fixes his gaze on the girl; he burns all the more for battle and briefly addresses Amata...
>
> > illum turbat amor figitque in uirgine uultus;
> > ardet in arma magis paucisque adfatur Amatam...
> >   (12.70–1)

Recently critics have been concerned with the aetiology of Lavinia's blush. Todd has argued that she blushes at the mention of Aeneas' name,[53] while Putnam believed and Lyne has argued emphatically that she loves Turnus.[54] Or, of course, as Cairns notes,[55] she may simply be embarrassed to be talked about so by her mother (whose own love is perhaps more in question!). Since Vergil chose not to specify the cause of the blush of this character, who is given no words to help us form a judgement, to ask what the blush "means" is possibly fruitless – and it is a question to which Vergil allows no clear response. It might be better first to change the focus and ask precisely how Turnus read the blush, for read it he certainly did. Clearly he took the blush as indicating an interest in him, fathering (or mothering) the disdain of Amata for Aeneas on to Lavinia: *illum turbat amor figitque in uirgine uultus;* | *ardet in arma magis.*[56] The fact that Vergil is deliberately obscure about the reason for the blush, but has it come immediately after mention of the name of Aeneas, allows the reader to do what Turnus did not, namely to connect the blush to the name of Aeneas. The possibility, suggested by Todd, that the blush is occasioned by the name of Aeneas, coupled with the possibility that Turnus misreads the blush

The Isolation of Turnus

which in reality is evoked by the word *Aenean*,[57] this possibility humanizes and renders intensely pathetic the whole sequence:[58] the "lover" for whom Turnus fought had her mind elsewhere. Cairns accepts Todd's reading but sees it as an Augustan feature, a sign of the greatness and triumph of Aeneas,[59] but in the context the focus is elsewhere: we are back in the world of supplanted lovers, of Alexis and Corydon, Lycoris and Gallus, as we will soon be back in the world of Meliboeus.

The need and the ability to prognosticate and to interpret comes with the age of Jupiter, as the *Georgics* teaches us. It is, perhaps, not surprising that Turnus, part of the race of Saturn, seems not to have these skills. It is time to look at Jupiter and his agents as they affect Turnus. The words of two critics are fairly representative: "[Turnus] causes tremendous suffering and loss as the principal human abettor of a war that Jupiter has forbidden and which he regards as basically impious. The evolved Jupiter [compared to the one who raped Io] whose will he opposes is no tyrant but a wise and just god."[60] Here is another: "Far from seeing in Turnus a hero dying for Italy, the *Aeneid* presents him as a rebel against the gods."[61] And the entire book of Hardie is a similar enterprise, positively depicting the triumph of Jupiter as Gigantomachy. Without denying any of this, I would like again to conclude by looking at this issue with a different focalization, for that is what Vergil did as he depicted the process whereby Turnus came to realize that he was the enemy of Jupiter.

After the wound of Aeneas has been healed by Venus, Aeneas rises up, and first instructs Ascanius in the lessons to be learnt from his father (435–6): "from me learn courage and the true toil, fortune from others", *disce, puer, virtutem ex me verumque laborem | fortunam ex aliis*. The contrast is between *labor* and *fortuna* in particular, a contrast which has a role in Vergil's larger cultural poetics. Aeneas here presents the superiority of *labor*, a term which necessarily conjures up the ethics of the age of Jupiter, the age of toil from the *Georgics*. Conversely the *fortuna* which unspecified "others" can teach, has a Saturnian look to it: so at 11.252 Diomedes had addressed the Italians: "*o fortunatae gentes, Saturnia regna...*" Aeneas's words, as he goes back out into the battle which will end with the death of the man who will recognize that Jupiter is his foe, are in fact the beginning of a process whereby the gap between Jupiter and Aeneas is elided; Aeneas in a sense *becomes* Jupiter, and is not simply his agent. This process Vergil effects by clear dictional suggestion. Juturna is the first to sense Aeneas as he thunders across the plain, as she retreats in fear (*prima ante omnis Iuturna Latinos | audiit agnovitque sonum et tremefacta refugit*, 12.448–9). This language, it seems to me, constitutes another instance of what some call "deviant focalization", that is the use of an epithet or description that conjures up an image outside the immediate logical narrative.[62] The words look like a description of Juturna's reaction not to Aeneas, but to Jupiter himself, in time gone by, when he raped her (12.141–2, 878). This possibility becomes stronger in the lines immediately following, one of narrative, followed by five of simile:

> Off he flies and sweeps his dark column across the open plain. As when heaven bursts and a storm cloud goes landward through mid-ocean (ah, the farmers long prescient shudder in their hearts: it will bring ruin to trees and destruction to crops, uprooting everything far and wide), before it fly the winds bringing the din to the shores.
>
> > ille volat campoque atrum rapit agmen aperto.
> > qualis ubi ad terras abrupto sidere nimbus
> > it mare per medium (miseris, heu, praescia longe
> > horrescunt corda agricolis: dabit ille ruinas
> > arboribus stragemque satis, ruet omnia late),
> > ante volant sonitumque ferunt ad litora venti.
> >   (12.450–5)

Various scholars have looked at the significance of storms, and Hardie in particular has useful observations on the significance of storms in the *Aeneid*, which he connects to the hurling of thunderbolts, *fulmina*.[63] But only Briggs has connected it to one which is perhaps more relevant than others, the great storm of *Georgics* 1.316–35, a storm which is likewise destructive of crops and strikes terror into the hearts of men.[64] Briggs notes of the *Aeneid* simile, "Aeneas himself becomes the storm." So he does, but there is more to it than that. What is significant about the storm of the *Georgics* is the central role played by Jupiter, paradoxically involved in destroying the agricultural works of his own culture. He hurls the thunderbolts (*fulmina molitur*, 329), and he terrifies the hearts of mortals (*mortalia corda*), just as Aeneas as storm would do in *Aeneid* 12: *miseris, heu, praescia longe horrescunt corda agricolis*. These farmers have even read the prognostic material of the *Georgics*, it seems; their hearts are *praescia longe*. Viewed from the perspective of this earlier Vergilian scheme, Aeneas not only becomes the storm, he becomes Jupiter.

Aeneas proceeds to destroy the city of Latinus, urging on his men, and here too the space between him and Jupiter becomes elided: "let there be no delay to my commands; here stands Jupiter" (*ne qua meis esto dictis mora, Iuppiter hac stat*, 12.565–9). *Iuppiter hac stat* – "we have God on our side". But a more ambiguous meaning emerges: "here stands Jupiter". The destruction of the city takes us back to the assault on Troy, and Aeneas himself (*ipse*, 579) joins in that destruction, just as long before, Jupiter himself (2.617–18 *ipse pater ... ipse*) joined in the destruction of Troy.

Readers will hardly be surprised, then, a few lines later when Saces comes to Turnus and informs him of Aeneas' attack on the city. The transformation of Aeneas is emphatic:

> Aeneas thunders in arms and threatens to hurl down the highest citadels of Italy and consign them to destruction, and already firebrands are flying at the rooftops.
>
> > fulminat Aeneas armis summasque minatur
> > deiecturum arces Italum excidioque daturum,
> > iamque faces ad tecta volant.
> >   (12. 654–6)

Fulminare inevitably conjures up Aeneas' ancestor, Jupiter; all other fulminators are metaphorical representatives of the god, whom we last saw performing precisely this act in the storm simile of *Georgics* 1 (*ipse pater media nimborum in nocte corusca | fulmina molitur dextra*, 328–9).[65] But it also conjures up his descendant, Octavian, at the end of the *Georgics* bringing his thunderbolts to the Euphrates after the Battle of Actium (*Caesar dum magnus ad altum fulminat |Euphraten, Geo.* 4.560–1). Jupiter, Augustus and Aeneas are all connected through this image, and it is the weight they amass that terrifies Turnus at the moment of his recognition. This nexus, moreover, renders a special force to Saces' words: *summasque minatur | deiecturum arces Italum excidioque daturum*. Would a Roman reader think of Perusia? Did Vergil? Small, an Augustan reader, observes of Turnus:

> The torment of his closing days on earth is barren. It only lays bare the fact that he is basically unworthy to participate in the new order of life in Italy. He lives just long enough to discover the shattering truth that all along he has been no more than an impediment to the making of a better world and that as such he is the enemy of Jupiter.

While the assessment of which world is better is a matter of point of view, these words seem true to Vergil's account of Turnus at the end of the *Aeneid*, as a version of them was true of Meliboeus at the end of the First *Eclogue*. It is one of the marks of Vergil's poetic genius that he insists on showing us how it feels to be the enemy of Jupiter.

R.F. Thomas

Notes

Professor Stahl was kind enough to invite me to a conference on "Vergil's *Aeneid*: Augustan Epic and Political Context" (Pittsburgh, 8/9 September, 1995), at which I delivered this paper; he subsequently provided thorough and challenging criticism, almost all of which I have taken to heart. The whole process of friendly collaboration within the context of frankly stated intellectual differences has been most encouraging.

[1] Cf. Stahl (1990) 174–211.

[2] Stahl (1981) makes very similar points. Older scholarship is generally for seeing Turnus simply as a figure of violence, in contrast to Aeneas the man of *pietas*.

[3] Cf. O'Hara (1990) *passim*.

[4] Pöschl (1977) 127.

[5] Pöschl (1962) 94.

[6] While Stahl (1990, 175) speaks of "sacrilegious Turnus who associates with such telltale characters as King Mezentius", Vergil in fact keeps the two apart; in the tradition of Cato, however (see Serv. ad *Aen.* 1.267, 4.620), they are closely linked. The two never meet in the *Aeneid*, and are at opposite ends of the Latin catalogue of *Aen.* 7.

[7] So Conte (1986) 157.

[8] Augustus, and the Augustan Vergilian, have an escape clause in the following sentence of the *Res Gestae*: *externas gentes, quibus tuto ignosci potuit, conservare quam excidere malui* – where *tuto* allows interpretation and justification of the withholding of *clementia*.

[9] This is particularly true of Galinsky (1988), (1994).

[10] Cf. Fordyce ad 7.56, with bibliography.

[11] The commentators refer to *Od.* 5.297 λύτο γούνατα (of Odysseus, also fearful), but Knauer rightly adds *Il.* 15.435 λύντο δὲ γυῖα (death of Lycophron) – in fact the more precise equivalent of *solvuntur (frigore) membra*.

[12] Putnam (1965) 200–1; also Nethercut (1968) 87.

[13] Nethercut (1968) 87.

[14] Stahl (1990) 200.

[15] On this, with references to the scholarship, see Feeney (1992) 35–7.

[16] As many have noted: e.g., Heinze (1993) 215, n. 25.

[17] Willcock (1983) 93–7.

[18] Gransden (1984) also has a good discussion of these lines, and of the way (noted by Willcock too) that Vergil intentionally confuses Turnus and Aeneas with his alternation of *hic...ille*, a confusion noted elsewhere by Servius, on 10.747–54 *hoc loco est confusio in aliquibus nominibus. nam quis sit Troianus, quis sit Rutulus, ignoratur*. For this see Willcock (1983) 94–5.

[19] Oddly, having shown pretty much the same sort of blending I claim here, Willcock reacts emotionally to Turnus' decapitation of two warriors (something Aeneas had done in Book 10, though without taking possession of the head; rather just taunting it): "How anyone can feel a strong sympathy for Turnus in his weakness at the end of Book 12 escapes me. The man is a thug." Would Willcock allow moderate sympathy? Willcock's words are used

centrally by Galinsky (1988) 323.

[20] Edwards, ad loc. (cf. 22.127-8, also in the mouth of Hector; 23.641-2).

[21] Certainly Knauer (1979, 429) indicates the connection.

[22] Cf. also *Il.* 2.690, 691; 19.60, where it is mentioned in connection with Briseis. It otherwise next appears once in the scholia to Eur. *Androm.* 1, in Strabo 13.584, 612, and here in Vergil. Cf. also *Aen.* 10.128: *Lyrnesius Acmon.*

[23] Stahl (1990) 193 n. 24 attempts to remove the parallels between Hector and Turnus as being meaningful in any way, but generally scholars allow the parallel; cf. Hardie (1986) 150.

[24] Austin prefers ablative *Latio* to dative, and of course syntactical obscurity is naturally a part of the Sibyl's style.

[25] See Pöschl (1977) 131-2 (= 1962, 98-9) for a useful listing of the various similes.

[26] Cf. Putnam (1965) 182-6.

[27] Again, well treated by Putnam from the perspective of amatory motivation.

[28] The style of 12.502 (*Turnus...Troius heros*) is inverted in 723 (*Aeneas... Daunius heros*), which again brings out their proximity to each other.

[29] 875, 901, 991, 992, 1023, 1063, 1104, 1129, 1194, 1274, 1277.

[30] *Anth. Pal.* 7.28, 134, 257 (rhyme in the pentameter); 292 (rhyme); 333; 350 (rhyme); 469 (rhyme); 474 (rhyme); 676.

[31] Cf. also O'Hara (1990) 82-5; Hardie (1993) 28-9.

[32] Pascal (1990) 251-68; Leigh (1993) 89-110.

[33] Leigh (1993) 104.

[34] *ThLL* 5.4.882.4-5 s.v. *devoveo*.

[35] A milder form of this type of metapoetics, and the chronological reverse of the current instance, is to be found at *Aen.* 3.158, 409, 505, where the use of *nepotes* by Aeneas, not yet on Italian soil, looks to the Roman future. The observations for Book 3 I owe to the paper by Reinhold Glei in this volume.

[36] Strikingly, Stahl (1990) at one point (182) has an interlocutor object that Turnus "had just before [going to war] been deprived of his sense by the Fury Allecto sent by Juno (7.406-66)". To which Stahl replies, "To such a sceptical reader I would, before explaining the Fury's allegorical character and function, suggest that he join me in tracing three other strands which likewise come together in the final scene of the epic." He never again, in the remaining thirty pages of his article, mentions or explains her character or function, although he informs me *per litteras* that this matter is addressed in the larger project from which the 1990 article is an "excerpted prepublication"

[37] Hardie (1986) 118-9.

[38] Small (1959) 243-52; Buchheit (1963) 111.

[39] Oddly, even the more balanced Pöschl (1977, 128-9 [= (1962), 96]) mentions only the Chimaera.

[40] Small (1959) 250-1 actually seems to allow some of these parallels, but see below.

[41] Small (1959) 249.

[42] Small (1959) 249; so does the Sibyl, of course (6.89-90).

[43] Cf. Otis (1964) 372-3.

[44] Pascal (1990, 268) wants to think of the Latins as the *venantes* and the *latro*

of the simile, an indication that *latro* bothers him. Any reader who identifies the *leo* as Turnus, as all readers surely do, and is then able to exclude Aeneas (cf. 12.14 *Dardanium*), works against the simile's Latin.

[45] *ThLL* s.v. *latro*, 1016.10.

[46] Here I differ from Putnam (1965, 199), for whom "the [Homeric] dream is really Hector's alone".

[47] Williams (1973) ad loc.

[48] Cf. Conte (1986) 156–7 for the point of view of the victim.

[49] Hardie (1986) 148; in his commentary he refers to the *audacia* (apparently bad) of Turnus at this point, although he does concede that the favorable interpretation of Turnus is a good piece of military tactics.

[50] Hardie (ad 9.19–21), suggests that Turnus is somehow deranged ("can we even be sure that he is not 'seeing things' [stars in broad daylight?], as the omen is not narrated directly?"), but there is no basis for this; the veil of day is parted to reveal the stars behind them, a reasonable if hyperbolic characterization of the rainbow.

[51] Cf. Williams (1973) ad loc. for the contrast between *Manes* and *superis*.

[52] Vergil seems to remove Turnus from this act.

[53] Cf. Todd (1980) 27–33. [On Lavinia's blush see also Fantham in this volume, p. 146 f. – editor's cross-reference.]

[54] Cf. Lyne (1987) 114–22, referring to an earlier work.

[55] Cf. Cairns (1989) 159.

[56] This perhaps explains why Vergil assigns Amata quasi-erotic language in her address to Turnus; that lays the foundation for the ambiguous blush.

[57] Cf. *OLD*, s.v. *vox*, 7, 10, for the ambiguity and the possibility that the *vocem* that evokes the blush could refer either to Amata's utterance, or to the "word" *Aenean*.

[58] So Todd (1980) 30: "He has added a poignant footnote to the self-delusion of which he is a victim." Cf. too Anderson (1969) 116: "We see how Turnus is moved, but his wild emotions may completely misinterpret the situation."

[59] Cf. Cairns (1989) 153.

[60] Cf. Small (1959) 251.

[61] Cf. Stahl (1990) 177.

[62] See Fowler (1990). I am not sure "deviation" is the ideal term; perhaps rather "focalizational trespass".

[63] Hardie (1986) 178 ff.

[64] Cf. Briggs (1980); he sees an "*hantise verbale*" in the similarity of *sata laeta*, *Geo.* 1.325, and *satis...late*, *Aen.* 12.454.

[65] See Hardie (1986) 148 for an Augustan reading of these same passages.

Bibliography

Anderson, W.S.
   1969   *The Art of the Aeneid*, Englewood Cliffs, N.J.
Briggs, W.W.
   1980   *Narrative and Simile*, Mnemosyne Supp. 58.

Buchheit, V.
   1963   *Vergil über die Sendung Roms*, Gymnasium Beiheft 3.

Cairns, F.
   1989   *Virgil's Augustan Epic*, Cambridge.

Conte, G.B.
   1986   *The Rhetoric of Imitation: Genre and Poetic Memory in Virgil and Other Latin Poets*, Ithaca.

Feeney, D.C.
   1991   *The Gods in Epic*, Oxford.
   1992   "Shall I compare thee…? Catullus 68B and the limits of analogy", in T. Woodman and J. Powell (eds.) *Author and Audience in Latin Literature*, 33–44, Cambridge.

Fordyce, C.J.
   1977   *P. Vergili Maronis Aeneidos Libri VII–VIII*, Oxford.

Fowler, D.
   1990   "Deviant focalisation in Virgil's *Aeneid*", *PCPS* 216, 42–63.

Galinsky, K.
   1988   "The anger of Aeneas", *AJP* 109, 321–48.
   1994   "How to be philosophical about the end of the *Aeneid*", *ICS* 19, 191–201.

Gransden, K.W.
   1984   *Virgil's* Iliad. *An Essay on Epic narrative*, Cambridge.

Hardie, P.R.
   1986   V*irgil's* Aeneid: *Cosmos and Imperium*, Oxford.
   1994   *Virgil* Aeneid *Book IX*, Cambridge.

Heinze, R.
   1993   *Virgil's Epic Technique* (trans. of *Virgils epische Technik*, 3rd edn 1928), Berkeley.

Knauer, G.N.
   1979   *Die Aeneis und Homer*, Hypomnemata 7, (2nd edn; 1st edn 1964).

Leigh, M.
   1993   "Hopelessly devoted", *PVS* 21, 89–110.

Lyne, R.O.A.M.
   1987   *Further Voices in Vergil's* Aeneid, Oxford.

Nethercut, W.R.
   1968   "Invasion in the *Aeneid*", *Greece and Rome* 15, 82–95.

O'Hara, J.J.
   1990   *Death and the Optimistic Prophecy in Vergil's* Aeneid, Princeton.

Otis, B.
   1964   *Virgil. A Study in Civilized Poetry*, Oxford.

Pascal, C.B.
   1990   "The dubious *devotio* of Turnus", *TAPhA* 120, 251–68.

Pöschl, V.
   1962   *The Art of Vergil*, tr. of *Die Dichtkunst Virgils* (1st edn), G. Seligson, Ann Arbor.
   1977   *Die Dichtkunst Virgils*, Berlin, (3rd. edn; 1st edn 1950).

Putnam, M.C.J.
   1965   *The Poetry of the* Aeneid, Cambridge, Mass.

Small, S.G.P.
   1959   "The arms of Turnus: *Aeneid* 7.783–92", *TAPA* 92, 243–52.

Stahl, H.-P.
   1981   "Aeneas – an 'unheroic' hero?", *Arethusa* 14, 157–77.
   1990   "The death of Turnus: Augustan Vergil and the political rival", in K.A. Raaflaub and M. Toher (eds) *Between Republic and Empire. Interpretations of Augustus and his Principate*, 174–211, Berkeley.

Todd, R.W.
   1980   "Lavinia blushed", *Vergilius* 26, 27–33.

Willcock, M.M.
   1983   "Battle scenes in the *Aeneid*", *PCPS* 29, 87–99.

Williams, R.D.
   1973   *The* Aeneid *of Virgil*, 2 vols., Glasgow.

14

THE END AND THE MEANING
Aeneid 12.791–842

David West

1. Preamble on the gods[1]

Denis Feeney's 'The Gods in Epic' discusses this passage on pages 146–55 and from his discussion there emerges an *Aeneid* teeming with insoluble theological problems, a 'dismaying poem' as he calls it on page 155. The starting point of his discussion is the observation that Juno here accepts the future greatness of Rome and yet fiercely resists it seven centuries later in the Punic Wars. Feeney, following Putnam and Johnson, deduces that her submission at the end of the *Aeneid* is insincere. This deduction leads them, and other scholars, to search the text of 12.791–842 for sinister, negative, threatening, nuances and opens the door to deep and prolonged consideration of Vergil's metaphysical thinking, from which I offer examples taken from the last four pages of Feeney's discussion.[2]

This seems to me not only to be one-sided, but also to make the *Aeneid* into a problem poem dealing with the ethics of the gods and the nature of their power, and thereby to subvert the obvious positive and celebratory tone of this dénouement of the epic, and there is no need for it. All that needs to be said about this apparent clash between Juno's submission in the *Aeneid* and her hostility to Rome in the Punic Wars was said in 1984 in a brilliant essay by E.L.Harrison. He points out that Juno does not meet her husband till the tenth book of the poem; that she has no knowledge of Fate apart from hearsay (*audierat*) at 1.20; and that her ignorance is essential for the plot. When she does eventually talk with her husband at the beginning of the tenth book, she is systematically deceived by him. At 10.12–13 he gives her to understand that Carthage will bring destruction upon Rome

> in time to come when cruel Carthage will open the Alps
> and send vast destruction upon the citadels of Rome.

> cum fera Karthago Romanis arcibus olim
> exitium magnum atque Alpis immitit apertas.

Harrison says, rightly, that this is 'the deception of Juno by a combination of hyperbole and omission'. Jupiter is predicting the Roman débâcle at Cannae and drawing a veil over the defeat of Hannibal at Zama in 202 BC and the destruction of Carthage in 146 BC. And he is equally economical with the truth in our passage in 835–9 where Juno is told that the Trojans will disappear, merged in the Latins, a race that will honour her more than any other people. 'Thus, at the end of the *Aeneid*,' writes Harrison on page 115, 'Juno is confident that...the descendants of the Trojans will in fact themselves succumb to her own Carthaginians' and leaves the *Aeneid* well satisfied with what she has heard. There is no point in hunting the text for Juno's doubts and hypocrisies and for deep analyses of the ethics of Jupiter's power. Jupiter has hoodwinked his wife, and Carthage is not mentioned here because it is inconvenient. Vergil has kept Juno in the dark in order that she may continue to provide the opposition to the hero throughout the story, and so that the end of her wrath may see the blessing of the gods conferred on the Julian future of Rome, Italy and the world. In this passage Vergil has far more important things to deal with than theology. This discussion on the conversation of Jupiter and Juno will deal with some of these. It will be divided into three parts: first the politics; second, the comedy; third, the politics of the comedy.

2. The politics

It is not difficult to read this passage in its political context. Vergil had certain obvious problems to solve at the end of his epic. His strategy of praising Augustus by praising his Trojan ancestor as founder of the Roman race, has in the end to face some discrepancies. If the Romans were originally Trojans, why are they not called Trojans? Why is there no trace of Phrygian in their language or in their culture, their clothes, and their character? And why are their gods not Phrygian gods? The whole Augustan message and purpose of the *Aeneid* is imperilled because of the absence of surviving Oriental elements in contemporary Latin culture. Vergil foresaw that objection and disposed of it in this conversation between husband and wife, by positing the stipulations of Juno that the Trojans be submerged in the Latin race and lose all their native Oriental characteristics.

The first of these is in lines 823–4, where Juno demands that native Latins should not lose their ancient name, should not be called Trojans or Teucrians. Buchheit (143) argues that this is part of

The End and the Meaning

Vergil's political strategy. The story in Livy 1.1.5–6 (see Ogilvie's note) gives credit to Aeneas for allowing the Aborigines to be called Latins. Vergil has chosen or invented a variant which deepens the aetiology and claims divine approval for the Latins by making their name a gift of the gods, not a condescension by a victorious Aeneas. Juno further insists that the Latins should keep their language. That will be discussed under Jupiter's reply at 837.

Her next stipulation is that the Latins should keep their native dress. The Augustan relevance of this is best shown by the story in Suetonius *Life of Augustus* 40 'He was eager also to revive the ancient style of dress, and one day when he saw a crowd of people wearing brown tunics at a public meeting, he was furious and shouted at them using a line from the *Aeneid* (1.282), 'Look at them,' he said, 'Romans, lords of the earth, the race that wears the toga', *en Romanos, rerum dominos gentemque togatam*. He then charged the aediles to see that this did not happen again. Patriotic pride was part of the Augustan programme, and in Augustus' mind the toga was a visible sign of it.

In 826–7 comes Juno's great concession in an ascending tricolon with anaphora:

> Let there be Latium, let the Alban kings live on through the centuries,
> let the stock of Rome be made mighty by the manly courage of Italy.

> sit Latium, sint Albani per saecula reges
> sit Romana potens Itala virtute propago.

These two lines contain two important Augustanisms. First, the Alban kings. According to Jupiter's prophecy at 1.268–71 the first of these was to be Ascanius Ilus, who was to change his cognomen to Iulus after the fall of Ilium. Iulus gave the Julian family its name and Augustus was the reigning Julian for whom the *Aeneid* was written. It has often surprised readers that the *Aeneid* does not refer to the *laudandus* until 1.286 or 289, but in fact the Julians receive their accolade in a clear allusion in the seventh line of the poem with the mention of the *Albani patres*. Dionysius of Halicarnassus (3.29.7) gives the names of the *Albani patres* who were enrolled in the Roman Senate in the seventh century BC and the first family on his list is the Julians (see Ogilvie on Livy 1.30.2, but see also Weinstock, 5 n. 4). Further, in Jupiter's prophecy at *Aen.* 1.274 we learn that the mother of Romulus and Remus was Ilia. Ilia was of the royal house of Alba, *regina sacerdos*, and was therefore a Julian. So therefore were her sons Romulus and Remus. Julius Caesar was not slow to make capital out of this connection. In 45 BC he was presented to the people as the new

Romulus and in that same year he took to wearing high red boots. Since high red boots were part of the regalia of the Alban kings (Dio 43.43.2) Julius was therefore claiming descent from Iulus (Weinstock, 324), and this claim is alluded to at *Aen.* 1.288, 'Julius, a name descended from the great Iulus', *Iulius a magno demissum nomen Iulo*. This line shows that Caesar's claim to be descended from the Alban kings was not forgotten twenty years later by Augustus or by contemporary Romans. Vergil, therefore, has praised the Julians as *Albani patres* at the beginning of his epic and as *Albani reges* at the end. When Juno and Jupiter agree that the Alban kings should reign through the centuries (or from generation to generation), *sint Albani per saecula reges*, Vergil's contemporaries would interpret that prophecy and see it as divine blessing for Augustus. This interpretation was to be demonstrated by Augustus in 2 BC with the dedication of the Forum Augustum, in the north apse of which there stood the statue of Aeneas with the Alban kings on his left and the Julians on his right, looking across at Romulus in the south apse with Augustus in the centre of the line joining them.

A further clear political message in these lines is the powerful anti-Orientalism at 825 and 827, a vital part of Octavian's propaganda in the thirties, which figures prominently on the Shield of Aeneas at 8.698 and 705–6. This will be discussed further in the second part of this paper, but here we may note the positive aspect, namely the praise of Italy. At 7.825 the Phrygians are effeminate, but the Italian stock is manly and they must not be asked 'to alter their voice, being men, or to change their manner of dress', *vocem mutare* viros *aut vertere vestem* (see Wiseman, 120). The sneer at the eunuch priests of the Phrygian goddess Cybele is confirmed in line 827:

> Let the stock of Rome become strong by the *manly* courage of Italy.
>
> sit Romana potens Itala virtute propago.

The peoples of Italy were an important part of Augustus' power base – and he was careful to cultivate them by policies which promised them respect, peace, prosperity, and the rule of law, in place of the exploitation, civil wars and anarchy of the preceding century. The clearest proof is in Augustus' own words at *Res Gestae* 25.2, 'The whole of Italy swore allegiance to me of its own free will and demanded me as its leader in the war in which I was victorious at Actium', *Iuravit in mea verba tota Italia sponte sua, et me bello quo vici ad Actium ducem depoposcit*. So too *Res Gestae* 10.2.

Vergil has another awkwardness to remove. The charge upon Aeneas was to establish the gods of Troy in a new city (1.6, 2.293–5 and

717, 12.192, and *Penatibus et magnis dis* at 3.12). It might be embarrassing to argue that the gods of Rome came from the east, but if they were Italian it would imply that Aeneas had failed in his duty. Vergil has several strategies for evading embarrassment. First, he has shown how Trojan culture is in fact Latin culture by tracing the foundation of Troy to the Italian Dardanus (3.167 and 503, 6.650, 7.207 and 240, 8.134). Second, he now lays the responsibility for Latin religious practices, *morem ritusque sacrorum*, on Jupiter. There can be no cavilling, and no suggestion that Aeneas has failed, if the Latin manner of ritual and worship is laid down by Jupiter, the King of the Gods.

There is yet another Augustan element. When Juno asks, and asks in Latin, for the retention of the Latin language and Jupiter gives his assent, there can be little doubt that Augustus, who saw a role in his settlement for the work of Horace and Vergil, would have approved. See also the Suetonius Life 86–8 for his interest in language. But perhaps there is an extra nuance. Over the preceding century Latin had throughout Italy become the official language of law, politics, and commerce. Now, people like Basques and Celts and the Italians of the first century BC, who live with powerful neighbours and see their own languages becoming extinct, tend to resent the loss. The words with which Jupiter grants Juno's request will have had a powerful contemporary relevance across Italy:

> I shall make them Latins, all speaking the same language.
>
> *faciamque omnes uno ore Latinos.*

Now, it is true, all Latium – and all Italy – speak Latin. The unspoken message is that such is the will of Jupiter.

3. The comedy

This episode starts with the king of all-powerful Olympus addressing Juno as she watches the duel between Turnus and Aeneas 'from a golden cloud' *fulva de nube*, where I believe that the cloud is golden (see *OLD* under *fulvus*), partly because in *Il.* 14.344 after a similar scene Zeus calls up a golden, χρύσεον, cloud to conceal his lovemaking with Hera.

This cloud is our first problem. It is important. Jupiter comments upon it at 796, and at 842 it ends the episode which it began. Feeney (1991, 150) sees in the cloud the etymological connection between *aer* and Hera (Juno), the goddess of our crass atmosphere as opposed to Jupiter the sky-god and god of the *aether*. So at 842, when Juno leaves the cloud, *nubemque reliquit*, 'Juno vacates her turbulent sphere as she

David West

moves closer to Jupiter, towards provisional equilibrium'. This frigid allegory seems to me to be a wrong turning. The *Aeneid* is a many faceted-poem, but it is absurd to find here a forecast of settled weather representing equilibrium between two gods. Besides, this intepretation of the second half of the line is excluded by the first half:

> Meanwhile she departed from the sky and left the cloud.
>
> interea excedit caelo nubemque relinquit.

If Juno is the goddess of the cloud, Jupiter is the god of the sky. If Juno is moving closer to Jupiter the god of the sky, why are we expressly told that she left it?[3]

Vergil's thrust here is not allegorical but comic. In 12.151, in a passage where Juno's treatment of Juturna demonstrates her cruelty and deviousness – she is the greatest liar in the *Aeneid* – she protests that she cannot bear to look at Aeneas fighting Turnus:

> My eyes cannot look upon this battle. I cannot look upon this treaty.
>
> non pugnam aspicere hanc oculis, non foedera possum.

She then urges Juturna to see what *she* can do to help her brother – 'go: it is right', *perge: decet*. Lines 792 and 796 which show Juno sitting in her cloud show also that her statement to Juturna was false, part of the shameless rhetoric by which she attempted to suborn Juturna to defy the will of the Fates, while keeping her own hands clean. Jupiter knows all this, and lets his wife know that he knows it. 'What are you up to?' he says – *quid struis* is fighting talk – 'what are you hoping for stuck there on those chilly clouds?', *aut qua spe gelidis in nubibus haeres?* We can almost see his great eyebrows rising. Juno picks up the point in a loud self-justifying bluster at 808–12. She does not take kindly to being teased.

But Jupiter's address to his wife is not all teasing. He is too subtle to make that mistake. He begins, shrewdly, not by telling her what she must do, but by asking her what she means to do, and reminding her that she has little freedom of manoeuvre. The Fates have decreed that Aeneas will become a god. Only then does he tease her about her ridiculous posture in the cloud. He then quickly changes tone and points out to her that she is completely in the wrong. It was not right that Aeneas should have been wounded at 318–23, and it was not right that Juturna should give Turnus back his sword at 785. Jupiter is omniscient. He knows exactly how Juno goaded Juturna into action.

At 800 Jupiter modulates again. He now appeals to Juno:

The End and the Meaning

> Make an end at long last, and give way to our entreaties.

> desine iam tandem precibusque inflectere nostris.

To his entreaties! That from the Omnipotent King of Gods and Men is an extraordinary gesture, almost a declaration of love, and such a declaration explicitly follows in the next line where he expresses his concern for her suffering – *dolor* being a husbandly euphemism for the fierce and unforgetting anger she has displayed since the fourth line of the poem, *saevae memorem Iunonis ob iram*. Even *tacitam* is part of the matrimonial dialectic, 'let not this great sorrow gnaw at you in silence', *ne te tantus edit tacitam dolor*. Although Juno has had a great deal to say throughout the poem, Jupiter pretends that she has suffered in silence. But rhetoricians and husbands do, on occasion, contradict themselves, and Jupiter lets her know in lines 801–2 that he is weary of her complaints, softening the rebuke with an amorous blandishment, mild and dignified, but still amorous:

> and do not let me hear
> the grievous cares streaming for ever from your sweet lips

> et mihi curae
> saepe tuo dulci tristes ex ore recursent.

Hear too his boredom in the long string of bisyllabic words, six accentual trochees in succession from *mihi* to *tristes*.[4]

The gentle admonition leads smoothly to the next modulation. At 803 he at last lays it on the line, 'The end is reached', *ventum ad supremum est*, and goes on to list what she has succeeded in doing, as a compliment to her powers, and at the same time as a reminder of the latitude she has already been allowed and a reminder of the licence she had taken upon herself (803–5):

> You have been able to harry the Trojans by sea and by land,
> to light the fires of an unholy war, to soil a house with sorrow,
> and mix the sound of mourning with the marriage song.

> terris agitare vel undis
> Troianos potuisti, infandum accendere bellum
> deformare domum et luctu miscere hymenaeos.

This is strong language, *infandum* in particular, and his final words repeat *ventum ad supremum est*. There is no varnish, no scope for protest or evasion even by Juno: 'I forbid you to go further', *ulterius temptare veto*. The King of the Gods has spoken, and has spoken like a loving husband,[5] tactfully but firmly imposing his authority upon a fractious, quarrelsome, jealous, and devious wife. Such family disputes are the very stuff of the divine comedy of manners which so enriches the *Iliad*. In this respect, as in so many others, Vergil is imitating Homer.

Juno replies at 808 with her head humbly bowed, *summisso vultu*. Well aware that disobedience is impossible, she begins by saying that she has already obeyed. But she rides with the hounds and runs with the hare. She has obeyed, but it was against her will, 'Against my will I have left Turnus and the earth', *et Turnum et terras invita reliqui*. Stung by Jupiter's teasing about the cloud, she continues the face-saving operation by boasting about how fierce she would be if she were fighting, and then slips in a wholly unjustified suggestion, refuted many times in the narrative of the last four books, that if you wanted to fight Trojans you had to drag them into battle 'and I would be dragging the Trojans into bloody combat', *traheremque inimica in proelia Teucros*. From bluster and insult to sophistry. Like Sinon in 2.78, where he confesses that he is a Greek, she is well aware that it is sound strategy when accused of serious crimes to establish one's *bona fides* by loudly confessing trivial offences which are already known to the court. So here she confesses that she encouraged Juturna to help her brother, but insists that she did not tell her to use weapons against Aeneas. This is technically true but serves to throw into clear light the cunning and callousness of her manipulation of Juturna at 12.142–60, and enables us to savour the legalistic nicety of her oath, carefully worded to avoid the wrath of the Styx, literally correct, but wholly false to the spirit and purpose of her treatment of Juturna. Vergil and his contemporaries were well versed in the difference between the word and the spirit, *scriptum* and *sententia* (*Rhetorica ad Herennium* 2.9.13–14).

At 818, again she talks of yielding and of abandoning the fighting. By now readers will know to take these assertions with a pinch of salt, and be surprised to hear that she leaves battles, hating them, *pugnas exosa relinquo*, – a sudden conversion from the warrior goddess of 810–11. Now come the face-saving stipulations, cunningly proposed with three heads of reasoning: first, that the Fates leave room for them (this meets Jupiter's opening point at 795 – 'Aeneas is being raised to the stars by the Fates', *Aenean...Fatis ad sidera tolli*; second, that her proposals would be to the benefit of Latium (she stresses the positive, drawing a veil over the fact that they would be detrimental to Troy); third, 'in consideration of the greatness of your kinfolk (or your people)', *pro maiestate tuorum*, a difficult phrase. Perhaps she means that Jupiter owes it to her not to humiliate her by establishing the Trojans in Italy, and also perhaps to himself. The humiliation of his queen, wife, and sister, would not be in his own interest.

The End and the Meaning

Juno is a shrew. At 821–2 she pointedly claims her own jurisdiction as goddess of marriage, and perhaps invokes the etymology of her own name, 'Juno from joining', *Iuno a iungendo*.[6] In 824 she speaks with a contemptuous jingle of two names for Trojans, 'do not order them to become Trojans and be called Teucrians', *Troas fieri iubeas Teucrosque vocari*. In 825 she reactivates the old slur on the effeminacy of the Phrygians, not only in insinuating that men should not speak like eunuchs (see above), *aut vocem mutare viros*, but also at *vertere vestem*, where she demands that they should not change into the effeminate garb of the Phrygians. They must wear the toga, not robes of Phrygian saffron and purple, no long-sleeved tunics, no ribbons, and no mitres. The anti-oriental satire of Iarbas at 4.215–7, of Numanus at 9.614–20, and of Turnus at 12.97–100 are the best commentary on these lines. In case the taunt of effeminacy is not perceived, she repeats it at 827, *sit Romana potens Itala virtute propago*, where *virtute* carries its etymological force (see above) in a dignified version of Numanus' words at 9.617, 'not Phrygian men. The truth is you are Phrygian women', *O vere Phrygiae, neque enim Phryges*.

Juno, then, is a shrew, but Jupiter, 'the discoverer of all men and all things', *hominum rerumque repertor*, as Vergil slyly entitles him at 829, sees her coming. He, who knows all things, even his own wife, smiles a little, *subridens*,[7] as he recognises in her the family traits she shares with her own brother, that is himself, and with their father Saturn with whom he had had his difficulties in the past as described in 8.319–20. In deference to this complex intimacy, even as he orders her to lay aside her anger, he makes it plain with weighty monosyllables that he is yielding to her wishes, *do quod vis et me victusque...remitto*. But the word I have omitted is crucial, *volensque*. He is yielding willingly, and that keeps her firmly in her place, because *she* yielded *against* her will.[8] *Volensque* is his riposte to her *invita* in line 809. He ends emolliently, appearing to concede more than she has asked, but this is economy with the truth. As we saw at the beginning of this discussion he has already given her to believe that Carthage will destroy Rome, and now he informs her that this new joint race in which Trojans will be submerged by Latins will honour her more than any other race upon the earth. No wonder she is pleased. But there is a strange phrase at 839, *supra ire deos pietate videbis*. How will mortals be able to surpass gods in *pietas*? *Pietas* is doing what ought to be done for gods, but also for one's city, one's friends, and one's family, and that includes proffering due respect and obedience. Jupiter may here be having a last glance at Juno's fractiousness. Throughout this whole Trojan episode her own *pietas* towards himself and the rule of Fate has left something to be desired – a point he made *en passant* with *infandum* at line 804. The dig, if it is there, is ignored or not understood. At 841 *mentem laetata retorsit*,[9] Juno rejoiced and changed her mind, but it was not easy for her. She did not simply change it. It had to be wrenched into its new disposition. *Retorsit* is an inspired translation of Homer's ἐπιγνάμψασα φίλον κῆρ at *Il.* 1.569 where Hera is cowed by Zeus.

Finita la commèdia, conducted in accordance with the comedy of the divine family as portrayed by Homer, providing before the dénouement of the poem a comic relief which admits of the full majesty and authority of an omnipotent god who is also as a husband a consummate manipulator of a difficult wife.

Sceptics may object that this analysis of the domestic comedy is an over-interpretation. The case for the defence rests on the Sinon episode in the second book. There Vergil explicitly and repeatedly states that Sinon's words are deceitful, at *versare dolos* 62, at *Danaum insidias* 65, at *scelerum tantorum artisque Pelasgae* 106, at *ficto pectore* 107, all culminating in the coda at 195–8:

> After such deceptions and such cunning from the lying Sinon,
> the story was believed. Treachery and false tears had ensnared
> men who had not been subdued by Diomede or Achilles of Larisa,
> by ten long years or by a thousand ships.
>
> Talibus *insidiis periurique arte* Sinonis
> credita res, captique *dolis* lacrimisque *coactis*
> quos neque Tydides nec Larisaeus Achilles,
> non anni domuere decem, non mille carinae.

Vergil is inviting us to look out for Sinon's lies and devices, and when we find them we notice that the 21 lines of Juno's speech use many of the same tricks. Like him, she begins by angling for our pity by saying how much she has suffered, *digna indignaque pati*; like him, she claims *bona fides* by confessing venial faults: 'I persuaded Juturna, I admit it, to go to the help of her unhappy brother' *Iuturnam, fateor, misero succurrere fratri suasi* at 813 (compare 'I escaped from death, I admit it, *eripui, fateor, leto me* at 2.134); oaths flow from both their lips (816–7; compare 2.141–4, 154–6). The *Rhetorica ad Herennium* 2.50 suggests that 'Pity, *misericordia*, is aroused...by explaining what will befall our parents, children, and other relatives as a result of our calamities.' It is not easy for Sinon to cite his children since he has already spun the tale at 87 that his father sent him to Troy in his earliest years, *pater primis huc misit ab annis*, (note too that he did not *come* to Troy, but *was sent*). Despite this handicap, by 138 he has acquired 'sweet children', *dulcis natos*, and Vergil must have hoped that we would catch him out in his lie. It is difficult for Juno also to appeal for *misericordia* for the sake of her relatives, but she makes a brave attempt to do so if *pro maiestate tuorum* at 820 means 'for the honour of your own kin'. Sinon's speeches, read with the interjected descriptions of the naïve credulity of the Trojans, are remarkably like the 'Friends, Romans, countrymen' speeches of Antony in Shakespeare's *Julius Caesar*, with the interjected descriptions of the fatuous credulity of the Roman mob. Vergil, and Shakespeare, are both satirising false rhetoric.

The same techniques are used elsewhere in the *Aeneid*. In 4.90–116 Juno uses them in trying to deceive Venus, but Venus is not an easy goddess to deceive – 'she realised that what Juno had said was all a pretence', *sensit simulata mente locutam* (105). Then again, after Venus' lengthy appeal to Jupiter on behalf of Aeneas at the beginning of Book Ten, Juno responds with a furious barrage of exclamations, rhetorical questions, and downright lies, as analysed in Stephen Harrison's commentary. At these, and other places in the *Aeneid*, Vergil is satirising the techniques of false oratory, and to point out the rhetorical devices is not over–interpretation. We have the advice of Aeneas to guide us – 'from this indictment learn the ways of all of them', *crimine ab uno disce omnes* (2.65–6). We also have Homer, as in the performance of Hephaestus in calming down the matrimonial strife at *Il.* 1.531–600, and the infinite amusement it provided the other gods; or the scene at *Il.* 14.292–353 where the 'brazen' Hera seduces her 'gauche' husband Zeus – the adjectives come from Janko's illuminating commentary.[10]

4. The politics of the comedy

Another objection that might be made is that the analysis of the comedy of manners has nothing to do with the subject of this conference, the political context of the *Aeneid*, but the relevance of this satire to the political situation in the twenties BC is surely obvious. The deployment of forum oratory to further the fierce ambitions of ambitious men was a characteristic feature of the last years of the Republic. The Republic was now restored, but it was restored without such public confrontations, an Augustan Republic. Augustus himself sometimes rushed out of the Senate 'because of the excessive violence of the disputants', *ob immodicas disceptantium obtrectationes* (*Vita* 54). This is no doubt some part of the explanation of the greatest snub in the *Aeneid*, the failure to mention Cicero at 6.849, *orabunt causas melius*. Glimpses of this Augustan attitude occur also in Horace. At *Odes* 1.1.7–8, for instance, we read that the fickle throng of Roman citizens strives to raise candidates to the three magistracies, *mobilium turba Quiritium certat tergeminis tollere honoribus*, and the point is made even more forcibly at 3.2.17–20:

> Virtue knows nothing of humiliation at the polls
> but shines with honours unsullied.
>   She does not take up the axes or lay them down
>   at the breath of the wind of public opinion.
>
>   Virtus repulsae nescia sordidae
>   intaminatis fulget honoribus
>   nec sumit aut ponit securis
>   arbitrio popularis aurae.

As Denis Feeney and Robin Nisbet have shrewdly observed (1983, 219), Aeneas and Augustus were both strikingly laconic in their utterances. Vergil's scathing satire on rhetoric applies to the cut-throat rhetoric of the late Republic and as such chimes with the Augustan settlement.

5. Postamble on the gods

The title of this paper is also an example of false rhetoric. The conversation between Jupiter and Juno is not the end of the *Aeneid* – Vergil has still a loose end to tie up (see Stahl's essay on the death of Turnus). Nor has this paper expounded the meaning of the *Aeneid*, whatever that might mean. But I hope it may have pointed to some of the diverse functions of the gods in the *poem*, of which I now select five:

1. The first is the political. By their prophecies and their decisions they attribute divine authority to contemporary phenomena.

2. They provide as a superplot a sublime view of human events, as when Jupiter in the heights of the aether looks down upon the sufferings of men at 1.223–9 or when the gods themselves grieve, as, for example, Jupiter and Hercules mourn the death of Sarpedon and Pallas at 10.464–73.

3. They provide as a subplot an extra dimension of personal relationships to add variety to the narrative. This subplot often shows divine persons behaving more meanly, spitefully, and dishonestly than the human characters in the epic. As in Homer, such scenes are often humorous, even as in our passage at the end of the *Aeneid*, where the gods are discussing decisions which to us are momentous in that they will confer untold blessings on individual human beings or nations, or will destroy them without pity.

4. The gods are sometimes seen as natural forces or human psychological impulses. This particular function, sometimes called 'double

motivation', shows clearly for example when the widow Dido falls in love with Aeneas as she dandles Cupid on her knee, believing he is Ascanius, *inscia Dido insidat quantus miserae deus* (1.718–9); or when Allecto visits Turnus in his sleep and he at first resists the temptation to war, but then succumbs to it (7.413–66). This can greatly enrich the texture of the epic, as when Aeneas comforts the beaten and bleeding Dares, and saves his dignity at 5.465–7:

> Unlucky Dares, what madness has taken possession of you?
> Do you not see that your strength is not as his
> and the divine will has turned against you?
> Yield to the god.

>> infelix, quae tanta animum dementia cepit?
>> non viris alias conversaque numina sentis?
>> cede deo.

Then again, it can be used to save the character of the hero of the epic. When in the twelfth Book Aeneas attacks a city inhabited only by old men, women and children, Vergil is careful not only to stress the provocation that Aeneas has endured, but he also exculpates his hero by attributing the responsibility to his goddess mother Venus (12.554–5):

> Now the mother of Aeneas, loveliest of goddesses, put it in his mind
> to go to the walls of the city.

>> hic mentem Aeneae genetrix pulcherrima misit
>> iret ut ad muros.

5. The divine element of necessity touches upon the insoluble problems of the relationship between irresistible Fate, omnipotent deity and human will. This aspect of the divine machinery is a rewarding narrative strategy, because it reminds us tangentially and disturbingly of the unknowable, of the frailty and brevity of man in a vast, callous, and incomprehensible universe. The *Aeneid* demonstrates the cruelty of Jupiter, the cruelty of life, but there is no point in scouring it to analyse motives that cannot be known or to search for explanations of what is beyond our understanding.

The fatal mistake is to choose between these five (and no doubt other) functions of the gods. Many scholars have ignored the first, the political function. Many have averted their gaze from the third, the divine comedy. Many deny the fourth, double motivation, as though it ruled out the participation of the gods as characters in the drama. As for the fifth, to overstress the theological problems and explore in depth what has been called 'the disharmony in the government of the universe' is to look for something which is not there. Necessity and fate

David West

and divine will are incompatible with the freedom of human beings. Jupiter 'resists quasi-theological exegesis' to borrow Feeney's judgement (1991, 145) of 10.112–13. These problems are insoluble. Vergil did not know the answer to them and is not trying to propose one or bury one in his narrative or even to reformulate the problems. He is using the mystery for the purposes of his story. To agonise in attempts to ferret out his view of such matters is to follow a will-o'-the-wisp which leads to a one-sided and impoverishing view of what is many-faceted, and to damaging misinterpretations of the detail of this brilliantly crafted epic story (see some of the footnotes to this paper). It is a scholastic weakness to go in search of profundities and lose sight of what is there, and a grave loss to expound this passage and pay no attention to its politics and its humour.

Notes

[1] My thanks are due to J. Griffin, E.L. Harrison, R.G.M. Nisbet, and H-P. Stahl who made valuable criticisms of earlier drafts of this paper.

[2] (with my italics) a) The *Aeneid* is preoccupied with power before any other subject, and Vergil was not the first poet to be exercised by *the problem* of how the power of divine violence could be used for harmony (Feeney (1991) 152–3).
b) The *dilemmas* involved in Rome's use of violence for order are a principal subject of the poem and they take their lead from *the problems* involved in the judgement of the state's patron god (ibid. 152–3).
c) Jupiter, to speak in social terms, is often seen in the poem presiding like a political superior over an emerging consensus, preferring, if possible, not to force the issue. Vergil's tactfulness in this matter creates *many unresolved areas of vagueness* around Jupiter, Fate, and Providence (ibid. 153–4).
d) …if it is *difficult* to glide over the implications of Jupiter's characterful participation, *it is also difficult*…to find in Jupiter a vantage-point from which to *dispel the problems created by the experience of reading the poem* (ibid. 154).
e) Every vantage-point the poem offers is *inextricable*, part of a competition of views… Jupiter's perspective is, naturally a commanding one… He regards events from a height that shrinks human values. *Yet it is not a perspective from which problems disappear*. In this *dismaying* poem, most readers want to find a vantage-point of comfort, and it is therefore tempting to construct a 'high' Stoic position in the portrayal of Jupiter, yet his participation in the narrative means that *it is never easy, and it becomes finally impossible* at the accommodation with Juno… The narrator is ultimately unable to commit himself to Jupiter's perspective (ibid. 155).

[3] This difficulty was seen by Feeney in 'The Reconciliations of Juno' (1984, 33), where he was tempted to emend *excedit* to *cedit*, 'she yielded to the sky'. But in *The Gods in Epic* (1991, 150) he mentions neither the difficulty nor his emendation.

[4] See West (1995, 106) on *mé nunc Thréssa Chlóe régit | dúlcis dócta módos*,

Horace *Odes* 3.9.9–10.

[5] The first word of Jupiter's speech, *coniunx*, is untranslatable. In English 'Wife' is an inflammatory vocative and in no way fits the tone of what follows. Day Lewis's 'My wife' is also quite dangerous. No doubt sensing this, Dryden has 'O Queen of Heaven' and Jackson Knight has 'My Queen', formal compliments which do no justice to the Latin. Fitzgerald has 'My consort, what will the end be?' which is dignified, but dead. West hazards 'O my dear wife' believing the tone of that to be more in harmony with the subtle diplomacy which follows, if the above analysis is anywhere near the truth, and consistent with the tone of *coniunx* elsewhere in the *Aeneid*. Vergil uses the vocative *coniunx* ten times: twice formally addressing Persephone, wife of Dis (*Culex* 286 and *Aen.* 12.178), and affectionately in all the other occasions (*Georg.* 4.456 with *rapta*, *Aen.* 2.519 with *miserrime*, where Hecuba appeals to Priam), 2.777 with *dulcis*, 8.377 with *carissime* where Venus is wheedling Vulcan, 10.607 with *gratissima*, and 611 where Juno returns the compliment with *pulcherrime*, and 11.158 with *sanctissima*). The tenth occurrence is here at 12.793.

[6] Vergil plays with the etymology of Juno's name at 4.126, *coniugio iungam stabili*, but Feeney (1991, 150) surely hyperallegorises. His argument is that Juno, the goddess of joining (*Iuno a iungendo*), is normally a goddess of strife and division in the *Aeneid* but is true to her etymology 'as the poem's principal force for structural cohesion', initiating the storm in the first book and a storm in the seventh, starting the poem and 'now at the last in the great mirror-scene to the first divine action contributing to a pattern of synthesis…'.

[7] For Johnson (126), Jupiter's smile is one of the most sinister moments in this increasingly sinister poem, 'touched with a nameless evil' and Feeney (1991, 148) finds it 'a chillingly suave acknowledgement of the anger she still feels'. But the same word, *subridens*, is used of Jupiter's smile when he replies to Venus' anxious complaints in the great mirror scene (1.254), and there surely it is an affectionate and amused acknowledgement of the temperament of his passionate daughter. The smile at 12.829 makes better sense along the same lines. The knowing smile of Zeus after Hera's mighty and dishonest oath at *Il.* 15.47 is equally perceptive.

[8] Jasper Griffin refers me to *Il.* 4.43 where Zeus yields to Hera willingly but with an unwilling heart, ἑκὼν ἀέκοντί γε θυμῷ.

[9] Johnson (127), suggests that in *adnuit his Iuno et mentem laetata retorsit* (841) *his* may be taken with both verbs so that the second half of the line could be ambiguous and carry the suggestion that she is turning her mind violently back from Jupiter's words and rejecting them, that 'her mental action would negate the outward sign that she makes'. This seems to be a doomed attempt to find support for his portentous reading of this scene. Feeney himself is right to reject it (1983, 184, n. 30), but makes an equally desperate attempt to support this general reading by finding intimations of Juno's part in the Punic wars in the 'loaded "meanwhile" that signals her departure' (1991, 148, n. 72).

[10] In a letter Robin Nisbet writes 'this comedy reveals something about the ancient ideas of the difference between the sexes (cf. *Aen.* 4): the man is statesmanlike and looks for compromises; the woman is uncompromising and

manipulative (as indeed women tended to be when they could operate most effectively through a man)'.

Bibliography

Buchheit, V.
    1953   'Vergil über die Sendung Roms', *Gymnasium Beihefte* 3.

Feeney, D.C.
    1983   'The taciturnity of Aeneas', *CQ* 33, 204–19.
    1984   'The reconciliations of Juno', *CQ* 34, 179–94.
    1991   *The Gods in Epic*, Oxford.

Harrison, E.L.
    1984   'The *Aeneid* and Carthage', in T. Woodman and D. West (eds.) *Poetry and Politics in the Age of Augustus*, 95–115, Cambridge.

Harrison, S.J.
    1991   *Vergil* Aeneid 10, Oxford.

Janko, R.
    1992   *The* Iliad: *a Commentary*, vol. 4 (Books 13–16), Cambridge.

Johnson, W.R.
    1976   *Darkness Visible. A Study of Vergil's* Aeneid, Berkeley.

Ogilvie, R.M.
    1965   *A Commentary on Livy Books 1–5*, Oxford.

Putnam, M.C.J.
    1965   *The Poetry of the* Aeneid, Cambridge, Mass.

Stahl, H.-P.
    1990   'The death of Turnus: Augustan Vergil and the Political Rival', in K.A. Raaflaub and M. Toher (eds.) *Between Republic and Empire*, 177–201, Berkeley.

Weinstock, S.
    1971   *Divus Julius*, Oxford.

West, D.
    1995   'Reading the metre', in S.J. Harrison (ed.)*Homage to Horace*, 100–7, Oxford.

Wiseman, T.P.
    1984   'Cybele, Virgil, and Augustus', in T. Woodman and D. West (eds.) *Poetry and Politics in the Age of Augustus*, 117–28, Cambridge.

INDEX

Roman proper names are placed according to their most familiar element; thus 'Ahenobarbus, L. Domitius' but 'Varius Rufus, L.'

Abas, shield of, 67–8
Accius, 262
Achilles, 38, 227, 257, 278–81
Acro, 233
Acron, 206
Actian Games, 7–8, 59, 62, 67, 71
Actian rams, 70–1
Actium, 15, 40, 48–9, 53–4, 56–8, 60–1, 63–8, 92, 179, 201–3, 209–11, 213, 232–5, 297; see also 'Nicopolis'
Actium propaganda, 49, 66, 74, 204, 208, 237
adultery, 88–9, 96–7
Aegyptus, 236
  sons of, 224, 227–30, 232–3, 235
Aeneadae, 48–50, 53, 56, 58, 206
Aeneas, 7–8, 186, 227–8, 230, 244, 247, 253–4, 314 and *passim*.
  and flight, 43
  in Homer, 12–13, 278–80
  mirrored by Hercules, 177, 180, 185
  shield of, ch. 10 *passim*, 258–9, 306. See also 'Vulcan, shield of'.
  taciturnity of, 246
  travel route of, ch. 3 *passim*
  and Turnus, 275–7
Aenus, 44, 48
Aeolus, 143, 278–80
Aerarium Saturni, 169, 171
Aeschylus, 226–9, 233–4
Agrippa, 57, 121, 123, 125, 128, 210
Ahenobarbus, Cn. Domitius, 45
Ahenobarbus, Lucius Domitius, 45–6
Ajax, 262
Alba Longa, 206

Alban kings, 305–6
Alexandria, 8–9
  Donations of, 90
Allecto, ch. 7 *passim*, 249, 285, 292, 315
Aloidae, 85, 98
Amata, ch. 7 *passim*, 294
Ambracia, 54
  Gulf of 56
Ames, Aldrich, 97
Anchises, 47, 260–1
  prophecy of, 108–11, 122, 124, 251–2, 259
Ancus Marcius, 102
Andromache, 44
Anio, river, 98
Anius, 47
'anti-types', 177–80
Antiate rams, 71
Antonia Maior, 45
Antonius:
  M. Antonius Antyllus, 45
  Iullus, 142
Antony, Mark, 15, 43, 56, 66, 70–1, 90–2, 94, 119, 177, 179–80, 210, 235–6
Anubis, 210
Apelles, 236
Apollo, 2–3, 13, 31, 47, 52, 58, 63, 72, 178, 203, 209, 232–3, 236
  Actius, 11, 13–14, 16, 61, 70–2, 74
  Karneios, 3
  Nomios, 2
  Palatine temple of, 71, 205, 211–2, 231–4, 236–7
  Sosianus, temple of, 211–2

319

Index

Thymbraeus, 47
Appian, 92–3
Appius Claudius, 102
Ara Maxima, 176, 187
Ara Pacis, 155
Ardea, 229
Argos, 229–30, 234–5
Aristaeus, 2
Aristotle, 87
Artemis, 232
Ascanius, 71–2, 126, 248, 258, 260
  Ascanius Ilus, 305
Assaracus, 12
Atticus, 85
Augustine, 104
Augustus, 1–3, 5–15, 101, 107–10, 112, ch. 6 *passim*, 142, 158, 160, 164, 169, 175–6, 178–180, 185, 189, 191, 202, 208, 210–13, 232, 235–6, 245, 261, 271, 273–4, 297, 304–7, 314
  and Aeneas' travel-route, ch. 3 *passim*
  domus Augusti, 205
  Forum Augustum, 306
  religion in the politics of, ch. 2 *passim*
  and requirements of propaganda, 180–3
  Res Gestae, 274
  statue (Prima Porta), 203
  and Vergil's Underworld, ch. 4 *passim*
Aventine Hill, 177

Bacchism, Bacchus, 143–5
Basilica Aemilia, 205, 208, 210
Basilica Fulvia, 210
Battus, 3
Bellona, 209–10
Belus, 239 n. 37
Berenice, 6–7
'Bremerhaven ram', 64–5
Brennus, 207
Briseis, 279
Britanni, 10
Brutus (tyrannicide of 510 BC), 103–4, 107
Brutus (tyrannicide of 44 BC), 103, 107
building programme, Augustan, 37, 231
Buthrotum 44–6, 48, 57, 61

Cacus 15, ch. 9 *passim*,
Caesar, C. (grandson of Augustus), 74, 128
Caesar, Julius, 16, 29, 89–90, 103, 107–10, 169–71, 184, 232, 235, 305–6
Caesar, L. (grandson of Augustus), 128
Caesarion, 43
Callimachus, 2–7, 9, 13–14, 261
Camilla, 228, 276
Camillus, 24–5, 107, 208
Campus Martius, 203
Cannae, 304
Capitoline Hill, 208, 210
Carrhae, 29
Carthage, 303–4, 311
Catilina, 15, 85, 91–2, 109, 206, 208–9, 245, 262
Cato the Elder, 136, 275
Cato (Uticensis), 85, 91, 109–10, 206, 209
Catullus, 108
Celaeno, 58
Cephallenia, 49, 51
Chimaera, 287
Chrysippus, 143
Cicero, 56, 85, 91, 109, 183, 245, 262, 313
Circus Flaminius, 203
Circus Maximus, 205, 207
civil war, 12–13, 15, 30, 107, 182–5, 190–1; *see also* 'Actium', 'Perusine War', 'Pompeius, Sextus'
Cleopatra VII, 7, 13, 119, 202, 210, 234–6
Clinton, Bill, 156
Cloelia, 206
'condensation symbols', 26–7, 29
consensus, 23–7, 29–30

320

Index

Constantine the Great, 30–1
Constantius II, 22
Consualia, 205
Cotison, 142
Crete, detour to, 47
Crinagoras, 120
Culex, 128
Cupid, 315
Curio (tribune of 50 BC), 89–90
Cybele, 306
Cyrene, 3

Daedalus, 124
Danae, 229
Danaids, ch. 11 *passim*
Danaus, 224–5, 232, 235–6
Dardanus, 46–8, 307
Dares, 315
Decii, 106, 284–5
Delos, 3, 5, 46–7
Dido, 103, 140–5, 147–9, 282–3, 289, 315
Diomedes, 254–7
Dionysius of Halicarnassus, 40, 44, 57, 137, 275, 305
Dionysos, cult of, 25
Dirae, 210
Discordia, 209–10
Divus Julius, temple of, 210
Dodona, 44
Donatus: Tiberius Claudius Donatus, 1, 16, 68, 78 n. 28, 111
Drances, ch. 12 *passim*
Drusus (son of Livia), 106, 128
Ducato, Cape, 55

Egypt, 233–4
Ennius, 8, 252, 258
Ephialtes, 98
Epicurus, 15, 167–8
Etruscans, 61
Euryalus, 228
Evander, 227–8, 261

Fama, 250–2, 258–9, 261–2
fire, 190–2
Flaminius, C., 22

Forum Augustum, 306
Forum Boarium, 5, 187
Forum Romanum, 64, 75
Fronto, 252
Fulvius, Marcus Fulvius Nobilior, 15
Furius, M. Furius Camillus, 21
furor, 165–6

Gates of War, ch. 8 *passim*
Gauls, 207–8, 232, 234–5
gigantomachy, 202, 207, 286, 295
gladiatorial *munus*, 187–90
Gods, Council of, 247, 258

Hannibal, 108, 304
Harpies, cattle of, 48, 58
Hector, 38–9, 147–8, 254, 278–9
Hecuba, 135, 147
Heldenschau, see 'Heroes, Parade of'
Helen, 143–4
Helenus, 44, 46
Hercules, 4–7, 15–16, ch. 9 *passim*, 236, 263, 314
Heroes, Parade of, 122, 258
Hesiod, 250
Hippomedon, 224–5
Homer, Homeric poems, 4, 6, 37–8, 75, 85, 98, 147, 247, 257–8, 260–1, 263, 276–80, 282, 290, 310, 312–14
Horace, 95, 103, 111, 230, 250, 307, 313
Horatius Cocles, 206
Hypermestra, 224

Iarbas, 259, 311
Icarus, 123–4
Ilia, 305
Ilioneus, 253, 261
invidia, 14, 87, 252
Io, 229, 287–8
Iphition, 279
Iris, 248, 291–2
Italians, Italy, 255, 306
Ithaca, 49, 51
Iulus, *see* 'Ascanius'
Iunius Brutus Pera, D., 187

321

Index

Ixion, 88, 208

Janus Geminus, temple of, 158–62, 171
Julia (aunt of Julius Caesar), 103
Julia (d. of Augustus), 45, 120–1, 125–6, 142
Julian (emperor), 190
Julian *gens*, 305–6
Julius Caesar, see 'Caesar, Julius'
Juno, 23, 143, 148, 165–8, 171, 230, 285, 292, 303–4, 306–13
 J. Lucina, temple of, 208, 210
 J. Moneta, temple of, 207
Jupiter, 23, 31, 48, 58, 165, 190, 202, 207, 247, 258, 287–8, 295–7, 304–11, 314–16; see also 'Zeus'.
 J. Feretrius, temple of, 206–7, 210
 J. Optimus Maximus, temple of, 204, 208, 210
 J. Stator, 209–10
Juturna, 148, 287, 289, 291, 293, 295–6, 308, 310

Kennedy, John F., 156

Laomedon, 13
Lapiths, 88, 208
Latin culture, 304, 307
Latins, 254–5, 304–5
 council of, ch. 12 *passim*
Latinus, 136–7, 141–2, 145–8, 168, 178, 243–4, 247, 255, 292
Lausus, 38–9, 276
Lavinia, 136, 142, 146–7, 293–4
Leucadia, (Leucas) 50–7
libertas, 104–5
Livia, 124, 128, 142
Livius: M.L.Salinator, 106
Livy, 101–2, 105–7, 110, 136, 275
London, Guildhall, 187
Lucan, 108, 110, 169
Lucius Caesar, 74
Lucky (Eutychos), donkey driver, 64
Lucretius, 15, 87, 186–7, 226, 255
Lupercal, Cave of, 204–5, 208
Luperci, 208

Lyrnessus, 278–80
Lyssa, 138

Maecenas, 1, 124
Magna Mater, 29
Manlius Torquatus, 106–7
Mantua, 9
Marcellus, C.Claudius (nephew of Augustus), ch. 6 *passim*
Marius, 98
Mars, 162–3, 204, 210
 Ultor, 31
Martial, 108, 187–8
Matronalia, 208
Meliboeus, 297
Messalla, Potitus Valerius, 176
Metellus, L., 169–70
Mettus Fufetius, 206
Mezentius, 15
Mincius, river, 9
Minerva, 209–10
Murena, Licinius (cos. 23 BC), 112
Musa, Antonius, 121
Myron, 232

Nekuia (*Odyssey* 11), 85, 98
Nemesis, 190
Neptune, 92, 209–10. *See also* 'Poseidon'.
Nero, 159
Nestor, 263
Nicopolis, 59–63, 69–72, 210
Nile, 210
Niobe, 232
Niobids, 234–5
Numa Pompilius, 159–60, 163
Numanus Remulus, 248, 258, 260, 311

Octavia, 122
Octavian, *see* 'Augustus'
Odysseus, 49–50, 248, 257, 260, 262
Olympia, 13
Oplontis, 73
Oppius, M., 93
Otos, 98
Ovid, 75, 136, 144, 171, 184, 230,

232–3, 235, 252, 260, 262–3

Palatine hill, 37, 47, 64, 72, 177, 204, 207, 236
Palatine triad, temple of, 212
Pales, 2
Palinurus, 186
Pallas, 38–9, 273, 276
  and sword belt, ch. 11 *passim*
Pandarus, 166
Paris, 227
Parthenon, 201
Parthians, 11–12, 158
Patroclus, 38–9
pax, 24, 26–7, 29–30
Pelops, 4, 6–8
Pergamon, 47–8, 207
'Perusine War', 97, 297
Phlegyas, 88, 99
Phrygian culture, 304, 306, 311
pietas, 21–30, 32, 88, 93, 99, 230
Piso, Cn. Calpurnius, 112
Pistoria, 184
Plato, 87, 164, 226, 246
plebs, 29, 31
Poetry, temple of (*Geo* 3), 261
Polydorus, 43
Polynices, 225
Pompeius:
  Cn. Pompeius Magnus, 93, 107–9, 184
  Sextus Pompeius Pius, 88, 92–4
Pons Sublicius, 207
Porsenna, Lars, 206
Poseidon, 278
Potitius, 176, 191
Praxithea, 135
Priam, sons of, 43–4
Primus, M., 124
prisons (British), 97–8
Procne, 144
Propertius, 73, 231–2
proscriptions, 93–5, 99
Ptolemy XIII, 235
Ptolemy XIV, 235

Quellenforschung, 38

Regia, 208, 210
religio, 21–2, 25, 28, 31–2
Remus, 177, 184–6, 305
rhetoric, ch. 12 *passim*, 314
rhipsaspia, 285–8
Romulus, 177, 184–6, 305
  Hut of, 205, 207–8

Sabines, rape of, 184, 205
Saces, 297
Salii, 208
Sallust, 184
Salmoneus, 88
Scipio:
  L. Cornelius Scipio Barbatus, 283
  M. Cornelius Scipio Hispanus, 284
Scopas, 236
senate, 28–9, 31, 313
Seneca, 187–9
Servius, 60, 86, 90, 108, 136, 158, 162–3, 205, 210, 224, 280–1, 289
Sestius, L., 112
Shakespeare, W., 313
shield:
  of Achilles (Homer), 200–1
  of Athena (Pheidias), 200–1
  of Herakles (Hesiod), 200–1
shrines, 24, 28
Sibyl, 280–1
simile, 276–7, 288–291, 296
Sinon, 258, 278, 310, 312–13
slaves, 93–4
Sparta, 96
Statius, 224–5, 235, 250
Strophades islands, 48–9
Sulla, 98
Syria, 11

Tacitus, 183
Tantalos, 98
Tarpeia, 207
Tarpeian Rock, 207–8
Tartarus, 14–15, ch. 4 *passim*
Tatius, T., 205
Tauromenium, battle of, 93
temple-robbery, 96–7
Tertullian, 189

Index

Teucrians, 311. *See* 'Trojans'.
Teucrus, 47
Thersites, 245, 248, 260
Theseus, 88, 99
Thrace, 43
Thucydides, 99
Tiberius (emperor), 128, 142, 246
Tityos, 98
Tolumnius, 293
Torquatus, Manlius, 207
Trasimene, Lake: battle of, 22
treasure trove, 95–6
triumphs, ch. 10 *passim*
  paintings for, 200
Triumvirs, 93
Troy, Trojans, 13, 44–8, 166, 275, 304, 306–11; *see also* 'Aeneadae'.
Tullianum, 204, 206–7, 210
Tullus Hostilius, 163, 206
Turnus, 15, 38–9, 75, ch. 7 *passim*, 166, 177–8, 186, chs. 11–12 *passim*, 307–8, 310–11, 315

Underworld (*Aeneid* 6), ch. 3 *passim*

Valerius Flaccus, 250
Varius Rufus, L., 90–1
Varro, 261
Venulus, 255
Venus, 141, 148–9, 210
  Genetrix, temple of, 16
  Marina, 203
Vergil: a republican?, ch 5 *passim*
Vesta, precinct of, 210
'Victor' (Nicon), donkey, 64
Vietnam War, and U.S. critics, 272, 275
Vulcan, 191–2, 260–1
  shield of, 57, 92, 104, 126, ch. 10 *passim*, 286

Zacynthus, 49–50
Zama, 304
Zeus, 13, 279–80. See also 'Jupiter'
  Z. Xenios, 228